Liquor in the Land
of the Lost Cause

Religion in the South

John B. Boles, Series Editor

LIQUOR

IN THE LAND OF THE

LOST CAUSE

SOUTHERN WHITE EVANGELICALS
AND THE
PROHIBITION MOVEMENT

JOE L. COKER

THE UNIVERSITY PRESS
OF KENTUCKY

Publication of this volume was made possible in part by a grant
from the National Endowment for the Humanities.

Editorial and Sales Offices: The University Press of Kentucky
663 South Limestone Street, Lexington, Kentucky 40508-4008
www.kentuckypress.com

11 10 09 08 07   5 4 3 2 1

Library of Congress Cataloging-in-Publication Data

Coker, Joe L., 1969–
  Liquor in the land of the lost cause : southern white evangelicals and the
prohibition movement / Joe L. Coker.
    p. cm. — (Religion in the South)
  Includes bibliographical references and index.
  ISBN 978-0-8131-2471-1 (hardcover : alk. paper) 1. Temperance and religion—
Southern States—History. 2. Prohibition—Southern States—History. I. Title.
  HV5187.C57 2007
  363.4'1097509034—dc22   2007025152

This book is printed on acid-free recycled paper meeting
the requirements of the American National Standard
for Permanence in Paper for Printed Library Materials.

Manufactured in the United States of America.

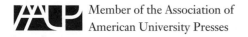 Member of the Association of
American University Presses

To Layton Edward Coker

Contents

Acknowledgments

Like all historians, I owe a large debt of gratitude to the numerous teachers, scholars, archivists, colleagues, and research institutions that contributed to the writing of this book. Many along the way helped me produce a final product that is far superior to anything I would have been capable of producing on my own.

The idea for *Liquor in the Land of the Lost Cause* took shape while I was a student working in the cataloging department at Pitts Theology Library at Emory University in Atlanta. It was there that I first became intrigued by the religious dimensions of the prohibition movement. Tasked with cataloging the library's enormous collection of American hymnals, I was fascinated by a unique subgenre of hymnody: temperance hymnals. This exposed me to the larger temperance and prohibition movement, and it tied in with my emerging interest in how religion and the surrounding culture impact each other. My curiosity about the temperance movement continued at Princeton Theological Seminary, where it coalesced into a dissertation topic. I was fortunate enough to be advised by James H. Moorhead, whose own work was largely responsible for my interest in the interplay between religion and culture. His guidance and input during the course of my research and writing were invaluable, and I am deeply indebted to him. Also serving on my dissertation committee were Paul Rorem and Richard Fenn, both of whom provided thoughtful analysis of my work and helped guide its development into a book.

The Southern Baptist Historical Library and Archives in Nashville, Tennessee, provided both archival and financial resources during the research process. Patrick Graham, director of Pitts Theology Library, was always generous with the library's wealth of archival material on southern Methodism. The library staff at Samford University was also hospitable and generous with its resources, and I am especially grateful for the help of Special Collections librarian Elizabeth Wells. Several scholars read the manuscript and provided input on the revision process. I deeply appreciate the comments of Paul Harvey and David Fahey, whose thoughtful analysis and helpful suggestions improved both the style and the substance of the book. I am likewise grateful to two anonymous readers whose critiques contributed to its final form. I would also like to thank John Boles and Joyce Harrison of the University Press of Kentucky for their commitment to seeing this work published.

On a personal level, I am indebted to the many friends and family members who supported and encouraged me during the long process of writing this book. I will be forever grateful for my father's endless support, optimism, and friendship. I thank Julia for her careful reading of the work along the way. I would also like to acknowledge two family members who always supported me in my academic pursuits but were unable to witness the completion of this project. Both my mother, Betty Jo Coker, and my brother, Yancy Lee Coker III, passed away during the writing of this book, but their love and support continue to sustain and motivate me. Finally, my deepest debt is to my son, Layton, who has brought more joy and happiness into my life over the past seven years than I ever thought possible.

Introduction

ON THE EVENING OF JULY 30, 1907, a spirit of revelry swept over the evangelical Christians of Atlanta, Georgia. Hundreds celebrated around the statue of Henry Grady, the famed post–Civil War booster of economic development in the New South. Lula Ansley, a leader of the Woman's Christian Temperance Union (WCTU) in Georgia, later recalled the jubilation: "The scene was indescribable—grown men sobbed like children, women threw themselves into each others' arms weeping—bells rang, horns blew, whistles screamed."[1] The celebrants also sang the doxology, although the blessing for which they praised God flowed, most immediately, from the Georgia state legislature. Earlier in the day Georgia lawmakers had passed a bill outlawing the manufacture or sale of alcoholic beverages anywhere in the state. This marked the first time that statewide prohibition legislation had ever been passed in a southern state.

The celebration was not simply the expression of Christians who were grateful that the government had struck a blow against the vice of drinking and the forces of evil. Most twenty-first-century Americans familiar with the South might fail to appreciate the momentous nature of that day's events. Indeed, the region is still known as a place where restrictions on the sale of alcohol linger, even though the United States abandoned its experiment with national prohibition more than seven decades ago. For Georgia evangelicals in 1907, however, the passage of this legislation was the culmination of decades of toil to build southern support for prohibition, and it provided a monumental victory for a movement whose success was far from guaranteed.

The struggle had been a long one, frequently contentious and bitter. It had taken place in pulpits, on political hustings, in denomi-

1

national meetings, in newspapers, and on street corners. It had pitted southern evangelicals against legends of the Confederacy such as Jefferson Davis; it had divided evangelicals internally and caused long-held theological beliefs to be reexamined, reinterpreted, and sometimes even relinquished. The movement had even seen the assassination of some of its leaders by anti-prohibitionists. The tide turned on that July day in Atlanta, and evangelicals at last found themselves victorious. Over the course of the next few years, the scene of celebration would be repeated across the southland as one southern state after another dried up and implemented statewide prohibition. Then, in 1919, the entire nation would embrace the legislative movement that had been erupting from southern statehouses over the previous decade. That year, the Eighteenth Amendment was ratified, and prohibition became part of the U.S. Constitution. Evangelicals in Georgia and across the South could congratulate themselves for launching the nation on its bold—though ultimately doomed—experiment.

The passage of statewide prohibition in Georgia marked a significant change for the South in terms of its attitude toward legal prohibition. During the antebellum period, the temperance movement enjoyed great success in the northeastern United States, and during the 1850s, more than a dozen northern states enacted statewide bans on liquor. But because of the temperance movement's Yankee origins—not to mention its strong ties to the abolition movement—it received a tepid reception in the antebellum South. Although many southern evangelicals supported temperance, they failed to make a deep impact on the larger southern society because they lacked sufficient numerical strength and cultural influence, both of which would wax rapidly after the Civil War. A more important factor in the failure to achieve prohibition in the antebellum South was the fact that the majority of southern evangelicals who supported temperance nonetheless balked at supporting legal prohibition. Using the state's power to reform the morals of sinners seldom found favor among antebellum southerners, evangelical or otherwise. Thus, no southern state enacted statewide prohibition prior to the Civil War; indeed, Georgia's 1907 legislation was the first of its kind in the South. Within a year, Alabama, Oklahoma, North Carolina, and Mississippi had gone dry, and Tennessee joined the ranks in 1909. By 1915, nine southern states had embraced statewide prohibition. Also key to this victory was the identification of the antiliquor cause with other social issues, especially race. Between 1880 and 1910, evangelicals successfully tied prohibition to these larger concerns within southern society, a development that proved essential to the movement's ultimate success in the region.

The aim of this book is to shed light on how southern evangelicals came to embrace this traditionally Yankee reform movement, make it their own, and transform the South into the standard-bearer in the agitation for national prohibition. Ultimately, prohibition in the South was achieved because of the tireless efforts of evangelicals—primarily Baptists, Methodists, and, to a lesser extent, Presbyterians—to make the legal prohibition of alcohol palatable to the white southern populace. This book studies the efforts of these southern evangelicals between 1880 and 1915 and examines the obstacles and adaptations that were part of their crusade. It turns out that their success was due in large part to their ability to adapt the prohibition message to the peculiarities of southern culture, particularly with regard to the issues of race, honor, gender, and separation of church and state.

Chapter 1 provides an overview of the rise of the temperance sentiment in New England in the early nineteenth century and its progress in the South from the antebellum period through the Civil War and Reconstruction. It then examines the shift that began in the late 1860s and early 1870s as southern Methodists and Baptists became increasingly aware of and concerned about alcohol consumption, especially within their own membership. The next chapter documents the shifts that took place in the 1880s in the vision, methodology, and involvement level of southern evangelicals with regard to the temperance issue. The simple desire to purify the church of drunkenness became a crusade to purge alcohol from all of southern society. This involved a move from reliance on moral suasion to advocacy for legal prohibition, as well as an increasingly active role for evangelicals in lobbying for legislation, endorsing candidates, and turning out the vote on election day.

The new political activism of southern evangelicals on behalf of prohibition ran afoul of a deeply held tenet of southern Christianity: the doctrine of the spirituality of the church. Chapter 3 examines the role of that doctrine within southern evangelical denominations, from its antebellum origins to its use as a justification for continued separation from their northern counterparts. It also explores the rising debate over ministers' involvement in political matters throughout the 1880s and 1890s and the underlying issues that led to changing attitudes toward the doctrine of spirituality. Some of these issues—such as the growing influence of holiness doctrine and the growing tension between low-church, egalitarian elements and the more elite, entrenched, and generally urban churchmen—were peculiar to southern Methodists. Other issues, however, were shared by all southern evangelicals. These included a growing dissatisfaction with the Democratic Party, the rise of Populism and other third-party movements within southern politics, and the threat such movements posed to the supremacy of the Democratic Party in the "solid South."

Racial tension—always a central element of southern culture—played a crucial role in the prohibition campaign. Chapter 4 explores how white southern evangelical prohibitionists' rhetoric and attitude toward African Americans underwent a significant metamorphosis between 1880 and the early 1900s. In the minds and language of these southerners, African Americans declined from a promising—though inferior—race in the 1880s to the "Sambo" of the 1890s, a childlike and irresponsible people unsuited for the responsibilities of suffrage. After 1900, in the eyes of white southerners, the black male deteriorated into the "black beast," a menacing animal who preyed on the virtue of white women and was fueled by cheap whiskey with salacious labels sold at saloons catering to blacks. Southern prohibitionists capitalized on the growing fear of black rapists and the increasing racial animosity in the early twentieth century to finally achieve prohibition throughout the South between 1907 and 1915. However, evangelical prohibitionists also offered a corrective to the rampage of mob justice toward African Americans that characterized this dark period, which historian Rayford Logan famously termed the "nadir" of race relations in the South.[2]

Another deeply ingrained aspect of southern culture—a commitment to the idea of honor—persisted into the postbellum era. Chapter 5 examines that concept of honor, the role it played in the Old South, the strained relationship between evangelicalism and the cult of honor in the antebellum period, and how that relationship changed in the postwar period. In the New South, Methodists and Baptists increasingly represented the middle and upper classes of southern society. At the same time, it was primarily poor, socially displaced white men who clung to many of the coarser aspects of the code of honor that had been rebuffed by evangelicals, including drinking, fighting, gambling, pistol carrying, and perpetrating racial violence. Southern evangelicals capitalized on their increasingly prominent role in society by reinterpreting the idea of honor and recasting it in bourgeois, Victorian terms, thus allowing them to lay claim to honor without forsaking their evangelical mores. The attempt to reclaim honor gave prohibition legitimacy as a truly southern reform movement, despite opposition from former Confederates such as Jefferson Davis, and it allowed evangelicals to portray those who opposed their moral reform agenda as dishonorable men.

The sixth chapter focuses on how prohibition opened new doors for southern women and expanded their sphere of influence and activity both in the church and in larger society. Most male evangelicals in the South supported women's vital role in the movement, but growing female participation became a two-edged sword as it threatened to bring other reforms such as women's suffrage, female preachers, and increased ecclesiastical rights for women. Chapter 6 also examines the activities of women's organizations, including the tactics and accomplishments of the WCTU and the problems its members faced when they were perceived as going too far and threatening male dominance.

Evangelicalism

The term *evangelicalism* in this study signifies a unique subset of American Protestantism, a movement born of the revivals that swept the nation in the eighteenth and early nineteenth centuries. Adherents of the New Light movement in the early eighteenth century reacted against the cold, rationalistic version of Christianity that they believed was dominating Protestantism in America. They offered a more experiential and emotional expression of faith that began to make inroads in the South prior to the American Revolution.[3] Although the effect of this movement in New England was to fragment churches, Mark Noll has noted that in the South, it served primarily to form new churches.[4] The New Light's emphasis on personal experience and revivalistic preaching made it a countercultural movement in the colonial South.[5] The first beachheads of New Light belief were established in Virginia and North Carolina by Presbyterians, but beginning in the 1760s, Baptists overtook them; after the American Revolution, the Methodists joined in the proliferation of evangelicalism across the South.[6]

At the dawn of the nineteenth century, a new wave of evangelicalism washed across the South, this time reaching further into the backcountry. For example, frenzied revivals of religious fervor erupted in camp meetings at Cane Ridge, Kentucky, in 1801. Over the next several years, similar revivals were sparked across the deeper South. In Georgia, the fires of revival burned fervently between 1802 and 1804.[7] In 1803 Lorenzo Dow, an itinerant Methodist preacher from New England, carried the evangelistic style and message to the frontier settlements of Alabama, becoming the first non-Catholic minister to preach there.

Although Presbyterians were the driving force behind the Kentucky revivals, and although evangelicals could be found in many denominations, including the Disciples of Christ and the Episcopal Church, the primary locus of evangelicalism lay within the Baptist and Methodist denominations. Less stringent in their educational requirements for clergy and more accepting of emotionalism in worship, Baptist and Methodist congregations multiplied rapidly during the first half of the nineteenth century. At the time of the American Revolution, Baptist churches accounted for only 10 percent of those in the South.[8] By 1850, that proportion had increased to nearly 35 percent, just slightly behind the Methodists, who could claim 37 percent of churches in the South.[9] By the end of the nineteenth century, Baptists and Methodists dominated the southern religious scene. In most southern states, those two denominations accounted for about 90 percent of the churches, with Presbyterians constituting another 5 to 6 percent.[10] The dominant white Baptist and Methodist bodies in the South, and the ones that receive the most attention in this study, were the Southern Baptist Convention (SBC) and the Methodist Episcopal Church, South (MECS), both formed in the mid-1840s.

Regardless of denomination, evangelical Christianity emphasized the individual's experience of a dramatic conversion event. The ensuing Christian life was viewed as a personal relationship with God and was expected to be marked by sincere religious devotion and personal piety. One's encounter with Christianity was supposed to be dramatic and life-changing, affecting one's morals and behavior in every aspect of life, both private and public. The purity of evangelical churches was maintained through strict discipline, and believers were expected to proselytize the lost and save sinners on both a local and a global scale. Evangelicalism was intensely individualistic, emphasizing the personal experience of salvation and the reformation of individual sinners rather than focusing on the aggregate sins of society or the endemic sins of social structures.

Scope of the Study

This study focuses on the prohibition movement in three southern states: Tennessee, Alabama, and Georgia. Admittedly, this involves some limitations. Drawing general conclusions about southern evangelicalism based on a sampling of only three states is bound to overlook certain nuances and unique conditions, especially in atypical southern states such as Florida and Louisiana, with their strong Catholic influence. Recent historians, however, have used such an approach with success. Daniel Stowell, for example, effectively used the study of Tennessee and Georgia to identify larger trends in southern religion during the Reconstruction era.[11] Furthermore, the three states I examine here reflect the southern context on a number of levels and capture much of the diversity of the South in terms of politics, geography, economic development, religion, wartime and Reconstruction experience, and social makeup. Each state contains the geopolitical divisions that marked so many southern states and resulted in rifts before, during, and after the Civil War.

Both Alabama and Georgia are intersected by the South's Black Belt, a designation with a dual connotation. In the antebellum period, it was a geographic term that referred to the crescent of rich (i.e., black) soil that traverses the South from Virginia to Texas. It runs east to west through both Georgia and Alabama, passing north of the sandy, coastal soil along the southern edge of each state and south of the less fertile wire-grass and hill country, where the Appalachian foothills intrude into the northern section of each state. Because this rich land was conducive to large-scale cotton production, the Black Belt also became the area where black slave labor was most beneficial to white landholders, resulting in a large African American population and accounting for the second connotation of the term. In the antebellum period, these geographic divisions created distinctions between the low-country planter aristocracy and the upland yeoman farmers; the former benefited most from slave labor, while the latter were less invested in the antebellum system. A similar geographic and political phenomenon was found in Tennessee. Whereas the flat, rich soil of the Tennessee Valley in the western and middle sections of the state historically lent itself to plantation farming and large slave populations, the mountainous eastern section benefited little from slave labor and contained a smaller African American population.

Following the 1860 presidential election, these distinctions impacted attitudes toward secession. South Carolina was the first state to secede from the Union, doing so on December 20, 1860. Alabama followed suit the next month, becoming the fourth state to secede. Southerners convened in Montgomery, Alabama, in February 1861 to write a constitution and form the Confederate States of America, and the city served as the new nation's capital until it was moved to Richmond the following summer. Hill-country regions with less to lose from the end of slavery were less inclined toward disunion, and strong Unionist tendencies ran through the mountainous regions of western Virginia, western North Carolina, eastern Tennessee, and northern Alabama and Georgia.[12] Upper South states such as Tennessee left the Union with less enthusiasm than their neighbors did, waiting until after the outbreak of hostilities to secede. By 1862, the war was effectively over for Tennessee. Key Union victories left the state under the military governorship of Andrew Johnson—himself from east Tennessee—who initiated the state's political reconstruction in 1862. Even before the Confederate surrender at Appomattox, Tennessee had abolished slavery and elected editor and Methodist minister William G. Brownlow as governor. Readmitted to the Union in the summer of 1866, Tennessee never experienced the harsher Reconstruction measures and military reoccupation implemented by the Republican-controlled Congress in 1867.

To a lesser extent than in Tennessee, Union sympathy existed in the hill country of northern Alabama and northern Georgia and persisted throughout much of the war. North Georgians resisted conscription into the Confederate army as late as 1863, and in northern Alabama the Alabama Cavalry of the U.S. Army was formed in 1862. More than two thousand Alabamians served in the cavalry during the war, eventually trekking through Georgia as part of General William Tecumseh Sherman's infamous March to the Sea.[13] Georgia was the most unified of the three states in terms of its support for secession and was not invaded by Northern troops until late in the war. Sherman left a swath of destruction—and lingering bitterness toward the

North—across the heart of Georgia. Although Georgia ratified the Thirteenth Amendment shortly after the war, its rejection of the Fourteenth Amendment caused the federal government to place the state under military rule again in 1867. Georgia was the last Confederate state to be readmitted to the Union, in 1870, and Federal troops did not evacuate the state until 1872.

When blacks in the South achieved voting rights during Reconstruction, the Black Belt took on greater political significance. Because African Americans constituted the majority of voters in Black Belt counties, they represented both a political threat to the white Democratic Party and a potentially valuable political resource to anyone who could marshal or manipulate their votes. For a time in the 1880s and early 1890s, many of these votes swung to the Populist cause, finding a brief biracial solidarity with the white yeomanry of the upcountry. Eventually, most Black Belt voters were swayed (or coerced) back to the support of the Bourbon Democrats, the old planter elite for whom most freedmen now found themselves sharecropping. But white Democrats continued to feel threatened by the black electorate, believing that the true loyalty of most freedmen still lay with the Republican Party. The potential of a neo-Reconstruction government reemerging in the South was an ever-present threat in the minds of white southerners.

Tennessee, Alabama, and Georgia also reflect the economic trends of the larger postwar South, as industrialization and urbanization finally found footholds in a region that had been almost completely ignored by the industrial and market revolutions of the early nineteenth century. New South industrialists created the city of Birmingham in 1871 in the iron-rich hills of northern Alabama. The city grew rapidly and became the leading industrial center in the South by the 1910s.[14] In Tennessee, Nashville and Memphis (and, to a lesser extent, the important rail centers of Knoxville and Chattanooga) became important commercial cities and stood in stark contrast to the rural nature of the rest of the state. The greatest success story of the postwar South was Atlanta, Georgia. As the central link in the supply chain of the Confederate army, the city had been a key target of Federal troops and emerged from the war a virtual wasteland. Afterward, Atlanta reemerged as the epicenter of the southern railway system and as the hub of the South's new economic order. In 1895 the city hosted the Cotton States and International Exposition, which instigated Atlanta's rapid growth as the home of most of the South's textile mills and other industrial plants.

In terms of religious composition, Tennessee, Alabama, and Georgia closely resemble one another and typify the religious changes that took place across the South during the nineteenth century. In all three, evangelical churches prospered following the revivals that occurred at the dawn of the nineteenth century, and they continued to grow for the next half century. In Georgia, Baptists grew in number from 9,000 members in 1790 to 55,000 by 1850, whereas Methodists advanced from just 5,000 members in 1790 to 50,000 in 1845. Presbyterians fared less well, increasing from only 200 members statewide in 1810 to about 5,000 by midcentury.[15] The rates of growth were similar in Alabama, where Methodist membership soared from 8,000 in 1832 to 40,000 in 1845, and Baptists increased from 5,000 in 1823 to 65,000 in 1860.[16] Likewise, in Tennessee, Baptists swelled in number from just 900 in 1790 to 46,000 in 1860, and Methodists went from 10,000 members in 1800 to 35,000 by 1830. Again, Presbyterians achieved slower growth, adding only 1,500 members between 1830 and the dawn of the Civil War, for a total of 8,500.[17] In the decades following the Civil War, Baptist and Methodist domination of the religious scene in the South grew stronger. By the time of the 1906 religious census, there were 160,000 white Baptists in Tennessee and 162,000 in Alabama; white Methodists numbered 140,000 in Tennessee and 191,000 in Georgia.[18]

Despite being the most unchurched region in the country during the eighteenth century, the South was transformed in the nineteenth century by the growth of evangelicalism and became known as a particularly religious region.[19] As noted by Donald G. Mathews, the southern United States has a long history of being "more orthodox, more racist, more traditionalist, and less rationalist than the rest of the country."[20] In the words of historian John Boles, the region has long been marked by an almost "tangible religious ethos."[21] In addition to its well-deserved reputation of having a more pronounced religiosity than the rest of the nation, the South has a unique form of evangelical Protestantism—one with a distinct "southern accent." Southern evangelicalism is distinct in part because it reflects the peculiar southern culture in which it exists. Based largely on its acquiescence to the institution of slavery in the antebellum era, its defense of that institution, and its "complicity in the hierarchical pattern of racial relations," southern Christianity has often been characterized as religion in cultural captivity, serving only to reinforce the values and institutions of the secular culture around it.[22]

By the late antebellum period, southern evangelical divines had become renowned for their unstinting defense of the institution of slavery. Their role as cultural apologists, however, was a far cry from the initial position they occupied in the South. As Christine Leigh Heyrman has demonstrated, evangelicals made deep inroads into the South during the colonial and revolutionary periods, but they did so as outsiders who often stood in opposition to the prevailing white culture of the region. Evangelicalism—especially as embodied by Baptists and then Methodists—was an iconoclastic movement in the South, relentlessly attacking the Church of England for its ceremonialism and lack of moral stringency. Furthermore, early Baptist and Methodist ministers in the South found themselves at odds with the prevailing culture because they often opposed slavery and held liberal views regarding the role of women in the church, often allowing them to teach and preach.[23] However, as evangelicals changed the religious attitudes of southerners, and as they grew in number, the movement increasingly embraced the social and cultural views of the region. Thus, by the time evangelicalism dominated the southern religious landscape in the early nineteenth century, it reflected the region's attitude toward women, race, and slavery.[24]

As my study of southern evangelicalism's post–Civil War efforts on behalf of prohibition demonstrates, southern evangelicals provided religious validation and underpinning to many impulses in southern culture, but they also worked to remake southern society in their own image. Their crusade against liquor reveals that evangelicals both shaped and were shaped by the culture around them. Prohibition served a multitude of functions for evangelicals and also reflected and exposed a number of impulses, tensions, and changes taking place within southern evangelicalism at the end of the nineteenth century. By accommodating and adapting their campaign for prohibition to the peculiar cultural baggage of the South, evangelicals were successful in transforming the South from a region with a natural disinclination toward governmental restrictions on drinking to one that led the United States in its experiment with nationwide prohibition in the 1920s.

Within the context of these three states, this study examines the prohibition message of white evangelicals, primarily members of the SBC and the MECS. Southern Presbyterians constituted a much smaller portion of white church membership and participated in the prohibition crusade less fervently than did Methodists and Baptists. The sources relied on for this study include denominational minutes and proceedings, denominational newspapers, sermons preached in white evangelical churches, and the personal papers and correspondence of white evangelicals. These sources allow for a thorough examination and understanding of the arguments, motivations, and justifications that influenced southern white evangelical attitudes toward liquor and prohibition. But these sources are not without limitations. The voices they contain belong primarily to white men, most of whom were middle class and educated and held positions of authority either in their churches or within the state denominational structure. The voices of women and African Americans are largely absent from these historical sources, or they are filtered through the press and denominational reports controlled by white men. In recognition of these limits, this study examines primarily the actions and attitudes of white male evangelical leaders of the southern prohibition movement; it does not presume that white sources can speak on behalf of black Christians or that male voices can speak on behalf of the multitude of women involved in the prohibition campaign.

Chapter One

"Distilled Damnation"

Temperance before 1880

HEMAN HUMPHREY PERSONIFIED the early phase of the movement to eradicate drunkenness in America. In 1813 the Congregational minister penned what was likely the first temperance tract in the United States, inaugurating a new genre of religious publication that would stream off printing presses for the next century.[1] Humphrey's tract embodied all the core characteristics of the nascent antebellum temperance movement, and he embodied the spirit of the New England evangelicals who launched it. A minister, revivalist, and later president of Amherst College, he represented a new breed of northeastern evangelical that emerged in the early nineteenth century. Humphrey was educated at Yale during the years when Timothy Dwight was leading spiritual revivals among the student body, and he carried into the pastorate the spirit of the Second Great Awakening and its attendant interests in evangelization, education, moral improvement, and missions. In the years immediately following the publication of his temperance tract, these impulses coalesced in the Evangelical United Front, a loose national network of evangelical benevolence societies such as the American Bible Society, the American Sunday School Union, the American Tract Society, the American Board of Foreign Missions, the Home Missions Society, and numerous other independent and denomination-based organizations formed in the 1810s and 1820s. These organizations represented the important role of voluntarism in post-Revolution American Protestantism

13

and did much to infuse American culture with a strong Protestant flavor.[2]

Antebellum Temperance in New England

Between the American Revolution and the War of 1812, alcohol consumption in the United States increased dramatically. After the turn of the century, a number of factors—including urban growth, economic instability, and profound changes in the social, political, and economic order—contributed to a pattern of Americans drinking more (and harder) whiskey than they ever had before or have since. In what historian W. J. Rorabaugh has called a "veritable whiskey binge" by Americans, consumption of distilled liquor almost doubled between 1790 and 1830, when it reached a per capita rate of 4.3 gallons.[3] Beginning in the 1810s, the northeastern United States underwent a fundamental shift from a subsistence economy to a market economy, stimulated by transportation and other developments that opened up large new markets to farmers and settlers in the previously isolated American backcountry. This market revolution encouraged farmers to produce more whiskey for exportation, which in turn made liquor cheaper and more plentiful both on the frontier and in eastern cities. Likewise, as travel increased, more taverns sprang up along newly built roads and canals, and the societal restraints on tavern keepers and their patrons weakened. In colonial society, drinking in a tavern had almost always been a local activity, done in the presence of friends and neighbors one would have to face the following day. But early Americans soon discovered that what happened in a distant roadside tavern stayed there, so they had fewer consequences to deal with if they partook of one dram too many.

There were also changes in terms of how people drank. The solitary binge became more prevalent than in colonial and revolutionary days, when drinking had primarily been a communal activity.[4] Along with this increased consumption came increased occurrences of drunkenness, a fact that did not escape the attention of evangelicals such as Heman Humphrey. He noted in his tract that a fellow New Englander had recently traveled to North Carolina and reported that drunkenness and raucous behavior among young men there were "considered as a thing of course."[5] Other early New England temperance advocates recognized more immediate threats to public order.

John Marsh, also of Connecticut, argued that ardent (or distilled) spirits unleashed criminality and animal instincts in a man and took him beyond the control of reason.[6]

As Americans' drinking patterns changed, so did the conventional wisdom regarding the benefits of alcohol. Throughout the colonial period, alcoholic beverages had been considered beneficial to the body and even, in the eyes of Puritans such as Increase Mather, a "good blessing from God."[7] During the revolutionary period, however, such assumptions began to be questioned. In 1774 Anthony Benezet, a Quaker, published a pamphlet charging that alcohol was detrimental to the body, soul, and society. A decade later Benjamin Rush, a Presbyterian physician from Philadelphia and a signer of the Declaration of Independence, published *An Enquiry into the Effects of Spiritous Liquors upon the Human Body, and Their Influence upon the Happiness of Society.* The work outlined the ways in which hard liquor was responsible for various physical and mental ailments and vices. Rush also dispelled popular myths regarding alcohol, such as the ideas that it kept one's body warm during cold weather, relieved fatigue, and aided in laborious work.[8]

Rush's writing received new potency and use after the first decade of the nineteenth century. In 1811 he reprinted a thousand copies of his pamphlet for distribution at the Presbyterian General Assembly, and the facts he compiled became the standard reference source for the early temperance tracts that began to appear. Humphrey's first tract, for example, emphasized the detrimental effects of alcohol on both the individual and society and relied heavily on Rush's writings. Although the Presbyterians responded by issuing a manifesto urging that societies be organized to promote morals and combat intemperance and Sabbath breaking, other denominations were not ready to embrace the temperance sentiment. In 1813 the Methodist General Conference attempted to pass a resolution prohibiting its ministers from selling alcohol, but the resolution failed.[9]

In the churches of New England, however, temperance was an idea whose time had come. Humphrey's tract was published in Connecticut in 1813, the same year that the first temperance society was formed in nearby Massachusetts.[10] The Massachusetts Society for the Suppression of Intemperance (MSSI) and others like it were formed in the 1810s in various urban centers of New England, primarily by Congregational ministers like Humphrey. Evangelicals were drawn to the temperance movement because they perceived intemperance as a threat on many levels. It was ruinous to the individual, destroying his mind and body and hindering his salvation. It tore families apart, as money that should have been spent on family necessities was wasted at the grog shop, and the drunken husband often abused and neglected his wife and children. It was damaging to society because it turned good, honest men into lazy, unproductive drunkards. Finally, it was a hindrance to the work of the church, because it kept the gospel message from reaching the men who needed to hear it most. For all these reasons, evangelicals became the core supporters of the temperance movement in its early decades and the main source of membership in organizations such as the MSSI.

Some historians interpret the formation of such organizations as a logical response to the changing conditions of society and the documented increase in alcohol consumption. Others, however, view the actions of Humphrey and others with more skepticism and charge that they were motivated by fear arising from their flagging social status and the decline of Federalism. Historians such as Joseph Gusfield, John Rumbarger, and Ian Tyrrell argue that the early temperance advocates were more concerned about maintaining social control and defending their "social allocation" than they were with stamping out inebriation. William Breitenbach has advanced a sort of post-Revolution declension theory, positing that temperance reformers were part of a generation haunted by the enormous legacy of their Revolution-era fathers. Temperance offered them an opportunity to "prove that they, too, had an important role to play in the history of the nation." Tyrrell asserts that early, short-lived groups such as the MSSI were concerned primarily with the growing immorality of the culture and the loss of their own social influence. He contends that the early temperance movement—which he calls a "surrogate Federalist crusade for social control"—lacked both a strong conviction about the liquor problem and effective organizational skills. These historians view the early northern movement as an effort by evangelicals to maintain their waning social prestige and recapture their place as moral authorities in the community, just as earlier historians such as John R. Bodo, John L. Thomas, and Charles I. Foster reclassified other postrevolutionary humanitarian efforts of northern evangelicals.[11]

The earliest temperance organizations, formed during the economically stressful period from 1812 to 1818, aimed their reforming message primarily at the upper class. Humphrey's tract, for example, called for the discontinuation of "the customary use of ardent spirits . . . particularly in pious families." This message was typical of early groups such as the MSSI, which were composed primarily of upper-class men who sought to influence those of equal social standing.[12] The movement was soon to be overtaken by the middle class, however. In 1826 the American Temperance Society (ATS) was formed in Boston. Although evangelical Christians were the driving force behind its founding, the ATS drew much of its support from manufacturers, entrepreneurs, commercial farmers, and members of the medical profession.[13] The evangelical Christians who founded the ATS were also active in other aspects of the Evangelical United Front, such as Bible societies, tract societies, and missions organizations. The ATS was one of the most successful and representative organizations during the first phase of the temperance movement. Its focus was on self-reform, and it called for abstinence only from distilled liquor, not from all alcoholic beverages. It was aimed at the middle-class businessman, who was expected to set an example of moderate drinking for the working class. The ATS reflected the evangelical ideology and methodology of other reform movements of the time, including the utilization of itinerant speakers, the widespread dissemination of literature, and the use of previously untapped sources of support such as women and young people. Also, the ATS still considered moral suasion, not legal coercion, as the best means of transforming society.[14]

During the 1830s the message and objectives of the temperance reformers shifted. Although they had traditionally remonstrated against only hard liquor, temperance advocates increasingly adopted a position of teetotalism, pledging to abstain from all forms of alcohol.[15] In 1836 a new organization committed to total abstinence, the American Temperance Union (ATU), emerged and soon became the dominant temperance society in the United States. Also during the 1830s, temperance advocates began to move beyond the tactic of moral suasion to embrace legislative means of limiting alcohol consumption. This activity started on the local level, where supporters of the "no-license" position attempted to limit the liquor trade by persuading local authorities to deny liquor licenses to applicants. The no-license effort met with varying degrees of success, but by the end of the decade, most northern temperance reformers accepted legal prohibition as their best hope for solving the liquor problem.

The next phase of the temperance movement began in 1840 when a new teetotal organization, the Washingtonians, appeared. This group, which was formed in Baltimore by six drinkers who had taken a pledge of total abstinence, included members from the middle class but also attracted many working-class men and women into the temperance movement for the first time. The ATU heartily endorsed the Washingtonian movement at first, but tension between the old and new wings of temperance advocacy soon developed. Washingtonians opposed legal prohibition and were often indifferent toward the evangelical religion that had always been a vital part of the movement. The Washingtonian movement itself soon split internally along class lines. Its middle-class members preferred the ATU style of temperance reform and wanted the group to be more socially respectable; many of them formed groups such as the Sons of Temperance that supported prohibition and embraced evangelical religion. The lower-class Washingtonians were primarily people who had been hard hit by the depression that began in 1837. Although they blamed alcohol for their economic plight, they were more sensitive to the tavern owner's right to make a living and were fearful of oppressive prohibitory laws. By the mid-1840s, however, middle-class members controlled most Washingtonian societies, and legal prohibition was again the main objective of American temperance crusaders.[16]

The final antebellum stage of the temperance movement came with efforts to enact statewide prohibition. Temperance reformers had begun their quest for legal prohibition in the 1830s by means of local licensing boards. Next came attempts at the county level to limit the sale of alcohol. By the 1850s, reformers in many states were optimistic that they could impose prohibition at the state level. Maine politician Neal Dow led the charge, drafting legislation that prohibited the sale of liquor in his state. The law was passed in 1851, and by 1855, twelve other northern states had enacted similar "Maine laws," and several others had passed limited versions of the law. But legal challenges to the constitutionality of the various Maine laws soon dealt a debilitating blow to the statewide movement. In addition, enforcement difficulties plagued most of the states that had passed Maine laws. By 1857, the prominent temperance lecturer John B. Gough ruefully announced that the agitation for statewide prohibition was now "a dead letter everywhere."[17] Enthusiasm for such laws faded even further as the nation's sectional conflict took center stage in politics. The temperance movement in the North thus experienced a lull during the late 1850s and throughout the 1860s.

Antebellum Temperance in the South

In the antebellum North, temperance became a powerful reform movement that was widely embraced by those both inside and outside the church. The South, however, was a different story. Measuring the strength of the temperance impulse there has been more challenging. Scholarly examinations of this period have arrived at very different conclusions regarding the movement's strength, vitality, and breadth of appeal in the South. Some historians view it as a strong counterpart to the movement in the North, with close parallels in terms of message, growth, and tactics. Others see the southern movement as a weak and ineffectual impulse with only "superficial and short-lived" parallels with northern temperance. They blame the South's lack of a market economy, its fear of abolitionism, and its distinct social patterns for retarding the spread of temperance sentiment there. Historians of this latter persuasion include Ian Tyrrell, who argues that southern temperance had "pockets of strength" but never compared with the northern movement in terms of enthusiasm or support. Tyrrell notes that although the southern states contained 44 percent of the nation's population in 1831, it was the source of only 8.5 percent of the pledges received by temperance organizations.[18]

One traditional explanation for the lack of widespread support for temperance in the South has been the movement's close affiliation with abolitionism in the North. Certainly, that connection was not lost on most southerners. Both movements shared similar origins in the Northeast. Benjamin Rush had served as a critical catalyst in the changing attitude toward liquor, but he had also been president of the nation's first antislavery society and played a major role in abolishing slavery in Pennsylvania.[19] The nation's first temperance paper, the *National Philanthropist*, had merged in 1829 with William Lloyd Garrison's *Investigator*. Thus, the temperance movement became associated with Garrison, whose antislavery rhetoric in the *Liberator* had led Georgia's governor to offer a $5,000 reward for his arrest in the early 1830s. Likewise, Heman Humphrey, a first cousin of the soon-to-be-infamous slave revolt leader John Brown, penned *Parallel between Intemperance and the Slave Trade* in 1828.[20] That tract blasted the South's peculiar institution and reinforced the connection between the two Yankee reform efforts—temperance and abolitionism—in the minds of many southerners. Humphrey argued that intemperance was a greater blight on the nation than was the trade in enslaved human beings, calling slavery a "mere sting of an insect" compared to the "fangs of a tyger" that intemperance represented. Although he viewed abolition as secondary to temperance in terms of importance, Humphrey's tract, which originated as a Fourth of July address, inextricably linked the two reform movements, and he called on his evangelical audience to engage in the fight to eradicate both evils.[21]

Figures such as Rush, Garrison, and Humphrey embodied the strong connection between temperance and abolitionism. The tie between the two movements became increasingly blatant in the 1830s. In Georgia, subscribers to the *Temperance Recorder* were bombarded with unsolicited abolitionist literature from the North.[22] The Connecticut Baptist Convention bound abolition and temperance together in an 1839 resolution that stated, "Every man has a right to be sober and a right to be free."[23] Historians have frequently blamed this connection for the South's ambivalence toward temperance and for the movement's sluggish performance there.[24] Northern leaders of the ATS recognized southerners' hesitance to embrace a movement tainted by abolitionism and sought to allay their fears. In 1833 they proclaimed that their only objective was temperance, and in 1836 the organization elected John Hartwell Cocke—a Virginia evangelical and hero of the War of 1812—as its president.[25] Yet such actions apparently did little to ease southern concerns. During the late 1820s, eight temperance societies associated with the ATS were formed in Alabama, but after 1833, no new Alabama society was affiliated with the national body.[26]

Nonetheless, Tyrrell and others consider the connection between temperance and abolitionism an insufficient explanation for the relative weakness of the movement in the South. Tyrrell concedes that by the 1830s, southerners were deeply suspicious of the temperance movement and its northern leadership, fearing that it was merely a front for abolitionism. He notes that although some of the strongest temperance supporters in the region were wealthy slaveholding planters, the majority were entrepreneurs and other middle-class residents of cities and small towns, very similar to the demographic group that supported temperance in the North.[27] Therein lies the cause of the movement's weakness in the South, according to Tyrrell. Northern temperance thrived in agricultural areas that were coming under the influence of a market economy. Because most of the rural South did not experience the same kind of market revolution, the key economic and social forces that drove northern temperance reform sentiment were largely absent from the South prior to the Civil War. Not until the 1850s, when railroads began to improve the transportation of goods from rural farms to larger markets, did temperance become more acceptable to the majority of southerners. Tyrrell argues that with these market improvements, rural farmers no longer had to distill their corn into whiskey for easier transportation; only then did opposition to temperance weaken and support for the movement begin to spread beyond the urban middle class. Tyrrell also contends that for most of the antebellum period, industrial entrepreneurs were largely lacking in the South. Thus, the preindustrial nature of the southern economy; the resistance of the agrarian majority, which had a vested commercial interest in continuing to distill their crops; along with a culture that valued the heavy consumption of alcohol kept temperance reformers from exerting significant influence in the antebellum South.

Rufus Spain likewise argues that "the South failed to keep pace with the rest of the nation in promoting temperance."[28] Stephen West agrees and, like Tyrrell, maintains that the movement in the South was crippled because southern society lacked the "emergence of capitalist economic relations and bourgeois culture" that flourished in the North following the market revolution earlier in the century. As evidence of the weakness of southern temperance relative to that in the North, scholars such as Tyrrell and West point to the fact that no southern state passed prohibition statutes prior to the Civil War, whereas a dozen northern states followed Maine with such legislation in the early 1850s.[29] Bertram Wyatt-Brown adds that those elements within the church that did wish to stem the rising tide of alcohol consumption simply lacked the power to do so in southern society. Even during the 1840s and 1850s, as the influence of evangelicals in southern society rose considerably, they had little success in changing the region's drinking habits. In the end, Wyatt-Brown argues, southern temperance efforts failed because of the economic and market factors discussed earlier and because southern churchgoers were not of one mind on the issue.[30]

Not all scholars of the subject have concluded that the antebellum temperance movement stagnated in the South because of the fear of abolitionism and the pursuit of economic self-interest. Jack Blocker notes that by 1831, temperance societies had been set up in every southern state except for Louisiana.[31] Douglas Carlson has examined the antebellum temperance movement in Georgia, Alabama, South Carolina, and Mississippi and observes that although the South had fewer temperance advocates, the southern movement was nonetheless a vibrant counterpart to that in the North. He cites its particularly rapid growth between 1828 and 1831, when the number of temperance societies in the South increased from 10 to 339.[32] Carlson concurs with the judgment of other historians that antebellum evangelicals constituted a conservative "culture church" that undergirded the status quo with theological justifications, and he notes that the influence of slavery on this agrarian culture prevented many evangelicals from being overly critical of the region's mores and practices. Nevertheless, he contends that there was significant southern participation in the movement.

Carlson argues against the "modernization paradigm"—the thesis that northern temperance grew out of the needs of the bourgeois class in the wake of modernization, industrialization, and market changes—and he rejects the common conclusion that the lack of such forces in the antebellum South led to a less vibrant temperance sentiment there. Rather, he emphasizes the central role of religious motivation in driving the movement, argues that the very existence of temperance activity in the South prior to 1840 was because of evangelical churches, and examines the religious rhetoric of southern temperance advocates.[33] In doing so, he finds that southern temperance literature was "indistinguishable in tone, content, and purpose" from that of the North.[34] Whereas one might expect to find an emphasis on the value of temperance as a means of reducing the threat of insurrection by drunken slaves, Carlson instead discovers that southern temperance advocates rarely utilized such arguments. He contends that although the antebellum South lagged behind the North in shifting from an agrarian economy to a market economy, southern evangelicals advocating temperance emphasized the same themes of optimism, reform, and improvement of society as did northern evangelicals.

Carlson notes that many southern temperance societies were indeed chafed by the amity between temperance and abolitionism in the North. For instance, in 1834 the Georgia state temperance society denounced any affiliation with such national bodies, and in 1849 it withdrew its invitation to have Father Mathew, a famous Irish Catholic temperance leader, speak to its members because he refused to renounce his antislavery stance. Nonetheless, Carlson observes that regional antagonism and the slavery issue played remarkably minor roles in southern arguments for temperance.[35] Furthermore, Carlson finds that southern temperance proceeded along a parallel path with the movement in the North. In contrast to the popular opinion that antebellum southerners rejected the reform movements of the North, he believes that the southern movement was both vibrant and in deep sympathy and accord with its northern counterpart. From the rapid growth of the temperance movement at the beginning of the 1830s to its decline following the economic depression of 1837, southerners paralleled their northern counterparts in pushing for reform—up to, but not including, the passage of statewide legal prohibition in the 1850s. Carlson notes that "if southerners shared with northerners in all other phases of the movement, they were more reticent to pass prohibition laws." Antebellum southern evangelicals were deeply committed to temperance as long as it was grounded in moral suasion. Once the emphasis shifted toward statewide legal prohibition, southerners balked.[36]

But southern antebellum temperance efforts were not merely the northern movement in miniature. The writings published in southern temperance newspapers such as Georgia's *Temperance Banner* and Alabama's *Crystal Fount* echoed the messages being published in northern papers, but they were original pieces written by southern temperance advocates, not simply articles that were imported and reprinted from northern sources.[37] Tyrrell notes that southern temperance advocates distanced themselves not only from northern temperance societies but also from northern temperance papers and writers, to avoid being associated with abolitionism.[38] Southern temperance papers published articles written by southerners that articulated the same arguments found in the North. Like their northern counterparts, these writings emphasized the theme of the ruinous impact of intemperance on three aspects of life: the individual, the family, and the community.

Thus, the picture of temperance reform in the antebellum South is mixed. Neither southern evangelicals nor reform-minded southerners in general maintained a consistent and united front against alcohol in the first half of the nineteenth century. There were moments of active agitation as well as moments of ambivalence and retreat. Tyrrell largely ignores the role of evangelicals in the temperance movement, especially in the South; instead, he emphasizes the need for a large contingent of middle-class manufacturers and entrepreneurs for any effective temperance reform to take root. In his view, the South did not have a strong antebellum temperance movement because it did not need one—at least not in terms of requiring its workforce to be punctual or to conform to the work patterns necessary for efficient industrial manufacturing. Carlson, in contrast, focuses exclusively on southern evangelical temperance literature. Whereas Tyrrell focuses on the overall size and success of temperance reform in each region, Carlson examines the movement only to the extent that it did exist in the South and compares its message to that of the North.

The bottom line is that a southern temperance movement, though smaller than its northern counterpart, did exist beginning in the late 1820s and was driven primarily by evangelicals. At the time, however, evangelicalism was still a much less influential segment of society in the South than it was in the North, and its power to effect change was proportionally less. In addition, southern evangelicals faced more social opposition than northerners did, in the form of a culture that strongly opposed temperance reforms and a preindustrial economic system that resisted any reduction in alcohol production and had little need for a sober workforce. Though not overwhelming in numbers, southern temperance advocates were energetic and deeply committed to their cause. They may have distanced themselves from the abolitionism of national temperance organizations, but there was little regional distinction in the message of southern temperance advocates. Only when southern evangelicals took up the temperance cause more fervently after the Civil War would they find it necessary to accommodate their message to the peculiarities of the surrounding culture.

The antebellum temperance movement lacked not only the will to use the power of the state but also the means of raising the liquor issue to a crisis level, so that the white male population would have no choice but to address it. Drinking was almost entirely a pastime enjoyed by white men. Drunkenness by slaves never presented a dire threat to the social order, as their access to alcohol was generally regulated by both the law and their masters, who possessed the absolute authority to punish any slave who committed a drink-induced transgression. In other words, whites effectively maintained social control over the African American population without any need for broad liquor legislation. Furthermore, southern cultural practices were still dictated largely by the planter elite, whose highly prized code of honor gave liquor a prominent role. Not until after the Civil War, when blacks experienced liberation and the planter aristocracy began to be eclipsed by a rising middle class, did conditions exist for prohibition sentiment to flourish in the South.

Southern Evangelicals and Temperance

It is clear that evangelicals took the early lead in promoting temperance in the South. The southern temperance movement began roughly a decade after it emerged in New England. In her study of antebellum southern social concerns, Anne Loveland states that the first temperance society in the region was formed in Virginia in 1826. An earlier study of North Carolina, however, found that temperance societies existed there in 1822, with calls for such organizations appearing in North Carolina newspapers as early as 1819.[39] It was not until the late 1820s that such societies emerged in Tennessee, Alabama, and Georgia. Aidel Sherwood, a Baptist minister, organized Georgia's first temperance society in 1827, which was soon followed by numerous others throughout the state.[40] In 1829 a statewide convention of temperance supporters was held in conjunction with the Baptist Convention. It passed a resolution praising the fact that it was no longer considered impolite to neglect to set out the dram bottle for guests in one's home or to harvest fields without the aid of liquor. One could even find "weddings in respectable families" where alcohol was not served. Some Georgia Baptist leaders, such as Jesse Mercer, were at first turned off by the new movement, claiming that its followers were too zealous in their attacks on alcohol. Mercer was one of the most prominent Baptist ministers in the state, as was his father before him. In 1822 he served as one of the principal organizers of the General Association of Georgia Baptists (which in 1827 became the Georgia Baptist Convention) and of what would become Mercer University, the state's largest Baptist college. For several years Mercer defended his medicinal use of brandy, but in the early 1830s he renounced all alcohol and embraced the temperance movement. In 1834 he established the *Temperance Banner*, the South's first temperance newspaper.[41]

Georgia Methodists established their first temperance society at their General Conference in 1832.[42] Early leaders in the Georgia temperance movement included Josiah Flournoy of Putnam County, who in the late 1830s crisscrossed the state in his buggy gathering signatures on petitions asking the state legislature to repeal local liquor license laws.[43] By the end of the decade, evangelical support for temperance had widened considerably. In 1839 temperance advocates from several denominations met at the Eatonton Baptist Church and issued an appeal to all Georgians to call on the state legislature to eliminate the current licensing system that permitted alcohol sales.[44]

In 1828 the first temperance society was formed in Alabama, followed by the first statewide organization—the Alabama State Temperance Society—in 1834. As in Georgia, Alabama temperance advocates began to petition for state intervention at the end of the 1830s. In 1838 a Baptist minister, Hosea Holcombe, presented a memorial to the state legislature asking for temperance reform; this memorial was repeated in 1840 by the Alabama Baptist Convention.[45] During the 1840s, however, there was a significant decline in the zeal of temperance advocates in Alabama, blamed largely on the increased political involvement of temperance organizations. As James Sellers has observed, once a temperance advocate in antebellum Alabama turned to supporting legal prohibition, "he ceased to be a harmless fanatic and became a menace to powerful interests."[46]

In Tennessee, temperance societies began to emerge in 1831, the same year that the state dropped its "quart law," which had limited liquor sales to quantities greater than one quart. Tennessee had copied North Carolina's quart law when it achieved statehood in 1796, but legislators abandoned it in 1831 in the hope that allowing the sale of liquor by the drink would increase liquor tax revenues. In a backlash against this action, temperance societies emerged across the state and quickly gained strength; by 1837, they had forced the reenactment of the quart law. Methodists were particularly active in temperance reform in Tennessee during the 1830s. They were led by John B. McFerrin, a minister in the Tennessee Conference who later became renowned for converting future president James K. Polk to Christianity at a camp meeting.[47] In 1833 the Tennessee Conference of the Methodist Episcopal Church (MEC) resolved not to use alcohol and urged all Methodist preachers to become agents of temperance reform.[48] In the 1840s and 1850s east Tennessean William G.

Brownlow—a Methodist minister, editor of the South's largest weekly newspaper, defender of slavery, supporter of the Union throughout the Civil War, and Reconstruction governor of the state—took the lead in the cause, writing and speaking extensively for temperance.[49] But Tennessee temperance advocates faced a setback in 1846 when the quart law was repealed by a new "tippling act" that once again allowed the sale of liquor by the drink. Although no Tennessee gubernatorial candidate in the mid-1850s advocated following Maine's example of statewide prohibition, the 1856 legislature reinstated the quart law again. Unfortunately for temperance supporters, legislators repealed it the following year.[50]

The message of evangelical temperance advocates centered, as Carlson has demonstrated, on the triple threat of alcohol to the individual, the family, and the community. But evangelical support for temperance was never unanimous in the 1820s and 1830s (or at any time during the antebellum period, for that matter). Holcombe called intemperance "the sin of sins in the Baptist church," but not all Baptists saw drinking in such negative terms.[51] Isham Peacock, a Georgia Baptist minister, was renowned for carrying a hollowed-out cane filled with whiskey. Peacock, nearly one hundred years old at the time, would swill from his cane in front of his congregation to prove that he could drink liquor without becoming drunk.[52] Some hard-shell Baptists who opposed temperance societies were reportedly "in the habit of 'saying grace' over their liquor before drinking." In Georgia, a Baptist minister in the late 1820s also ran the local grog shop.[53] One southerner in the 1820s observed that "it was the fashion in those days for very nice people, even clergymen, to drink in moderation."[54] Because of their rigid Calvinism and pessimistic, premillennial vision, hard-shell Baptists rejected the idea of improving society in any way or of transmitting any code of personal piety and morality to the larger culture.[55]

Both Baptists and Presbyterians faced resistance from within. Primitive Baptists and other antimission Baptists strongly resisted the temperance cause, particularly because it relied on the use of external societies for its promotion. Primitive Baptists had no use for such "modern innovations" as Bible societies, Sunday schools, and seminaries.[56] Many Baptists of this persuasion in the 1820s and early 1830s broke off to form separate bodies, such as the Two-Seed-in-the-Spirit Predestinarian Baptists. Yet antimission sentiment continued to exist within mainline state Baptist conventions in the South. They were a frequent source of opposition to temperance societies and were reluctant to discipline or expel members who continued to drink alcohol. Those who opposed such extraecclesial organizations were often referred to as "antieffort" Baptists. They maintained that institutions such as Sunday schools, temperance societies, and mission societies were "destroying the independence of the churches and taking away their keys."[57]

When the Ebenezer Baptist Association was formed in Alabama in 1838, its constitution included an article forbidding fellowship with any congregation that supported temperance, tract, or missionary societies, as well as any affiliation with state conventions or theological schools. The Tallassahatchee Baptist Association, comprising Baptist congregations in both Alabama and Georgia, split in the late 1830s when a group of churches within the association refused to have fellowship with churches that supported such societies. The breakaway churches declared, "We . . . believe the benevolent institutions to be unscriptural, viz: the missionary society, Bible society, tract society, temperance society, Sunday School Union, and the abolition society."[58] Likewise, the Yellow River Baptist Association in Georgia included abolition societies in the list of organizations it denounced. Given that no abolition societies existed in the state at the time, their inclusion was likely intended to further disparage temperance and other societies by their association with abolitionism.[59]

Presbyterians in the South took an active role in the temperance crusade in the 1820s and 1830s, but their enthusiasm began to wane toward the end of the latter decade. This was due in part to a concern similar to that of the primitive Baptists regarding the church's increased reliance on external societies. Southern Presbyterian leaders such as James Henley Thornwell argued against using such bodies to carry out the work of the church. In Thornwell's view, the question of temperance societies fell under the larger issue of church boards. He argued that scripture required all church affairs to be controlled directly by the church, not delegated to outside organizations such as mission boards. Although many northern Presbyterians sided with Charles Hodge, who characterized Thornwell's position on boards as "hyper, hyper, hyper high church Presbyterianism," southern Presbyterians largely embraced the Thornwellian view.[60] In 1848 the General Assembly resolved that the church should not link itself with such external societies.[61]

Similar arguments can be found in all southern evangelical denominations, and they represent a kind of conservative opposition that would beleaguer the movement in both the antebellum and postbellum eras. Thornwell has been called "the Calhoun of the church," although Eugene Genovese has suggested that it may be more accurate to refer to John C. Calhoun as "the Thornwell of the state." Conservatives such as Thornwell and the antieffort Baptists held to a very strict construction of the Bible, which led them to argue against extrabiblical innovations such as mission and temperance societies. Calhoun's similar interpretation of the Constitution led to ideas such as states' rights and popular sovereignty in the South—ideas that had political consequences for the entire nation after his death. These ideas also led many conservatives both inside and outside the church to oppose temperance and prohibition in the antebellum period on the grounds that it violated individual rights and local sovereignty. Political heirs of Calhoun, such as Jefferson Davis, would echo these objections to prohibition in the New South era.[62]

After the mid-1840s, support for the temperance movement began to decline in the South, even within its evangelical base. As sectional antagonism over the slavery issue became increasingly heated and divisive, the weight of temperance's genealogy as a northern movement with ties to abolitionism became more difficult to ignore. In 1849 the Liberty Baptist Association in Alabama refused to admit the Rechab Baptist Church because it was a "test church," meaning that members were required to take a pledge of total abstinence. The admission of such a church, the association explained, was likely to create internal strife because many member churches did not embrace temperance.[63] Later apologists for southern temperance maintained that had it not been "for the overshadowing slavery controversy," Georgia's early evangelical temperance workers would "have cleared the state of the liquor traffic before the secession conflict."[64] As it was, however, evangelicals grew uncomfortable with the increasingly secular and political nature of the movement. Taking the cause into the political arena was risky and unpopular in most of the South, and temperance organizations that meddled in politics often suffered for it. For example, the national group Sons of Temperance boasted a strong organization in Alabama until it began to support the Know-Nothing Party and blended politics into its temperance message, after which the group's support dwindled. This was also true of other nonchurch temperance organizations in the South, such as the Washingtonians, which disintegrated after embracing legal prohibition in the 1850s.[65]

Among Methodists, internal tensions contributed significantly to the waning support for temperance beginning in the late 1830s and especially after the mid-1840s. Prior to the rupture of the Methodist Episcopal Church, temperance was caught up in ongoing internal denominational struggles regarding slavery and the power of the episcopacy. In 1816, before temperance sentiment had taken root in either the North or the South, the MEC had amended its general rules to lessen restrictions on church members regarding the use and sale of alcohol. Charles Wesley had implemented the original rule in 1743, which required all members of the church to avoid drunkenness and enjoined them not to buy, sell, or drink liquor. The new rule implemented in 1816 merely forbade ministers to sell alcohol. In 1836 the General Conference voted to extend this rule to deacons and elders, but there was also an effort afoot to discard the 1816 rule entirely and reinstate Wesley's original, more stringent rule. A motion to do so was defeated in 1836 and again in 1840, largely as a result of southern opposition to the change. Although many Methodists in the South strongly supported the temperance movement and may have preferred the stricter rule, these votes became part of larger ongoing debates within the denomination.[66]

These disputes involved the issues of slavery and the strength of the episcopacy, both of which divided the denomination along regional lines. In both 1836 and 1840 the resolutions regarding temperance were overshadowed by abolitionist-sponsored resolutions that called for a total separation of all Methodists from the institution of slavery. Likewise, debates in both years concerning the power of the General Conference over bishops distracted attention from the temperance issue. Both the slavery and the episcopacy questions drove the delegates into regional voting blocs. The slavery issue did so for obvious reasons, and the episcopacy question had been entangled with the slavery issue since the 1820s. Northern Methodists wanted to strengthen the conference's authority over bishops; southerners saw this as a back door through which abolitionists could impose their will, so they desired a stronger and more independent episcopacy. At the next General Conference of 1844, these two intertwined issues would come to the fore again and cause the southern conferences to withdraw from the MEC.[67]

The 1844 MEC General Conference took up the case of Bishop James O. Andrew of Georgia, who had inherited two slaves as part of his deceased wife's estate. Because church law forbade a bishop to hold slaves, the conference demanded that Bishop Andrew resign from his position. Southern Methodists were outraged at this assault on Andrew. Their prediction that northern Methodists would use the conference's power over the episcopacy as a means of attacking slavery seemed to be coming true. In defending Andrew, they viewed themselves as fighting not for the institution of slavery but rather for the church's constitution and due process. In the aftermath of the 1844 General Conference, southern conferences met to condemn the action taken against Andrew, and in 1845 they met in Louisville and formed the Methodist Episcopal Church, South.[68]

At their first General Conference as a denomination sans southerners, the MEC in 1848 overwhelmingly voted to eliminate the current rule regarding liquor use and reinstate Wesley's original 1743 rule. Without resistance from southern delegates, the General Conference was able to strengthen its stance against drinking. Southern Methodists made no such alteration and retained the less stringent rule for another four decades. Although many southern Methodists may have wished to clamp down on intemperance, the regional divisiveness and defensive mentality of the conferences constituting the MECS, and the bitter nature of their separation from their northern brethren, made it unlikely that the new southern denomination would follow the example of the MEC and reinstate Wesley's rule. This would have required them to concede that they had voted wrongly on the issue in 1836 and 1840. In the years between their secession from the MEC and the Civil War, southern Methodists became increasingly silent on the subject of temperance.

Unlike the Presbyterians and the Methodists, southern Baptists continued to actively support both temperance and prohibition into the mid-1850s. Like the Methodists, they had disaffiliated with their northern brethren, forming the Southern Baptist Convention in 1845. For the Baptists, however, the issue of temperance had never been entangled in or tainted by the debates over slavery and missionary appointments that led to their division. Some southern Baptists even sought to emulate the 1851 victory of statewide prohibition in Maine. Thus, in 1855 the Georgia Temperance Society nominated its own candidate for governor: Methodist minister Basil Hallam Overby of

Atlanta. Overby ran on a prohibition platform, but his sound defeat by both the Democratic and Know-Nothing candidates marked the final antebellum foray of southern temperance advocates into politics.[69]

Just as southern evangelical interest in the temperance movement reached its nadir, the region's political and economic fortunes also began to decline. As sectional antagonism increased and war commenced, temperance activity dwindled in both the North and the South. However, the South's experience in the Civil War and the economic devastation and political turmoil that followed would serve as a catalyst for renewed interest in temperance in the region. During the Civil War, the Confederacy faced serious food shortages and implemented wartime measures restricting the production of alcohol from corn or grain, except for a limited amount to be used in hospitals.[70] These prohibitions were motivated not by moral concern but rather by the necessity of conservation,[71] and they were lifted soon after the war. However, they gave southern states their first experience with large-scale prohibitory legislation, demonstrating that such laws could be implemented.[72]

Southern Temperance after the Civil War

As the Confederacy began to suffer more and more military defeats, southerners sought to understand and explain why the tide had turned in favor of the Union. Most southern evangelicals interpreted the decline and fall of the Confederacy as God's punishment for the region's sins. Some identified this sin as the cruel and abusive practices of southern salveholders in the antebellum period (not the actual institution of slavery—just its unbiblical administration). Others identified excessive drinking as the major moral failing of the southern nation. Even during the Civil War, the use and abuse of alcohol became a popular scapegoat for the Confederacy's military setbacks. Evangelical jeremiads attempted to convince southerners of their wrongdoing and called for repentance so that the Confederacy could resume its divinely appointed path. One such tract blamed the drinking of Confederate leaders and army officers for the South's misfortunes on the battlefield. "No wonder that disasters have befallen our arms," the author wrote, "when in defiance of the mandates of heaven . . . reeling inebriates are appointed to lead our brave cohorts to the charge." The writer went on to explain that it is "no wonder that God had forsaken us" and has brought devastating droughts and crop failures to the South, whose people had consumed "the bountiful supplies of providence, in past years, in distilled damnation."[73] The idea that alcohol abuse was to blame for the South's troubles was so widespread that one Confederate general allegedly remarked during the war that "if the South is overthrown, the epitaph should be: 'Died of Whiskey.' "[74]

Once the Confederacy was, in fact, overthrown, whiskey production in the South resumed and grew rapidly, despite postwar poverty. The South was a scene of physical, economic, and psychological desolation after the war.[75] Writing in 1868, Alabama poet Sidney Lanier described the days of Reconstruction as the "dark Raven days of sorrow." Lanier gave voice to a sense of brokenness and humiliation shared by many southerners during the postwar period, writing, "Our hearths are gone out and our hearts are broken."[76] Not surprisingly, perhaps, an increasing number of southerners turned to alcohol during this period. Historians have noted that the despondency of defeat and the increased availability of liquor as towns and cities grew only exaggerated the traditional southern drinking patterns.[77] As alcohol consumption increased, concern about the prevalence of intemperance rose among evangelicals. Frequent drinking became common among church members and even ministers. One Methodist minister in Tennessee was renowned for his practice of drinking a glass of brandy with a raw egg broken into it prior to each sermon.[78] A Baptist minister in Tennessee wrote of seeing "a Baptist preacher so drunk that he could not stand alone. He was obliged to hold to the pulpit to avoid falling down, and his speech was so incoherent that many of his congregation did not understand him; and when the church attempted to discipline him he declared that he was not drunk because he did not fall down."[79] The inebriated minister went on to chastise his congregation for pointing their judgmental fingers at him. Referring to liquor, he told them, "You know it makes a man more spiritual." He then warned his congregation that if he were disciplined he would publicly expose comparable sins of individual church members. In the end, the minister was not punished, and according to the writer of the story, the church eventually "died of strong drink."[80]

Such excesses aroused the latent temperance sentiment of southern evangelicals. As the 1860s came to a close, they began to recognize that they had backslid on the issue of temperance and sought to mend their ways. By 1869, Georgia Baptists had established a temperance committee, which conceded in its report, "That there has been a marked decline in the interest once felt in the temperance reformation, is a fact too evident to be denied." Because of the apathy of temperance workers, there was now a total absence of temperance societies in communities where they had once flourished, and churches were increasingly lax in disciplining intemperate members. "The consequence is that the sin of drunkenness is on the increase among our church members as well as in the country at large," the committee claimed, and it urged Georgia Baptists "to abstain from all such indulgences themselves, and by all prudent measures to persuade others to the same course."[81] The committee believed that the lack of temperance advocacy in recent years was likely "due to the demoralization of war." In 1870 the committee members explained that "immediately after the war, influences of a baneful character were working a great destruction, and the sudden upheavals of society had engendered a recklessness truly formidable to the temperance reform." Sounding an optimistic note, however, they contended that "now, as the public mind is being restored to quiet, we see flattering signs of a return to soberness, in habit as well as in thought."[82]

As the 1870s progressed, Methodists and Baptists in particular began to take note of the increase in drinking, especially among their own membership. Conventions, conferences, and associations drew attention to this misbehavior and called on local congregations to discipline and expel members who drank to excess and refused to reform. By 1873, the Holston Conference of the MECS created a temperance committee, and in 1875 it proclaimed that "the chief, if not the only successful, way to free humanity from the demon spirit of intemperance, is to wage a fierce and constant war upon it . . . from the pulpit, in the pastorate, and from the press." The conference urged its preachers to enforce the discipline on any church members who were intemperate so that the church might be purified and serve "as a city that is set on a hill."[83]

There was no consensus among southern Methodists regarding the liquor traffic, however. During the first half of the 1870s, they refused to declare liquor trafficking a sin. An attempt to make such a declaration failed in 1870. In 1874 the General Conference of the MECS sought to amend the general rules to declare both buying and selling liquor immoral, but the proposal failed to be ratified by the state conferences. Not until 1886 did the denomination reinstate Wesley's original rule regarding alcohol consumption and make both the manufacture and sale of liquor immoral and punishable by the church.[84]

Georgia Baptists were warned that "our success in purging the churches of this unholy leaven has not been complete; and that there is scarcely one of them that is not sometimes afflicted by the misconduct of some of its members in this respect." The state convention's temperance committee observed that the work of fighting intemperance was on the shoulders of the preachers and should not be taken lightly. It warned that "the amusing anecdotes, and frequent mirthfulness of many" temperance addresses made them less effective. Ministers were admonished to take a more serious tone, employ less levity, and make more scriptural arguments when preaching the temperance message. "Bring the authority of the Bible to bear . . . a carefully prepared and thoroughly scriptural exhibition of truth and duty in this behalf is a thing rarely if ever heard."[85] By 1874, Georgia Baptists claimed to be seeing the fruits of their stern and solemn approach to the issue. Comparing the current state of affairs to that immediately after the war, the temperance committee reported: "Then, many of our church members manufactured, sold, and freely drank ardent spirits, without incurring discipline; now, but few, if any churches, will tolerate such conduct. Then, many brethren censured pastors if they preached sermons on intemperance, or took an active part in temperance work; now, all such efforts are warmly commended, with but few exceptions."[86]

By the end of the decade, the cause was being pursued with more vigor than ever, and the dormant southern evangelical animosity toward the demon rum was roused from its slumber. Southern Methodists and Baptists increasingly turned their attention to the problem of drinking in the church and, more importantly, in the larger society. This marked the beginning of a new period of southern evangelical agitation on behalf of temperance and prohibition. During the decades that followed, the renewed southern temperance movement would dwarf anything the region had experienced in the prewar years and would reverse the antebellum order of temperance enthusiasm:

before the Civil War, the South had lagged behind the North in temperance zeal, but after 1880, southern evangelicals proudly renewed the charge against intemperance and, in the process, led the nation into its twentieth-century experiment with nationwide prohibition.

Chapter Two

"It Is Not Enough That the Church Should Be Sober"

Drying Up the South, 1880–1915

"THE GLOOM WHICH HAD SO LONG been on the affairs of the denomination was now rapidly giving way, and brighter prospects were everywhere evident," wrote B. F. Riley, reflecting on the atmosphere of the early 1880s.[1] The Alabama Baptist leader recognized that as the post–Civil War malaise began to fade in the South, evangelicals became increasingly optimistic about their mission to redeem and transform society. Beginning around 1880, southern efforts to end intemperance became vitalized as never before, and evangelicals turned increasingly outward in orientation. Though still concerned about disciplining church members who imbibed, evangelicals set their sights on the larger society around them. As a letter to the editor of the *Alabama Baptist* expressed in 1882, evangelicals felt a growing sense of duty to amend not just their own morals but those of their neighbors as well. The writer explained that a Christian "must not only protect his church by keeping its membership pure, but he must to the extent of his ability and influence protect society and the state from any evil which threatens their well-being. This is a duty which he owes to himself, as well as to society and to the state."[2] This sense of Christian duty to make others sober was echoed by the North Georgia Conference of the MECS, whose temperance committee argued that "it is not enough that the church should be sober. It is her duty to help others get sober, and stay so."[3]

During the final decades of the nineteenth century, evangelicals went to new extremes to "help others get sober"—whether the "others" wished for their help or not. Thus, after 1880, southern evangelicalism began to transform from a body seeking internal purification and demanding stricter morality of its membership to a vociferous force aimed at purging society of what evangelicals perceived as its most menacing threat: alcohol. By the turn of the century, they were deeply immersed in a moral and political crusade that was sweeping the South, and by 1915, the region that had once repudiated sumptuary legislation had been transformed into a nearly saloon-free zone from Virginia to Texas. The newfound duty of evangelicals to impose morality on the larger society involved several modifications, including a widespread embrace of teetotalism; a shift from moral suasion alone to legal suasion; the emergence of several key evangelical leaders who made prohibition the primary focus of their ministry; multiple lines of argumentation aimed at convincing both the faithful and those outside the church of the rightness of prohibition; increased political activity and lobbying; and an evolving, pragmatic advocacy of increasingly broad legislation culminating in statewide prohibition.

Teetotalism

As of the 1870s, southern evangelicals had not reached universal agreement on the issue of total abstinence from alcoholic beverages. Some denominational papers at the time even printed recipes for homemade wine.[4] In 1878 the GBC conceded, "Whether total abstinence or the general introduction of domestic wines be the proper remedy, it is not for us to inquire; this is a matter of individual opinion, on which men will probably never agree."[5] Nor did evangelicals attack the use of alcohol for medicinal purposes. An 1876 article in the *Alabama Baptist* encouraged temperance but noted, "We do not condemn its medical use."[6] In 1879 the editor of the *Holston Methodist* of east Tennessee criticized advocates of total abstinence. Although the paper supported prohibition efforts and the editor praised the good work of temperance advocates in the church, he faulted teetotalers who "bind their members to abstain from sweet cider, dried apple beer, Mexican beer, etc.—drinks that are not only innocent, but in many instances useful."[7] Many southern evangelicals continued to eschew teetotalism throughout the 1880s and even into the 1890s. In 1892 the East Tennessee Association of Baptists had to admit, "The humiliating fact stares us in the face, that many church members insist that it is not wrong to patronize barrooms to a small extent."[8]

By the 1890s, however, evangelical church bodies no longer considered abstinence to be a "matter of individual opinion," as the Georgia Baptists had in 1878. Teetotalism became the established doctrine of southern evangelicals, who had accepted a new definition of temperance: "the moderate use of all things that are helpful, and the total abstinence from all things that are harmful."[9] When recounting the development of the temperance movement in a 1902 sermon, I. O. Rust of Tennessee observed that "there was many a brawl and battle between the moderationists and teetotalers, but after awhile total abstinence won the day and entirely occupies the temperance idea of this time."[10] The Georgia Baptist Convention (GBC) praised the fact that "there seems to have dawned a new and better day for the cause, not of temperance alone, but of total abstinence and prohibition."[11] In 1908 northerner William Garrott Brown observed of southern evangelicals, "Temperance they have virtually ceased to preach, demanding instead that government compel all men to become teetotalers."[12]

Southern evangelicals were increasingly intolerant of even moderate drinking. In their worldview, there was no middle ground between the teetotaler and the drunkard. The barroom must be eliminated from society, they argued, because once a man began to drink, he would very likely become a drunkard.[13] This conviction that no one could be trusted to drink responsibly might appear to be a hyperbolic argument aimed at further demonizing alcohol. Given the existing cultural patterns of drinking and violence in the South, however, the evangelical mistrust of southern drinkers had some basis in reality. The confluence of cultural drinking patterns and the southern propensity toward violence made the existence of the saloon a particularly acute threat to the community.

A northern writer condescendingly noted in *Century Magazine* that "of wines, the common people in the South know so little that they use the term 'wine' as if there were only one kind of wine in the world." He went on to note the relative absence of beer in the South, especially outside of the cities, and concluded that southern drinking patterns were "as unlike as possible to those of southern Europe."

Walter Hines Page, a southern journalist who moved to New York when he became owner and editor of *World's Work*, likewise wrote in a 1907 editorial that the working-class southerner "knows few sports and has few mild drinks."[14] Brown observed that these drinking customs continued into the early twentieth century and remarked that in the South, "to drink means ordinarily to drink whiskey, and not at table or in the restraining company of women, but in surroundings the least conducive to moderation and decency. It means, therefore, deplorably often, not merely drunkenness, but rowdyism."[15] All these writers recognized that drinking patterns in the South differed significantly from those in the North. Therefore, the evangelicals' fear that any drinking would inevitably lead down a slippery slope to alcoholism might have been driven in some measure by an understanding of the way alcohol was consumed in southern culture. It might also reflect their concern about the potential for "rowdyism" and violence, which always lay just below the surface in southern society, and which alcohol tended to rouse.

The distinctiveness of southern drinking patterns can be attributed largely to the cultural influences on the region. During the colonial and early republic periods, immigrants settling in the North hailed primarily from England and from western European and Mediterranean countries, and these immigrants brought their respective cultures with them. Beer, wine, and cider tended to be their alcoholic beverages of choice, and these drinks were consumed chiefly at mealtimes.[16] The influence of such cultures was minimal in the South. Grady McWhiney has demonstrated that the antebellum South was populated mostly by immigrants from the Celtic regions of the British Isles (primarily Ireland, Scotland, and Wales) and that the Celtic folkways and customs implanted by these settlers in the Old South gave birth to a distinctive culture that distinguished the South from the rest of the nation.[17] One aspect of this culture was the predisposition to drink harder, distilled alcoholic beverages such as whiskey rather than the lighter, fermented beers and wines favored by the English and the continental Europeans who were shaping the culture of the northern states.[18] Southern drinkers also tended to partake of their preferred alcoholic beverages at any and all times of the day. For instance, southerners believed that whiskey acted as a stimulant when performing strenuous physical work, and northern visitors to the antebellum South were frequently shocked to find that men drank hard liquor from early in the morning until late at night, even on Sunday. Although all southern states had laws prohibiting slaves from drinking alcohol, they were generally loosely enforced, and the extent to which African Americans indulged in drinking is debated among historians. Some, such as Kenneth Stampp, argue that slaves took solace in heavy drinking; others, such as Eugene Genovese, argue that they were actually more temperate than their masters.[19] The public establishments and events at which drinking tended to take place, however, were generally off-limits to both blacks and women.[20]

Conspicuous consumption of alcohol was a part of southern culture not only among the laboring class but also among the planter aristocracy. As Bertram Wyatt-Brown explains, sociability was key if a man hoped to achieve public recognition of his gentility within the southern culture of honor. A man of wealth and honor was expected to be a gracious host who always offered his guests alcoholic refreshments. Failure to extend such a courtesy was a flagrant affront and a sign of disrespect and dishonor, as was the refusal to accept a drink when offered.[21] Thus, sharing an ice-cold cocktail—usually a rum-based julep—with visitors to one's home in the heat of summer was more than mere southern hospitality; it was part of a complex of social interactions by which one defined oneself as a man of gentility, of ease and luxury, and of honor. As Ian Tyrrell states, "social drinking, at the very least, was essential to the lives of the southern gentry." Southern colleges gained a reputation in the antebellum era for training young men for the social obligations of the leisure class. One antebellum student at Virginia's William and Mary College described the students' daily routine of drinking mint juleps in the morning and gin twists in the middle of the day. A northern observer noted that instead of "manly sports," southern college students' greatest source of pleasure was getting drunk.[22]

Southern culture was noticeably different from that of the North not only in its drinking patterns but also in its tendency toward violence. Historians have proposed a multitude of explanations for this predisposition. McWhiney, naturally, sees it as an inheritance from southerners' proud and savage Celtic ancestors. Others claim that the institution of slavery created a culture in which violence was a part of the established social order. Wilbur Cash attributes southern violence to the frontier individualism of the region's settlers, while Edward Ayers argues that the southern cult of honor is the key element in understanding violence in the South. Still others posit that anything from sexual frustration to an obsession with weapons to the oppressively warm climate undergirded southerners' propensity to resort to violence more rapidly and more frequently than the average northerner.[23] Customs such as dueling died down in the South only after the Civil War, and even then, it reflected merely a change in the concept of how respectable gentlemen should settle disputes, not a societal shift away from violence (as the number of lynchings in the South at the end of the century demonstrates).

Thus, southern prohibitionists had a peculiarly southern set of cultural issues to deal with—cultural traits that, in their view, made the embrace of teetotalism particularly important. Because of the high probability that social drinking would lead to drunkenness, and that drunkenness would unleash violent tendencies, southern evangelicals warned their listeners that they were "pitching their tents towards Sodom" when they indulged in even the smallest bit of alcohol consumption.[24] Even taking "a little wine for the stomach's sake," as the apostle Paul had recommended, was proscribed. One Georgia Baptist preached against women using wine in cooking, lest it awaken the dormant drunkard surely lurking within the husbands and sons who would eat the food.[25]

Legal Suasion

A more dramatic shift took place in the final two decades of the nineteenth century when southern evangelicals embraced the idea of legal suasion. Whereas evangelical prohibitionists in the antebellum South had balked at using the state to impose their moral strictures on society, they increasingly warmed to the idea in the 1880s and 1890s. As both the desire and the sense of obligation to eradicate intemperance in society grew at the end of the 1870s, evangelicals were confronted with the question of how best to accomplish that feat. The editor of the *Alabama Baptist* in 1881 recognized that the question of whether to use legal or simply moral suasion was "troubling the minds and hearts of men."[26]

During the 1870s, most southern evangelical groups remained reluctant to endorse legal prohibition. The Holston Methodist Conference had formed a temperance committee as early as 1873, but its annual reports steered clear of advocating the use of legal means to promote temperance. Reports during the 1870s emphasized the gospel as the most effective way to change the hearts and attitudes of drunkards. In addition to increased disciplinary enforcement against offending members, they vowed to fight the temperance battle "from the pulpit, in the pastorate, and from the press."[27] In 1880, however, the conference broke with tradition and memorialized the Tennessee legislature to enact a local option law.[28] By 1883, its vision had greatly expanded, and the body resolved "that we are of [the] opinion that the only effectual way to extirpate the great evil of intemperance is by a national prohibitory law backed by an enlightened Christian senti-ment, and that we, as a conference, pledge ourselves to preach, pray, work and vote with reference to that end."[29]

This speedy evolution from moral suasion to absolute nation-wide prohibition was rare among southern evangelicals in the 1880s. Among the Southern Baptist Convention, the Alabama Baptist Con-vention was the first to advocate a nationwide prohibition law, also in 1883.[30] Most evangelicals did not follow suit until the 1890s; however, demands for local option laws and other mechanisms for prohibition became increasingly common among Baptist and Methodist bodies in the early 1880s. In 1881 the Tennessee Baptist Convention (TBC) passed its first temperance resolution, which—among other things—expressed its approval of "all legislative action looking to the sup-pression of the traffic." In Alabama, Baptists embraced the concept of prohibition in 1881, and the Methodist conference did the same the following year.[31] The Tennessee Conference of the MECS made it clear in 1889 that it was changing course with regard to prohibi-tion, although it did not condemn its forebears who had been reluc-tant to end drinking by legal means. "Our fathers walked in the light they had," the conference resolved. "We propose no censure on them when we say that in dealing with the liquor traffic in the past many of its infamies have been winked at, but now God by the light of to-day commands in unmistakable terms all men everywhere to repent." The conference went on to call for national prohibition as the only effec-tive solution to the problem.[32]

Prohibition was also promoted as the best way to clean up the political system. In 1881 the Tallassahatchee and Ten Island Baptist Association in eastern Alabama passed resolutions recommending that members "refuse to support, by their suffrage, any man who is before the people for office of honor or profit, who does habitually drink, vend or offer spirituous liquors to his fellow citizens to gain their votes."[33] The practice of "treating" was a long-standing political tradition wherein political candidates would "treat" voters to free liquor on election day as a means of winning their support before sending them staggering into the voting booth.[34] This confluence of the demon rum and corrupt politics was the bane of temperance advocates. Henry H. Tucker, editor of the *Christian Index*, Georgia's state Baptist paper, attacked the use of alcohol in electioneering in 1878, charging that "a few gallons of the fateful liquid" had been known to "float" a man into public office. It had become an axiom among political candidates that "a certain amount (the more the better) of intoxicating beverages—chiefly whiskey—is essential to the successful conduct of a campaign," Tucker added.[35]

Not all Baptist bodies embraced legislative endorsements on the same schedule. For example, in 1878 the GBC noted that various courses of action existed for fighting intemperance, but that "as a convention, we have no pet theories to advocate."[36] In 1881 the GBC conceded, "As to the plan upon which to operate, and the best means to be used in the accomplishment of this work, there is a great diversity of opinion as has been manifest in the long and labored discussions in this Convention." In the end, the temperance committee concluded that it "will make no suggestions in regard to a plan of operation or means to be used." Instead, the convention called for the continued discipline of members who drank and issued a vague suggestion that Georgia Baptists "unite with their fellow-citizens in devising and executing some plan for the suppression of intemperance."[37]

Unlike their Baptist brethren in Tennessee and Alabama, Georgia Baptists remained reluctant to support legal suasion throughout the 1880s. In 1889 the convention's committee argued that "legislation is in some respects valuable, yet the most appropriate remedy for intemperance is moral suasion."[38] In 1891 the temperance report explained, "Intemperance is more a personal than a social evil. It deals more with individuals than with the masses."[39] Therefore, the temperance efforts of the convention should target individuals, not society at large. Not until the late 1890s did the GBC begin to pass resolutions endorsing local option laws and encouraging its members to vote for men who would fight the liquor traffic. It was in 1900 that the Georgia Baptists finally conceded, "We have found by experience that the most efficient method of dealing with this gigantic evil is to invoke the strong arm of the law . . . a general prohibitory law is the only measure ever presented to the public that will successfully exterminate the accursed traffic in our state."[40]

In 1889 the *Christian Index* of Georgia also expressed reticence about turning to the state as a means of effecting moral reform. The gospel was the one and only cure for what ailed humankind, Tucker argued. "Prohibition and education are very good things in their way," he explained, but "the gospel is the world's great reliance."[41] Likewise, that same year the *Alabama Christian Advocate* expressed concern that reliance on the state to reform individuals was overshadowing reliance on the gospel. The editor maintained that "temperance societies and prohibition movements are good in their place," but only the gospel could ultimately quench the thirst of the intemperate.[42]

By the turn of the century, however, such lingering reticence regarding the use of legal means had faded. Southern evangelicals were now almost unanimous in accepting legal prohibition—in conjunction with continued moral suasion—as the key to defeating intemperance. In 1899 Tennessee Baptist Edgar Estes Folk declared, "Some say use moral suasion against the saloon, and tell their boys to keep away from the saloon. That is good, but let us have legal suasion too, which will keep the saloon away from the boys. Let us have both kinds of suasion."[43] The North Georgia Conference declared in 1888 that the principle of prohibition "is a sound one, and must finally prevail."[44] Even the GBC declared in 1903, "We believe in the providence of God, that the time has come when there should be a state law upon the subject of prohibition."[45]

Evangelical Leadership

A vital component in the rise of prohibition sentiment among southern evangelicals and its subsequent acceptance by the larger public was the emergence of denominational leaders who made prohibition a central element of their ministry. These individuals played a critical role in making prohibition a defining characteristic of southern evangelicalism. In Alabama the undisputed leader of prohibition agitation was Washington Bryan Crumpton, who actively raised awareness of and support for the prohibition movement from 1880 to passage of the Eighteenth Amendment and beyond. After serving as a lieutenant in the Confederate army, Crumpton entered the ministry in 1866 and pastored churches throughout Alabama; he then became a state evangelist and corresponding secretary for the state Baptist mission board from 1883 until 1913. It was Crumpton who, in 1881, made the first temperance report to the Alabama Baptist Convention since the Civil War. While serving as secretary of the mission board, Crumpton held three-day "Baptist rallies" at churches across the state, where he promoted causes such as missions and prohibition. After hearing numerous stories of the damage being done by liquor, he resolved, "By the help of god, if it takes my life, liquor in Alabama shall go."[46]

Crumpton's first public stand for prohibition took place in the late 1870s. He discovered that a local Jewish merchant was selling liquor within five miles of a church, in violation of an old statute restricting such sales. Crumpton went to the grand jury and had the man indicted. "Soon he burned down his store and moved away," Crumpton recalled. "I made the Jew my enemy, but it broke up the business." In 1878 Crumpton came across an old magazine article that explained the history and effectiveness of Maine's 1851 statewide prohibition law. This was Crumpton's first exposure to the idea of widespread legal suppression of the liquor traffic, and it inspired him to preach his first prohibition sermon. He recalled the widespread opposition to such a position at the time:

> I screwed up courage to preach a sermon on the subject in a growing little city, where the Jewish element was very strong; they and the Catholics were favorable to the traffic, most of the prominent corners were occupied by saloons, and almost the whole country filled with people who drank, or excused drinking—none of them believed in suppression. If anybody in the audience, the day I preached, believed a word I said in that sermon, I never heard of it—probably my wife was an exception, though she might have been skeptical.[47]

Crumpton noted that after this sermon, support for prohibition flourished in the city, even within the Jewish community. From that point onward, Crumpton became the premier prohibitionist in the state of Alabama and one of its most respected Baptist leaders.[48] As a special traveling correspondent for the *Alabama Baptist*, Crumpton worked the prohibition cause into almost every speech he made. "Every day of the week and Sunday, too, I talked and reasoned and prayed" on behalf of prohibition, he stated.[49] Crumpton also became a lobbyist in Montgomery, the state capital, when a Dallas County church asked him to petition the legislature for prohibition in the county. Crumpton said that he had been afraid not to accept, "for it seemed to me a call from God."[50] He continued to pursue his lobbyist avocation and gained widespread influence among both evangelicals and politicians in the state.[51]

Crumpton himself had been a moderate imbiber of wine until a young Baptist preacher, Benjamin Franklin Riley, rebuked him for drinking. (Crumpton clearly took the reprimand to heart.) Riley, another leader of the prohibition movement, had pastored churches in both Alabama and Georgia in the 1870s and 1880s and then served as president of Howard College, Alabama's Baptist college (later Samford University). Riley then taught English at the University of Georgia before moving to Texas for nine years, where he pastored and served as president of that state's Anti-Saloon League. A devoted, if paternalistic, advocate for the better treatment of African Americans, Riley returned to Alabama and in 1910 wrote *The White Man's Burden*, which chronicled the injustices suffered by blacks in the South, praised the advances made by blacks since emancipation, and challenged whites to aid in the further uplift of the black race.[52] A key component of said uplift, Riley believed, was prohibition. He stated that "the better class among the colored people was engaged in stoutly opposing strong drink," and in 1909 he organized the Southern Negro Anti-Saloon Federation to further inculcate such values among the African American population. Solving the "race problem" that was plaguing the South, Riley argued, was dependent on first resolving the liquor problem.[53]

Tennessee was rich with prominent and vociferous prohibition advocates at the end of the nineteenth century. Edgar Estes Folk, however, was undoubtedly the movement's preeminent spokesman there. Folk had served as a Baptist minister in both Tennessee and Georgia before becoming owner and editor of the *Baptist and Reflector* in 1889 (where he remained until 1917). He was also president of the Southern Baptist Sunday School Board. Folk came from a family of politicians and ministers. His brother Joseph W. "Holy

Joe" Folk was a reform-minded governor of Missouri from 1905 to 1909; another brother, Reau Folk, was Tennessee's state treasurer from 1901 to 1911. E. E. Folk helped form the Local Option League in Tennessee in 1896; in 1899 this was reorganized as the Tennessee Anti-Saloon League, and he served as its president for twelve years.[54]

Another prominent prohibitionist in Tennessee was Methodist minister David C. Kelley. A colonel in the Confederate army, Kelley was a middle-Tennessee preacher who advocated greater evangelical involvement in the political sphere. Toward this end, he abandoned his ministerial post in 1890 to run for governor on the Prohibition Party ticket. Other Tennessee Methodists who were prominent in the struggle for prohibition included B. F. Haynes, editor of the *Tennessee Methodist*, and Elijah Embree Hoss, who, before becoming a bishop, pastored in Knoxville, edited the *Christian Advocate*, and taught at Vanderbilt University in Nashville.

In the antebellum South, Georgia Baptists had been some of the most fervent proponents of temperance. In the Georgia of the New South, however, the Methodist Church furnished some of the hardest-hitting prohibition clergyman-activists in the southland, including two distinguished bishops and two alcoholics-turned-revivalists. Bishops Atticus Greene Haygood and Warren A. Candler were both involved in the temperance movement, especially during the 1880s.[55] Both men also served as president of Emory University—Haygood from 1875 to 1884, and Candler from 1888 to 1898. Haygood was a key promoter of the economic rejuvenation of the New South, and he made prohibition a central component of his message. Candler, brother of Coca-Cola founder Asa Candler, was chairman of the North Georgia Conference's temperance committee in the 1880s, even though he enjoyed wine on occasion and his wife used alcohol for medicinal purposes later in life.[56]

Sam Jones, born in Alabama and raised in Cartersville, Georgia, began drinking alcohol as a teenager. He practiced law until 1872, when his dying father urged him to change his ways. So Jones joined the Methodist Church, became a minister, and was soon the South's most popular traveling preacher. He took his revival tent from city to city across the South—as well as Boston, Chicago, San Francisco, and cities in between—preaching a fiery brand of "masculine Christianity." In a twelve-month period in 1885 and 1886, Jones traveled more than twenty thousand miles and preached a thousand sermons to a cumulative audience of three million people. He became a national celebrity and even earned the distinction of having a candy bar named after him. He was famed for his stinging yet witty attacks on his opponents. Jones liked to tell audiences, "I may be alone [in my beliefs], but I'm still in good company."[57]

Jones was deeply committed to the cause of prohibition, and he taught that drinking alcohol was completely incompatible with Christianity. "A man can't drink whiskey and be a Christian, and don't you forget it," the former alcoholic admonished his listeners. Jones's hard-line stance and his caustic attacks on those who disagreed with him won him both widespread popularity and numerous enemies. In response to his crusade for prohibition, some anti-prohibitionists in Cartersville threatened Jones's family and even blew up his buggy with dynamite. After that incident, Jones sent his family away for the rest of the campaign, and his home was guarded by a group of African American volunteers. Jones enjoyed strong support in the black community and was known for paying his black and female employees the same wages he paid the white men who worked for him.[58]

One of the most dramatic of Jones's many converts to Christianity was Tom Ryman of Nashville, a wealthy businessman and the owner of dozens of riverboats. At his tent meeting in Nashville, Jones railed against the drinking, gambling, and showgirls aboard these "floating dens of iniquity." Ryman had gone to the meeting intending to confront Jones, but by the end of the evening, Ryman confessed that Jones had "whipped me with the gospel of Christ." Ryman embraced Christianity and ceased selling liquor on his boats, the best of which he rechristened the *Sam Jones*. The converted businessman also paid to have a meetinghouse constructed for the use of churches and religious speakers—an auditorium that would eventually become known as the Grand Ole Opry.[59]

Another man who came away from a Sam Jones revival with a changed heart was Sam Small. Small, a reporter for the *Atlanta Constitution*, had been sent to Cartersville to cover one of Jones's tent meetings for the newspaper. By the end of the meeting, Small, an alcoholic, had given up the bottle and given himself to the ministry. He returned to Atlanta and took up the cause of prohibition with a vengeance. Raised on a plantation outside of Knoxville, Small now stood atop empty whiskey barrels on Atlanta street corners preaching the gospel of prohibition to passers-by.[60] News of his preaching reached Jones, who went to hear him in Atlanta and asked Small to join him on the revival circuit. Together, the two men, along with exuberant music leader E. O. Excell, packed churches and auditoriums across the nation.[61] Small eventually ran for governor of Georgia on a prohibition platform.

Despite the GBC's slowness to embrace legal remedies to address intemperance, several Georgia Baptists stood up to lead the cause. Among them were John E. White, pastor of the Second Baptist Church in Atlanta; James B. Gambrell, a former scout for General Robert E. Lee and president of Mercer University (his son, Roderick Dhu Gambrell, was killed by an anti-prohibitionist in Mississippi); James B. Hawthorne, who pastored Baptist churches in Montgomery, Nashville, and Atlanta; and Len Broughton, founder of the Baptist Tabernacle Church in Atlanta.

Besides these prominent denominational leaders and revivalists, all of whom were men, evangelical women played a crucial role in altering public opinion about prohibition in the late nineteenth century. In Alabama, well-known reformer Julia Tutwiler was a leader in the crusade. Tutwiler had a remarkable education for a southern woman of her era, having studied at Vassar as well as in Germany and Paris. She was a leader of both educational and prison reform in the state of Alabama, as well as a staunch advocate of prohibition. Rebecca Latimer Felton of Georgia, wife of Populist leader William Felton, was a popular political activist and reformer. A harsh critic of both conservative Democrats and the Methodist hierarchy, Felton worked tirelessly to reform not only southern society but also southern politics and the southern Methodist Church.

The Woman's Christian Temperance Union provided southern evangelical women with a rare opportunity to participate in the public discourse on prohibition. Deemed the protectors of the home and the domestic sphere, women had a greater voice in the prohibition debate than in any other issue involving religious belief or public policy in the nineteenth century. Crumpton expressed a growing sentiment among evangelicals in 1884 when he wrote that women were "the worst sufferers from the effects of liquor, and they have a right to be heard on this question, and work in the front ranks of this movement."[62]

Evangelical Arguments for Prohibition

Evangelical prohibitionists made their arguments along several different lines: biblical, emotional, social, and economic. Biblical arguments were surprisingly rare, especially after 1880. Two factors may explain why evangelicals, for whom scripture was so central in matters of faith, worship, and right living, utilized biblical arguments so sparsely: their goal of legal prohibition, and their devotion to teetotalism. In advocating prohibition to a mostly Christian audience through sermons and the religious press, evangelical prohibitionists hoped to convince their hearers and readers not only that Christians should not imbibe but also that they should support the legal elimination of alcohol from all of society. One might argue that even if the Bible condemns drinking, why should that restriction be imposed on the entire secular community? The Bible, after all, denounces many sinful activities, yet the church does not demand that the government make all citizens subject to those teachings. Thus, prohibitionists emphasized instead the social and economic harm being done by liquor. Evangelicals also recognized that biblical passages regarding alcohol could be thorny, especially for those advocating teetotalism. Although the Bible does prescribe total abstinence for priests, kings, and even John the Baptist, most of its references to wine condemn only drunkenness.[63] Furthermore, scripture praises wine as a gift from God in the Psalms and depicts Jesus making wine at a wedding feast and consuming wine with his disciples at the Last Supper.[64] Given the inherent problems in trying to ground an argument for teetotalism entirely in scripture, it is not surprising that evangelical prohibitionists relied more heavily on other forms of argumentation to make their case.

One area where evangelicals could not escape the issue of wine drinking in the Bible involved the use of wine in communion, or the Lord's Supper. In the 1880s both southern evangelicals and evangelical prohibitionists in the North debated what was known as the two-wine theory. The theory had its roots in the antebellum temperance movement, when Moses Stuart speculated about the nature of the wine consumed by Jesus and the disciples at the Last Supper.[65] Biblical scholars began to argue that two different types of wine are spoken of in the Bible, even though the English word *wine* was used to translate both. One type of wine was alcoholic; this was the kind of wine that made Noah drunk and that was warned against in Proverbs.[66]

The other type of wine was unfermented; this was the kind of wine praised by the psalmist and commended by Paul as being good for the stomach.[67]

Two-wine theorists sought to demonstrate that the use of fermented wine at the Lord's Supper was not historically accurate. "In the wine used by Christ in the Lord's Supper there was not a drop of alcohol," A. C. Dixon said in an 1891 sermon, summarizing his support of the two-wine theory.[68] They argued that Christ and his disciples had not consumed wine at the Last Supper, pointing out that the Bible refers only to "the cup" or "the fruit of the vine" in the Last Supper narratives, not specifically to wine. Two-wine advocates also relied on Jewish experts regarding the historical practice of the Passover supper. The *Alabama Baptist* ran a story making the case that "the Jewish Passover was to be observed with unleavened things. Therefore the wine must be unleavened or unfermented."[69] For many temperance advocates, the idea that God could condone the use of alcohol—"the enemy of the human race"—in any form was unthinkable.[70]

Not all evangelical prohibitionists embraced the two-wine theory. The *Baptist* of Memphis admonished its readers in 1888, "It would be a great lift to the temperance work to persuade our temperance men that they had better let that two-wine notion go, and put total abstinence on simple, practical grounds. The two-wine bridge will certainly break down."[71] Some evangelicals who rejected the two-wine theory reconciled Jesus's drinking habits with their own antialcohol stance by citing the cultural context of his time. For example, John R. Broadus, the New Testament professor at Southern Baptist Seminary, argued that Jesus drank wine only because of the culture in which he lived. Had Christ lived in the nineteenth century, Broadus supposed, he would have drunk coffee or tea instead. The cultural superiority implied by Broadus was made explicit in the writing of Gerrit Smith, a New York philanthropist who explained that Jesus drank wine because he simply did not know any better.[72]

In 1869 an alternative solution to the problematic issue of communion wine was introduced by a Massachusetts dentist and Methodist layman, Thomas D. Welch. By applying Louis Pasteur's new process for preventing microorganisms from developing in milk, Welch used grapes to produce a nonalcoholic drink that would not ferment.[73] Welch's son, Thomas E. Welch, began to produce and bottle the grape juice. In 1893 he set up a display at the Columbian

Exposition in Chicago where visitors could sample his unfermented juice, and grape juice sales subsequently exploded.[74] The substitution of grape juice for wine in the communion cup spread rapidly as the nineteenth century came to a close. An 1885 *Alabama Baptist* article argued, "There should be a rigid and radical reformation in all our churches in the prohibition of the use of fermented wine at the Lord's Supper, for the good of the church."[75] In 1887 the General Conference of the MECS recommended the use of unfermented juice when churches celebrated the Lord's Supper.[76] But fear of upsetting biblical literalists led the TBC in 1891 to table a resolution that would have called for the use of only unfermented wine in the Lord's Supper.[77] In 1900 the North Georgia Conference did urge its membership to use only unfermented wine for Holy Communion,[78] but seven years later, it was still making the same plea to member churches.[79] Southern evangelicals who opposed the use of wine in communion also argued that giving a man a taste of wine at the Lord's Supper could lead him to slide into alcoholism. In 1900 the editor of the *Alabama Baptist* warned, "Let us not put any strong drink to the mouth of our brother, for we know not to what it may lead."[80] Instead, the paper advocated the use of unfermented grape juice for communion, and then it recommended that Alabama Baptists procure said juice from the Fruithurst Grape Juice Company in Cleburne County, Alabama.

Prohibitionists loved to recount heart-wrenching stories of drinkers' despair, destitution, and death and their families' abuse and abandonment. In 1878 Henry Tucker described the devastating impact of drinking on a man's family, leaving a "heart-broken mother" and petrified children who "bathe their cheeks with tears" when their father returns home from the saloon inebriated.[81] The *Baptist and Reflector* ran a story in 1905 depicting the squalid living conditions that resulted from drinking, where "mamma can't make a fire without coal; papa spent all his wages for drink last night and we all have to go to bed to keep warm. The mother turns to the bed to find only a few old ragged quilts in which to wrap her freezing children." The writer lamented the heartache brought on by drink and the lives and souls it destroyed.[82] Charles White of Elizabethton, Tennessee, described the scene of misery and despair when visiting the home of a drunkard: "You see the grim monster of destitution and want as it starves the babe at its mother's breast. You see the fireless hearth, the shivering forms, and the empty cupboard, and wonder why God, in his infinite wisdom, should doom these innocent victims to a living grave, while the man behind the bar revels in his gains."[83]

In 1905 the wife of an alcoholic wrote a letter to a judge in Cleveland, Tennessee, pleading with him to somehow relieve her hardship. She recounted the abuse and neglect she endured as a result of her husband's drinking, and she threatened suicide if something were not done. The *Baptist and Reflector* printed her letter, noting that she was only one of thousands suffering in silence throughout the state. The solution to her troubles, the editor argued, was to take the temptation of liquor out of her husband's way and thus save both him and his family.[84]

Secular papers that supported the prohibition movement, such as the *Nashville Tennessean*, also emphasized the connection between drinking and personal tragedy. In a front-page article entitled "Suicide Winds up Period of Drinking," the paper informed its readers that a man in Montgomery, Alabama, had "fired a fatal shot into his brain this morning." The death of a streetcar conductor in another state usually did not warrant front-page coverage in the *Tennessean*, but the paper seized the opportunity to link alcohol with personal ruin and misfortune. The paper reported that the gentleman had "been drinking heavily at intervals recently," leaving its readers to conclude that the man's latest binge had led directly to his decision to take his own life. "He leaves a large family," the report concluded—yet more victims of the liquor traffic.[85]

As early as 1881, the editor of the *Alabama Baptist* became convinced that the use of emotional arguments to make the case against alcohol was ill-conceived and pointless. "The pathetic rehearsal of touching stories of broken hearts, starving children, ruined fortunes, and blasted families have done little more than arouse the emotions of the listening congregations," he argued.[86] Although evangelicals increasingly made use of other types of arguments as the nineteenth century ended, moving stories of personal ruin and families in despair remained a reliable staple of writers and speakers who condemned liquor.

Evangelicals also employed arguments emphasizing the social costs of drinking to persuade the public of the rightness and reasonableness of prohibition. Many evangelical prohibitionists touted prohibition as a panacea for the ills of southern society, a balm that would relieve a multitude of sufferings. The Reverend G. W. Garner of Georgia wrote in 1900 that he supported prohibition "because state prohibition would cleanse the ballot, purify the political machinery, untrammel the great cause of religion, clothe the drunkard's widow, feed and educate his children," and generally resolve most of the problems facing Georgia society. Garner posited that preventing grain from being distilled into whiskey would also create a greater supply of both bread and meat for those in need.[87] The editorials on temperance and prohibition in the *Alabama Baptist* continually emphasized the social impact of alcohol.[88] An 1894 editorial, for example, lamented "the ruined homes, the pauperism, insanity and self-murder" directly attributable to alcohol.[89]

In this vein, prohibition was widely promoted as a cure for crime. The *Baptist and Reflector* estimated that between 72 and 90 percent of criminals in U.S. jails were there either directly or indirectly because of liquor, and it laid the responsibility for almost all homicides at the feet of alcohol.[90] "Another man shot in Nashville, probably fatally. Where? In a saloon, of course. Every murder happens in and around saloons," the paper claimed.[91] In an 1884 prohibition sermon, Atticus Haygood focused on the social consequences of alcohol. He argued that the liquor traffic made men idle and led to "pauperism," and he said that it was more harmful to the poorer classes than to the wealthy, because it made basic economic transactions such as establishing credit at a store more difficult for the former.[92] The Tennessee Conference in 1889 echoed the argument that alcohol "creates very largely the pauperism, the lunacy, and the crimes of the country, whose care or cure, or conviction and punishment, impose enormous burdens of taxation on the state."[93]

The TBC accused the saloon not only of being the center of many social problems but also of being a barbaric and "un-American" institution. It was, many southern evangelicals contended, the greatest social evil that the country had ever faced. Tennessee Baptists called it "an evil greater than ever slavery was, that enslaved the body only; this enslaves the body, mind, and soul." In a praising tone one might not expect from southerners, Tennessee Baptists argued that prohibition needed the same kind of great leaders that had championed abolitionism, calling for "the eloquence of a Wendell Phillips, the pen of a Harriet Beecher Stowe, and the zeal of a Lincoln." The saloon, Tennessee Baptists declared, must meet the same fate as did slavery: "as it was with slavery, so shall it be with the saloon; it must go from every town in our beautiful State."[94] G. W. Perryman, pastor of Deaderick Avenue Baptist Church in Knoxville, explained that the saloon was at the root of both poverty and crime in the region. He asked, "What kind of fruit is the saloon bearing. Look around and see, and behold poverty, wretchedness, ignorance, despair and death. Who fills our jails? The saloon. Who fills our workhouses? The saloon. Who at last fills hell with perishing souls? The saloon."[95]

Along with social arguments, prohibitionists also utilized economic arguments. Evangelicals and other drys ceaselessly highlighted the monetary cost to society of alcoholism and higher crime rates resulting from drunkenness. Anti-prohibitionists also relied on economic arguments, such as the threat of lost tax revenue for schools and public works, to combat calls for widespread prohibition. In a sermon on the eve of an important prohibition election, Chattanooga minister G. C. Rankin tried to persuade his audience that the cost of prosecuting and imprisoning alcohol-fueled criminals greatly surpassed any revenue generated from liquor taxation.[96] Similarly, in Knoxville, Methodist minister J. W. Perry preached a sermon on the topic and said, "I do not want to be known as one of the citizens of Knoxville who puts himself in the attitude of begging the saloon man to educate my children." He argued that prohibition would channel the estimated $1 million spent in Knoxville each year on alcohol into economic growth that would easily replace any lost liquor tax revenue. Perry pointed to the city of Cleveland, Tennessee, where, he said, "within three years after saloons had been put out, two hundred and fifty homes were built, the tax on which was much more than the revenue previously derived from saloons."[97] Evangelicals also highlighted the fact that railroad companies and other businesses frequently imposed temperance on their employees, whether they were on duty or not. "Business is joining religion in advocating prohibition," it was reported, not out of any moral or religious conviction but because businessmen recognized alcohol's destructive impact on workers.[98]

Evangelical Political Activism

Another significant change for evangelicals in this period was their increased involvement in the realm of secular politics. Tired of merely talking about effecting political change, evangelical prohibitionists became increasingly engaged in the political process. This involvement took two main forms: mobilizing Christian voters and lobbying state legislatures. The former involved efforts to ensure that church members voted on election day—and that they voted correctly. The latter generally entailed denominational bodies memorializing the state legislature in support of pending prohibition legislation and sending representatives to petition legislators in person.

Resolutions passed by denominational bodies became increasingly aggressive as the century drew to a close. Gone were the diffident temperance resolutions of the 1870s and 1880s that apologized for seeming to suggest how church members should vote. In 1882 the *Holston Methodist* expressed its opinion that "many Christian men are not sufficiently governed by the morals and conscience of Christianity in politics" and that more attention should be paid to the morals and character of those in politics.[99] This conviction that there should be no separation between personal morality and public morality became a recurring theme among southern evangelicals as the nineteenth century ended and the twentieth century began. In 1911 the Holston Conference of the MECS rejoiced in the fact that candidates for public office were increasingly being held to higher moral standards in both their public and private lives. It noted: "The time was when politicians took the position that the private moral character of an aspirant to office was not to be considered; intellectual qualifications and a good public record were the only qualifications, but our people are beginning to realize that there cannot be two standards for morals, one for private life and the other for public life, and that the man who does not lead an exemplary private life can not be trusted in public positions."[100] In 1904 Tennessee Baptists announced, "we will not vote for any man of any party of any office who is known to be or supposed to be in sympathy with the saloon."[101]

In 1893 a Methodist minister from Harriman, Tennessee, told an audience, "It is not sentiment that makes a man a prohibitionist; it is his vote."[102] The Holston Conference reiterated this sentiment in 1904 when it resolved that the church should "resolve less and vote more, it being the vote and not the resolution that makes the saloon power tremble."[103] E. E. Folk echoed this idea a year later, urging his readers: "You may preach until your head is gray, you may pray until your knees are as hard as the camel's, you may adopt all the temperance reports and pass all the temperance resolutions you choose, but saloon-keepers and gamblers care nothing for all that, so long as you will walk up to the polls on election day and vote for their men for office. But when Christian people learn to vote as they pray, then the saloon-keepers and gamblers will tremble and saloons and gambling dens will be banished from our land."[104]

A. T. W. Lytle, a Methodist from Atlanta, wrote in the *Wesleyan Christian Advocate* that Christians should not blame the saloon for the drunkenness and ruined lives that surround them. Instead, Christians have only themselves to blame, because they elect the men who license the saloons and allow them to operate.[105] Likewise, William J. Albert of Atlanta argued, "If it be morally wrong for a Methodist steward or Baptist deacon to run a barroom, then it is morally wrong for him to vote for a law or license that permits another man to run the business, and the pulpit which fails to denounce such inconsistency is itself wrong. Shall we call it moral cowardice?"[106]

For George Brewer of Lafayette, Alabama, the biblical admonition to be the light of the world became a rallying cry for Christians to turn their antialcohol sentiment into action. He warned his fellow Baptists that the many resolutions being passed by religious bodies calling for prohibition "are not worth the paper written upon if they lead to no action." He announced that the time for the "strangulation of the monster of intemperance" had arrived.[107] Another Alabama Baptist, James D. Dickson, made a similar plea in the pages of the *Alabama Baptist*, saying, "It is the duty of every citizen . . . to do all he can, by use of the ballot, and in any other way, to rid the state and this whole country of the foul blot now resting upon it by reason of the 'legalized and licensed' traffic in intoxicating drink."[108]

In Tennessee, the state prohibition committee enlisted ministers, such as itinerant Methodist preacher A. B. Wright, to serve as local speakers for the movement. Wright spent the weeks prior to the 1887 Tennessee prohibition referendum speaking in churches and schoolhouses in east Tennessee to drum up support for the prohibition initiative.[109] Some evangelical ministers went even further, running for public office themselves and making prohibition the centerpiece of their platforms. As mentioned earlier, Methodist minister David C. Kelley of Tennessee left his ministerial charge in 1890 to run for governor on the Prohibition Party ticket. W. R. Whatley of Alexander City, Alabama, claimed that in 1892, Baptist preachers were on the ballot in every county in the state.[110]

Evangelicals increasingly invoked their spiritual authority to manipulate people's votes. When voters arrived at a polling station in Valdosta, Georgia, on election day, they were greeted by a large banner that read:

Vote as if the master waited at the door.
Vote as if tomorrow your voting would be o'er.
Vote as if you met the Master's searching look.
Vote as tho it were his hand your ballot took.[111]

By creating mental images of Jesus working the polls and processing each ballot, evangelical prohibitionists sought to drive home the eternal implications involved in exercising one's civic duty. On the eve of an important prohibition referendum in Tennessee, one Baptist editor advised his readers to think carefully about how they cast their ballots, because the consequences were tremendous. He went on to make the dire prediction that "the man who refuses to vote, or the man who votes for the vile traffic with its fruits, will have the curse of God upon him and his family while his generations bear his name."[112] Tennessee Baptist G. L. Ellis warned in a sermon, "Remember that God's hand is against the man who stains his hand with a whiskey ballot."[113] If divine wrath were not enough of a motivator, some evangelical ministers threatened that their own wrath would be visited on those who voted wrongly. G. W. Perryman of Knoxville warned his congregants in a sermon, "I want you one and all to understand that if any of you are for the saloon, high or low license, that I will make it so warm for you that you will not have to sit close to the registers in this church."[114]

Denominational bodies also became lobbyists, not only sending memorials and petitions to their state legislatures but also appointing delegations to lobby legislators in person at the state capital. In 1880 Crumpton urged Alabama Baptists to get involved in the campaign for legal prohibition by petitioning the state legislature. "The legislature will adjourn in a few days, to reassemble in February; this gives us more time to work in," he advised. "Let every friend of temperance consider these as golden moments and work to secure as many names against the traffic as possible. Every petition will have its weight."[115] Baptists in Fort Deposit, Alabama, heeded Crumpton's appeal. A dozen citizens gathered at the Baptist church there "to consider the adoption of such measures as would secure prohibition for our town and country," they reported. They circulated petitions and gathered signatures in both the city and the surrounding countryside, and they sent the church's pastor, J. M. Fortune, to Montgomery to lobby the legislature for a local option law. A few months later, Fortune reported to the *Alabama Baptist* that the community's efforts had been successful and rejoiced that Lowndes County "will be free from the baneful liquor traffic" beginning the following January.[116]

As the nineteenth century drew to a close, southern evangelical denominations became increasingly comfortable with flexing the political muscle afforded by their large memberships. At the 1893 TBC, the Reverend W. D. Turnley noted that evangelicals had the numerical power to make a difference in the South and asserted, "I would put a prohibition plank in every platform of every political party. . . . We believe that every child of God owes it to his church to do what he can to rid the country of this curse."[117] In 1896 the Baptists reminded the state legislature that they represented "125,000 white Baptists" and formed a small committee to lobby for the application of a four-mile law (a saloon-free zone around schools and sometimes churches) to all towns and cities with five thousand or fewer inhabitants.[118] Southern evangelicals acknowledged that a major change was taking place in their approach to prohibition, but they deemed it their duty to pursue a new line of attack in the war against intemperance. Atlanta Baptist minister John E. White viewed the church's use of its power and influence to address social problems such as intemperance as "a revival of the prophetic spirit in the ministry."[119]

Legislative Approaches to Prohibition, 1880–1900

During the 1880s and 1890s, various legislative approaches to prohibiting the sale of alcohol emerged. Southern evangelical support for these different mechanisms was marked by both pragmatism and an ever-expanding vision of prohibition. One of the earliest means of limiting the sale of alcohol had been "high license"—the imposition of steep licensing fees on both liquor wholesalers and saloons. License laws emerged in the 1860s and 1870s that both placed some controls on saloons and generated revenue for the government. Tennessee governor William Brownlow, lamenting the rising number of distilleries and saloons in the state following the Civil War, urged the legislature to tax the liquor business out of existence.[120] Forcing sa-loon keepers to pay a license fee to stay in business subjected to some governmental regulation, such as limiting their hours of operation and prohibiting the sale of liquor to minors. The stated goal of the high-license approach was to elevate license fees to the point where fewer saloons could afford to stay in business. Those that did pay the higher fees would, in theory, be forced to raise their prices and cater to a more well-heeled and responsible clientele.

As southern evangelicals became more outspoken in support of legal prohibition of liquor in the 1880s, they began to express greater dissatisfaction with the high-license approach to controlling saloons. They denounced it as not only ineffective but also immoral, since it made the state a partner to the debauchery of the saloon. The tem-perance committee of the Holston Conference declared in 1885 that "the time has come when high-license and all other compromise measures should be abandoned and heroic measures adopted."[121] Two years later the Tennessee Conference of the MECS charged, "The license system in any shape is an evil, and an evil can never be twisted into a remedy for the ravages which flow from itself as a cause."[122] Evangelist Sam Small spoke in Knoxville in 1887 and charged the license system with doing great damage to the morality of the state. If given a choice between the high-license system and "free whis-key," Small claimed that he would prefer the latter.[123] George Brewer challenged Alabama Baptists to declare publicly that they would not vote for any politician who supported the licensing system.[124] Judge Job Harral of Tennessee wrote to the *Baptist and Reflector* to propose strict legal penalties for those involved in the liquor traffic. Drunk-ards should be jailed for six months, he wrote, but the saloon keeper should be incarcerated for six years and the distiller for ten years; the legislators who voted to license saloons should received the harshest penalty of all: life imprisonment.[125]

Opposition to the high-license system continued to grow in the late 1880s and early 1890s. The Holston Conference reiterated in 1889 that it was "unalterably opposed to license, high or low."[126] The North Georgia Conference argued in 1891 that "the highest, as well as the lowest," form of license "is the sale by government of indulgences to sin against God." Combating the argument that the revenue raised from saloon licenses provided essential funding for valuable state pro-grams, the conference retorted: "The plea that these barrooms should be allowed, and therefore protected, because public schools may be sustained and highways built with the purchase of money of a people's blood, is the refinement of Iscariotism."[127] When the GBC finally embraced prohibition in the late 1890s, it simultaneously rejected the high-license approach. "The license system is in league with hell and the devil, and must die," the convention resolved in 1897, "but prohibition dwells in the light of God's word and under divine favor, and must succeed."[128]

Some evangelicals were less harsh in their judgment of the licensing system, however, and embraced a more pragmatic approach. In 1889 the editor of Georgia's *Christian Index* noted that a new high-license system had recently been implemented in Boston that would eliminate 70 percent of that city's saloons. The editor criticized his fellow evangelicals, complaining that they "argue and preach and vote against such a measure as this, on the grounds that it is compromising with evil." The *Christian Index*, he assured his readers, "is not much given to theories and never runs wild on isms, and takes a practical views of things." He drew the analogy of having 2,630 mad dogs (the number of saloons in Boston) running loose in a city and having the power to kill all but 780 of them. The only reasonable approach, he concluded, was to "get rid of the dogs first and go to hair-splitting afterwards—if at all."[129]

By the 1890s, supporting high license had become synonymous with being an anti-prohibitionist. In 1895 Crumpton chastised Alabama's Democratic governor William C. Oates for favoring high license over outright prohibition, arguing that support for the license approach would serve as "an encouragement to the friends of the liquor traffic." He went on to explain: "The worst enemies we have are weak-kneed prohibitionists, who are ready to yield to the high-license arguments, politicians who favor high-license 'for revenue only,' and the liquor dealer's association who to a man are in favor of high license for monopoly only. All the dealers, except the small fry, favor high license, because it dignifies the business and makes friends among the tax payers and the friends of the public school."[130] Another recurring complaint about the licensing system was the existence of "blind tigers"— unlicensed, unregulated saloons supplied primarily by moonshiners. If all saloons were abolished, prohibitionists reasoned, such establishments—viewed as a particularly insidious source of debauchery—would be easier to detect and eradicate.

As alternatives to high license, prohibitionists offered several more restrictive approaches, including local option, mile laws, and state-run dispensaries. Different approaches thrived in different states, but the most popular legislative means of prohibiting the sale of alcohol in the South between the 1880s and 1907 was local option. By 1890, every state in the South had utilized this approach to some extent.[131] It was deemed the most democratic approach because it allowed local voters to impose prohibition on their own community or to reject it. Some—generally those less ardent about prohibition—saw this as the great strength of the local option approach. The editor of the northern *Outlook*, writing about prohibition in the South, argued, "It is one of the virtues . . . of local option that it presents the saloon to the voters for their judgment upon it again and again. . . . The voter cannot escape the responsibility for a decision for or against the saloon. Public opinion is kept keen upon the subject."[132] In some cases, such as in Birmingham, it allowed rural voters in the county to impose prohibition on the residents of larger cities near them.[133]

In Georgia, local option was the main instrument of the prohibition forces for the three decades prior to statewide prohibition. Atlanta experimented with local option, briefly going dry in 1886 and 1887 before reverting to licensed saloons. Although prohibition was short-lived in Atlanta, the Georgia legislature passed a local option bill in 1887 that allowed many counties and smaller cities to ban saloons. By the middle of the first decade of the twentieth century, 125 of Georgia's 145 counties had gone dry under the state's local option law.[134] Even before the GBC embraced legal suasion, it endorsed local option as the best legal approach to prohibition.[135] The *Wesleyan Christian Advocate*, the organ of the Georgia MECS, stated in 1886, "We thoroughly believe in the wisdom and expediency of the local option movement, and think it beyond all question the best for the friends of temperance to adhere to this method."[136] Methodist bishop Warren A. Candler abandoned the "moral suasion alone" approach in the 1880s and embraced local option as the best means of fixing Georgia's drinking problem. As chairman of the North Georgia Conference's temperance committee, he maintained that the saloons in the state outnumbered the churches three to one, and under such circumstances, the powerful arm of the law must be utilized to advance the prohibition cause.[137]

After the turn of the century, however, evangelicals in Georgia became increasingly dissatisfied with the local option approach. They began to recognize its limits and its ultimate inadequacy. Sam Jones, who had long been a local optionist, came to conclude that local option laws were "too local and too optional."[138] Although an area could vote out the saloons, liquor manufacturers and distributors found that they could skirt local restrictions by shipping their wares from "wet" counties or from other states—known as the "jug trade." The GBC complained that the jug trade and the continued advertisement of mail-order liquor in dry-county newspapers were undermining local option in the state. It called on the governor to back legislation that would prohibit the shipment of liquor from wet to dry counties.[139]

As prohibitionists increasingly rejected local option in favor of statewide prohibition, anti-prohibitionists increasingly endorsed local option as the most reasonable course of action. Just as supporting high license had become synonymous with being anti-prohibition in the 1890s, by 1905, any political candidate who advocated local option was considered a wet candidate. As Alexander McKelway noted, "The two systems for controlling the saloon evil, local option and state prohibition, are generally regarded as mutually antagonistic."[140] In 1913 the northern temperance paper *American Issue* likewise said of an Alabama gubernatorial candidate, "Mr. Henderson is for local option. In Alabama that means saloons."[141]

Although the local option approach was widely popular throughout the South, prohibitionists in some states favored a different method of restricting liquor sales. Tennessee evangelicals were especially fond of mile laws, which created saloon-free zones (usually four miles in diameter) around schools or churches. In Tennessee, such laws had existed as early as 1824, when the legislature prohibited the sale of liquor within one mile of a church building.[142] After the Civil War, mile laws began to proliferate. Recognizing that the saloon was "the alma mater of criminals," legislators sought to keep them away from schools and colleges. Several acts were passed in the late 1860s, each banning the sale of alcohol within two miles of specific institutions, including the Baptist college at Mossy Creek (later Carson-Newman College) in 1867. In 1877 the law was expanded to include any private educational institution that was outside an incorporated town, and the radius of prohibition was extended to four miles. This extension of the law virtually eliminated saloons from rural areas in the state, but the battle for the larger towns and cities remained.

Tennesseans' partiality for the four-mile law was due in part to the state's constitution. In 1873 Governor John C. Brown had vetoed a local option law because he believed it violated the Tennessee Constitution. Since the constitutionality of local option was an unsettled question, most prohibition activists viewed the four-mile law as the best means to avoid the problem altogether.[143] In 1906 the editor of the *Baptist and Reflector* cited the constitutionality issue when explaining why Tennessee Baptists favored the Adams (four-mile) law over the more precarious local option approach. The four-mile approach was also favored because it increased the likelihood of imposing prohibition in areas where it would likely be rejected if left to a popular vote of the residents. Persuading a majority of the state legislature to place a large portion of the state under prohibition by means of the four-mile law, evangelicals reasoned, would be easier than convincing the majority of voters in incorrigibly wet areas to impose it on themselves via local option. Finally, it was argued that the four-mile approach gave prohibition more permanence. Folk pointed out that, under local option, the issue could be put on the ballot every two years by either side, giving rise to "constant strife and turmoil and confusion." Under the four-mile system, the only way for saloons to return to a dry area was for the legislature to repeal the law for the entire state.[144]

In the late 1880s evangelicals put increased pressure on the Tennessee legislature to toughen and expand the four-mile law. In 1886 the Tennessee Conference of the MECS announced that it was "heartily in sympathy with and emphatically indorse the Four-Mile Law, and exhort our people as good citizens to assist in its rigid enforcement."[145] The push to broaden the law to larger cities remained the main focus of Tennessee evangelicals until 1907. The first major expansion of the law came in 1887, when it was extended to all schoolhouses, both public and private, whether school was in session or not. In 1889 the TBC called on the legislature to extend the four-mile law to the whole state, including all incorporated towns.[146] As noted earlier, in 1896 the Baptists called for its expansion to all towns and cities with five thousand or fewer inhabitants.[147] Such requests continued through much of the 1890s in Tennessee, but neither the Democratic nor the Republican Party would endorse any form of prohibition—not even the four-mile law.

Despite this predilection for mile laws, one of the key organizations pushing for the extension of prohibition in Tennessee during the 1890s was called the Local Option League. Its leadership came primarily from the evangelical ranks, including *Baptist and Reflector* editor E. E. Folk, *Nashville Christian Advocate* editor E. E. Hoss, *East Tennessee Baptist* and *Anti-Saloon Journal* editor Samuel W. Tindell, and Methodist minister David C. Kelley. In 1899 the Local Option League and other evangelical prohibitionists in Tennessee increased the pressure on the state legislature to extend the four-mile law. Hoss warned legislators of the political ramifications of continued indifference toward prohibition:

> We speak soberly and earnestly when we say that if the present Legislature adjourns without taking any action in response to numerous petitions that we have sent to that body, the disgust of the good people will be too deep to find adequate expression in mere words. We are living in a period of social and political disorganization. Men are not as much bound by party ties as they once were. There is a growing tendency toward independence and self-assertion. It is well for those who are in power to reflect a long time before they turn a deaf ear to the pleas that come from so many thousand homes in favor of some further restriction of the promiscuous sale of ardent spirits.[148]

The state legislature responded in 1899 by extending the four-mile law to cities with two thousand or fewer inhabitants, provided the town reincorporated after passage of the bill. In that same year, the Local Option League reorganized as the Tennessee Anti-Saloon League (ASL) and continued to campaign for expansion of the four-mile law. It pushed again in 1902 to extend the law to cities of five thousand residents, urging evangelicals not to vote for any candidate who did not support such an extension. Republicans, hoping to capitalize on the issue, added support for extension of the four-mile law to their platform.

In 1903 prohibitionists in Tennessee won a major victory with the passage of the Adams law, which granted that extension. Evangelicals were overjoyed, and Folk wondered, "Is the millennium nearby?"[149] Evangelicals did not halt their push to further expand prohibition in the state, however. In 1905 only twelve of Tennessee's ninety-six counties remained wet, and the TBC promised that "an aggressive fight will be made to secure the election of a governor and legislature next time who will favor the extension of the Adams Law to every place in the state."[150] The Holston Conference of the MECS that year called "special attention to the effort to extend in Tennessee the Four-Mile Law to all towns and cities of the state."[151] The Tennessee Conference, which covered the middle and western portions of the state, likewise endorsed the Adams law and announced that it "favor[ed] its extension so as to include the cities and larger towns of the state" and vowed to support only candidates who were committed to prohibitory legislation.[152]

In 1907 evangelicals had a bill introduced in the Tennessee legislature that would extend the Adams law to cities with populations of 150,000 or fewer. The bill was sponsored by Senator I. L. Pendleton of Davidson County and became known as the Pendleton bill, but it had been written by Baptist editor and ASL president E. E. Folk.[153] A similar bill had been defeated in 1905 ("by trickery," claimed Folk), but in 1907 the bill passed.[154] The only cities in Tennessee that remained wet were Nashville, Memphis, Chattanooga, and LaFollette, a small mining town in the hills of eastern Tennessee. Despite their success in having the Adams law extended in 1907, evangelicals celebrated only a limited victory, since the cities that remained wet served as sources of liquor for residents of surrounding dry counties. Folk wrote, "If the sale of liquor were confined within LaFollette and Chattanooga and Nashville and Memphis, if it could be sold only to the citizens of these cities, then it would be to a large extent a local question. But as long as these places are allowed to send their liquor in jugs to the surrounding counties and make the boys in those counties drunk . . . it is a question in which every citizen of the state is interested."[155] The only recourse, evangelicals believed, was to push once again for statewide prohibition.[156] As with local option, the four-mile laws' weakness was that they did not prohibit the shipment of alcohol from wet areas to dry ones, and the TBC asked for both state and federal legislation that would prohibit such importation.[157] Folk noted that actions by Governor Malcolm Patterson, such as vetoing a "jug bill" in 1908, put the ninety-two dry counties in Tennessee "at the mercy of the four remaining counties of the state," and he called for a renewed fight for statewide prohibition.[158]

Tennessee was not the only state to enact mile laws, but this approach was more dominant in Tennessee than elsewhere. The Georgia legislature did pass a three-mile law in 1891 that prohibited liquor sales within three miles of both schools and churches. Georgia evangelicals heartily approved the new law and fought an almost immediate attempt by wets to reduce the coverage to one mile.[159] Similar laws also existed in Alabama in the 1870s and inspired Crumpton's crusade for prohibition in that state. He recalled meeting a pastor of a small Baptist church who had successfully lobbied the Alabama legislature to pass a law prohibiting liquor sales within one mile of his rural church. This became one of the few places in the state where prohibition prevailed during the 1870s, and the old pastor was determined to continue lobbying in Montgomery until he got another half mile added to the law. Crumpton credited that pastor with convincing him "that prohibition was the thing that good men every where ought to labor for."[160]

The Alabamian approach to prohibition was more piecemeal than that of its neighbors. The state not only implemented local option and mile laws but also experimented with state-run liquor dispensaries as another alternative to high license. In 1891 the city of Athens, Georgia, implemented a government-run dispensary after growing frustrated with the ineffectiveness of local option laws. That system caught the attention of other city leaders across the nation, and those in both Boston, Massachusetts, and Sioux Falls, South Dakota, studied the Athens approach to see if they could copy it.[161] Governor Ben Tillman of South Carolina was also impressed by the system, and in 1893 he implemented a statewide network of liquor dispensaries based on a model being used in Sweden at the time.[162] Advocates of the dispensary viewed it as a more realistic way to reduce the sale and consumption of alcohol than outright prohibition, which they viewed as ultimately unenforceable.[163] The dispensary promised to cut alcohol consumption while still generating revenue for the state.[164] Five years later, Alabama state senator Frank S. Moody, who had been captivated by South Carolina's system, convinced the Alabama legislature to begin experimenting with a dispensary program. In 1900 legislation was passed that allowed counties not under local option to close all the saloons and establish government-run liquor dispensaries in their place. The dispensaries could not sell liquor by the drink and were to be closed on Sundays and election days.[165]

Evangelicals initially rationalized the dispensary approach as being the least of various evils. They viewed one liquor establishment per town as preferable to the dozens allowed to exist under the license approach. But after the turn of the century, Alabama evangelicals became increasingly alarmed at the spread of dispensaries, seeing them as a threat to their previous prohibition victories. "If this movement continues to grow as it has in the past two years," a writer in the *Alabama Baptist* stated in 1902, "all of that part of the state which has been won for prohibition will be lost and the battle will have to be fought again on the same fields." O. C. Doster of Newton, Alabama, wrote to the *Alabama Baptist* to proclaim, "The dispensary is a gigantic monster." He warned his fellow Baptists not to compromise with evil or condone it by supporting the dispensary system. Lida B. Robertson of Mobile argued that it was better for the state to be just a "regulator" of the liquor traffic, as it was under the high-license approach, than to become a buyer and seller of liquor too.[166]

By 1907, the prohibition scene in Alabama was eclectic: twenty-one counties had adopted total prohibition through local option, twenty-one counties still employed high license as the only form of liquor restriction, sixteen counties had abolished saloons and established dispensaries, and the nine remaining counties had established dispensaries that coexisted with licensed saloons.[167] Support for dispensaries in Alabama had waned significantly, and in 1908 the approach was abandoned. The dispensary ultimately failed in Alabama, as well as in South Carolina and North Carolina, due to not only opposition from hard-line prohibitionists but also widespread corruption within the dispensary system itself.[168]

Campaign for Statewide Prohibition, 1900–1915

Shortly after the turn of the century, evangelicals increasingly rejected intermediate approaches such as local option, mile laws, and dispensaries as both insufficient and a compromise with the liquor traffic. These approaches were inadequate because they failed to fully prohibit the sale of alcohol in any given area. Furthermore, because such schemes allowed for the continued sale of alcohol in some parts of the state—those outside the four-mile limit, those that rejected local option prohibition, or those where alcohol was dispensed under the auspices of the government—evangelicals viewed them as unacceptable concessions to the liquor industry. These methods of prohibition made the state an accessory to the continued consumption of alcohol and complicit in the moral, social, and economic consequences thereof. The push for absolute statewide prohibition of the manufacture, sale, and consumption of liquor thus gained new momentum among southern evangelicals. The decline of third-party political movements, the disfranchisement of African American voters, and the decreased threat of Republican resurgence in the South made statewide prohibition legislation more realistic after the turn of the century, and evangelicals were confident that they could now be victorious.[169]

The campaign for statewide prohibition was aided greatly by the Anti-Saloon League, which became the dominant prohibition organization in the South after the turn of the century. In 1893 Howard Russell founded an ASL in Ohio. Russell, a Congregational minister, was a graduate of Oberlin College, a hotbed of midwestern prohibition sentiment. Two years later the Ohio ASL joined with a similar organization based in Washington, D.C., and formed the national ASL, filling a growing need for a nonpartisan prohibition organization.[170] In the 1880s and early 1890s the Woman's Christian Temperance Union, under the leadership of Frances Willard, had become intimately connected with the national Prohibition Party. This political affiliation created internal division—in 1889 Ellen Foster founded the Nonpartisan Woman's Christian Temperance Union as an alternative to Willard's WCTU—and caused many outsiders to withdraw their support from the organization. Seeking to avoid the trap of partisanship, the ASL envisioned a nonpartisan and pragmatic approach to the liquor problem. A separate league was established in each state and formulated strategic policies for achieving incremental legislative successes in that state. Unlike the Prohibition Party, which had been launched in 1869 as a separate political party attempting to draw support from disaffected Democrats and Republicans, the ASL embraced an omniparty approach. Its goal was to work precinct by precinct to get politicians elected who supported its prohibition agenda, and it proved enormously successful at uniting evangelical prohibitionists across denominational boundaries and avoiding the albatross of party affiliation. Perhaps more importantly, the ASL avoided civil rights issues that continued to separate northern and southern prohibitionists. It also brought to the prohibition struggle a modern, bureaucratic, and highly organized operating system.[171]

The ASL's motto, "The Church in Action against the Saloon," expressed its church-based approach. Local congregations were embraced as both the primary means by which to disseminate the league's message and the key source of funding. The leadership of the state leagues was drawn primarily from evangelical leaders, and 75 percent of the state ASL superintendents were clergymen.[172] Sometimes state leagues brought in experienced superintendents from other states. For instance, Brooks Lawrence, a Presbyterian minister from Ohio, came to Alabama in 1906 to serve as superintendent of that state's league, while Alabamian W. B. Crumpton served as its president. The league often co-opted existing temperance organizations, such as the Local Option League in Tennessee. By 1908, ASLs had been established in all but four states. Despite the strong presence of prohibition sentiment and evangelical support in the South, the ASL was slow to establish itself there. The league's northern leadership had difficulty grasping and accommodating the unique features of the South, including its one-party politics, race relations, and social customs. The ASL's organization was strong in some states, such as Tennessee and Alabama, but almost nonexistent in other states, such as Georgia.[173]

The first state where the drive for statewide prohibition bore fruit was Georgia. The major turning point occurred in September 1906, when violent race riots broke out in Atlanta. Racial tension had been building in the city for months, fueled by an epidemic of reports of black men raping white women and by an intense gubernatorial race wherein the candidates capitalized on the racial fears of whites. Four sexual assaults were reported on September 22, and the floodgates of emotion opened, resulting in a four-day spree of race-based lynchings, shootings, beatings, and property destruction at the hands of white mobs.[174] More than ten thousand white men roamed the streets of the city, unimpeded by police, in a wave of violence that ultimately left ten black and two white Atlantans dead and countless more beaten and wounded before six thousand troops restored order to the city.[175] In the immediate aftermath of the riots, Georgia prohibitionists rushed in to provide an explanation for the underlying cause of the violence. The epidemic of rapes, they argued, was an outgrowth of saloons that served black men. Statewide prohibition had not been a campaign issue for either gubernatorial candidate in 1906, but after the riots, it became the first order of business for the new legislature.

Georgia became the first southern state to enact statewide prohibition, and it launched a new call for Maine laws—this time centered in the Southeast rather than the Northeast. The state became a model for evangelicals elsewhere and energized campaigns for statewide laws across the region.

Many looked to Georgia as a test of whether statewide prohibition could work in the South. In March 1908 Booker T. Washington compared current crime and court statistics with those from the preceding year, when Atlanta had still been wet. He reported a "remarkable reduction" in the crime rate in Atlanta, which had been cut in half since prohibition took effect.[176] The *Baptist and Reflector* reported that for the first time in Atlanta's history, the jails were empty.[177] A correspondent for *Our Home Field*, a Baptist publication, reported that one Atlanta policeman had not seen a single drunk person on the city's streets in four weeks, whereas prior to prohibition, he had seen four or five per day. Only 65 persons appeared before the city court accused of drunkenness in January 1908, compared with 553 who had faced such charges the previous January.[178] The northern magazine the *Independent* also examined Georgia's newly imposed law and found that within days of its going into effect, the crime rate in Atlanta had been cut in half. Bars were being converted into coffeehouses, the paper reported, and breweries into factories. The positive effects of statewide prohibition were impossible to deny, the *Independent* declared, noting that "even the rumheads are beginning to say it is a good thing."[179]

Tennessee followed Georgia's lead in 1908. Although it did not experience an outbreak of racial violence, the events contributing to the passage of statewide prohibition involved a shocking martyrdom for the cause and a full-scale political realignment in the state. As Thomas R. Pegram observes, "Nowhere was the liquor question more intense, more violently divisive, and more central to state politics than in Tennessee between 1908 and 1914."[180] Tennessee evangelicals found a political champion in the person of Senator Edward Ward Carmack. Carmack had not always supported statewide prohibition, stating as late as 1906 that he opposed it.[181] But Carmack, the son of a Campbellite minister, eventually changed his mind, saying in 1908 that the saloon had "sinned away its day of grace" and declaring himself fully supportive of statewide prohibition legislation.[182] In 1906 Tennessee elected Democrat Malcolm Patterson as governor. Patterson, a congressman from Memphis, was strongly opposed to statewide prohibition, and in 1907 he blocked several antiliquor measures. In 1908 the dry forces sought a challenger to take on Patterson. Carmack, whose Senate term had recently ended, agreed after much cajoling by prohibitionists to run against Patterson in the Democratic primary. When Carmack returned from Washington to challenge Patterson's reelection, a bitter campaign ensued; it centered on prohibition, which had become an increasingly divisive issue in Tennessee politics. During the course of the primary campaign, Patterson and Carmack held a series of fifty debates, and prohibition took center stage in each one.[183]

The Anti-Saloon League endorsed Carmack. Its president, E. E. Folk, was a close friend of the senator's and campaigned tirelessly on his behalf. Folk had used the editorial pages of the *Baptist and Reflector* to vigorously criticize Governor Patterson's stance against prohibition during the past two years. In a close contest, Patterson emerged victorious in the June primary election. The Alabama-born incumbent received 85,000 votes to Carmack's 79,000. Folk called the election "a perfect carnival of corruption," accusing Patterson supporters of stuffing the ballot boxes and voting multiple times. In one precinct that had only 52 registered Democratic voters, Folk reported, Patterson somehow obtained 207 votes.[184] Carmack accepted the results of the primary, but he proposed that because of the widespread support for prohibition, the state Democratic Party insert a statewide prohibition plank into its platform. In response, the Democratic leadership—all Patterson supporters—changed the process for nominating delegates to the state party's convention. The new arrangement placed one man, who happened to be the attorney for the Chattanooga Brewing Company, in charge of appointing all delegates. Thus, the 151 delegates that Carmack had picked up in the election were unseated and replaced by Patterson-supporting anti-prohibitionists. When the convention assembled in July, it surprised no one when the party declared itself opposed to statewide prohibition.

Tennessee prohibitionists, including Carmack, were incensed. Carmack accepted a job as editor of the *Nashville Tennessean*, and during the months leading up to the general election, he used the editorial pages to savagely attack Patterson and the wet forces supporting him. The Republicans nominated George N. Tillman, who was endorsed by Folk and the ASL. Patterson won reelection, however, which caused Carmack to amplify his rage against the "machine" politicians running the Democratic Party in Tennessee. Many of Carmack's scathing editorials focused on Colonel Duncan B. Cooper, a close adviser to Patterson. Cooper warned Carmack to cease his attacks, but Carmack refused to relent. On the afternoon of November 9, 1908, Carmack encountered Cooper and his son, Robin, on a street in downtown Nashville. The Coopers approached Carmack and drew pistols. Carmack was armed as well, and a gunfight ensued. Robin Cooper shot Carmack, who died instantly. Almost as instantly, Carmack became a martyr for the cause of statewide prohibition. Evangelicals, along with all Republicans and dry Democrats, were incensed at the violent attack on Patterson's political nemesis, and the evangelical press was livid.

Carmack's role as a martyr for the cause of prohibition was quickly established. Folk, when eulogizing Carmack, described him as a Christ figure who had been "shot down like a dog by the hands of men not worthy to touch the hem of his garments." He described the funeral procession, where "strong men, unused to weeping, shook with convulsive sobs, and swore they would avenge his death." Folk's grief at the death of a friend and the loss of the chief political ally of the prohibition cause was obvious. "O Carmack, Carmack," he lamented, "could we but call you back to earth again, there are thousands of us who would willingly lay down our lives for yours."[185] Evangelicals charged that Carmack had been assassinated as part of a conspiracy that included Patterson himself. "The evidence seems strong that there was a conspiracy," wrote Folk, and that it included at least the bodyguard and next-door neighbor of the governor.

Just when it seemed impossible to do so, Patterson enraged Tennessee evangelicals even further. Shortly after Carmack's shooting, both Duncan and Robin Cooper were convicted of murder, even though the elder Cooper had never fired a shot. The case was appealed to the state supreme court, which upheld the conviction. Governor Patterson immediately pardoned both men. In the wake of this action, the prohibition cause reached the zenith of its popular appeal and political support in Tennessee. Republicans in the state legislature embraced statewide prohibition, and the Democratic Party split into two factions: "independent" and "regular" Democrats. The regular Democrats were those who supported Patterson and opposed statewide prohibition. The independent Democrats had been Carmack supporters and were now more committed than ever to obtaining statewide antiliquor legislation. When the legislature convened in January 1909, the independent Democrats and the Republicans joined forces to form a fusionist majority that passed a law extending the four-mile law to every city in the state, thus putting all of Tennessee under prohibition. Governor Patterson vetoed the bill, but the coalition of Republicans and independent Democrats was able to override his veto.[186]

The Carmack shooting, combined with Patterson's pardons and veto, sealed the governor's political fate. A well-known liquor dealer is alleged to have remarked, "When Cooper shot, he killed Carmack, Patterson, and whiskey at the same time."[187] Even the liquor industry now considered Patterson a liability. Patterson withdrew from the 1910 gubernatorial race, and his replacement was defeated by Ben Hooper, a Republican who supported prohibition.[188] Not until 1914 did regular Democrats relent, embrace prohibition, and work with independent Democrats to nominate a prohibitionist gubernatorial candidate.

Just as the race riots in Atlanta had given Georgia prohibitionists the additional popular support they needed to achieve their goal of statewide prohibition, so Carmack's death allowed Tennessee evangelicals to succeed sooner than would have been possible otherwise. Following the passage of statewide prohibition in Tennessee, letters poured in to Folk congratulating him on the campaign's success, and most writers recognized that Carmack's death had tipped the scales in their favor. Baptist minister J. B. Gambrell, former president of Mercer University in Georgia but now living in Texas and working for prohibition there, wrote, "I do not doubt that the killing of Carmack helped to clear the atmosphere. Splendid man he was." Gambrell did not take lightly the idea of designating Carmack a martyr for the cause; his own son had been gunned down by a liquor dealer in 1887 while campaigning for prohibition in Mississippi.[189] Another correspondent speculated that Carmack, "looking down from the celestial heights, sees that his martyr's blood was not shed in vain."[190]

Alabama lacked the kind of cataclysmic event that benefited the prohibition movement in both Georgia and Tennessee. Also unlike its neighbors, Alabama vacillated between being dry and being wet between 1907 and 1915. When Georgia implemented statewide prohibition in 1907, Alabama was still experimenting with a limited dispensary system. With the disfranchisement of black voters and the emergence of a strong ASL in the state, however, Alabama prohibitionists became increasingly confident that their state could finally rid itself of liquor altogether. The ASL, under the direction of Brooks Lawrence, continually agitated for local option legislation, and immediately after Georgia's move to statewide prohibition, the Alabama legislature acceded to popular pressure and passed a local option law. In October and November 1907 local option elections were held across the state, and nine counties went dry. The biggest victory for prohibitionists came in Jefferson County, which housed the booming industrial city of Birmingham. Rural residents of the county—who referred to the nearby city as "Bad Birmingham" because of its association with immorality and vice—successfully outvoted city residents, who largely voted against prohibition.[191]

Evangelicals praised the legislature for its 1907 local option law, but they soon demanded more. In November 1908 the legislature passed, and Governor B. B. Comer signed into law, a bill prohibiting the sale of liquor anywhere in the state. Fearing successful challenges to the constitutionality of legislative prohibition, the ASL pushed for constitutional prohibition in Alabama. In August 1909 Governor Comer approved an amendment that would make statewide prohibition part of the Alabama Constitution. When the proposed amendment was put to a popular vote for ratification, however, it failed in all but six of Alabama's sixty-seven counties. Although legislative prohibition was still in effect after the amendment's failure, the tide was turning against the dry forces in Alabama. Emmet O'Neal, an opponent of statewide prohibition, was elected governor in 1910, and in 1911 the state legislature replaced statewide prohibition with a local option law. The new statute allowed each county to decide whether it wanted local prohibition, a dispensary, or licensed saloons. Crumpton immediately challenged the law in court on technical grounds, appealing the case to the state supreme court but ultimately losing to the local optionists. Alabama retreated from the ranks of dry states and remained under local option for the next four years. Within the first year of the local option law's taking effect, seventeen counties held elections, and nine of them voted in saloons. By 1914 Jefferson County went from being totally dry to having eighty-three licensed saloons, twenty-seven wholesale liquor establishments, and thirteen liquor-serving social clubs.[192]

The election of 1914, however, gave Alabama prohibitionists new hope of returning the state to the dry column. A majority of the legislature was sympathetic to the cause of statewide prohibition, and the churches, led by the ASL, renewed their agitation. In January 1915 a statewide prohibition bill—almost an exact duplicate of the state's 1908 legislation—passed both houses of the legislature. It forbade the manufacture or sale of anything that "tastes like, foams like, or looks like beer," as well as the sale of any beverage in a bottle shaped like a whiskey flask.[193] Brooks Lawrence launched a letter-writing campaign to get evangelicals across the state to deluge the new governor, Charles Henderson, with correspondence urging him to sign the new prohibition bill. Henderson still vetoed the bill, but his veto was successfully overridden, and Alabama was once again under statewide prohibition.

After 1880, evangelicals in the South manifested a renewed commitment to the cause of prohibition and embraced new tactics to achieve victory over the demon rum. The key shift in the evangelical attitude toward drinking after the Civil War was the conviction that it was "not enough that the church should be sober." Southern pastors were no longer content to chide only members of their own congregations for their immoderate consumption of alcohol. Rather, the years between 1880 and 1915 were marked by a deep sense of urgency to totally eradicate alcohol from the diets of all southerners. This was an important shift driven by a number of forces. In a time of rapid social, economic, and political change, prohibition became increasingly valuable and important to evangelicals as a perceived cure-all for every ill faced by the region. The post-Reconstruction era was also a stressful and unnerving time for southern white evangelicals because of the presence of African American voters, who proved to be unfriendly toward prohibition and hindered white prohibitionists within the Democratic Party from reforming its wet stance. Also, in the postwar era, southern evangelicals were vying for a level of cultural dominance and prestige that had been denied them during the antebellum period. Now they, rather than the planter aristocracy, were in a position to define what it meant to be a man of honor and respectability. Finally, the late nineteenth century was marked by significant changes in the role of women in American life, which prompted southern evangelicals to reconsider women's part in the prohibition movement and to use that movement to reaffirm their own masculine roles as the protectors and guardians of women. All these factors were instrumental in driving southern evangelicals to embrace prohibition with unprecedented fervency after 1880 and to demand the abolition of liquor from the entire South.

Like evangelicals across the South, those in Tennessee, Alabama, and Georgia became increasingly energized as the nineteenth century closed and the twentieth century began. As a result, between 1907 and 1915, these states as well as five other former Confederate states implemented statewide prohibition.[194] But ultimately, after all their struggles to achieve statewide prohibition, evangelicals still found it insufficient. Just as the jug trade had rendered local option ineffectual, interstate commerce made statewide prohibition insufficient. Thus, evangelical prohibitionists in the second decade of the twentieth century, led by the ASL, amplified their call for nationwide prohibition.[195] After Congress passed the Eighteenth Amendment in December 1917, southern legislatures were quick to ratify it.[196] The nation's patience with the noble experiment would eventually wane, but on the eve of nationwide prohibition, evangelicals in the South could be confident that their devotion to the cause had been instrumental in leading the nation to its new undertaking. And southerners such as Alabama ASL superintendent Brooks Lawrence recognized the region's role, proclaiming to an Alabama WCTU meeting, "The South is BRINGING temperance to our land."[197]

The southern evangelical vision of enforcing sobriety beyond the confines of the church and into the larger society had expanded from the town level to the county level to the state level, and finally to the entire nation. Several significant changes among southern evangelicals between 1880 and the early 1900s aided in this expansion, including an increased emphasis on teetotalism, the embrace of legal suasion, a group of leaders devoted to the cause of prohibition, increased and unapologetic political activism on the part of the church, and a shift from milder, more localized forms of prohibition to statewide prohibition. One of these elements in particular—the increased involvement of evangelicals in secular politics—was key to the ultimate victory of the prohibition cause. The move into the political realm, however, was not achieved without first overcoming significant resistance from both inside and outside the church.

Chapter Three

"Why Don't He Give His Attention to Saving Sinners?"

Prohibition and Politics

THE EVOLUTION OF SOUTHERN evangelical prohibitionists from moral suasionists to political activists met with serious resistance from both without and within evangelical circles. Several other issues became deeply intertwined with prohibition after 1880, especially during the politically turbulent 1890s. Southern evangelicals' increasingly strong prohibition stance placed them on a collision course with a revered principle: the doctrine of the spirituality of the church. This conviction that church and state are distinct spheres that should never overlap had become entrenched in southern denominations in the mid-nineteenth century, simultaneously distancing them from their antebellum support of slavery and justifying their continued separate existence. Prohibition fervor among evangelicals also coincided with the emergence of a third-party Populist movement that threatened the hegemony of the Democratic Party in the South. Thus, during the 1890s, declaring oneself to be a prohibitionist suggested disloyalty to the Democratic Party and to white political supremacy. As a result, evangelicals committed to prohibition had to negotiate the South's unique cultural and religious traditions as well as the political realities of the region.

Resistance to Evangelical Political Activism

As William Link observes in *The Paradox of Southern Progressivism*, social reform movements in the late-nineteenth-century South placed the traditional commitment to individual autonomy in conflict with a new desire to intervene in the private lives of individuals.[1] Prohibition was no exception, and southern evangelicals who began to advocate prohibition in the 1880s immediately faced opposition from those both inside and outside the church. Among those who attacked evangelicals for pushing their temperance crusade into the realm of legally mandated prohibition were anti-prohibitionists and political conservatives. In 1885 Senator Richard Coke of Texas engaged in a heated debate with a Baptist prohibitionist. In a soon-to-be-infamous remark, Coke declared, "scourge the preachers back to their pulpits and cut off their rations." Coke's "scourge the preachers" remark was used for years by evangelicals as evidence of the contempt secular politicians had for ministers and of their determination to keep men of faith "in their place."

E. E. Folk was similarly attacked for his political activities in his capacity as president of the Tennessee Anti-Saloon League. Jesse Littleton, a wet Tennessee politician against whom Folk campaigned, called Folk a "political parson," a "careless divine," and a "political boss preacher."[2] One Methodist wrote that "second-class politicians" were increasingly espousing the idea that ministers should not meddle in politics because preachers had not been outspoken enough in advocating their right to influence legislation.[3] By applying the states' rights argument—a core tenet of the defense of the old Confederacy—to the individual, conservatives attempted to brand the prohibition movement as antithetical to southern values and beliefs. "Some demagogues claim it would be trespassing upon the liberty of the people," noted J. B. Hawthorne in a sermon, "but not so, it would, on the contrary, deliver the people from its most horrible taskmasters; it would give them more liberty, more freedom." Hawthorne likened the government's interference in the sale of liquor to its already established right to regulate the quality of meat sold by a butcher.[4]

No less a symbol of the Old South than Jefferson Davis, former president of the Confederate States of America, entered the fray in 1887 when he attacked prohibitionists pushing for statewide legislation in Texas. Methodist bishop Charles Betts Galloway criticized Davis's refusal to support statewide prohibition, which infuriated the former Confederate president. The two men became embroiled in a long and public debate via letters printed in the press. The clash between Galloway of Mississippi and Davis of Texas was also widely reported in the evangelical press throughout the South. Davis's attacks on evangelical prohibitionists reflected the attitude of unredeemed Confederates who were still committed to the political philosophy of states' rights. From that doctrine Davis extrapolated a corollary idea of "community independence," which, he claimed, precluded the state government from imposing prohibitory legislation on local communities.[5] Davis referred to existing local prohibition laws as "wooden horses in which many a disguised enemy to state sovereignty as the guardian of individual liberty was introduced."[6] Davis's sentiments were widely quoted by anti-prohibitionists to strengthen their case. Galloway responded that the old idea of states' rights had overtaken Davis's mind and clouded his thinking, and he pointed out the logical fallacy of Davis's argument, which would render state governments impotent to legislate on any matter that affected local communities.[7]

Many southern evangelicals reacted with dismay and anger at the position taken by their former president. Loyalty to the old regime and its statesmen clearly had its limits.[8] Judge Job Harral, a Tennessee Baptist, recognized the damage that such a high-profile figure could inflict on the prohibition cause. "I hear some people say: 'I was a prohibitionist, but when I see a great man like Jeff Davis come out against it, I think it must be wrong,'" Harral reported to the *Baptist and Reflector.* Davis's "silly talk about sumptuary laws and the curtailment of human liberty" had no doubt cost the movement some support, but Harral was confident that a reform movement was afoot that would sweep away opponents such as Davis "and consign them to the oblivion they so much deserve."[9] In Alabama, Methodist W. A. McCarty speculated that Davis and other conservatives had led to setbacks at the ballot box for prohibitionists. "There can be no doubt that the personal influence and the 'personal liberty' notions of Jefferson Davis contributed to the defeat of prohibition in Texas and Tennessee," he wrote. McCarty explained the limits of southern loyalty to Davis, saying, "As Jefferson Davis represented our cause and suffered for it we will honor him. But on moral questions we will follow him only as he follows truth and righteousness." He pointed out that there were other Confederate heroes who could serve as moral authorities for the region, including Robert E. Lee and "Stonewall" Jackson, two men "whose moral grandeur eclipses even their peerless fame as soldiers." McCarty attacked the inconsistency of Davis's opposition to statewide prohibition but his support of local option. If a state cannot prohibit the consumption of alcohol without trampling on the rights of individuals, McCarty reasoned, how can a county enact the same prohibition without violating the same rights?[10]

O. P. Fitzgerald, editor of the *Christian Advocate* in Nashville, likewise speculated that Davis's attacks had influenced recent prohibition elections in both Texas and Tennessee. In the end, however, he believed that Davis's stance against prohibition had done greater harm to his own legacy than to the prohibition movement. The editor wrote: "Our opinion is that he who might have died enjoying the warmest affection of the best people of that section of country which in the past so greatly honored him has alienated the esteem of many friends by supplying the liquor interest with campaign literature deriving its effectiveness not from the force of the argument, but from the name of the writer. His best friends are mortified at this use of his influence." Like McCarty, the editor challenged "the hackneyed, shattered plea of 'personal liberty'" and attacked Davis's flawed logic by pointing out that "if prohibition adopted by a vote of the people of a state is wrong in principle, so also is prohibition by a vote of the people of a county."[11]

Evangelicals waved off the personal liberty argument raised against their efforts on behalf of prohibition, but this was not the only argument advanced by wet politicians. As Senator Coke's "scourge the preachers" comment implied, there was a strong sense among some politicians that ministers had no business meddling in the affairs of the state. Politicians' argument about the proper sphere of ministers struck a more resonant chord within evangelicalism. In his quarrel with Bishop Galloway, Jefferson Davis branded the clergyman a "political parson" and accused him of having "left the pulpit and Bible to mount the political rostrum and plead the higher law of prohibition." Prohibition's advocacy by ministers of the gospel, Davis declared, was "an enemy to the spirit and practice of true Christianity."[12]

A significant number of evangelicals were inclined to agree with Davis about the proper relationship between ministers and secular politics, and similar criticisms could even be found within the denominations. Southern evangelicals' decision to embrace legal means of sobering up the South put them at odds with a principle held dear by the three dominant southern white denominations: the strict separation of church and state. This tenet went by different names in different denominations and had different origins in each, but it served the same important function for Methodists, Baptists, and Presbyterians. Frequently referred to as the doctrine of the spirituality of the church (especially by Presbyterians and Methodists), the idea that church and state exist in two distinct and wholly separate spheres was especially important in the southern denominations because it vindicated their original secession from their northern brethren and justified their continued existence as separate, regional denominations.

The Doctrine of the Spirituality of the Church

During the antebellum era, the issues of slavery and abolition had both political and moral implications, causing much consternation and strife within any denomination with a significant southern membership. The issue became increasingly divisive during the 1830s, and by the mid-1840s, the major national denominations reached the breaking point. The years 1844 and 1845 witnessed the division along regional lines of both the Methodists and the Baptists as a result of agitation over the slave issue.

In the Methodist Episcopal Church, the General Conference of 1844 was the watershed event. At that year's conference, two unpopular decisions led to a split in the church. In the first case, Francis Harding, an itinerant Maryland minister, had acquired slaves through his recent marriage and was subsequently suspended from his ministry by the Baltimore Conference. The General Conference agreed with the Baltimore Conference that Harding had violated church regulations by refusing to manumit his slaves.[13] The second decision involved Bishop James O. Andrew of Georgia, one of only five bishops in the MEC at the time. Andrew had come into possession of two slaves as part of his deceased wife's estate and through his remarriage to a slave-owning widow. Andrew had little choice in the matter, because Georgia law forbade his emancipation of the slaves. At the General Convention, a motion was made that Andrew be forced to resign if he continued to own slaves, despite the fact that such ownership was not strictly proscribed by church rules. Southern Methodists were especially upset by the treatment of Andrew, in part because he was one of their own, and in part because his case involved constitutional issues that clouded the role played by slavery. In defending Andrew, they believed that they were fighting not for the institution of slavery but rather for adherence to the church's constitution and for due process. In the aftermath of the 1844 General Conference, southern conferences met to condemn the actions taken against both Andrew and Harding, and in 1845 they met in Louisville to form the Methodist Episcopal Church, South.[14]

The year 1845 also demarked the beginning of a separate southern denomination for Baptists. Up to that point, Baptists in the South had cooperated with northern Baptists as part of the Triennial Convention —formally known as the General Missionary Convention of the Baptist Denomination in the United States—whose activities centered on a foreign mission society and a home mission society. From its founding in 1814 until the early 1840s, this mission society sought to avoid division over the slavery issue. In 1841 it adopted a statement of neutrality, but the issue of whether the convention would appoint a slaveholder as a missionary became increasingly divisive. As with the Methodists, it was the case of a Georgian that proved to be the turning point. In 1844 Georgia Baptists nominated slaveholder James E. Reeve for appointment as a missionary with the home mission society. When the board refused to either appoint or reject Reeve, the Alabama Baptist Convention pressed the issue, demanding that the president of the board explicitly state whether slaveholding disqualified candidates for ordination as missionaries. The board replied that slaveholders would not receive appointments, and in May 1845, southern Baptists met in Augusta, Georgia, where they decided to form the Southern Baptist Convention and establish their own mission boards.[15]

While Baptists and Methodists were busy rupturing in 1845, the ingenious Old School Presbyterians—the largest Presbyterian body in the South—formulated a doctrine that would stave off their own disunion until after the outbreak of the Civil War. Facing the same internal divisions over the slavery issue as the other national bodies, the General Assembly of the Old School Presbyterian Church passed a resolution in 1845 declaring that "the church of Christ is a spiritual body," and as such, it was not within its purview to take a stand on the issue of slavery.[16] Whereas the New School Presbyterians split over slavery in 1857, the doctrine of the spirituality of the church, as it became known, proved successful in keeping the Old School Presbyterians united until the secession of southern states in 1861—a decade and a half longer than the Baptists and the Methodists.[17] Perhaps more important, when disunion did visit the Presbyterians, they were able to invoke the doctrine of spirituality as the primary justification for their secession.

During the fifteen years following the enunciation of the doctrine of spirituality, the South's leading Presbyterian divine, James Henley Thornwell, explicated and radicalized the doctrine. He argued that the church "has no mission to care for the things, and to become entangled with the kingdoms and the policy, of this world."[18] Northern Old School Presbyterians such as Charles Hodge considered Thornwell's interpretation both extreme and inconsistent with traditional Presbyterian belief. As Ernest Trice Thompson has pointed out, the doctrine was a clear deviation from the theology of John Calvin in Geneva, John Knox in Scotland, and the Puritans in both England and America, all of whom understood that the mission of the church was to engage and transform both society and its government in light of Christian morality.[19] Nevertheless, the Thornwellian version of the doctrine became increasingly popular among Presbyterians in the late antebellum South, and they were particularly fond of defending its strict separation of church and state whenever the issue of slavery arose.[20]

The most importance facet of the Presbyterian resolution of 1845 was not its ability to postpone denominational division for fifteen years; rather, it was the fact that it established a doctrine that for more than half a century would be an important element in the self-understanding and self-justification of all southern evangelicals, not just Presbyterians. It formalized into biblical doctrine a conviction that was shared by many antebellum southern evangelicals but that, prior to 1845, had existed only as a vague idea that lacked clear and reasoned formation. Southern Methodists and Baptists knew that they did not want their northern counterparts to broach the issue of slavery, but they had failed to crystallize a sound biblical argument for *why* it should not be brought up in national assemblies, in missionary appointments, or in issues of denominational polity. It was occasionally hinted at in less sophisticated terms, such as the Baptists' 1845 pledge that they would "not interfere in what is Caesar's" and Bishop Andrew's 1844 statement that "Methodist preachers instead of spending their time on politico-religious lecturing . . . ought to do the one work of preaching the gospel of the grace of God."[21]

For the most part, southern Methodists and Baptists in 1845

couched their arguments against interjecting the slavery issue into church matters in terms of how it violated church polity. Both denominations emphasized that important scriptural and ecclesiastical principles had been "trampled under foot" by their northern brothers and that their schism was purely an attempt to preserve those principles.[22] The Baptists argued that the constitution of the Triennial Convention "knows no difference between slaveholders and non-slaveholders" and that the northern Baptists had betrayed the spirit of that document by forbidding the appointment of slaveholding missionaries.[23] Likewise, among resolutions passed by the southern Methodist conferences in the months following the 1844 General Conference, the chief complaint against the northerner participants at that conference was that their actions in the case of Bishop Andrew had been unconstitutional and an "extrajudicial" violation of church rules.[24]

Yet Baptists and Methodists in the South soon became enchanted with the doctrine of spirituality as formulated by the Presbyterians in 1845 and as elucidated by Thornwell afterward. It enunciated what they had long felt or desired: that the church simply had no business speaking to the issue of slavery.[25] And after 1861 they were given a model of how the doctrine of spirituality could serve as a biblical justification for severing relations with the bothersome northern, antislavery half of one's denomination. When the Old School Presbyterians finally split along regional lines in 1861, the southern seceders were adamant that the rift had been instigated by a violation of this doctrine of spirituality.

At the 1861 General Assembly of the Old School Presbyterian Church in Philadelphia, a set of resolutions (known as the Gardiner Springs resolutions) was adopted, pledging that body's loyalty to the government of the United States. The southern delegates strongly opposed this action, as did some northerners such as Charles Hodge, who objected to the General Assembly taking such a political stance, especially given the divisiveness of the issue.[26] If Hodge and other northerners were reticent about the church making political pronouncements, southern Presbyterians influenced by Thornwell were incensed by the General Assembly's action and interpreted it as a blatant violation of the doctrine of the spirituality of the church. The southern churches withdrew from the assembly and launched a separate Presbyterian denomination.

At the inaugural assembly of the Presbyterian Church in the Confederate States of America (PCCSA) in 1861, the violation of the spiritual nature of the church was a central theme. The opening sermon reminded those present that the General Assembly had attempted "to place the crown of our Lord upon the head of Caesar" and to bind itself to the state. Such conduct, the preacher warned, was contrary to the spiritual mission of the church.[27] Likewise, the assembly asked Thornwell to pen an address to all Christian churches to justify the fledgling denomination's existence. In these remarks, Thornwell blamed the schism on the northern Presbyterians' passage of the Gardiner Springs resolutions. Had the delegates not taken this action, he speculated, "it is possible that the ecclesiastical separation of the North and the South might have been deferred for years to come."[28] In the years that followed, many southern Presbyterians claimed that they had wanted their denominational union with the Old School Presbyterian Church to remain intact despite the political division of the southern states from the United States. Southern Presbyterians maintained that the Confederate states had seceded over political differences, which should have had no bearing on the spiritual union of northern and southern Presbyterians. However, when the northern delegates at the 1861 General Assembly insisted on equating loyalty to the United States with loyalty to Christ, they were forced to withdraw and form their own denomination.

Southern Presbyterians' assertions that they intended to stay in communion with their northern brethren have been treated with skepticism by modern historians, who have also questioned to what extent southern Presbyterians were truly committed to the doctrine of spirituality. Jack Maddex, for example, claims that antebellum southern Presbyterians were very active politically and worked "through the church to defend slavery and reform its practice." He rejects the idea that the 1861 Old School General Assembly was not committed to an apolitical denominational union and maintains that Thornwell's reputation as a protector of the spirituality of the church is undeserved.[29] Likewise, E. Brooks Holifield maintains that the antebellum southern clergy never truly abstained from addressing societal and political issues. "Their self-described isolation was merely a protective gesture during the slavery controversy," he argues.[30]

Maddex and Holifield are correct in their assertion that southern

Presbyterians were not wholeheartedly committed to the doctrine of spirituality before the Civil War. Indeed, there is evidence that antebellum southern Presbyterians invoked the doctrine only when it was beneficial to do so. In addition, the validity of southern Presbyterians' commitment to remaining united with their northern brethren even after southern states had seceded from the Union is undermined by the lack of southern participation in the 1861 Old School General Assembly. Lewis Vander Velde's research reveals that less than half of the southern presbyteries bothered to send representatives to the Philadelphia gathering, and only two presbyteries lying within the thirteen states of the budding Confederate States of America were represented at the General Assembly.[31] Such unwillingness to participate in the national assembly raises serious questions about the southerners' purported commitment to unity. Evidence from the inauguration of the PCCSA in 1861 suggests that its founders had a strong desire to both entrench the doctrine of spirituality within the nascent denomination and depict it as the principle on which they based their decision to separate from the old denomination. In this effort, it appears, they were quite successful. As the war progressed, the northern church denounced slavery and the rebellion of the southern states in stronger terms, which reinforced the southern Presbyterian commitment to the doctrine of spirituality. Later generations came to view the doctrine as the key reason for their forebears' decision to establish a new denomination.[32] By the post-Reconstruction era, this questionable version of the denomination's nativity was widely accepted by southern Presbyterians, and the doctrine of the spirituality of the church became a core tenet of the PCCSA's heir, the Presbyterian Church in the United States (PCUS).

Although historians might rightly question how sincerely antebellum southern Presbyterians embraced the idea of the spirituality of the church, it is clear that, beginning in 1861, the doctrine became an increasingly integral part of their self-understanding and underlay their refusal to reunite with northern Presbyterians for the next half century. By the turn of the twentieth century, the doctrine of spirituality had become a distinctive characteristic of southern Presbyterianism.[33] Articles appearing in the *Presbyterian Quarterly* occasionally repeated the argument for the strict separation of church and state. In 1890 Alfred Jones, a Virginia minister, argued that the Bible clearly teaches that "under the New Testament dispensation, church and state are intended by our saviour to be absolutely separate and distinct. They are different spheres, touching at no point."[34] Another article in the same journal in 1900 reiterated the spiritual limits of the church's authority and urged that "[she] should ask no favor of the state except to be let alone as she seeks to call and train men for the kingdom of grace and glory."[35] As late as 1910, Presbyterian Samuel Spahr Laws argued in a sermon that the PCUS should continue as a separate denomination from the northern Presbyterian Church in the United States of America (PCUSA) because it serves as "an organized protest against the church meddling with State and political or secular affairs, and as such deserves perpetuity." He explained that the PCUS was especially devoted to the idea of "the absolute spirituality or non-secularity of the Christian church" because it had been the "pole star" of the denomination since its inception.[36]

Southern Presbyterians were convinced that the key principle driving the birth of the PCCSA was the spiritual nature of the church, and they believed that the role played by slavery and states' rights was merely peripheral. This understanding of the importance of the doctrine of spirituality is exemplified by a speech given in 1911 titled "The Origin, Doctrines, and History of the Presbyterian Church in the United States." In South Carolina, W. H. Frazer complained to his listeners: "It is no uncommon thing to hear those who should know better declare that the northern and southern Presbyterian Churches separated over the subject of slavery. Let me say to you that they did not. . . . Neither was it primarily a question of 'states' rights.' The separation came upon the issue as to the scope of the Church's right and function."[37] Frazer claimed that none of the southern commissioners at the 1861 General Assembly had wanted to splinter from their northern brethren. But the resolution demanding obedience to the Union as a sign of loyalty to the church had made it painfully clear that in order to be true to their convictions regarding the commingling of church and state, southern Presbyterians must secede and form a new denomination. According to Frazer, the spirituality of the church, not slavery, was the primary force behind the formation of the PCCSA, and it remained a defining characteristic of the PCUS. It was also the reason why the southern church had not reunified with the Presbyterians of the North.

It was not just southern Presbyterians, though, who utilized this doctrine to put a revisionist spin on their denominational genesis and to justify their continued postwar independence. The issue of reunification haunted all southern denominations after Appomattox, and the doctrine of spirituality provided a soothing balm to southern churchmen facing the difficult decision of whether to reconcile with their northern counterparts. Southern Methodists and, to a lesser degree, southern Baptists realized after the Civil War that the doctrine of spirituality was the then-unnamed principle that had been violated in 1845 and for which they had stood when they severed relations with the North. In the summer of 1865 a conference of Methodist pastors and laymen assembled in Palmyra, Missouri, to discuss the matter of postwar reunification. The group determined that the MECS should resist any efforts to reunite with the MEC and produced a brief document laying out the argument for continued disunion. In what became known as the Palmyra Manifesto, southern Methodists presented pragmatic arguments for continued separation, such as the fact that many members had come into the MECS during the twenty years since separation and should not be asked to join a denomination they had never been part of. More important, the document offered a philosophical and theological explanation for why the schism had occurred and a rationale for continuation as a separate southern body. The statement explained, "The question upon which the Church divided was not whether the institution of slavery was right or wrong, per se, but whether it was a legitimate subject for ecclesiastical legislation." Southern Methodists accepted that the question of slavery was a political one that had now been answered by the war and abolished by federal and state legislation, but they still insisted that it should not have been brought into the church by the northern Methodists in 1844. To rejoin that denomination now, they warned, would be to "compromise the essential principles of the Gospel" by "accepting political tests of church-fellowship," and it would condone the northern Methodists' actions. The Palmyra delegates urged their fellow southern Methodists to "oppose the prostitution of the pulpit to political purposes" and to reject reunification with the northern church.[38]

Thus Methodists found a new justification not only for the original breach with the MEC but also for their continued existence as a separate denomination. Antebellum southern Methodists had never clearly articulated the doctrine of the spirituality of the church, although it was in line with the traditional American Methodist attitude toward church-state relations.[39] Yet following the circulation of the Palmyra Manifesto, southern Methodists emphasized their commitment to keeping the church purely spiritual and nonpolitical as the primary catalyst for disunion, and the doctrine became deeply entrenched within southern Methodism.[40] The message of the Palmyra Manifesto was reiterated in Columbus, Georgia, just weeks later when three southern Methodist bishops met there to discuss the task of resuscitating the Methodist Church in the South. Although the late war may have settled the political questions of slavery and secession, the bishops declared that the ecclesial questions that had split the denomination in 1844 remained alive. Because northern Methodists "have incorporated social dogmas and political tests into their church creeds," the bishops argued that reunion was still out of the question.[41]

For the Baptists, too, the doctrine of spirituality was a welcomed enunciation of what distinguished them from their northern brethren. The doctrine fit well with their long history of advocating church-state separation, from the time they were a persecuted minority in England and colonial America to their role in the formation of the First Amendment. Though less tied to their justification for remaining a regional body, southern Baptists saw the belief in a strict separation of church and state as a defining element of their identity. They viewed themselves as pioneers in opposing the commingling of church and state, and their claim to early champions of the cause such as Thomas Helwys, Roger Williams, and John Leland often led Baptists to exude a certain sense of owning the doctrine. By the 1880s, the principle of the spirituality of the church was firmly entrenched within southern Baptist thought. To their long legacy of opposition to state involvement in the church southern Baptists added their opposition to church involvement in the state and portrayed it as a longstanding element of the denomination.[42] The editor of the *Baptist Beacon* in Knoxville noted in 1880 that in the South, "the temper of our people has always been averse to politics in the house of God," unlike Christians in the North.[43] In 1891 the *Baptist Expositor*, a short-lived Alabama publication, described "the separation of Church and State" as being a "distinctive" doctrine of Baptists.[44]

Although some doubt can be cast on how important the doctrine of the spirituality of the church was to Methodists, Baptists, and Presbyterians at the time denominational division occurred, it is clear that in the years following the Civil War, the idea of a nonpolitical church took on new life in the lore and self-understanding of southern evangelicals. Following military defeat and the period of Reconstruction, southern bitterness toward the North deepened, even in areas of the South that had been strongly Unionist early in the war. Though the claim to military superiority had eluded them, southerners were eager to lay claim to moral superiority over the North.[45] Southern evangelicals did this in part by charging that settling the national issues of slavery and secession was irrelevant to the issue of reunion with their northern counterparts. They maintained that the original impetus for denominational disunion—both in 1844 and 1845 for the Methodists and Baptists and in 1861 for the Presbyterians—involved theological and ecclesiological differences between the regions. In short, the northern contingents had prostituted the church for political purposes and made "political hucksters" out of its ministers.[46]

Internal Challenges to Spirituality

The growing appetite among evangelicals in the 1880s for legal prohibition challenged the now-ingrained doctrine of spirituality within southern denominations. The political activism of evangelical prohibitionists was in direct conflict with the idea of ecclesiastical noninvolvement in politics. A significant impediment to those evangelicals who wanted to free themselves from the restraints of the doctrine came from conservatives within their own denominations. As legal prohibition became an increasingly important cause to many southern evangelicals in the 1880s, a confrontation with the doctrine of spirituality was assured.

One of the earliest challengers of the spirituality of the church was David C. Kelley, a Methodist minister in middle Tennessee. Kelley had been an early exponent of the use of legislation in the fight against alcohol. In an 1873 sermon to the Tennessee legislature he had denounced the evils of the liquor trade and called on the lawmakers to "make liquor dealers responsible for the legitimate results of their iniquitous trade."[47] Then in 1882 he wrote a response in the *Quarterly Review of the Methodist Episcopal Church, South* to an earlier article by C. W. Miller. Miller had reiterated the argument that the doctrine of spirituality was central to both the antebellum division of the Methodist Church and the southern church's continued identity. Embracing political abolitionist views had driven the northern church away from the "conservative position, always occupied by the church, into an attitude the most radical and revolutionary," explained Miller. Without making any specific reference to prohibition, he argued that southern Methodists, both then and now, should reject such politicization of the pulpit.[48]

In response, Kelley assailed the idea that the church has no business involving itself with social and political reform. The "true" doctrine, he explained, is that "wherever a moral question has been adversely acted upon by the state, the necessity for fearless, outspoken truth becomes the more urgent upon the part of the church." In an unapologetically iconoclastic tone, Kelley assaulted the very foundations and founders of the doctrine of spirituality. He protested the idea that, "because some of our fathers—good and wise men—should have, in great pressure, in the midst of the smoke and confusion of battle, declared that slavery was a civil institution, and drawn therefore the false conclusion that the church must maintain toward it a perpetual silence, that we at this late day shall be held bound to regard their declaration as the lamp of truth."[49] The prohibition movement, Kelley argued, was a prime example of why the church should shirk old restrictions regarding its involvement in political matters. Clinging to the old idea that civil questions are beyond the domain of the church "dissevers us from some of the mightiest moral movements of the age," he explained. Kelley wrote that the tide was turning away from the old attitude that the nature of the church was purely spiritual, noting that conferences now routinely passed resolutions on the subjects of prohibition and Sunday closing laws. These issues were just as political in nature as were the northern abolitionists' resolutions that had caused such strife at antebellum General Conferences, he argued. Kelley recognized that this new political activism on the part of the church was a break from the past, but he concluded that "we had rather be right than consistent." If it continued to adhere strictly to the old doctrine of spirituality, he warned, the church would be "blind to the most brilliant light of the historic present."[50]

In 1887, as Tennesseans prepared to go to the polls to vote on a statewide prohibition referendum, Kelley continued to drum up political support for prohibition as well as to criticize those who would have ministers like himself remain silent on such matters. "An obscuring fog is attempted to be raised in view of the question being at the same time moral and political," he told an audience in Nashville. "A moral question does not in any way change its character because it has become the subject of political discussion or legal enactment." He argued that Christian ministers cannot remain silent on a moral issue just because it has entered the political realm. The church cannot be silent, he explained, "The preacher of the gospel of the lord Jesus Christ has no option left him but to fight that evil whenever, wherever, and however he may."[51]

Some traditionalists, such as Kelley's fellow Tennessee Methodist E. E. Hoss, opposed this new evangelical political activism. Hoss lamented that "discussions of current issues" were replacing the emphasis on personal salvation in many churches and made clear his position that the Methodist Church should rely exclusively on "spiritual forces and agencies to secure the extermination of the traffic in strong drink."[52] But a rapidly increasing number of evangelical prohibitionists soon joined Kelley in challenging the spirituality doctrine. The editor of the *Alabama Baptist* proclaimed in 1884, "We do not belong to that class of men who are afraid of the combination of temperance and politics." The paper looked forward to the day when prohibition would become the dominant issue in politics.[53] That same year, a writer to the paper observed, "There seems to be a great horror on the part of some people of mixing religion and politics. As to myself I do not care to have much politics in my religion, but I do want a good deal of religion in my politics."[54] Tennessee minister T. S. Eastes wrote that he believed himself to be "under the same obligation to fight sin in the partisan policies of the country as anywhere else." He further believed that ecclesiastical involvement in politics would serve to "purify and elevate the civil government."[55]

Many evangelical prohibitionists increasingly viewed political involvement as essential to living out their Christian faith. "How a man can be a Christian and a good citizen and not be interested in the peace and safety of his country, is a mystery to me," wrote one Alabama Baptist. "The fact is," he maintained, "you can't separate a man's religion from his politics. . . . I can not be a Christian in church and the Devil's own dog at the polls."[56] At a conference in 1896, one Tennessee Methodist minister announced his willingness to be maligned for the cause of prohibition and his confidence that he was not the only Methodist clergyman to feel this way, saying, "If to preach the doctrine of temperance and to preach against the open saloon as the source of most of our social, industrial, and moral evils, and therefore the greatest enemy of the Christian religion and of the church of God, is to be a 'political partisan,' you may publish me as one not only in your papers, but on the house tops, and by me stand over three thousand Methodist preachers, not a dozen of whom would refuse to vote for a measure to prohibit the matchless evil of the age."[57] Another Alabama Baptist went so far as to call political noninvolvement by Christians a sin. "You cannot neglect the politics of the state without sin. If bad men rule by your negligence, you shall be held responsible for it," he wrote.[58]

Throughout the 1880s, evangelical prohibitionists met with some internal resistance from conservative evangelicals who viewed their activities as a jettison of the traditional southern doctrine of the spirituality of the church. An 1879 editorial in the *Holston Methodist* warned, "Churches that allow politics proper in their press and pulpits are sowing the wind, and will reap the whirlwind."[59] At the 1888 Southern Baptist Convention, two delegates attempted to introduce temperance resolutions. The convention's president, Dr. James P. Boyce, ruled that the delegates were out of order because they were introducing a political question. Such issues were outside the purview of the Baptist denomination, Boyce argued, and the convention delegates upheld his ruling.[60] That same year, the Holston Conference of the MECS advocated continued adherence to the doctrine of spirituality in the campaign against liquor, recommending that the church "keep herself disentangled from all political alliances, and continue to labor, in her proper sphere, for the propagation of temperance doctrines."[61] In 1894 the bishops of the MECS reiterated, "Our church is strictly a religious and in no wise a political body."[62]

M. J. Webb of Parrott, Georgia, expressed his fear that "Baptists are drifting away from the true idea of the separation of church and state." His concern had been aroused by the increasing frequency of Baptist associations and conventions memorializing state legislatures to pass further prohibition laws. In the view of some southern Baptists, the use of state power to enforce temperance violated not only the Baptist tradition of church-state separation but also its long heritage of freedom of conscience and local church autonomy.[63] Although he claimed to support prohibition, Webb believed that "it is not part of the work of a church to regulate the conduct of those outside its pale. . . . A matter may be right but if it be political it should not be once considered by a Christian in connection with ministerial duties or receive the expressed sanction of a religious meeting."[64]

A popular argument among adherents of the doctrine of spirituality was that entering the political sphere damages the effectiveness of a minister. Following increased church involvement in the 1887 Tennessee prohibition referendum, a Presbyterian minister issued a warning against such activity. "The minister who openly advocates prohibition forecloses his influence over a large class of men to whom he has been sent," he wrote in the *Nashville Daily American*. "When he preaches prohibition he forsakes his own legitimate weapons and ruins his own cause."[65] The editor of the *Alabama Christian Advocate* cautioned in 1888, "Even prohibition may be bought at too high a price . . . if it costs the usefulness of the minister and the purity of the church."[66] Lemuel O. Dawson, a Tuscaloosa Baptist minister known throughout Alabama, stated that "when a preacher enters politics in the vast majority of cases his work in the ministry is ended."[67] The *Christian Advocate* of Nashville attacked the idea that "the preacher in his official relations shall be the exponent of political and social movements" as "one of the most dangerous and insidious of modern progressive religions' claims." The editor claimed that Wesley never knew of such an admixture of the pulpit and politics, and modern Methodists should stay true to his example.[68]

In response, Georgia Methodist S. P. Richardson attacked the doctrine of spirituality and blamed it for the present moral corruption in American politics and society. Ministers are called to be salt and light to the world, he reminded readers of the *Wesleyan Christian Advocate*, but the doctrine of spirituality is flawed because it prevents that salt from being applied where it is most needed. "How can the salt save the carcass when the pulpit refuses to apply the salt to the carcass. The cry comes up we are spiritual, but is it not a fact that the spiritual preaching has not saved the carcass from putrifaction. We declare in their presence that the attitude taken by the pulpit of this country toward the politics of the nation has been the cause of all former corruption in politics."[69] Regardless of the objections raised by "small preachers" and "narrow-minded laymen," Richardson declared that it was time to "let the broad-minded, thinking pulpits and churches of the nation unite on definite lines and fight to the death the battle of social and political morality."[70]

The new attitude toward political involvement exhibited by evangelical prohibitionists such as David Kelley and others was part of a larger trend. This new breed of southern evangelical advocated a more proactive brand of Christianity that impacted all aspects of life. No one epitomized this new impulse better than Sam Jones. In 1886 Kelley wrote an article praising Jones, calling the Georgia evangelist "a symptom of an epoch which is close at hand . . . the incoming age of practical, earnest preaching, the center of which will be *this life and its duties.*" Jones "does not seek to build in the emotions or imagination, but in the practical duties of everyday life."[71] Kelley heralded Jones as a harbinger of "a new type of Christianity."[72] Although Jones was known as "the Moody of the South," his practical Christianity was a departure from northern evangelists such as Dwight L. Moody, who declined to bring politics into their religious message. Jones never hesitated to draw clear connections between the Christianity he preached—which he called "practical religion" or "positive religion"—and the political issues of the day.[73] In fact, he often went out of his way to see that his revivals influenced political contests. In 1899 he took his revival tent to Toledo, Ohio, during election season to combat the city's anti-prohibition mayor (coincidentally named Sam M. Jones) and garner support for the dry Republican candidate.[74]

Sam Jones argued that "a preacher must be a patriot," and part of being a Christian patriot meant championing "every clean method and every right aim which results in good government." The new style of evangelicalism emphasized practical, everyday application of the gospel, and political involvement for the cause of righteousness was a natural outgrowth of this philosophy. Jones declared: "The sweet by-and-by preacher is about out of a job and almost out of a congregation, but the true now-and-now preacher, who is handling with gloves off the corruption in politics and the corruption in society, has a large audience, a large place in the hearts of his countrymen, and a home awaiting him in heaven." Jones was not afraid to attack political parties that refused to embrace prohibition. "The Democratic Party, with its 'nonsumptuary plank,' has sold out to liquor from snout to tail, and the goods have been delivered. The Republican Party claims that it is a temperance party, but it never loses a chance to gain a vote by concessions to breweries and distilleries," wrote Jones.[75] Sam

Small, Jones's associate, argued that "if the preacher is true to his mission, he cannot avoid political questions." Both Small and Jones maintained that being a Christian necessitated taking a public stand for prohibition. In 1887 Small lamented to a crowd in Knoxville, "It is a sad sight to see Christians who do not take sides in the great prohibition fight."[76] "I've been a prohibitionist ever since I got religion," Jones explained, "and if you're not, you need another dip."[77]

Methodists such as Kelley and Jones reflected the growing gap between rural evangelists and holiness-influenced pastors on the one hand and urban ecclesiastical leadership on the other. Members of the former group generally hailed from rural areas and favored the traditional, strict Wesleyan discipline and the old-time practice of religion, and they accused the latter group of being lax on discipline and pandering to wealthy Methodist patrons such as the Candlers (of Coca-Cola fame) and the Vanderbilts. The urban denominational leaders were "modernizers," as Christopher Owen puts it, in contrast to the traditionalist instincts of those Methodists influenced by holiness and leaning toward populism. Whereas the traditionalists wanted Methodists to remain a strictly disciplined and "peculiar" people, modernizers embraced growth, progress, higher education, and a larger, more bureaucratic denominational structure.[78] Although Jones never accepted the holiness doctrines of sanctification, Owen has pointed out that many southern evangelists found themselves allied with holiness preachers as they clashed with the more urban, sophisticated, and entrenched leadership of the MECS.[79] Among rural Methodists, anti-intellectualism and opposition to centralized government fueled disdain of the "dewdrops"—or doctors of divinity—who controlled the denominational infrastructure and pastored the prominent urban "First Churches." These city preachers were viewed as less devoted to the strict traditional discipline and values to which rural Methodists were committed.[80]

Attempting to make clear-cut distinctions between rural and urban factions is a difficult and often problematic exercise when dealing with southern prohibitionism, however. The very use of the term *rural* as if it represented one homogeneous whole is misleading. Within the white population, a distinction must be made between Black Belt rural whites and upcountry rural whites. The former were largely heirs of the planter aristocracy, and they still owned large tracts of land on which freedmen now sharecropped. They were Bourbon

Democrats, meaning that they were entrenched conservatives who resisted social change and profited from maintenance of the status quo.[81] They aligned with urban whites known as the "Big Mules" to form the heart of the Democratic Party in the South. The Big Mules were urban middle- and upper-class whites who lived in industrialized areas and had vested interests in railroads, industry, and banking.[82] Upcountry rural whites, in contrast, formed the core of the Populist political movement that flourished at the end of the nineteenth century. They were generally small-scale farmers who felt the pinch of high tariffs, the crop-lien system, high railroad freight rates, high interest rates, and other economic conditions that benefited Bourbons. Consequently, these rural whites desired political and economic reform.

The category of "evangelicals," of course, overlapped all three of these white constituencies. Evangelical Christian churches could be found in cities, towns, and the backwoods, and so could prohibitionists, especially during the 1880s, when prohibition support ran high among both rural and urban evangelicals. Urban modernizers such as Atticus G. Haygood and Warren A. Candler led the prohibition cause, as did rural evangelicals such as Sam Jones and W. B. Crumpton. Indeed, it was in rural areas where movements such as the antimissionary primitive Baptists and a younger cousin, Old Landmarkism, persisted and created some resistance to prohibition within evangelical circles.[83] Therefore, it was never a simple matter of backcountry Puritans embracing prohibition while big-city libertines rejected it.

It was not until the 1890s that an urban-rural split occurred within the ranks of prohibitionists. The primary catalyst for this division was the rise of populism, which threatened the Democratic Party's hold on the region. Just as many rural hill-country farmers felt driven to revolt against the Democratic Party in the 1890s and vote for the Populist Party, many evangelical prohibitionists became disillusioned with the Democrats' failure to embrace the cause. Sam Jones spoke for many when he said, "I had as soon go to Alaska for grapes, or to the moon for cheese, as to go to a Democrat Convention for temperance legislation."[84] This dissatisfaction on the part of evangelical prohibitionists, especially those in the rural upcountry, contributed to their decision to rebel against the Democrats. Throughout the rural South, many evangelicals had a strong moral commitment to prohibition— as well as sympathy with the economic policies of the larger Populist cause—that caused them to denounce the Democratic Party during the 1890s.

The Threat of Populism

Between 1886 and about 1896, the issue of whether and to what extent the church and its ministers should involve themselves with prohibition as a political issue became particularly divisive within southern evangelicalism. A growing number of evangelicals asserted that it was the duty of Christians to engage the evils of the liquor traffic, even if it led them into the political realm. Not only were they increasingly active politically, but they were also increasingly aggravated by the Democratic Party. Evangelicals had grown deeply committed to the legal prohibition of alcohol during the 1880s, but the Democratic Party did not share their enthusiasm. By 1890, many evangelicals were so exasperated with the Democrats' refusal to embrace prohibition that they began to threaten desertion, and these disgruntled prohibitionists were pitted against those evangelicals who remained loyal Democrats. At the same time, Democratic dominance in the South was being threatened by the rise of the Populist Party. In southern elections between 1890 and 1896, both the Populist Party and the Prohibition Party threatened Democratic hegemony by running candidates for local, state, and national offices. Bourbon Democrats warned that by splintering the Democratic base, third parties opened the door to a neo-Reconstructionist Republican resurgence that would result in black rule of the South. Likewise, Bourbon evangelicals relied on the doctrine of spirituality as a chief tool for reining in maverick prohibitionists.

This "outburst of long-repressed radicalism" in the South, as C. Vann Woodward has characterized populism, originated in Kansas and the Midwest in the 1870s, where a third-party movement arose to challenge Democratic and Republican political candidates.[85] A second wave of Populist political revolt emerged in the mid-1880s and took root in the South, initially taking the form of farmers organizations seeking to alleviate the hardships they faced. Cooperatives such as the Agricultural Wheel and the Farmers' Alliance emerged in almost every county in the South, representing aggrieved farmers whose complaints included low cotton prices, high railroad shipping rates, a dearth of marketing facilities, and an oppressive crop-lien system.[86] Most early agrarians and Populists did not view industrial and market development as antithetical to their interests as farmers. They did, however, feel that an unresponsive and corrupt political machine beholden to the rising corporate class was ignoring the changing economic order's injurious impact on small producers in the South.[87]

For most of the 1880s, Populists in the South remained an internal faction within the Democratic Party that sought to liberalize the party's stance on economic and political issues that were of concern to the agrarian class. By 1890, it became apparent to many in the Farmers' Alliance that working for reform from within the Democratic Party system was futile. The economic situation of rural southerners was declining rapidly, with cotton prices dipping to a thirty-year low. Members of the Farmers' Alliance increasingly defected from the organization, which they considered incapable of effecting the kind of change that would benefit southern yeomanry. Emboldened by the political victories of Populists in Kansas in 1890, southern agrarians moved into the political arena by creating a political party to challenge the Democratic establishment and seek redress of their grievances. Across the South, Farmers' Alliance supporters moved outside the Democratic Party and merged with the People's Party—also known as the Populist Party—to challenge the two major parties in general elections.[88]

Politically, 1892 turned into an extremely contentious year for the South. The national People's Party nominated James Weaver, a former Union general, for president. Weaver had no strong support in the South and soon abandoned his campaign there altogether. The real battleground in the South, especially in Alabama and Georgia, was for state and local offices. In the end, the Democrats were largely victorious over the Populists, but the margin of victory was slim and was achieved through widespread corruption and voter fraud. For example, in the Alabama gubernatorial election, Populist candidate Reuben Kolb lost to his Democratic opponent by 12,000 votes, but Kolb claimed victory nonetheless and contested the election. Although he ultimately lost his appeals, it became evident that the Populist claims of fraud were valid.[89] In 1894 Populist candidates in Alabama were successful in winning numerous local and state offices, as well as congressional seats. Kolb ran against Bourbon Democrat William C. Oates for governor, and again the election was riddled with fraudulent voting practices. Kolb once again refused to concede defeat and even held his own inauguration around the corner from Oates's official ceremony.[90] In Georgia that same year, Populist candidates won the governorship as well as three-fourths of the state's legislative seats.[91] Populist candidates in Tennessee took control of the governor's mansion and almost half of the state legislature.[92]

Coinciding with the rise of the Populist movement was the emergence of the Prohibition Party. Methodist minister John Russell and his colleagues founded the party in Michigan in 1868. They believed that a separate political alternative was necessary if there was to be any hope of maintaining and extending Maine laws in the United States.[93] The Prohibition Party received scant national attention until the presidential election of 1884, when the party's candidate received 25,000 votes in New York, causing Republican nominee James G. Blaine to narrowly lose both the state and the overall election to Democrat Grover Cleveland. For the next decade, the Prohibition Party was recognized as a more serious third-party player on the national political scene.

During this period the party also began to make inroads into southern politics, primarily via evangelical prohibitionists seeking an alternative to the Democratic Party.[94] R. A. Moseley of Talladega, Alabama, wrote that he was "astonished that any reading, intelligent Christian man can keep out of the Prohibition Party."[95] Though not a powerful force in southern politics as a whole, the Prohibition Party had a widespread influence on the prohibition debate within evangelicalism. Wayne Flynt notes that in Alabama a surprisingly large number of Baptists followed their ministers into the Prohibition Party. By 1892, however, the Prohibition Party had already been overshadowed nationally by the People's Party; after 1896, the Prohibition Party splintered internally, and its influence in national politics waned.[96] In the South, the Prohibition Party's strong appeal was due to the Populists' refusal to embrace prohibition. For example, the 1892 Georgia Populist Party Convention rejected a prohibition plank. The delegate who proposed the plank was none other than evangelist Sam Small, who proceeded to run for governor as a prohibition-supporting Populist. This threatened to split the party's vote, and the other Populist candidate eventually withdrew from the race. Four years later, Georgia Populists added a moderate prohibition plank to their platform, which they then blamed for their subsequent political defeat.[97]

Since the redemption of southern state governments during Reconstruction, Democrats had enjoyed an almost undisputed monopoly on political power in the South. Their legislative programs were aimed primarily at aiding the former planter elite and the emerging industrial and railroad elite in the South.[98] Fresh in the memories of white southerners, however, was a Reconstruction period marked by Republican control of southern politics and widespread African American representation at the local, state, and federal levels. Populism represented dissent within the white Democratic ranks, and nervous Democratic politicians warned white voters of the potential consequences of such internal division: the emergence of a neo-Reconstruction government run by black Republicans.

Populism was particularly threatening to the Democratic establishment because it not only harnessed the voting power of disgruntled rural whites but also appealed to black voters. The Readjuster movement in Virginia in the 1880s, led by William Mahone, managed a rare moment of biracial unity in the South when it overthrew conservative Democratic control of the state government. Populist leaders William H. Felton and Tom Watson sought to import the biracial approach of "Mahonism" into Georgia in the late 1880s.[99] Populists embraced reforms, such as ending the convict lease system, in an effort to entice black support, and Watson advocated allowing African Americans to serve on juries.[100] Even ardent white supremacists such as Reuben Kolb in Alabama sublimated their personal biases in an attempt to broaden the appeal of the Populist ticket to blacks.[101] Democrats capitalized on the role that African Americans were being allowed to play in this new Populist movement, warning that these apostate Democrats were opening the door to black rule of the South. Democrats opposing Mahone in Virginia told voters that the "continuation of white rule in Virginia" depended on all whites supporting the Democratic Party.[102] Evangelicals also incurred Democratic wrath for valuing prohibition over white solidarity. When Virginia Baptist minister John R. Moffett proclaimed in 1889 that he "would rather have good Negro rule than the rule of the alcoholic devil," Democratic newspapers retaliated by warning white voters that "good Negro rule" was an oxymoron and that returning African Americans to political power was akin to releasing smallpox or yellow fever in a community. The *Danville (Virginia) Times* also admonished Moffett to get back to "his sphere" and to stay out of "ours," employing the now-familiar argument that ministers had no place speaking out on political issues. Moffett joined the Prohibition Party, and in 1892 he was murdered by a Democratic Party operative who opposed prohibition.[103]

Splitting the White Vote

The Populist movement increasingly threatened the solid South in the late 1880s and early 1890s, and evangelicals contributed greatly to this situation. Evangelical prohibitionists had given notice of their dissatisfaction with the Democratic Party. Job Harral warned that evangelicals in the South "hold the balance of power, and if the great political parties are too cowardly, or too corrupt" to support prohibition, then evangelical prohibitionists would find others to support at the polls.[104] L. C. Coulson declared his dissatisfaction with the Democrats, saying, "I repeat it now, that the Democrat party in Alabama, as well as out of the state, is in the hands of the liquor devils of the country." Coulson argued that given the political dominance of the party in Alabama, it could easily eradicate the liquor traffic without risking its political power. If the Democrats would take this step, there would be no need for any talk of a third party advocating prohibition.[105] One Alabama Democrat warned Crumpton that prohibitionists' attacks on the Democratic Party threatened to return the state to Republican rule. Crumpton replied that if that happened, the responsibility would lie with the Democratic Party for not nominating candidates who were acceptable to evangelical voters, not with evangelicals for following their principles in the voting booth.[106]

The denominational press, which had been supportive of the prohibition movement, denounced the extremism of those who would allow their prohibition sentiments to undermine their party loyalty. The editor of the *Alabama Christian Advocate* attacked the Prohibition Party in 1888 and advised readers: "As citizens beware of third party movements. As ministers, keep politics out of the pulpit and preach the gospel, for it, not prohibition platforms, is the power of God unto salvation." Demonstrating the solidarity of Alabama's evangelical press against the Prohibition Party, the *Alabama Baptist* reprinted the editorial on its front page, noting that it "so nearly expresses our sentiments that we publish it in full" and stating that the "exhortation to the Methodists is equally applicable to Baptists."[107] The *Wesleyan Christian Advocate* of Georgia likewise denounced "the so-called political preaching," noting that "our church is a spiritual church."[108] The

Alabama Baptist condemned Democratic deserters "who bolted and voted for a prohibition candidate" in a recent election, and although the editor looked forward to a time when all citizens would be able to vote for prohibition and at the same time "imperil no grand interest," that time had not yet arrived in the South. The "grand interest" of Democratic and white political supremacy must not be jeopardized by those who let their enthusiasm for prohibition override their loyalty to the Democratic Party.[109]

Samuel Henderson warned in 1886 that "a 'third-party' movement dooms us to utter and hopeless failure."[110] He and the *Alabama Baptist* argued that Alabamians should embrace the local option approach of Georgia and suggested a truce between prohibitionists and Democratic lawmakers. The editors wrote, "We propose leaving all parties just as they are—only give us 'local option.' We will do the rest. Whatever is accomplished in our state in this respect must be accomplished through the dominant party." They bargained that if Democratic lawmakers made local option available throughout the state, evangelical voters would not make an issue of whether these lawmakers supported prohibition.[111] For many evangelical prohibitionists, however, it was not enough for a legislator to support local option; he had to personally support the prohibition cause. John Orr, a Baptist from Alabama, declared that his religious convictions would prevent him from voting Democratic in the upcoming election. "I expect to vote the Prohibition ticket," he informed his fellow Alabama Baptists.[112] Likewise, E. T. Smyth of Anniston, Alabama, proclaimed, "I will vote for no man, to fill any office, if I know that he is a friend to the worst enemy of our race."[113]

The editors of the *Alabama Baptist* continued to insist that prohibitionists should not impose such a litmus test on legislators. They warned readers not to complicate prohibition with politics.[114] Loyal Democrats within the evangelical ranks supported the editorial position of the *Alabama Baptist*. One such supporter from Birmingham decried as extremists those who supported prohibition to the point of forsaking the Democratic Party and called for them to abandon their hopeless third-party campaign and return to the fold. "It is a bootless task to 'run a muck' against the Democratic Party, especially in the South," he observed, where memories of Republican rule still lingered and would consign any such rebellion against the Democrats to failure.[115]

But many evangelical supporters of prohibition recoiled at the paper's admonition to remain loyal to the dominant political party despite its unreceptive attitude toward prohibition. "I cannot say that I am pleased with the editorial position of the *Alabama Baptist* in regard to keeping prohibition out of politics," wrote A. S. Worrell. He argued that "prohibition, if it is anything, is political; and, if it is political, it must enter politics, or remain a dead letter."[116] Prominent minister J. J. D. Renfroe questioned, "Are we to understand [the editors] as meaning that prohibitionists are to be remanded to the back seats, or to no seats at all, or into silence, to keep it out of politics?"[117] M. J. Turnley of Gadsden warned his fellow prohibitionists not to be deceived by the "keep it out of politics" argument. To him, the position embraced by the editors of the paper was the same one taken by the chief advocates of the liquor trade. "All the whiskey saloonists everywhere, and all the red-eyed, purple-nosed politicians in the country echo the words, 'keep it out of politics,' you will ruin the party and prohibition, too," Turnley wrote. The only way to "keep it out of politics," he said, was to "fill politics brim full of prohibition," for if both the Democratic and Republican parties would put a prohibition plank in their platforms, there would be no cry for a third party. But, Turnley noted, the Democratic Party "now lies debased at the feet of whisky."[118]

In 1893 B. F. Haynes's *Tennessee Methodist* hosted a long-running debate between those who supported the Prohibition Party and those who viewed it as a threat to southern society. The debate began with a series of articles by J. D. Smith of Paducah, Kentucky, who advocated the formation of a "suitable political home" for Christians who desired the prohibition of liquor.[119] The series elicited a strong response from J. T. Millican, a Methodist minister from Turkeytown, Alabama, who sought to dissuade other evangelicals from deserting the Democratic Party in favor of the Prohibition Party. Toward this end, Millican invoked the time-honored principle of the spirituality of the church. "One peculiar distinction of the M. E. Church, South," Millican wrote, "is that it is a *non-political church*. This view is the basis of her existence as a separate ecclesiastical body." True to the legacy of the Palmyra Manifesto, Millican reminded his readers that "'twas a political question that divided us in 1844"; thus, the church must ever steer clear of political issues. According to Millican, the church "is a *spiritual* institution for the spiritual uplifting of the race."[120]

In response to Millican's claim that the church is solely a spiritual institution, J. D. Smith replied, "Is that all?" Smith questioned whether Millican thought that Christians should not vote in secular elections. He speculated that most Methodists do vote, and he added that Millican probably "sticks in a ballot himself sometimes." Smith's point was that because most Christians voted, of necessity, for politicians, the church is inescapably political; further, a moral responsibility comes along with voting, and a moral culpability comes along with voting for men who aid and abet the liquor traffic. Though disavowing any intent to urge Methodists to join the Prohibition Party, Smith clearly thought that they should abandon the Democratic Party if it refused to embrace prohibition. He said, "I do not care a cent whether you join the existing Prohibition Party or not, if you will just get out of your old liquor-soaked, liquor-ruled, and liquor-cursed party, and organize an anti-liquor party of your own. I do not care if there are a thousand anti-liquor parties organized."[121]

A Methodist layman, Horace Merritt of Lewisburg, Tennessee, joined in the debate to support Smith's position against that of Millican. He too made the argument that Christians who supported the Democratic Party with their votes were politicizing the church and making it guilty by association. He echoed Smith's argument that, by voting, Methodists were dragging the church into politics. Merritt concluded that he "would rather have a pure, clean political church than to have what my brother would call a non-political church, whose members were guilty by their votes of complicity in the liquor business of drunkard making."[122]

Millican continued to argue that political support of prohibition violated the core tenet of southern Methodism: the doctrine of the spirituality of the church. The nonpolitical nature of the southern church, he maintained, "constitutes almost the sole distinction between her and her great sister" in the North.[123] Referring to the church's 1844 split, Millican warned that "if a political question divided the church, severed it in twain, once, it will do it again." The idea that the church could stray into the political realm without becoming soiled and compromised was absurd, believed Millican.[124] Like other evangelicals who were also loyal Democrats, Millican invoked the old spirituality doctrine in an attempt to quell prohibition enthusiasm that might threaten Democratic supremacy.

Prohibitionists against Bourbonism

As Populist-minded evangelical prohibitionists became increasingly outspoken and politically active around 1890, evangelicals who were also loyal Democrats attacked them for letting their zeal for prohibition lead them out of the party. Rather than using the race-driven arguments of secular Democratic politicians about the threat to white supremacy, conservative evangelicals relied on the doctrine of the spirituality of the church to undercut the growing current of single-issue prohibition voters. The question of whether loyalty to prohibition should override one's commitment to the Democratic Party—a debate often cloaked as an issue of adherence to the doctrine of spirituality—became a cantankerous one within southern Methodist and Baptist life between 1888 and 1896. Three episodes in the early 1890s highlight this use of the spirituality doctrine against prohibitionists, especially those supportive of third-party politics: the trial of David Kelley in 1890, the Tennessee Baptist Conference's temperance resolution of 1890, and the firing of professor Henry Scomp in 1894.

One of the earliest and most outspoken critics of the idea that the church should be nonpolitical was David Kelley, who created controversy in 1890 by leaving his pastorate to run for governor of Tennessee on the Prohibition Party ticket. Though he received a greater number of votes than any other Prohibition Party candidate in any Tennessee election, he failed to win. The real contest for Kelley began after the gubernatorial election was over. Because he had left his ministerial charge without obtaining official permission, the Tennessee Conference of the MECS suspended Kelley. His suspension was followed by a contentious trial overseen by Bishop Robert K. Hargrove, who reportedly opposed prohibition, strongly disapproved of ministerial involvement in political matters, and was generally hostile to third-party political movements.[125] Although the conference largely supported Kelley's actions and voted 168 to 25 against putting him on trial, Hargrove appeared to be determined to punish Kelley for his political run and moved ahead with the trial anyway. The bishop appointed an investigation committee and a trial committee, selecting the latter's members entirely from the 25 who had constituted the minority in the original vote. The trial committee convicted Kelley, and Hargrove suspended him from the ministry for six months; he also required that the punishment be carried out before Kelley had exhausted the appeals process. Hargrove penalized Kelley's main supporters as well, including presiding elder B. F. Haynes, by reassigning them to remote and low-paying pastoral duties.[126]

Haynes, who embraced holiness theology, became editor of the conference's new paper, the *Tennessee Methodist*, in 1891. Whereas the *Nashville Christian Advocate* and its editor, E. E. Hoss, defended Hargrove and gave minimal coverage to Kelley's appeals, Haynes used his paper to keep the case in the public eye over the next several years. Kelley was finally vindicated at the 1894 General Conference, where the Committee on Episcopacy overturned his conviction and censured Bishop Hargrove for maladministration.[127] Kelley's supporters, including Haynes, emphasized the technical irregularities in the case and the bishop's procedural transgressions, but they also argued that Kelley had been punished primarily for his political stand for prohibition and against the Democratic Party. The case received a great deal of attention from Baptists as well, who viewed the trial as revenge for Kelley's political support of the prohibition cause. Tennessee Baptists seized the opportunity to attack what they viewed as the authoritarian and undemocratic polity of the Methodist Church. "The action of Bishop Hargrove in the Kelley case . . . was unjust, unfair, dictatorial, and tyrannical in the extreme," wrote the *Baptist and Reflector.*[128]

The *Alabama Christian Advocate* defended the decision in the Kelley trial and in similar cases. Its editor noted in 1890 that "several itinerant preachers have been before the public as candidates for political office," and most of them were disciplined. But, the editor argued, they were punished not for their political involvement per se but rather—as in the Kelley case—for eschewing their ministerial duties. Regarding Kelley, the editor stated, "Whether he abandoned his work to run for governor, or to run a foot-race, or to run a sawmill, or not to run at all, was never involved in the question before the conference." Nevertheless, there was widespread public perception that Kelley had been punished by a presiding bishop with a well-known disdain for third-party politics. Even the *Birmingham Daily News* summed up the case thusly: "Dr. Kelley was deposed for running for governor."[129]

In the same year that Tennessee Methodists were dealing with the Kelley case, a Tennessee Baptist employed the spirituality doctrine to put the brakes on the state convention's advocacy of prohibition legislation. The controversy was spurred by the resolution presented to the Tennessee Baptist Convention by its temperance committee in Chattanooga. Every year since 1881, the convention's temperance report had expressed support for prohibition and, in recent years, had called on the state legislature to pass prohibition legislation. When the committee presented its report in 1890, however, the delegates received a surprise. Under chairman S. E. Jones, a pastor, newspaper editor, and professor of math and natural science at Carson-Newman College in east Tennessee, the committee had decided not to call for such resolutions. In fact, the report declared: "We most emphatically . . . do not favor the passing of any resolution or resolutions which can by any reasonable interpretation be construed as a delegated church act, and, therefore, as by this convention to in any way convert the Baptist denomination into, or identify it with, any party or political measure looking to low or high license, to local, state, or national prohibition. From an ecclesiastical or Christian stand-point we believe the whole thing impracticable and absurd." Jones went on to reiterate the spirituality doctrine, proclaiming that "to preach repentance toward God and faith in the Christ is the duty of the church and that alone." The business of the church is to make men temperate by means of the spread of the gospel, not by use of the law, Jones's report reminded the convention.[130] The reading of the report provoked great consternation among the delegates. In the end, the convention rejected the committee's report and passed instead a brief resolution favoring "the absolute prohibition of the manufacture and sale of intoxicating drinks."[131]

Debaters on the floor of the convention were allotted only five minutes apiece to express their feelings about the issue, but the debate continued in the pages of the *Baptist and Reflector* for months. Critics argued that, in dealing with the temperance issue, the convention "must not evade the question, nor give forth any uncertain sound."[132] Jones wrote an article for the *Baptist and Reflector* defending his position and his rejected report. He felt that he and his supporters had been mistreated at the convention, claiming that many delegates "began to shake their heads and almost hiss" before he had read even one-third of the report. But he was defiant in stating that his report was true to both Baptist doctrine and the teaching of the New Testament. He laid down a challenge to his Baptist brethren, offering $50 to anyone who could show him where the New Testament allows a Christian church to make the kind of appeals to the state that his opponents sought. "It is a great point with Baptists to insist that we go no further in our teaching or practice than we have New Testament precept or practice for," Jones explained, and there existed no such biblical warrant for the kind of ecclesiastical reliance on the state that was becoming increasingly common among Baptists and other evangelical churches.[133] In making this argument, Jones revealed that his opposition to political involvement by the church may have been fueled in part by Landmarkism. That movement, which emerged in Tennessee during the mid-nineteenth century and deeply impacted southern Baptists well into the twentieth, taught that the only true churches were those descended from an unbroken line of Baptist churches that could be traced back to the first century. Landmarkers were also primitivists who believed that only those institutions established in the New Testament were valid; thus, they refused to cooperate in mission societies and temperance organizations. Hence Jones's claim of the lack of a biblical warrant for the church's appeals to the secular government.[134]

In response to Jones, George A. Lofton, who had pastored Baptist churches in Georgia, Alabama, and Tennessee, argued that resolutions in support of prohibition legislation did not constitute an excessive intermingling with the state, nor did it violate the spirit of the New Testament. "Our temperance resolution committed no one to any party," Lofton explained, but was merely the exercise of the duty Baptists have to "preach, and pray, and resolve against public evils which require legislative control or prohibition for the general and universal good." Baptists had long recognized the church's right to lend moral support to the state without crossing the line into inappropriate organic union with the state, he observed.[135] The Reverend William Huff of Bellbuckle, Tennessee, likewise wrote to the *Baptist and Reflector* to cite precedents for such resolutions. Huff noted that as early as 1775 the Baptists of the General Association of Virginia had memorialized the state's colonial legislature concerning freedom from the British and freedom of religion within the colony.[136]

A supporter of Jones responded to Huff's letter by arguing that prohibition resolutions were entirely different from resolutions regarding religious freedom or even temperance. Prohibition is "a principle upon which the church is divided. It is a political principle, as it seeks a legislative remedy," wrote W. P. Maury. Such action on the part of the church undermined the whole meaning of Christianity, according to Maury, who noted that "for a Baptist convention to wipe out the line of demarcation between Christ and Caesar, and to place itself upon Caesar's territory, and to usurp Caesar's functions, is virtually saying that Christ has died in vain."[137] Jones concurred with Maury, claiming that with the resolution passed in Chattanooga the convention had "allied itself to politics and to the state, or took a long step in that direction." Jones cited the controversial action taken by the Methodist Kelley and argued that this was the next logical step for Baptist ministers who supported such a resolution. "What is prohibition but the shibboleth of the third party—a political party for all intents and purposes?" asked Jones.[138]

Jones's Landmarkism continued to enter into the debate over prohibition legislation. Lofton argued that some aspects of the life of the church are not strictly provided for in the New Testament, such as the development of conventions, seminaries, and mission boards. Church resolutions about prohibition and other subjects fell under this category, which Lofton called "the undefined operations of Christianity." Jones responded that the New Testament "knows nothing" of Lofton's "undefined operations" and that such inventions were an example of men adding to the word of God. In another article he labeled any such extrabiblical practices that might exist in the Baptist Church "heterodoxy and antichrist" and prayed for their eradication.[139] Lofton nevertheless continued to argue that the convention's prohibition resolution was consistent with both Baptist history and the practice of the primitive church.[140]

The back-and-forth between Jones and Lofton continued into 1891. Jones remained resolute that the church had no business petitioning the state on behalf of its moral crusade to end intemperance. "The church of Jesus Christ as such has no more to do with state legislation, good or bad, than Jupiter's moons," he wrote. Even the renowned Georgia Baptist minister J. William Jones, an architect of the religion of the Lost Cause, weighed in on the matter.[141] Although *this* Jones favored prohibition and supported resolutions calling on legislators to pass prohibitory laws, he firmly opposed the third-party approach.[142] When the Tennessee Baptists convened again in October 1891, S. E. Jones was no longer on the temperance committee. The new committee presented a report, passed by the convention, stating that it was "heartily in favor of whatever means or methods will foster or promote in a scriptural way the cause of temperance or prevent the sale and use of intoxicating liquors," and it recommended that "Baptist Churches make every possible effort to secure legal prohibition."[143] Nevertheless, one speaker at the convention conceded, "This is a live issue on which we are not one, as we should be."[144]

The fate of Henry A. Scomp, a professor at Emory College, provides a third example of how supporting the Prohibition Party rather than the Democratic Party could bring a southern evangelical under significant fire. In 1888 Scomp had written a popular book entitled *Alcohol in the Realm of King Cotton,* which provided a history of the growth of temperance and prohibition sentiment in the region. The book received widespread support from the Methodist hierarchy in Georgia. Atticus Haygood wrote the book's introduction and believed that the work would hasten the arrival of "universal prohibition by law."[145] At the North Georgia Conference in 1888, Emory College president Warren A. Candler called Scomp's book "perhaps the most valuable treatise extant upon the subject of temperance movements in this country, and especially concerning the temperance reform in Georgia. We feel sure the cause of prohibition will be furthered by its extensive circulation among our people."[146] But by the early 1890s, Scomp, like many evangelical prohibitionists in the South, became frustrated with the Democratic Party and sought another party that mirrored his views on prohibition.

In 1892 Scomp became increasingly supportive of the Prohibition Party and its candidates. When evangelist Sam Small, who was running for Congress on the Prohibition ticket, came to speak in Covington, Georgia, Scomp agreed to chair the meeting. Scomp later recalled that "Mr. Candler's wrath was terribly aroused at this. Two days later he threatened that if I persisted in . . . my prohibition course, I should lose my chair in the college." Scomp retorted that he would not "surrender my convictions or my right to champion them" for his position on the Emory faculty. Scomp rejected the idea that ministers should steer clear of political involvement, and he reminded Candler that in 1855 one of Emory's professors had chaired the election campaign of Basil Overby, a Methodist minister running for governor of Georgia on a temperance platform. "Preachers have since then, as well as before, oftentimes been candidates for office," wrote Scomp.[147]

Scomp's employment at Emory, where he had taught Greek for eighteen years, was based on a renewable three-year contract; each time the contract expired, Scomp had to be renominated by the college president. When Scomp's contract expired in 1894, Candler nominated another individual instead, and Scomp was fired. This proved to be a controversial decision on Candler's part, having the appearance of being retaliation against the professor for his involvement with the Prohibition Party. According to Scomp, his political activism on behalf of the prohibition cause had initiated the bad blood between Candler and himself, along with a disagreement they had regarding the WCTU. These disputes "generated the deep hostility which Mr. Candler has so long cherished against me," explained Scomp, and "I soon found that he was actively at work against me to drive me from the college." The enmity between the two men was obvious. Candler allegedly declared that the town of Oxford, Georgia, was not big enough for the two of them and, according to Scomp, told several people that "he and I could not remain in the same college—one of us must go." Scomp wrote, "He never dared refer any charge, for that would have involved an open fight in the boards. He preferred to wait until my sixth term of three years would expire." As a result, Scomp found himself "consigned long ago to the outer darkness, whither are gathering prohibitionists, populists, Woman's Christian Temperance Unions, Atkinson Democrats, rich men who give Candler no largesses, and fashionable women who pray."[148]

For his part, Candler explained his actions as simply getting "rid of a professor whom we had carried too long." He ·characterized Scomp as a fanatic who "sought to make sympathy for himself by talking of his temperance views, claiming they displaced him though they had absolutely nothing to do with his case. Hence all this ado."[149] The "ado" that Candler refers to was the storm of protest aroused by Scomp's dismissal. Between the supporters of prohibition and the enemies of Candler (who were not few), the result was a public assault on both the college and its president. One of the most outspoken defenders of Scomp was Mrs. W. C. Sibley, president of the WCTU in Georgia from 1883 to 1900. Sibley and Candler had their own ongoing feud, which had erupted in 1892 when Candler attacked the state WCTU for its connection with the national WCTU and that body's support for women's suffrage. In the wake of Scomp's dismissal, Sibley wrote a newspaper article charging that Candler had been motivated purely by his personal dislike of Scomp's efforts on behalf of prohibition and the WCTU. Candler had attempted "to throttle and curtail professor Scomp's political action," she stated, and she characterized Scomp as a "man who refuses to sacrifice principle and self-respect for position." Sibley also accused Candler of hypocrisy for trying to quash Scomp's political support for Prohibition Party candidates "while reserving to himself as a president of the institution and prominent minister in the Methodist church free course as a pronounced Democrat, and of course supporter in that way of the liquor traffic."[150]

Despite his ardent support for prohibition legislation during the previous decade, Candler's commitment to the cause was called into question after Scomp's dismissal. An editorial in Tennessee rejected Candler's explanation that it was "simply a case of a professor who was a failure as a teacher." The editor questioned why Scomp's contract had been renewed six times over the course of eighteen years if he were such a poor teacher. Sarcastically, the editorial said, "Dr. Candler says he is also a prohibitionist. If this be true, injustice has been done him." The editor then inquired, "Will the doctor please write us the number of times he has voted the Prohibition Party ticket, since its organization in 1880?"[151]

Supporters of the Prohibition Party were beginning to appropriate the label *prohibitionist* for themselves alone. As the *Daily Advance* of Harriman, Tennessee, explained, "a Democrat is said to be a Democrat because he votes the Democratic ticket. A Republican is said to be a Republican because he votes the Republican ticket. Similarly, professor Scomp is a prohibitionist, because he believes in the principles of the Prohibition Party, and votes the Prohibition ticket."[152] The *Voice*, the national paper of the Prohibition Party, also publicized Scomp's termination and lambasted Candler and Haygood for their anti-prohibition actions. "The truth of the matter is apparent in the fact that Dr. Candler and Bishop Haygood, as professed prohibitionists but voting Democrats, could not tolerate Scomp as a professed and voting prohibitionist," editorialized the paper.[153]

Candler was not, in fact, a strict and consistent adherent to the principle of spirituality. In the 1880s he had vocally supported local option and had authored many of the temperance reports of the North Georgia Conference calling for statewide prohibition laws. Candler openly supported some Democratic candidates for office, such as Senator Augustus O. Bacon and Governor William Y. Atkinson. He was even criticized by hard-line adherents to the doctrine of church spirituality. In 1894 Candler received a letter from a friend reprimanding him for a recent "political interview" he had granted to the *Atlanta Constitution*. The writer noted that he had heard several other men express their disappointment in Candler's involvement in political issues. "I think it is a very grave mistake for a minister in active service to go into politics or appear to the world as being even in the smallest meshes of the net," wrote Candler's critical friend.[154]

Yet when prohibition candidates challenged wet Democrats, Candler became an outspoken advocate of political noninvolvement. For instance, he announced the day before a Fulton County election that Methodist clergy had no business getting involved in politics. The next day, the wet Democrat defeated the dry candidate, and Candler was accused of contributing to the prohibitionist's loss.[155] Likewise, in 1896 Candler refused to support the Prohibition Party's candidate for governor, Seaborn Wright; this was widely viewed as lending support to Wright's wet, Democratic opponent.[156] In 1894 Candler refused to allow a student that he deemed "too third party" to give a speech and declared that Emory was a Democratic institution.[157]

Candler was not alone in his opposition to Scomp's political activity or to the Prohibition Party in general. Bishop Atticus G. Haygood, who had been a tireless supporter of prohibition in the 1880s, also attacked Scomp and called the Prohibition Party "extreme if not fanatical."[158] Haygood had expressed the opinion in 1886 that temperance supporters must resist the rising urge to join a third-party movement in the name of prohibition. "Stand by local option," Haygood had warned, "and don't go into politics."[159] A supporter of Candler's actions wrote to say that he agreed that Scomp was "deranged." "I am glad that Scomp is out of the college," wrote the Reverend Frank Eakes. "My own opinion is and has been, that he wanted to get into the papers and pose as a martyr to the cause of prohibition and make capital of that." Eakes believed that Haygood should go even further in his condemnation of Scomp, writing to Candler, "I think the matter has progressed so far that the bishop ought to slay him. . . . Kill him (figuratively, of course) and let it be done with."[160]

The Scomp controversy and the larger conflict between prohibitionists and hard-core spirituality adherents pitted "establishment" Methodists against a more rural element with less loyalty to the Democratic Party. Scomp's rhetoric during the controversy played on larger Populist themes. Statements such as "the era of ecclesiastical bossism is here" resonated with a society pregnant with a popular resentment of politicians who were entrenched in the party machinery and who were viewed as doing little to address the needs and concerns of rural, working-class whites.[161] Scomp's parallel between the bosses of the state's Democratic political machine and the likes of Candler and Haygood within the state's Methodist hierarchy was especially intended for the evangelical subset of the Populist movement. The leaders of the Methodist Church in Georgia, Scomp argued, were "down on almost every phase of modern reform and real advance."[162]

As the examples of Scomp, the TBC temperance report, and Kelley demonstrate, during the early 1890s, prohibition became a contentious issue for southern evangelicals. Staunch support for the cause raised questions about one's loyalty to the Democratic Party and to white hegemony. Opposing it raised questions about one's moral fortitude and one's credentials as a Bible-believing evangelical. Conservative evangelicals negotiated this quandary by relying on the doctrine of the spirituality of the church, which allowed them to profess support for prohibition but maintain that prohibition sentiment should not become a political issue that caused one to question the Democratic Party. As they struggled with the issue of prohibition and its implications for party loyalty, the doctrine became a tool employed by Bourbon evangelicals to safeguard white Democratic rule in the South. Evangelical prohibitionists, in contrast, came to regard it as an impediment that stifled reform and preserved the status quo.

By the turn of the century, the Populist and Prohibition parties' threat to Democratic supremacy in the South had waned, and agrarianism became the South's "second Lost Cause," as Woodward puts it.[163] The threat of a Republican resurgence powered by black votes and a fractured white electorate was further allayed by disfranchisement schemes after 1900. And as Dewey Grantham observes, after 1900, the Democratic Party increasingly "accepted the Populist concept of the positive state—of a more active governmental role in promoting economic growth and protecting society."[164] Only after these threats associated with populism had diminished, however, could all southern evangelicals—rural and urban, Bourbon and Populist—reunite firmly behind the cause of prohibition.

Final Decline of Spirituality

Even after 1900, many conservative southern evangelicals were still devoted to the old doctrine of spirituality, and evangelicals who spoke out in support of prohibition as a political matter often faced internal opposition and had to defend themselves for taking up the cause. During the 1902 governor's race in Georgia, Atlanta Baptist minister Len

Broughton actively backed prohibition candidate Dupont Guerry, "the only candidate for governor who says the saloon must go down." Broughton reported that at one of his speaking engagements, where he intended to discuss "the moral and immoral issues of the pending campaign," he was sitting near two ladies who were talking about his upcoming speech. According to Broughton, "One of them, speaking evidently so I could hear her, said, 'He has no business messing with politics—why don't he give his attention to saving sinners.'"[165] The *Alabama Baptist* observed in 1905 that there were still many in southern society "who think that the preacher should have as little to do as possible with politics."[166] The Reverend W. B. Rutledge, a Baptist from east Tennessee, noted in 1908 that to this very day it is "a dangerous thing for a preacher to 'meddle' in politics, or to interfere with the methods of the politician."[167]

For the most part, however, most southern evangelicals embraced the idea of the church becoming involved in the political arena when questions of moral reform were at stake.[168] Alabama Baptist leader A. J. Dickinson argued in 1907 that "the old notion of the opposition of the sacred and the secular as antagonistic and exclusive spheres of life is now refuted and proven fallacious. There is no act which is not both secular and sacred."[169] In 1908 the Reverend E. K. Cox of Howell Memorial Baptist Church in Nashville preached a sermon titled "The Church and the Liquor Traffic," a large portion of which was spent defending a minister's right to speak out on political subjects from the pulpit. Cox asserted:

> I resent with all the power of my manhood the insult to my integrity and patriotism in the cry that says that while the Negro has his political rights, and the most corrupt ward heelers alive may be as active as they please, I must hold my peace concerning the matters which affect myself, my country, and my home. I have been listening to this cry for about fifteen years, and have been struck with two things about it: the noise comes mainly from those who are identified either directly or indirectly with evils entrenched in our political life to which the preacher's opposition is being felt.

Cox admitted that not all those who opposed ecclesiastical involvement in politics were motivated by personal self-interest, but even so, they were "ignorantly echoing the cries raised to drive the minds of men away from the great issues involved."[170]

The Reverend G. W. Perryman of Knoxville remarked at the Tennessee Baptist Convention, "The whiskey Democrats and whiskey Republicans have lost sight of party lines in their efforts to save the accursed traffic. Why can't temperance people drop these lines to drive out whiskey?" He also defended the church's increased involvement in the political struggle over prohibition, saying, "They make a fuss about preachers being in politics. Who got 'em into it? These low-down whiskey fellows did it."[171] W. B. Crumpton of Alabama argued that preachers were involved in politics because the liquor interests went there first, and that if preachers "are true to their high calling, [they will] go after [liquor] until it is driven out of politics and off the face of the earth."[172] By 1909, even E. E. Hoss, who had opposed Kelley's iconoclastic attitude toward party loyalty in 1890, was willing to contemplate abandoning the white man's party if circumstances demanded it. Regarding the martyrdom of Edward Carmack in Nashville and the subsequent fusion of dry Tennessee Democrats with Republicans, Hoss declared that it was better to "ruin the party than let liquor ruin the people."[173]

Allegiance to the doctrine of the spirituality of the church persisted most strongly within the PCUS. It was only natural that the last bastion of staunch adherence to the doctrine should be among the southern Presbyterians who gave birth to it. In 1909 the Presbytery of North Alabama passed a series of resolutions endorsing the state government's efforts to pass statewide prohibition. In response, Birmingham minister W. I. Sinnott filed a complaint with the denomination's General Assembly. Sinnott argued that the resolutions improperly meddled in the affairs of the secular government and contravened the church's commitment to the doctrine of spirituality. Unlike other southern evangelical denominations, the PCUS had never passed resolutions endorsing prohibition or appointed a permanent temperance committee, fearful that such moves "would involve the possibility of political entanglement." The PCUS had issued only ambiguous temperance resolutions, steering clear of direct endorsement of prohibition legislation.[174] But Sinnott's complaint to the 1910 General Assembly forced the denomination to confront the matter. Its judicial committee heard Sinnott's case and ruled against him, saying that the North Alabama Presbytery's actions were consistent with the church's stance against the evil of intemperance.[175]

The decision in the Sinnott case marked a significant change in the southern Presbyterian interpretation of the doctrine of the spirituality of the church that it had embraced since 1845. Antebellum Presbyterians had done much of the theological "heavy lifting" of expounding the doctrine, fitting it to the needs of southern churches and employing it as a justification for sectional division of the major denominations. Southern Methodists and Baptists subsequently embraced the doctrine because it served them well, absolving them of their antebellum support of slavery, vindicating their secession from national denominations, and justifying their continued separation. But it was also within these two evangelical denominations that prohibition sentiment took firm root, and soon the doctrine began to interfere with new evangelical priorities; it could not coexist peacefully alongside the growing urge of late-nineteenth-century evangelicals to purge society of alcohol. By the 1880s, for some Baptists and Methodists in the South, the doctrine of spirituality had become as much of an inconvenience as it was an asset.

The emergence of the Populist threat to the Democratic Party simultaneously disrupted the prohibition efforts of southern evangelicals and provided new usefulness for the spirituality doctrine in some quarters. Prohibition efforts had gotten off to a grand start in the 1880s, with widespread evangelical support in both cities and rural areas. By 1887, Atlanta had been dried up—at least temporarily—and Tennesseans got a statewide amendment on the ballot, as did other southern states such as Texas. During that decade, urban evangelicals were just as likely to support prohibition as were rural evangelicals. With the introduction of populism, however, the momentum of the prohibitionists was temporarily derailed, but not because they lost enthusiasm for the cause. In fact, quite the opposite was true. Some evangelical prohibitionists became increasingly frustrated at the Democratic Party's refusal to embrace prohibition. Spurred, no doubt, by the rising drumbeat of Populist attacks on the Democratic Party as a corrupt and incorrigible institution beholden to corporate interests, the party loyalty of many prohibitionists was eclipsed by their loyalty to the cause. By the time evangelical prohibitionists began to state that they would rather see blacks elected than wet

Democrats, prohibition had taken on a more radical and threatening air in the South.

This triggered a reaction among those evangelicals who, though they heartily supported prohibition in the 1880s and still wanted it to succeed eventually, did not lose sight of a higher priority: the maintenance of white political superiority via the Democratic Party. These evangelicals of the Bourbon and Big Mule persuasion cooled toward prohibition because it became a sign of a lack of Democratic fealty. They were thus put in an awkward position: outright opposition to prohibition was a morally unacceptable position for evangelical Christians in most churches, yet ardent support for prohibition put them in opposition to the Democratic Party. Adherence to the doctrine of the spirituality of the church proved to be an optimal alternative for Bourbon evangelicals; it allowed them to continue to support prohibition in principle but to fight against its becoming an issue that might undermine Democratic hegemony. In their pursuit of a dry Dixie, evangelical prohibitionists had to overcome not only the obstacle of the doctrine of spirituality, which made the advocacy of prohibition legislation a questionable endeavor for ministers, but also the threat that prohibition posed to Democratic domination in the South. Not until the Populist challenge was resolved would southern evangelical prohibitionists again present a united front—united not only by their opposition to liquor but also by their shared fear of what they considered an equally dangerous threat to southern society: African American men.

Chapter Four

"But What Seek Those Dark Ballots?"

Prohibition and Race

IN ADDITION TO OVERCOMING the political obstacles facing their cause, southern evangelical prohibitionists found it necessary to accommodate their campaign to the peculiarities of southern culture. One of the most persistent and pernicious problems in the South's history has been that of race relations, and the southern prohibition movement coincided with what has been termed the "nadir" of race relations in the South.[1] Between 1880 and 1910 the southern white view of blacks, and the language used by whites to describe blacks, declined steadily. Evangelicals contributed to this deteriorating racial rhetoric. An examination of the rhetoric of the prohibition movement between 1880 and 1910 reveals that the cause was greatly shaped by the racial attitudes of its white advocates; at the same time, prohibition played a significant role in shaping and informing evangelical attitudes toward blacks.

In the 1880s prohibition was a key element of the New South agenda as envisioned and promoted by evangelicals. It encouraged a more optimistic and accommodating attitude toward blacks, who were expected to be supportive of prohibition and vote accordingly. Beginning in 1890, prohibition played an important and twofold role in leading evangelicals to support the disfranchisement of black voters. Evangelical prohibitionists came to realize that African American voters were not as supportive of prohibition as had been hoped, and by the mid-1890s, it also became evident that the mere existence of a black voting bloc made it impossible for white voters to divide over the issue of prohibition. So long as the threat of black political resurgence remained, prohibition would take a backseat to Democratic Party loyalty for the vast majority of white voters. This accounts for the evangelical embrace of the neo-Sambo description of African Americans, which characterized black men as unfit for the responsibilities of full citizenship. After the turn of the century, prohibition continued to influence deteriorating racial attitudes. White evangelicals played on the popular image of the "black beast," in part because alcohol was the central ingredient in the perceived degradation of black males. The white hysteria about black brutes assaulting white women that swept the South in the early 1900s put the prohibition cause back in the public spotlight. Evangelical prohibitionists capitalized on this renewed public concern over alcohol and successfully pushed prohibition as the solution to black savagery. Whereas most whites advocated rope and fagot as the ultimate solution to black attacks on white women, evangelicals promoted a more preemptive solution: cutting off the liquor supply. At each point along the way, evangelicals participated in this decline in racial rhetoric, sometimes critiquing the prevailing racial attitudes of the region, but often embracing and utilizing them for the advancement of prohibition.

1880s—The New South

"The Old South rested everything on slavery and agriculture, unconscious that these could neither give nor maintain healthy growth. The New South presents a perfect democracy . . . a hundred farms for every plantation, fifty homes for every palace, and a diversified industry that meets the complex needs of this complex age."[2] With these words, a new era in the American South formally began. They were spoken by Henry Grady, publisher of the *Atlanta Constitution*, before the New England Society of New York in 1886. He represented a new movement, dubbed the "New South," that sought to redirect the South's focus away from past hurts and perceived injustices and toward the future instead. New South advocates envisioned a southland modeled on the industrialized northern states. They emphasized economic development, education, and a new attitude toward both the Yankee in the North and the freedman in the South. Although the movement is frequently dated from Grady's 1886 speech, both the term *New South* and the principles it embodied predate this event. In what was likely the first public use of the phrase to designate the postbellum South, a northern magazine ran an article in 1870 called "The New South: What It Is Doing, and What It Wants."[3] Grady actually credited Georgia senator Benjamin Harvey Hill as the inspiration for his ideology. Hill was an opponent of secession who nonetheless served as a senator in the Confederate States of America. In 1871 he addressed the University of Georgia alumni association and voiced ideas that, coming from the mouth of a former Confederate leader only a few short years after the Civil War, were revolutionary. The Old South had been a failure, Hill announced, due to social errors that must be eradicated from southern society. The antebellum South had tied itself to an immoral and inefficient slave labor system, and that system had stalled the economic development of the region.[4] The themes of Hill's 1871 address—that slavery had been a failure and that the future of the South lay in industrial development and the cultivation of an educated free labor system—found fruition when the New South movement emerged full force in the 1880s.

A diversified economy, agricultural efficiency, and the elimination of encumbering practices such as sharecropping and farm tenancy were key economic aspects of the New South program touted by southern boosters such as Grady. But the message did not consist entirely of economic and industrial reforms. Other elements attracted evangelicals to the New South movement, and it was there that some of its strongest advocates emerged. Foremost among these was Atticus G. Haygood, president of Emory College in Oxford, Georgia, who titled his 1880 Thanksgiving Day sermon "The New South." Haygood asked the students of the Methodist school to consider what the South had to be thankful for on that Thanksgiving Day and, in the process, launched his avocation as a New South spokesman. The first thing the South should be thankful for, said Haygood, was its remarkable economic recovery over the past fifteen years. Religion, he contended, was the key reason that the South had experienced such a powerful recovery since the devastation of the war. Then Haygood cited another cause for southern thankfulness that likely surprised his hearers: the fact that slavery no longer existed in the region. He announced, "There is one great historic fact which should, in my sober judgment, above all things, excite everywhere in the South profound gratitude to Almighty God: *I mean the abolition of African slavery.*" Haygood went on to briefly defend the practice of slavery, noting that "its worst features were often cruelly exaggerated, and that its best were unfairly minified." Nevertheless he reiterated "the one great historic fact, that *slavery exists no more.* For that fact I devoutly thank God this day!"[5]

Haygood admitted that he had changed his mind about slavery and that he now had "new light" on the subject. "I do now believe many things that I did not believe twenty years ago," he said. Haygood explained that the end of slavery was a blessing to the South and to all its denizens, black and white. The benefit to the freedmen was obvious. The benefit of free labor to the white population of the South, he argued, was equally evident in the growth of industry and business. As a result of the end of slavery, Haygood saw southern whites becoming more industrious, efficient, and prosperous. Carrying on the theme that Hill had initiated almost a decade earlier, Haygood blamed slavery for the lack of antebellum development in the South. "But for slavery, Georgia would be as densely populated as Rhode Island," he lamented. Haygood closed his historic sermon with a parting admonition to "cultivate industry and economy, observe law and order, practice virtue and justice." Southerners in the New South must look forward, not backward. "This is not 1860, it is 1880," he reminded his listeners; "the true golden day for the South is yet to dawn."[6]

Like Haygood, other evangelicals embraced the New South message and were not afraid to suggest that both slavery and secession had been mistakes. Georgia evangelist Sam Jones, whose father had owned slaves, did not lament the passing of the peculiar institution. In 1886 he said, "I am sorry that America has it in her history . . . I am glad that is done away with forever."[7] One of the best-known revivalists in the country and one of the most indefatigable proponents of prohibition, Jones traveled frequently to northern cities, where he reassured Yankees that the Old South was dead and encouraged investment in the burgeoning southern industrial economy.[8] Like other New Southites, Jones sought to heal sectional animosities. He claimed that he now loved and honored Union heroes such as Ulysses S. Grant, just as he was sure that northerners loved and honored southern heroes such as Robert E. Lee and Stonewall Jackson. Now that the war was over, he assured his audiences, "We can be friends though our fathers have been enemies."[9] Sam W. Small, Jones's revival partner, had grown up on a plantation in Tennessee, but in the 1880s he too denounced secession and hailed the downfall of slavery. He criticized not only the folly of slavery but also the folly of the war waged to preserve it, lamenting the "misguided men in the South" who had fired on Fort Sumter. The only good thing to result from four years of fratricide, he continued, was that it "struck the shackles from six million slaves."[10]

Another New South supporter was Methodist minister David C. Kelley of Tennessee. Regarding the old institution of slavery, Kelley echoed Haygood by stating that "we have new light, and in it we rejoice in common with the whole Christian world." For Kelley, this new light regarding slavery demanded that southern evangelicals reengage with their black brothers and aid in their uplift. "We thought we were right," Kelley explained, but "many of us mistook a temporary purpose of God . . . for an absolute right. We all came to acknowledge the mistake, and rejoice in the greater light." Kelley speculated that God had brought Africans to America in slavery for the same reason he had brought the Israelites to bondage in Egypt: for a brief period of "tutelage" and "as a preparation for future growth." The mistake made by many southerners, according to Kelley, was that "this temporary need of the Negro many good men mistook as indicative of a permanent divine purpose." Always willing to stir up controversy, Kelley even went so far as to posit that God had used the work of antebellum abolitionists just as he had used Moses to free the children of Israel.[11]

A Tennessee Baptist minister writing to the *Baptist and Reflector* in 1890 echoed this theme of contentment with the end of slavery. He admitted to having spent many years prior to the Civil War confidently proclaiming that abolition would never triumph in America, but he was now comfortable with having been wrong. "We would not alter that prohibition of slavery in the Constitution if we could," he stated. "We now feel and see that it is all for the best, and that the South is prospering much better every way—physically, mentally, morally, and religiously—with free than she did with slave labor."[12] New Southites argued that slavery had hindered the progress and industrial development of the Old South and that abuses in its administration had tainted the institution. The focus of New South prophets was to forget about slavery, get over any lingering resentment about its demise, and move forward with the establishment of a new era in the South founded on industrial development and the principles of science and efficiency. Instead of ascribing the South's Civil War defeat to any moral failings on the part of the region, New Southites blamed it on an antebellum political economy that had for decades retarded the region's development. Had the South not been mired in an antiquated and inefficient labor system, it might have been victorious.[13] The promise of the New Southites was that if the region now embraced technical and industrial advancement—given its already confirmed moral superiority—the South's future prosperity would be limitless.

Other evangelical New South advocates espoused a similar message. Alabama Baptist J. J. D. Renfroe chastised politicians who cultivated sectional animosity for political gain. He used the occasion of the Fourth of July—a holiday that southerners had largely abandoned since the war because of its association with Confederate defeats at Gettysburg and Vicksburg—to laud the downfall of slavery and the rise of new race relations and economic opportunities in the South since Appomattox. He assured his listeners on that day that slavery had been an "indefensible burden" on southern society and its economy, and he urged a new era of national harmony.[14] Jabez Curry of Alabama had served as both a soldier and a legislator for the Confederacy, but he became a Baptist preacher after the war and in the 1880s embraced the new vision for the South. Speaking in 1882, Curry said of slavery, "The South rejoices that it is gone—irrevocably gone."[15]

The attitude of New Southites toward blacks was one of optimism and confidence. They said good riddance to slavery and welcomed universal male suffrage. But the themes of evangelical New Southites included more than the renunciation of slavery. Their central elements were the healing of sectional animosity; the encouragement of industrial development and economic reform in the region; the solicitation of northern capital investment in the South; a commitment to educating African Americans; an optimistic view of the potential of blacks, including their right to vote; and an emphasis on prohibition as the key social reform. Haygood's 1880 Thanksgiving sermon launched a decade in which many southern evangelicals would embrace a new and forward-looking attitude toward the region's economic development, toward their northern victors, and toward blacks. Haygood, Grady, and others spoke throughout the North, soliciting Yankee capital for investment and development as well as for philanthropic work in the region. Atlanta held an International Cotton Exposition in 1881 to demonstrate to the world its ability to efficiently develop and utilize its natural resources. Atlanta even gave General William Tecumseh Sherman—who less than twenty years earlier had burned much of the city to the ground in his March to the Sea—a hero's welcome. The city announced that it was "a new place; modern, democratic, a fresh production, wholly practical, without antiquities or prejudices."[16] Just as Atlantans would proclaim themselves "too busy to hate" almost a century later, New Southites in the 1880s worked feverishly to set old racial animosities aside and boost the South and all its inhabitants through economic development.

Yet it was the moral element of the New South agenda—the moral uplift of southern blacks and of the region as a whole—more than the economic elements that stimulated evangelical support. Their optimistic view of African Americans drove New South evangelicals to expect great things from the freedmen. Grady boasted, "In the South, there are Negro lawyers, teachers, editors, dentists, doctors, preachers, multiplying with the increasing ability of their race to support them."[17] Given the opportunity, New Southites believed, African Americans had the intellectual and moral capacity to achieve much. Haygood dedicated himself to a program of moral and economic uplift of blacks in the South, and the two key elements were improved education and temperance reform. In 1881 Haygood published *Our Brother in Black*, which called the old slave trade "the sum of all villainies" and lamented the lack of effort by southerners to educate blacks. Haygood called for a new attitude among white southerners to support "the elevation of our black brother" through education.[18] New Southites argued that African Americans, though still deemed inferior to whites, were nonetheless full of potential and capable of being educated and raised up considerably. Their potential had never been fully tapped, and it was the responsibility of white southerners to encourage their growth. Haygood devoted much of the 1880s to promoting the two causes he believed were central to southern prosperity: prohibition and black education.

From 1885 to 1891 Haygood served as general agent for the John F. Slater Fund, which had been established in 1882 by a Union army veteran and industrialist who donated $1 million for the education of freed slaves in the South. Former president Rutherford B. Hayes, one of the directors of the fund, selected Haygood to serve in this role, which involved disbursing $40,000 per year to black educational institutions in the South.[19] During these years Haygood canvassed the region, preaching and speaking to raise public support for black colleges. Haygood's correspondence with Hayes during this period reveals both his deep commitment to educating the South's black citizens and his belief that the issues of education and temperance were intertwined. "I am seeking to create and foster sentiment in favor of the work of teaching these poor people among southern white people. I do not believe that I can do anything so important for the southern Negro as this," he wrote to Hayes in 1885. Haygood's letter explained, "I believe with all my soul that God's hand is on me for these poor people. It is to me a sacred work." Haygood knew that the majority of southerners were disinclined to support educational efforts for freedmen, but he was confident that the tide was turning toward the more optimistic vision that he and other New Southites promoted. He assured Hayes that he was beginning to see evidence of change even in areas where "Bourbon sentiment has been supreme," such as the Black Belt of Alabama.[20] He also noted stronger support for educational efforts within the church, especially as the older generation of southern Methodists, such as Bishop George Foster Pierce, retired. Pierce was not of the same racially optimistic mind-set as Haygood and viewed African Americans as incapable of benefiting from the kind of liberal arts education that Haygood advocated; he described such attempts to educate blacks as contrary to nature.[21]

Along with the educational uplift of blacks in the South, Haygood saw temperance as the other key reform needed. He used his position as the Slater Fund agent to further his prohibition crusade, just as he used his role as a popular temperance speaker to raise support for black education. Haygood often used the more popular issue of prohibition as a means of getting an audience to listen to his plea for educational support. "I spoke to a great crowd Saturday night in the opera house on a local option prohibition issue," he reported to Hayes in 1887, "and improved my opportunity to set before the leading people of Raleigh the importance and value of the right education of the Negro race." In the same letter he reported that on another occasion he had made two speeches in support of local option at a courthouse and had discussed the education issue in both.[22]

Haygood was not alone in making the connection between prohibition and black education. Jabez Curry, who also served as an agent of the Slater Fund, likewise dedicated himself to the cause of improving educational opportunities for all southerners, black and white. He saw free, quality education as essential for the rise of a New South, and he believed that blacks possessed the potential to be part of that picture. Curry saw the fate of the whole South as tied to the fate of its black citizens, warning, "If we do not lift them up, they will drag us down."[23] The northern American Missionary Association, which established black colleges in the South for freedmen, also made temperance a central part of the educational environment. In 1882 the association reported on the role of temperance in its institutions. For instance, at Fisk University in Nashville, "every student was required to sign the total abstinence pledge or to leave the institution." At Atlanta University, "all of the 310 students had signed the same pledge."[24]

White southern evangelicals of the New South persuasion were optimistic about blacks' potential to be educated and to contribute to society and the economy. Most of them espoused the twin themes of a reconciliatory attitude toward African Americans and a confidence that prohibition would advance the South as a whole. Thus, a key aspect of turning blacks into valuable members of southern society involved inculcating the principles of temperance in them and aligning them politically behind prohibition. Blacks were seen as important players in the ultimate victory of statewide prohibition, and black religious leaders were viewed by white prohibitionists as valuable and welcome helpmates in the struggle against alcohol. New Southite prohibitionists were also optimistic about the potential boon the black populace offered to their cause, convinced that the legion of black voters in the South would—after training in evangelical schools and guidance from black religious leaders—guarantee political victory over the liquor interests.

As Edward Ayers has observed, "blacks enjoyed their greatest political activity and visibility of the entire New South era in the prohibition movement." John Hammond Moore concurs that the prohibition campaign of the 1880s "witnessed a degree of integration and free association which has rarely been equaled since."[25] At prohibition rallies, African Americans received warm receptions when they spoke before white crowds on the subject of this important political and moral issue. White religious leaders routinely praised their black counterparts for their important role in leading the masses of black voters to support local option initiatives. Thus, for many black Christians, actively participating in the prohibition movement in the 1880s was an opportunity to gain respectability and acceptance in white society.[26]

When a constitutional amendment to enact statewide prohibition in Tennessee went on the ballot in 1887, white prohibitionists brought blacks into the campaign and praised their work on the amendment's behalf. They organized black WCTU chapters and brought in prominent African American speakers. Bishop Henry Turner of the African Methodist Episcopal Church spoke to black audiences in Knoxville, telling them that a vote for prohibition was in their own best interests. When Joseph C. Price, the African American president of Livingston College in North Carolina, traveled to Knoxville to speak in support of the amendment, several white churches canceled their Sunday morning services so that their members could attend his lecture. Price warned his black hearers that they must vote for prohibition to preserve the gains they had made in the South since the war.[27]

Although the amendment failed to pass, white evangelicals praised the efforts of black leaders on its behalf. The editors of the *Christian Advocate* reminded readers that even though most blacks had voted against the amendment, "a small minority of colored men strove nobly to arrest the tide that carried the mass of their people for whiskey." The editors, O. P. Fitzgerald and Warren A. Candler, went on to wax optimistic, saying that this group had "reassured the minds of some who were taking desponding views of the future of the Negroes in this country, and they have exhibited in vivid contrast the advantage of intelligence and morality over ignorance and vice." In closing, the editors shared a moving interracial moment they had experienced on election day. "It was a thrilling scene at the opening of the polls," they recalled, and "prayers [were] offered by both a white and a colored minister of the gospel. That black preacher's prayer for his people—his 'poor, ignorant, deluded people,' as he expressed it—will not be forgotten by those who heard it, and its pathos touches us as we recall it."[28]

In Alabama too, white evangelicals lauded black leaders who spoke out in support of prohibition. William Councill, president of a black college in Huntsville, told his fellow African Americans that prohibition was essential to their full emancipation. Likewise, the well-known Alabama educator Booker T. Washington promised that the benefits of prohibition for blacks would be "second only to the abolition of slavery."[29] In Georgia, the ultimately successful campaign to close the saloons in Atlanta in 1885 was launched at a rally held by black prohibitionists at the Lloyd Street Methodist Church, and white prohibitionists owed much of their success in Atlanta to the black voters of the city.[30]

The Lost Cause

Although the New South message was forward-looking, its messengers did not forsake white southerners' proud past. A corollary to the rise of the New South orthodoxy was the mythos of the Lost Cause. The concept of an unapologetic veneration of the Confederacy and all it stood for had debuted long before the 1880s. Indeed, the Confederate cause had scarcely been lost when the term *Lost Cause* was coined by E. A. Pollard in 1866. His book by that title laid out a defense of antebellum slavery and the constitutional political principles that southerners clung to and that led, in Pollard's view, to the inevitable sectional conflict. In the 1880s, however, the Lost Cause idea began to take on more mythic qualities and serve as a sort of southern civil religion, complete with its own saints, holy days, and institutions. The most extensive chronicler of this religion of the Lost Cause is Charles Reagan Wilson, who examines the central role that Christian clergymen played in blending Christian symbols with the imagery of the Confederacy in order to preserve southern culture. As "the prime celebrants of the religion of the Lost Cause," he explains, ministers "used the Lost Cause to warn southerners of their decline from past virtue, to promote moral reform, to encourage conversion to Christianity, and to educate the young in southern traditions."[31] Wilson's work has been seminal in establishing a framework for understanding the admixture of evangelical Christianity and neo-Confederate ideas that made southern culture unique in the postwar period (and continues to do so today, to some extent).

Nonetheless, Wilson pays little attention to the New Southites, describing them simply as a paternalistic subset of Lost Cause clergy that flourished in the 1880s.[32] More recent scholars of the New South movement have found its leaders to be both more distinct from those

Lost Cause devotees who dwelled on the injustices of the "war of northern aggression" and more deeply involved in promoting some Lost Cause ideas along with their New South agenda. Paradoxically, it was these forward-focused New Southites who played a major role in establishing this regional cult of the Lost Cause. To a great extent, this was done to provide cover for their Yankee-based economic vision for the southland. According to Robert Mathisen, the New South advocates used romanticized myths of the Old South to undergird and strengthen their New South vision.[33] They both harked back and urged forward, concurrently chastising the backward economy of the Old South, shackled by agrarianism and slavocracy, and extolling the virtue and moral superiority of antebellum southern yeomanry. Both Dan Frost and C. Vann Woodward go so far as to credit the New South prophets with creating the concept of the Lost Cause as a way to embrace and praise the old ways but also to set them aside and push the South forward in a new direction.[34] It was Henry Grady, after all, who brought Jefferson Davis out of exile and reinvented him as a living saint of the Lost Cause.[35] New Southites were proud of their southern heritage and thought that reverence for tradition had an important place in the southern mind, but they did not believe that the past should serve as a model for the future of the region.

The tension between these two mind-sets—forward-looking New South and backward-looking Lost Cause—was a contradiction deeply embedded in the movement, though it seems not to have troubled New South prophets such as Haygood and Grady.[36] As Joel Williamson has argued, there developed a "profound division in the southern sense of self, the division between the 'New South,' as it was called, and the Old." For New Southites, the Civil War had taught the lesson that industry and commerce were the keys to the future. For Old Southites, the war had demonstrated that whatever the weaknesses of the old economic order, the South's moral system had been vindicated.[37] In his 1886 New South address, Grady paid homage to the warriors of the Lost Cause: the "hero in gray with a heart of gold" who returned with an undefeated spirit to rebuild the region.[38] In addition to praising the common man of the Lost Cause—the yeoman who had left his small farm to serve as a lowly private in the Confederate army— apostles of the Lost Cause beatified the saints of the region's new civil religion. In 1870 Alabama Baptist J. J. D. Renfroe, who had served as a chaplain in Lee's Army of Northern Virginia, said that the youth of the South were not without statesmen and heroes to look up to. "There is a star-lit sky above, studded with the savants of other days," he told an audience, and he named Generals Lee and Jackson as two of the brightest stars in the constellation of southern heroes.[39] He highlighted the moral superiority of those Confederate leaders and imbued the Lost Cause of the Confederacy with moral righteousness. The death of Jefferson Davis in 1888 and his subsequent reinternment in Richmond's Hollywood Cemetery in 1893 were particularly momentous events that reawakened and strengthened southern sectionalism.[40]

The Lost Cause sought not only to glorify the noble but ill-fated cause of the Confederacy but also to revamp the image of the South's antebellum slave society. This emphasis by New Southites on the idyllic days of the Old South was well received by audiences in both the South and the North. In the South it functioned as a "soothing salve," reassuring southerners that they had done nothing shameful.[41] Military defeat did not equal moral inferiority; southerners could still hold their heads high as they moved boldly into the future. As a poem popular in the postwar South put it, the Confederacy had been, and the South continued to be, a "gallant nation, foiled by numbers."[42] By the 1880s, northerners too had developed a soft spot in their hearts for the romanticized mythos of the splendorous bygone South. In what one historian has called "a national love feast for the Old South," plantation-themed literature became immensely popular in the North.[43] As Kathleen Minnix explains, "Yankees longed for the balm of mythology, for tales of chivalrous knights in gray and belles who moved gently through a magnolia-scented world."[44] Northern authors became the primary producers of works praising the cavalier legend of life in the Old South as a new genre of "plantation romance" developed after the war.[45] In her 1886 novel *Atlanta in the South*, Maud Howe—whose mother had penned the "Battle Hymn of the Republic," which had inspired Union soldiers as they crushed the southern rebellion a generation earlier—lauded the bucolic plantation life of the Old South, where blacks had enjoyed greater happiness than they would later find in freedom.[46]

Foremost among those authors whose work influenced the popular conception of plantation life in the Old South was northerner F. Hopkinson Smith. His 1891 *Colonel Carter of Cartersville* helped establish in the northern imagination a stereotype of the antebellum southern aristocrat as chivalrous, well-mannered, hospitable, resistant to modernity, courtly toward women, and faithfully served by amenable, happy slaves who were almost part of the family.[47] The "new cavalier literature" that came out of the post-Reconstruction South lacked the anti-Yankee tone that had characterized much of the plantation-themed literature of the late antebellum South. "It glorified the South, but not at the expense of the North," says Lawrence Friedman.[48] Thus northern audiences and writers found it easy to embrace and emulate the glorification of Old South plantation life and its depiction of a kinder, gentler slavocracy. And, by extension, they found it easier to tolerate the latent racism that reemerged in the 1890s, when the Lost Cause ideology began to eclipse the New South optimism of the 1880s.

The Force Bill of 1890

As the 1880s drew to a close, the New South movement lost two of its key leaders: in 1889 Henry Grady passed away, and in 1890 Atticus Haygood was elected bishop of Los Angeles. Haygood had been elected bishop by the MECS in 1882 but turned down the appointment to continue his work for black education and prohibition in the southern states. When he was elected a second time, and by the largest vote ever cast for a bishop in the denomination, Haygood felt compelled to accept the honor and assumed his new assignment on the West Coast.[49] Haygood's absence from the South was brief; he departed for California in 1891 but returned to Georgia in 1893 due to failing health. But that interstice saw significant changes in southern race relations. When Haygood returned, he found that southern evangelicals' positive attitude toward blacks that had dominated the 1880s was quickly reversing course. During the remaining two years of his life, he would see a significant decline from the New South model of optimism and promise that he had done so much to establish since his 1880 Thanksgiving Day sermon.

The year 1890 marked a significant turning point in southern race relations as congressional actions fanned southern fears of African Americans' increased political power. Southern whites were rightfully worried when former Union general Benjamin Harrison won the presidency in 1888 and Republicans recaptured both houses of Congress in that election. In 1889 the new Republican majority launched an investigation into whether southern whites were suppressing the black vote, and in 1890 Senator Henry Cabot Lodge introduced a bill to end election fraud in the South and guarantee the full political participation of African Americans.[50] Known as the "Force Bill," because it authorized the use of military force to ensure compliance, Lodge's proposed legislation enraged southerners, who feared that it would usher in a black-dominated neo-Reconstruction government.

Southern evangelicals were no less incensed by the legislation than the rest of southern society, and many of them took to the pulpit, press, and platform to denounce what they saw as northern meddling in the South's race problems. In the process of defending southern handling of the race issue to date, these evangelicals revealed that a racist, Lost Cause–driven attitude was beginning to eclipse the more benevolent paternalism that had dominated 1880s evangelicalism. They also exposed a changing posture toward African Americans in relation to the prohibition movement and an increased advocacy of prohibition as the primary cure for the South's "Negro problem." With regard to racial issues, the common message that southern evangelicals sought to convey to the North in 1890 was one that defended the institution of slavery, lamented the enfranchisement of blacks, warned the North not to interfere in southern racial matters, and proposed that prohibition was the solution to the race problem.

Southern evangelicals in 1890 still held on to some of their old New South optimism with regard to blacks. "It is our deliberate conviction that the Negroes are making progress," wrote E. E. Hoss in an editorial entitled "Our Brother in Black," a reference to Haygood's 1881 book by the same title. Nevertheless, in the message of evangelicals such as Hoss, Lost Cause rhetoric played a greater role, most notably in the defense of slavery. Hoss, another editor of the *Christian Advocate*, still declared that he was pleased that slavery had ended. "That 'peculiar institution' has no more interest for us than a last year's bird's nest. From our heart we are sincerely glad that it belongs to the past, and not to the present or the future," he wrote. Hoss quickly followed this statement with a "nonetheless" and laid out a long defense of the bygone institution. Other evangelicals tended to skip the approval of emancipation and jumped straight to a defense of the ultimately beneficial nature of bondage for African Americans. "In spite of all the evils that were connected with it and flowed from it," Hoss explained, "it was, on the whole, a lifting force to the Negroes from the day they landed in America to the day of their emancipation."[51]

The thesis that slavery was a flawed but advantageous institution was a popular one among southern evangelicals in 1890. Another Tennessee Methodist, S. A. Steel, gave an address at a Chautauqua meeting in Bayview, Michigan, and argued that "God overreached the evil of slavery for the advancement of the Negro race." Likewise, the editor of the *Alabama Christian Advocate* elucidated, "we did not say there were in those days no cruel masters, any more than we say there are no cruel husbands and fathers." But despite the negative experiences blacks had in bondage, "slavery became a school to them in which they were civilized, instructed in the arts of life, the habits of industry and the religion of Christ." The editor claimed that, in the end, blacks had benefited from the experience of slavery because it brought them into contact with Christianizing and civilizing influences. Steel, pastor of McKendree Methodist Church in Nashville, asked, "where will you find 4,000,000 of the descendents of Ham outside of the United States who know the English language, who understand the arts of civilized labor, who are under the salutary influence of the Christian religion and who stand where the southern Negro stood when he received the gift of freedom?"[52]

In April 1890, O. P. Fitzgerald, coeditor of the *Christian Advocate* of Nashville, gave a speech before the National Reform Association in Washington, D.C., titled "The Southern Race Problem." Fitzgerald reminded his audience that "there are more professed Christians among the Negroes in these southern states than in all the world besides." Hoss reiterated that "the average Negro of the southern states, in the year of our Lord, 1865, stood on a higher level than any large number of his kinsmen had ever occupied in any part of the world in any age in human history." W. C. McCoy, editor of the *Alabama Christian Advocate*, expressed many of the same themes as Fitzgerald and Steel. He sought to soften the popular image of slavery and give it a paternalistic spin, noting that "the parental method of settling difficulties between the slaves, even with the lash, after each party had made his statement, gave him an idea of justice." He went on to argue that other aspects of plantation life instilled in African Americans "an idea of the proper relationship between God and man" and "fixed in them the basis of a civilization which was infinitely better than their fathers have ever worked out in Africa." In the end, McCoy justified slavery, saying, "The old slave code does look bloody, but in actual administration it was not half so bloody as it looked, being mitigated and softened by the pecuniary interest and benevolent feelings of the masters." Even Haygood referred to slavery as a "ministry" that had raised Africans out of barbarism.[53]

By the early 1890s, even the most optimistic New South evangelicals began to argue that the burden of suffrage might be too great for African Americans to bear. Steel believed that granting the franchise to freedmen was a "stupendous mistake." He observed, "Even the North seems to be coming to realize that this measure was a mistake." Likewise, Fitzgerald declared, "When the suffrage was suddenly thrust upon the Negroes in the South the great body of them was unprepared to meet its responsibility." The current problems regarding black voting in the South should not come as a surprise, he said. It "was bargained for when ballots were placed in the hands of a vast body of men unable to read them, and who were manifestly disqualified to perform the duties of electors with advantage to themselves or with safety to the state." Like Steel, Fitzgerald believed that people in the North now recognized that postwar enfranchisement was a mistake. "Our fellow citizens of the North are themselves groaning under the burdens and alarmed at the increasing dangers of indiscriminate suffrage, and are now seeking to discover some means of relief," he observed, saying that this was "a fact which should cause them to exercise some patience and charity toward their fellow countrymen in the South who are dealing with the same problem in another form."[54]

Southern evangelicals assured their northern listeners that despite any malicious reports they might be receiving about the state of African Americans in the South, the lot of southern blacks was in fact steadily improving. Much of this progress was owed to the selfless and magnanimous work of southern whites, they reminded their hearers. Blacks in the South were becoming wealthier and more educated landowners, Fitzgerald reported. "The Negroes are free and prosperous and happy," Steel promised his Michigan audience, "they are making more rapid progress than any other people ever made from barbarism to their education."[55] Blacks were painted as the beneficiaries of the great generosity of southern whites.

"Since the Negroes were set free," McCoy explained, "millions of dollars [had been] raised annually by voluntary taxation upon the property of the whites to educate the blacks," and "thousands [were] given privately every year to aid in building churches and for almost every other object of Negro fancy or want." Blacks were treated as fairly as—or even more fairly than—anyone else in legal matters, McCoy wrote. "Whenever a Negro has to be tried in the courts he invariably prefers a white jury to a black one," he explained, because of the whites' attitude of pity and forgiveness toward blacks in southern culture.[56] McCoy argued that lack of social equality did not constitute a denial of civil rights.[57] He was confident that intermarriage and total social equality between blacks and whites would never occur because no matter how wealthy, educated, and cultured a black man might become, no white woman would ever marry him. She would always prefer a man "of white skin and pure Caucasian lineage." But contrary to what some "fanatical minds" might believe, that did not mean that blacks were being denied their civil rights. "There is no hostility in the southern white man toward the Negro, nor in the Negro toward the white man," McCoy maintained.[58]

Evangelical writers in 1890 were confident that the one thing the southern race situation did not need was meddling by the federal government. Steel questioned the wisdom of legislation that would "rend asunder people who now love and trust and help each other and embroil them in a deadly antagonism by an effort to redress imaginary wrong." McCoy added, "If outsiders would be content to attend to their own affairs and let us alone, these mutual feelings of good will would never be disturbed." Fitzgerald concurred, writing, "There is no need for interference from the federal government in the management of the race problem in the South." Making a political issue out of the race problem was a mistake, said Steel, just as it had been with slavery in the past. He was confident that "if we could have kept the question of slavery out of the hands of politicians, the Christianity of America would in time have set the Negroes free without shedding a drop of blood." Likewise, he was confident that the Christians of the South would resolve any lingering racial strife in the region, as long as the North did not interfere.[59]

Southern evangelicals made it clear that they feared the Force Bill would lead to a black-dominated neo-Reconstruction government in the South. Southern whites had endured such a system once, and now that the southern governments had been redeemed, they vowed never to stand for it again. The threat of federal legislation to guarantee the full political participation of blacks led New South evangelicals to call into question blacks' right to vote at all. Although they had never been fully convinced of the wisdom of postwar enfranchisement, their opposition to black voting rights had been muted during the 1880s. This was due in part to their optimistic hope that, through education and moral instruction, black votes could be marshaled into a bloc supportive of prohibition and other reforms. Southerners in the 1880s were also generally agreeable to black suffrage because, as the decade wore on, fewer and fewer blacks exercised their voting rights. Steel explained that blacks had realized that "their interests are identified with ours . . . that they have nothing to gain from politics." The fact that they "quietly and wisely acquiesce in the inevitable supremacy of the whites," Steel believed, was "one of the most favorable conditions of their progress" and was "largely due to the growth of a better feeling towards the whites."[60] Favorable to whom, Steel did not say.

Patience, not officious legislation, was what the South required, said southern evangelicals. Steel warned that the Force Bill would "make the solid South more solid" by subjugating the many causes that currently divided southern Democrats (including silver, prohibition, tariffs) and unite them "along the lines of self-preservation." White southerners would never again acquiesce to black political supremacy. "We know from experience that Negro rule is intolerable," Steel explained. The bitterness of postwar feelings might have excused its implementation in the 1860s, but not in 1890. "We will not submit to Negro rule," Steel promised his northern audience. "We are willing to lift the Negro up; we are resolved he shall not drag us down." Steel and other evangelicals in 1890 began to express a much stronger advocacy of a Herrenvolk democracy—a democratic society dominated by whites, regardless of whether they enjoyed numerical superiority. McCoy expressed these sentiments well in the *Alabama Christian Advocate:* "The whites will hold and exercise the power both of making the laws and of executing them, even in states and counties where the majority of voters are black." The postwar experience of black political ascendancy "cleared away all the clouds, and revealed plainly the ground which the whites are obliged to take."[61]

If federal intervention was not the solution to the racial problems in the South, what was? Beginning in 1890, evangelicals increasingly promoted prohibition as the principal remedy for the region's racial strife. Fitzgerald said, "Of the so-called race troubles in the South whisky has been the cause of almost every case that has come within my personal knowledge. . . . What are called race troubles in the South are mostly whisky troubles . . . close the saloons, and the race problem is half solved."[62] One finds this remedy proposed by Alabama Baptists in 1890 as well. "We don't remember to have seen a single account of a riot or trouble between the races except where it was precipitated either by drunken white or Negro men," wrote the editor of the *Alabama Baptist.* "Nearly every Negro who kills one of his color is maddened by liquor, and the same is true of the whites."[63] In Georgia, Senator Alfred H. Colquitt began to advocate prohibition "as the best and surest solution of the Negro problem." Colquitt, a former Methodist preacher, former Confederate general, former Georgia governor, and ardent New Southite in the 1880s, said in 1890 that "it is a liquor conflict, not a race issue." The editor of the *Alabama Baptist* wrote that abolishing the saloons "would very nearly put an end to those crimes of violence which are now attributed to race prejudices."[64] Prohibition thus took on a new role: the cure for the region's "Negro problem." Whereas in the 1880s it had served as a needed moral reform to aid the New South in its journey toward productivity, efficiency, and thrift, in the 1890s it was increasingly promoted as a silver bullet to end the region's racial woes.[65]

1890s—The Return of Sambo

After 1890, the Old South ideology and outlook began to dominate southern thought, and the southern white attitude toward blacks continued to become progressively more pessimistic, negative, and distrustful. The southern evangelicals' view of their black neighbors began to resemble the so-called Sambo image that had flourished in southern culture during the final decades of slavery.[66] Williamson describes how Sambo—a common name given to second-born sons in many African cultures, and a popular name among southern slaves—became an antebellum southern stereotype of slaves as simplistic, childlike creatures. The black man was "an adult black body with a child's mind and heart" who had the potential either to be amiable and obedient like a white child or to revert to his unruly, barbaric nature. It all depended on how the white master—Sambo's adopted parent—cared for, nurtured, and disciplined him.[67] As Stanley Elkins has explained, Sambo had a childlike personality, "docile but irresponsible, loyal but lazy, humble but chronically given to lying and stealing."[68] Sambo's infantile qualities and his utter dependence on his master for guidance and instruction dominated the late antebellum white mind and provided fodder for the paternalism of the age.

A sort of neo-Sambo image of southern blacks emerged in the 1890s. Southern writers, politicians, and preachers increasingly portrayed African Americans as childlike creatures who must be protected and parented by white men—the "adults" in society, as it were—for their own good. This was also seen as being for the good of society, for in the 1890s, whites became convinced that blacks were regressing instead of progressing. It was widely believed that if not properly restrained and guided by his betters, the black man would quickly revert to his barbaric nature and become a menace to society. Southern evangelicals also embraced the more pessimistic view of the possibility of black improvement embodied in the Sambo image of African Americans. Whereas New South evangelicals in the 1880s had pushed for black education based on a belief that African Americans had significant potential for mental and moral advancement, by the late 1890s, such sanguinity had largely been replaced by condescending paternalism.

The editor of the *Alabama Baptist* wrote, "A little learning is a dangerous thing for the Negro, and but a few of them have the capacity, the brain power, to get more than a little." African Americans were simple beings designed by God for simple labor, the writer explained. Perpetuating the Sambo image of a simpleton who could be docile if correctly supervised, the editor wrote, "He is not of a vicious, spiteful race, when properly treated . . . he is, as a race, a hewer of wood and a drawer of water, made so by the unalterable decree of God."[69] Rudyard Kipling's poem "The White Man's Burden," published in February 1899 to encourage America to become the imperial caretaker of the Filipinos, offered imagery that southern evangelicals quickly seized on to describe white southerners' task in overseeing these volatile black creatures. A. J. Dickinson, pastor of Birmingham's Fist Baptist Church, explained in April 1899 that in addition to whites' burden overseas, southern whites had their own special burden to bear: the ignorant black man.[70] Like many other southerners, evangelicals embraced a more sinister paternalism that viewed blacks not as men of great untapped potential but rather as childlike creatures trapped in perpetual ignorance and dependency.[71]

As the southern evangelical view of African Americans became more pessimistic in the 1890s and 1900s, prohibition was thought to be the solution to the region's racial woes. John E. White, a Baptist minister in Atlanta, summed up the Sambo image several years later, observing that southerners were becoming increasingly aware that "the Negro constitutes a child-people element in our population, that the great mass of the Negroes are ignorant and weak and therefore are to be thought for in government and protected from the perils of liberty."[72] One of those "perils of liberty," it turned out, was the franchise. It was not a great leap from the premise that blacks were childlike and immature to the conclusion that they had no business being in the voting booth. Already, the almost universal belief among white southerners was that blacks should not have been enfranchised so quickly after emancipation. To this was added the widespread conviction that blacks were no more qualified to cast a ballot now than they had been immediately after the war and that, by and large, they were incapable of making such an advancement. The movement to disfranchise the black man in the South gathered steam throughout the 1890s. In the 1880s many New Southites had seen education as "the great panacea for the South."[73] By 1890, the *Memphis Avalanche* observed that white men no longer sat around trying to devise ways to raise money for schools for the black man; instead, they were now "restlessly employed in searching for some means to make him a nonentity in politics."[74] Two developments in the 1890s proved especially important in driving southern evangelicals to embrace disfranchisement: the realization that black voters would not support prohibition, and the political lessons learned from the failed attempts by the Populist and Prohibition parties to pry white voters away from the Democratic Party.

At the beginning of the 1880s, most whites in the South had accepted black suffrage as a fact of life. In 1879 Georgia native and Mississippi senator L. Q. C. Lamar claimed that no southern man of influence believed in the possibility of disfranchisement. Wade Hampton, South Carolina's senator and former governor, concurred that it would be impossible to disfranchise black voters now, and he claimed that southerners would not do so even if it were an option.

In 1880 the *Atlanta Constitution* proclaimed that black suffrage was here to stay and that the southern people accepted this reality.[75] In the 1890s, however, southerners rejected the permanence of this political reality. Southern evangelicals increasingly embraced the premise that blacks were not capable of managing the responsibility of voting.

In 1889 Henry A. Scomp, one of Georgia's leading evangelical prohibitionists, began to suggest that black suffrage was at the root of many of the South's racial problems. The simple fact that African Americans had the right to vote was not troubling to Scomp; the problem was what blacks, as a group, tended to vote for. Scomp posed the question to his readers: "But what seek those dark ballots?" What they sought, he concluded, was to vote en masse against anything supported by whites. He believed that if the majority of whites supported something—prohibition, for example—that was enough to convince the black population to oppose it. Each election therefore devolved into "simply an opportunity for division of races." The result was heightened racial antagonism, with blacks consistently voting against the best (i.e., white-supported) candidates and legislative measures.[76] A writer to the *Alabama Baptist* in 1899 argued that repealing the Fifteenth Amendment was "the only permanent solution of the race problem."[77]

The process by which blacks were excluded from the democratic process varied from state to state. In 1889 Tennessee lawmakers implemented a poll tax, voter registration restrictions, and the Australian (or secret) ballot, all with the express purpose of restricting African American voting rights. The last of these measures, the Dortch secret ballot bill, was one of the most effective means of restricting black suffrage. Although it was initially applied only to the districts with the largest black populations, the Dortch law was extended in 1897 and again in 1901. In 1893 Alabama also passed a secret ballot law. These laws drastically diminished black voting rates by forcing African American voters to enter the voting booth alone. No party operative could assist them in reading and marking their ballots, which listed only the candidates' names, not their party affiliation.[78] In 1901 Alabama held a constitutional convention that resulted in the imposition of poll taxes, literacy tests, and residency requirements to disfranchise black men almost completely. After the new constitution took effect, the number of eligible black voters in the state dropped from 181,000 to less than 3,000. Georgia was the only southern state to have a poll tax in place throughout the 1880s, which stultified black participation in elections there. For the 1900 elections, the Georgia legislature mandated that all candidates be nominated by all-white primaries; this left black voters who could pay the poll tax free to vote for the white-picked candidates of their choice in the general election. Not until 1908 were black Georgians fully disfranchised via constitutional amendment.[79]

Northern whites in the 1890s served as enablers of the southern attitude that black voting rights could and should be curtailed. Just as northerners in the 1880s had been enamored of visions of a grand and genteel Old South, in the following decade they began to question the wisdom of universal male suffrage in the southland. In 1890 Henry C. Vedder, editor of the *Baptist Quarterly Review* in New York, conceded that "to give the ballot to the Negro was one of those gigantic blunders that are worse than crimes." He criticized southern politicians for their use of fraud and intimidation to quash the Negro vote in the South, but in the end, he absolved them. They were, after all, merely attempting to regain "the political supremacy they should never have lost." Vedder expressed optimism that the color line in the South would gradually diminish and blacks would catch up with whites in terms of intellectual and moral development. In the meantime, the proper course of action was to undo the wrong the North had done by enfranchising freedmen, and he suggested that limiting the right to vote solely to those who "have the intelligence necessary for its proper exercise" would not violate the Constitution.[80] The *American Missionary* also sympathized with the southern predicament. "In some of the states the colored voters outnumbered the whites, and when they had the reins of power their rule was disastrous," the magazine's editor noted in 1892. He added that "the southern problem is to prevent this."[81] Such a view of black voting rights became increasingly widespread in the North during the 1890s. In the 1896 case of *Plessy v. Ferguson,* the Supreme Court endorsed the principle of separate but equal, and two years later in *Williams v. Mississippi,* it sanctioned the disfranchisement of black voters in Mississippi by means of a literacy test.[82]

Both Populists and Bourbon Democrats had motives for disfranchising African Americans. Although the Populist movement had a strong biracial quality in its early stages, by the mid-1890s, most

Populists had come to believe that blacks were the greatest hindrance to their goal of toppling the Democratic Party. Bourbons had successfully used the rhetoric of white supremacy and racial fear-mongering to dissuade many would-be Populists from joining a movement that allowed a place at the table for blacks. Furthermore, Populists realized that through corruption and intimidation, Democrats had been able to use the massive number of black voters in the Black Belt counties to offset the turnout of Populists in the hill counties, thereby denying many statewide victories to the Populist Party.[83] Bourbon Democrats, meanwhile, sought to disfranchise black voters because of the constant threat they posed to Democratic hegemony in the region. Both Reconstruction-era Republican rule and the near victories of Populists in the mid-1890s made Bourbons painfully aware of the precarious nature of their political control, and in both cases, control of the black vote was the crucial factor. In addition, Democrats wanted to disfranchise many of the poor, upcountry, rural whites who harbored habitual animosity toward the Bourbon elites. Thus, they were hopeful that disfranchisement mechanisms such as poll taxes, literacy tests, and property ownership requirements would eliminate threats both black and white.

Evangelical prohibitionists, whether Democrat or Populist, had other reasons for endorsing disfranchisement. They were convinced that African Americans would not become a dry voting bloc, after all. They also believed that an open and productive debate on the issue of prohibition, free of racial demagoguery, could not take place until blacks were no longer allowed to vote. In 1898 Presbyterian Alexander McKelway defended the southern aspiration to disfranchise blacks. He deemed it unfair and dangerous for a constituency that owned less than 5 percent of the property in a town to possess the political power to make the town's laws and run its government. Speaking to a northern audience, McKelway sought to elicit their empathy by drawing the following analogy: "Suppose the Chinese should elect by their own votes, in New York City, a governor who should prevail upon the legislature to change the charter so as to turn the city government over into the hands of the Chinese, owning five percent of the property, and utterly unfit to rule, how long would the Revolution be deferred?"[84]

In 1900 the *Alabama Baptist* editor proclaimed, "the great trouble growing out of the Negro problem is the right to vote." He explained that "the trouble lies in the want of a knowledge of the power and the sacredness of the ballot." The editor urged his readers to vote for a state constitutional convention to disfranchise blacks, saying, "This is a government of the white man, and the welfare of both races demand that it shall remain forever in the hands and under the control of white men."[85]

During the 1880s, Sam Jones, a champion of the New South ideology, had warned his fellow Georgians that preventing African Americans from voting was a damnable offense in the eyes of God.[86] But by 1900, Jones endorsed Georgia's new all-white primary system. According to Jones, African American Georgians had brought this loss of suffrage rights upon themselves. "The Negro is to blame largely for this state of things," he explained, "for if the Negro had realized that the best white people of the South were his best friends and he had quit ganging with the liquor crowd and let Yankee-Doodle alone he would have been much better off today."[87] These two issues—the perception that black votes were routinely being bought by wet candidates, and the belief that outside agitators from the North were fomenting southern blacks' animosity toward whites—were common themes among southern white evangelicals.

Jones was not the only southern evangelical to draw a direct connection between disfranchisement and black opposition to prohibition. Southern evangelicalism's shift in thinking about black potential and black suffrage was driven in large measure by its continued desire to pass prohibition legislation. By the end of the 1880s, evangelicals' optimism that blacks could be nurtured and educated into a voting bloc supportive of prohibition began to fade. They increasingly came to believe that black men were puppets of the saloon interests and consistently voted against prohibition measures and dry candidates. W. B. Crumpton, the leading prohibition crusader of Alabama, argued that disfranchising blacks would remove "the single most powerful political weapon of the saloon interests."[88] In 1891 a Birmingham minister complained to the *Alabama Baptist* about the negative impact of black voters on the issue of prohibition, grousing, "the vote of the ignorant Negro who works as a porter in the store of the upright and enterprising white man, makes the law which is to govern the society which must surround and inevitably touch the very characters of the sons and daughters of the Anglo-Saxons."[89] The growing perception that blacks largely voted wet, combined with anger over this constituency's power to prevent the passage of local option laws and the election of dry politicians, led many evangelicals to embrace disfranchisement as the only hope for the success of prohibition.

The defeat of statewide prohibition in Tennessee in 1887 and the repeal of local option in Atlanta the same year fed this assessment that most blacks voted wet. The leader of the Young Men's Prohibition League in Atlanta immediately blamed the defeat of local prohibition on the desertion of "thirsty" blacks from the temperance ranks.[90] Examining the results of the 1887 vote in Tennessee on a prohibition amendment, Joseph Cartwright argues that a majority of both blacks and whites voted against the amendment.[91] Nevertheless, prohibitionists targeted black voters as the source of the defeat, which galvanized support among southern prohibitionists for the removal of blacks from the political process. After the defeat of the prohibition amendment, the editor of the *Christian Advocate* in Nashville wrote, "The liquor men in Tennessee owe their temporary escape to the black voters they sent to the polls, inflamed with whiskey, feed with their money, and wearing their badges." He and other prohibitionists were becoming increasingly convinced that high black turnout on election day meant disaster for the prohibition cause. "Wherever the Negro vote was strong prohibition was weak," the paper concluded.[92]

Furthermore, prohibitionists were hopeful that disfranchisement of black voters would aid the cause by allowing white voters to freely challenge and even desert the Democratic Party without fear of a Republican takeover. With the rise and fall of populism in the early and mid-1890s, prohibitionists had learned that attempting to rebel against the Democratic Party because of its failure to embrace prohibition was a losing battle. Bourbon Democrats would respond with threats that any such division of the Democratic ranks would open the door for black-supported Republicans to defeat both the Democratic and third-party candidates. Prohibitionists believed that factoring the African American vote out of the equation would allow white Democrats to split over the liquor issue and facilitate the victory of prohibition. Following the passage of a disfranchisement amendment in North Carolina in 1900, McKelway praised the removal of "the shadow of Negro domination." He reported that "the Liquor Dealers' Association in the state is in despair" and predicted that disfranchisement would soon spell victory for prohibition.[93] In Alabama,

S. O. Y. Ray was likewise confident after the adoption of Alabama's new constitution in 1901. He declared, "The stronghold of the whiskey power in the state has been eliminated by the disfranchisement of the Negro, and others like them, and now with a fair fight and a fair count we can carry the state."[94]

Evangelicals and Lynching

Concurrent with the rise of an increasingly negative view of blacks in the 1890s came a dramatic increase in mob violence by whites, primarily targeting blacks. An epidemic of lynching began to sweep the southern states in the 1890s. Between 1885 and 1903 there were 3,337 mob killings in the United States, 2,585 of which transpired in the South. This figure does not include acts of terrorism that did not result in death; these acts, known as charivari, included beatings, whippings, and tar-and-feathering.[95] Most victims of mob action were black, but not all. Between 1882 and 1913, 402 lynchings took place in Georgia, 310 in Alabama, and 240 in Tennessee. Blacks accounted for more than 90 percent of the victims in Georgia, 85 percent in Alabama, and slightly less than 80 percent in Tennessee.[96] Lynching, though not a uniquely southern form of violence, was disproportionately practiced by southerners and rapidly increased during the final decades of the twentieth century.[97]

The church, which had become a powerful institution in southern culture by the end of the nineteenth century, has long been implicated in this rash of racial violence. In 1929 Walter White, an assistant secretary of the National Association for the Advancement of Colored People (NAACP), investigated lynching in the South and accused southern evangelicalism of being culpable for the carnage that took place in the region beginning in the 1880s. "Not only through tacit approval and acquiescence has the Christian church indirectly given its approval to lynch-law and other forms of race prejudice," White wrote, "but the evangelical Christian denominations have done much towards creation of the particular fanaticism which finds an outlet in lynching."[98] Recent historians have a more nuanced view of the complicity of southern evangelicals in the lynching epidemic. Although southern evangelicalism certainly functioned to a large extent as a "culture church," validating the practices of the larger society around it, there is also a striking tradition of southern evangelicals challenging the values and racial attitudes of southern society.

The evangelical response to lynching was neither universal nor resolute. One can say that southern evangelicals, as a whole, simultaneously censured lynching and were sympathetic to and often forgiving of the emotions and societal forces that led to such lawless acts. Evangelicals often took an ambivalent stance on the issue. Sam Jones, for example, condemned mob justice but understood that some crimes—the rape of a white woman, in particular—were so heinous that any response other than lynching was unacceptable to most white men. As Jones put it, "rape means rope in every state in the Union."[99] Historian Hugh Bailey charges that many evangelicals "encouraged lynching by accepting the lyncher's rationale—the contention that the Negro was a beast and that such action was the best defense against rape."[100] A Georgia Baptist editor provided a good example of this when he explained, "We do not defend the lynching, but he who commiserates [with] the brute is far more despicable than the lynchers!"[101] When the Southern Baptist Convention passed a resolution condemning lynching in 1906, members were careful to note that they also condemned "with equal emphasis, and in many cases with much greater emphasis," the crimes that precipitated most lynchings.[102] In 1899 the editor of the *Christian Index* in Georgia noted that "by common consent, lynching for rape has been made an offence to be condoned." Rather than challenging this societal approbation, however, the Baptist editor sought only to limit its extension. He wrote, "But only when, by common consent, all other forms of mob violence are utterly repudiated, can we justify ourselves among civilized people." Some evangelicals were willing to grant that mob justice in retaliation for rape was excusable, so long as it did not encourage people to settle other disputes by extralegal means.[103]

Southern evangelicals did speak out against the act of lynching beginning at the end of the 1880s. In 1889 the editor of the *Alabama Baptist* applauded an Alabama couple who tried to prevent the lynching of a black man, even though he was accused of raping the woman.[104] In this editorial, as elsewhere, lax law enforcement was blamed for much of the lynching in the South. "I honestly believe that fifty percent of the lynchings in Alabama is due to the tardiness of the law," sermonized the pastor of a Baptist church in Mobile.[105] In 1890 the *Alabama Baptist* delighted in the news that more criminals were being executed by the state, believing that the stern enforcement of the law would squelch extralegal justice.[106] Still, a reader wrote to the paper expressing dismay that it had not been more vocal in condemning mob violence. "I'm opposed to lynching," he proclaimed, and urged the state to act decisively against lynchers and treat them as the murderers they are.[107] In 1894 the *Alabama Baptist* ran two editorials praising the increasing rejection of lynching by Alabamians and blaming the slow judicial process for much of the epidemic. The editor wrote, "The law's delays and the consequent uncertainty in the public mind have had much to do with the increase of lawlessness of late years."[108] Haygood condemned lynching in no uncertain terms. "A country given over to lynch law is damned," he said, adding on another occasion that "lynching is anarchy." Haygood, whose tireless advocacy for and support of the black community had earned him the nickname the "nigger bishop" in some quarters, urged the formation of Law and Order Leagues to guarantee that the legal process was carried out fully, fairly, and swiftly.[109] This conviction that mob violence was an assault on the authority of the government and the orderliness of society was popular among southern evangelicals.[110]

There were, however, limits to how much criticism of mob justice the southern masses would take from evangelicals. The most notable example of an evangelical who crossed this invisible line was Andrew Sledd, a Methodist minister and professor at Emory College in Oxford, Georgia. He was also the son-in-law of Methodist bishop Warren A. Candler, a powerful family tie that did not, in the end, protect him from the wrath of a public offended by Sledd's attack on lynching. The "Sledd affair," as it became known, began when Sledd published an article in the *Atlantic Monthly* called "The Negro: Another View"; it ended when he was fired from Emory and briefly exiled from the South. In the 1902 article, Sledd proposed to present a "calm, unbiased" examination of the black man, one that fell somewhere between the "two extremes" represented by the typical northern and southern views of African Americans. His basic argument was that blacks are inferior to whites, but they nonetheless possess inalienable rights. Sledd had been motivated to write the article after finding himself on a train with several marshals who were rumored to be transporting an African American prisoner accused of murder. As the train stopped at various stations along its route, it was met by angry mobs prepared to "mete out summary vengeance" to the accused man. Fortunately, the prisoner was not actually on the train. At about the same time, however, another accused black man in Georgia was not so fortunate. Sledd's article highlighted the brutal execution of Sam Hose at the hands of an angry mob on a Sunday afternoon in rural Georgia.[111] Trains loaded inside and out with passengers made special trips to the scene of the atrocity, where they eagerly witnessed the execution and subsequent mutilation and burning of Hose. Sledd decried how such mobs, made up of "coarse, and beastly, and drunk" lower-class whites, became filled with "a blood lust that wild beasts know" and gathered to view "the indescribable and sickening torture and writhing of a fellow human being." Afterward, they took home his charred bones as souvenirs.[112]

Sledd denounced lynching as "the purest savagery" and went on to attack discrimination against respectable blacks.[113] Lynching was an indefensible crime, he argued, even in defense of the virtue of southern white womanhood. Sledd also expressed a sentiment that, by the turn of the century, had become almost extinct in the South: that blacks possessed a remarkable potential for progress and betterment. Historian Henry Y. Warnock has argued that Sledd represents "a current of racial interest beginning to run strongly in the Methodist church by 1900."[114] However, Sledd's views more accurately represent not a current that was "beginning to run strongly" but rather one that was beginning to run out of steam in the midst of a larger culture that was beginning to run out of patience with evangelical optimism about blacks and condemnation of white vigilantes. Sledd stood as one of the few heirs of the optimism of the New South movement at the end of the century. At the very least, he represented one of the few southern evangelical voices calling for racial and sectional reconciliation and cooperation as the nadir of evangelical racial attitudes rapidly approached.

Sledd's article failed to cause a stir in the South until it was attacked by a fellow Georgia Methodist and a major radical political figure, Rebecca Latimer Felton. She had the article reprinted in the *Atlanta Constitution* and stirred up a firestorm of angry protests aimed not only at the young professor, whom she branded a traitor, but also at Emory College and Felton's longtime nemesis, Bishop Candler. By the next day it had become a front-page controversy, and the trustees of Emory began to feel the pressure, led by Felton, to rid themselves of Sledd. Emory president James Dickey asked Sledd for his resignation, but Sledd refused. In the end, a compromise was reached, and Sledd was granted enough money to subsidize the pursuit of his Ph.D. at Yale in return for his resignation. Although he was offered teaching positions at both Stanford and Syracuse universities, as well as the presidency of a college in Ohio, Sledd chose to return to the South after finishing at Yale. He took a position at Southern University, a Methodist school in Alabama.[115]

Scholars have proffered several explanations of why Sledd's article aroused such widespread antipathy toward its author. Its antilynching theme was, after all, not unheard of within the evangelical ranks. Evangelical pastors continued to condemn the brutality and lawlessness of lynch mobs, generally without being fired and banished from the region. Why, then, did Sledd's article touch off such controversy? Most historians have focused on the ill will between Felton and Sledd's father-in-law, Candler. Felton had long been a vocal critic of the Candler family and the Georgia Methodist hierarchy, calling them all despots. This animosity stemmed in large part from political differences between Felton, a Greenback-turned-agrarian-turned-Populist, and the Candlers, conservative Democrats whose fortunes were continually on the rise.[116] The Candler family represented the kind of urban, newly rich Bourbon Democrats that Felton and her husband, Populist politician William H. Felton, had devoted their lives to removing from political and ecclesiastical power. Although Felton claimed to have been unaware of Sledd's relation to Candler when she launched her assault, Candler was certain that she had used the article as an excuse to attack him.[117]

As Sledd's experience demonstrates, evangelicals walked a fine line when they denounced lynching. Most evangelicals who condemned lynching did not face repercussions as severe as those felt by Sledd. They were, however, frequently chastised by those outside the church, and sometimes by those within. When one Georgia minister went so far as to expel a congregant for participating in a lynching, twenty-five members walked out of the church. In 1897 the local paper of Dalton, in northern Georgia, lambasted Atlanta preachers, saying that they "seem to have run entirely out of gospel subjects to preach on. Last Sunday several of them preached against lynching, and not one of them preached against rape."[118] Many people in southern society felt that such mob actions were necessary, especially when a black man was accused of raping a white woman, and did not deserve condemnation by ministers.

The issue of rape—more specifically, the rape of a white woman by a black man—played a central role in the lynching epidemic at the turn of the century. Between 1882 and 1930, 90 percent of lynchings in the South were precipitated by the commission of a crime. Forty percent of the time, the person was accused of murder; 30 percent of the time, the alleged crime was sexual assault.[119] This latter charge, however, served as whites' primary justification for the practice of lynching. Beginning early in the 1890s, more and more black men were accused of—and summarily executed for—raping white women. By the middle of the 1890s, southern whites were convinced that this crime had reached epidemic proportions. Accusations of sexual assault by black men on white women increased in frequency during the 1890s and exploded after 1900, as did white mob retaliation.

1900s—The Black Beast

In 1900 Charles Carroll's book *The Negro a Beast* was published in the South. It caused a sensation by using both biblical and pseudo-Darwinian arguments to demonstrate that African Americans were not human beings at all but were, in fact, more closely akin to apes.[120] Carroll's book also revealed where southern thinking about blacks was headed. Two years later, Thomas Dixon Jr., a Baptist minister from North Carolina, wrote his novel *The Leopard's Spots*. That book sought to counter the more sympathetic view of African Americans that Dixon believed wrongly dominated the American mind. As these books demonstrate, the white image of black men devolved from the childlike Sambo of the 1890s to the increasingly popular "black beast" figure during the first decade of the twentieth century. Likewise, southern white rhetoric no longer portrayed blacks as childlike innocents needing guidance and protection; it now reflected the belief that black men had regressed to the savage beast that was an inescapable part of their nature. And with the rising number of rape allegations against black men, it became widely held among whites that blacks had a natural predisposition toward sexual immorality.[121]

Evangelicals perpetuated this new perception of African Americans as much as other white southerners did. A 1903 editorial in the

Alabama Christian Advocate warned that "there is going on a degeneracy among the Negroes that is appalling." The editor explained, "We are developing a new type of Negro unheard of until recent years, a conscienceless, lawless, fearless brute, led only by his strong animal nature fired by these devilish influences, and ready for rape, robbery, and murder."[122] The conviction among southern evangelicals that blacks were reverting to a more barbaric nature, leading to their commission of rape and other atrocities, was widespread. Dickinson argued that African Americans were regressing not only morally but also physically.[123] Haygood denounced the "gorilla ferocity" displayed by African Americans who attacked white women. The theory of black degeneracy came to dominate southern white evangelical thinking. Southern evangelicals argued that a grave process of retrogression had taken place; blacks were now more barbarous and a greater threat to society than when they had been under the ameliorating and restraining influences of slavery. Haygood had noted in 1893 that he could not recall a single incident of a black man attacking a white woman in the antebellum period.[124] McKelway in 1906 likewise wrote that such attacks had been unheard of in the days of slavery. "The Negro of slavery days or war times who would have attempted such a crime would have been torn to pieces by his fellow-slaves," claimed McKelway.[125]

Recent historians such as Edward Ayers have argued that the explosion of rape hysteria among white southerners, and the proliferation of lynchings in response, "began by a sort of spontaneous combustion fed by racial and sexual fears."[126] Joel Williamson has elaborated on this, presenting an intriguing, if perhaps over-psychoanalyzed, explanation of the rape hysteria in the 1890s and 1900s and the intensely violent response. He argues that the combination of economic depression, industrial change, and Victorian gender ideals coalesced into an outburst of unprecedented vengeance by southern white men. The worldwide economic depression that began in 1893 rendered many men incapable of supporting their families, as demanded by Victorian gender roles. Furthermore, these Victorian ideals elevated womanly virtue to an unprecedented level. According to Williamson, southern white men embraced the notion that because white women did not enjoy sex, men were obligated to abstain from such relations with white women—even their wives—as much as possible. Thus, southern white men, already feeling vulnerable because of their inability to meet the financial needs of their families, were particularly sensitive to the idea of black men having sexual relations with white women because it meant that "black men had achieved what white men, in the Victorian infatuation, had lost"—guilt-free sex. The white male reaction was fierce. "Black men were lynched," Williamson argues, "for having achieved a sexual liberation that white men could not achieve without great feelings of guilt." He suggests that blacks served as scapegoats for the frustrations whites were experiencing at the turn of the century. Whites constructed an enemy—a black beast against whom they must protect the women in their care—to give themselves the "illusion that they were indeed managing their lives in important ways."[127]

This image of lynching as a cathartic act, expunging southern white men of the deadly combination of racial hatred and frustrated sexual longing, comes out in William Faulkner's *Light in August*. The novel tells the story of Joe Christmas, a mixed-race man who kills a white woman. When Christmas escapes from prison, he is pursued relentlessly by Percy Grimm, who had longed after the murdered woman but had never possessed her. When he finally catches Christmas, Grimm shoots him and then castrates him. The act of lynching, Williamson and others would argue, represented a symbolic castration of black men in retaliation for their ability to obtain that which white men were unable to possess. Fitzhugh Brundage concurs that the idea of black men raping white women "represented a sexual liberation" that white southern men wanted but could not experience. To deal with their sexual desires impeded by Victorian mores, southern white men "projected their thoughts upon black men and symbolically eradicated these desires by lynching hapless blacks."[128] Wilbur J. Cash's *The Mind of the South* also recognizes this deadly combination of race and sex. In examining what he calls the southern "rape complex," Cash explains that the new legal opportunities available to black men after the Civil War jeopardized the old taboo against any kind of sexual approach toward white women. White men were anxious about what this meant for white women, who had long been identified with the purity of the South itself, and for their heirs, whose pure white lineage they desperately wanted to preserve. Thus, white men justified to themselves their violence toward African American men.[129]

The rape hysteria among whites and the idea of black degeneracy did not escape the attention of evangelical prohibitionists. In fact, it fed directly into their warnings about the dangers of liquor and served as a catalyst for a new wave of prohibition activity after the turn of the century. The evangelical critique of race-driven mob justice began to shift after 1900, and prohibition resurfaced as an important element in evangelical racial attitudes. Evangelicals offered prohibition as an alternative solution to the "Negro problem" (or "Negro menace," as they perceived it after 1900). Rather than arguing that lynching was morally wrong because it was brutal and violated the human rights of the accused black man, evangelicals argued that prohibition was a better way to stop blacks from raping white women. Eventually, much of the white male electorate in the South became convinced of the merits of this solution. It can be argued that prohibitionists both capitalized on racial fears to promote their cause and used prohibition to redirect the anger of white racists in a less violent, more moral direction.

The "rape narrative"—an account of how some Negro brute had attacked and ravished a defenseless white female—had become commonplace in southern society and was integral to the justification for lynching the accused and any other African American who stood between him and the mob.[130] During the first decade of the twentieth century, liquor became an important part of the rape narrative. A typical tale was this one published in the *Nashville Tennessean* in 1908: "Margaret Lear, fourteen years old, was walking home from the Shreveport High School . . . and her way took her past a Negro saloon. Out of that saloon staggered a Negro named Coleman— 'drunken,' ran the testimony at the trial, 'on cheap gin.' He followed her to a ditch on the edge of a field, assaulted her, and shot her."[131] Alcohol became a central ingredient in what James Morone has termed the "White Sermon," the familiar, recurring narrative of how a liquor-crazed black man had ravaged and killed yet another innocent white woman. As he says, "liquor, lust, and lynching all ran together, especially in the dangerous cities."[132] Evangelical prohibitionists used the centrality of liquor in the rape scourge—and the fury surrounding it—to marshal broad popular support among whites for statewide prohibition. They also emphasized the beast-making properties of the low-grade alcohol marketed to blacks, with its obscene and inflammatory packaging, and they promised that prohibition was the best way to eradicate sexual assaults on white women.

Evangelicals made a particularly strong connection between black lawlessness and the need for prohibition following the Atlanta race riots of 1906. Daily reports of black sexual assaults filled the Georgia secular press in the late summer of 1906.[133] These reports, combined with a gubernatorial campaign that saw an unprecedented degree of race-baiting, increased the racial tensions in Atlanta. On September 22 violence broke out, and for four days thousands of white men beat, shot, and lynched African American men in and around the city. Atlanta police did little to impede the violence, and troops had to be called in to restore order. In the end, ten blacks and two whites were reported killed in the riots.[134] The violence in Atlanta played right into the hands of evangelicals who were pushing for statewide prohibition legislation, and they redoubled their efforts. Immediately after the riots, the *Alabama Baptist* blazed the headline: "Atlanta Riots a Terrible Indictment of the Saloon." Northerner John Corrigan observed, "Had it not been for 'riot week' in Atlanta the state prohibition bill would not have been enacted this year. The lessons of that week were the most effective clubs in the hands of the prohibitionists, and furnished them most timely and unanswerable arguments."[135] Evangelicals immediately named liquor as the primary cause of racial violence, and they increasingly marketed statewide prohibition as the cure for the region's racial violence and the wave of black attacks on white women.

In the immediate aftermath of the Atlanta riots, Georgia evangelicals took the moral high ground. The editor of the *Wesleyan Christian Advocate* expressed dismay at the white mob violence and remorse for the innocent black victims, noting that "the better element of our population are deeply humiliated." The Methodists also observed that had their warnings about the dangers of alcohol been heeded, the riots could have been avoided. The editor reminded his readers that petitions had been signed prior to the riots, asking city officials to "close up the low, dirty dives around which Negroes loafed, alleging these places as one of the causes of the shocking number of assaults on white women by Negroes," yet they had been left open.[136] Georgia evangelicals also seized on the fact that during the riots, city officials had ordered all the saloons closed. "We close the saloons when the mob is on the rampage of blood," wrote the *Wesleyan Christian Advocate*, "but when the mob is out of sight, 'for revenue' we tolerate a business that makes mobs."[137] A group of evangelicals met at the Wesley Memorial Church in Atlanta just after the riots to mount an offensive against the saloon. "For the largest prosperity and good order of our city and county and the protection of our women from the assaults of criminal Negroes," they resolved, Fulton County must embrace prohibition on a permanent basis.[138]

The Atlanta riots were explained as a direct consequence of the flood of black-on-white rapes being reported in the Georgia press during the summer of 1906. McKelway explained, "If there had been no assaults upon white women in and near Atlanta, there would have been no mobs and no riots. That is a truism." In November 1906 he wrote an article about the riots for the *Outlook* subtitled "A Southern White Point of View." As he had a decade earlier when defending disfranchisement, McKelway drew an analogy between southern blacks and New York City's Chinese population, hoping to evoke northern understanding of and empathy for the situation in the South.

> May I suggest here a comparison? . . . Suppose in New York City there had been, say, four hundred and eighty assaults, or attempted assaults, upon white women of the city, by Chinese brutes—two hundred and forty in three days, one hundred and sixty in one afternoon; that the New York papers, yellow or otherwise, had published extras describing these assaults; that the police, with the best will in the world, had succeeded in arresting only a small number of these criminals . . . and that the whole white population of the city had come to believe that the different Chinese quarters of the city were hiding and protecting these criminals of their own race. . . . What would the New York mob have done under those circumstances? What could have prevented their indiscriminate slaughter of the Chinese?[139]

If the premise that black rapists were to blame for the riots had become a truism, as McKelway asserted, it was equally accepted that liquor was to blame for black rapists. McKelway elsewhere argued that local option was no longer sufficient; absolute prohibition across the state was needed to protect the "weaker race" and thereby protect white women from attack.[140]

The post-riot campaign by prohibitionists proved successful. Though he had not strongly supported statewide prohibition as a candidate in 1906, once he took office, Georgia governor Hoke

Smith increasingly embraced it as the best solution to what he called the direst threat to the state: the combination of liquor and blacks.[141] Georgia adopted statewide prohibition in 1907, which emboldened evangelicals across the South in their efforts to push prohibition as the solution to the threat of black brutes.[142] Evangelical prohibitionists ceased to rely solely on the argument that blacks were reverting to their bestial, uncivilized nature—that they were "lapsing into barbarism," as one evangelical put it in 1903.[143] After 1906, they began to focus on the external stimulus that turned the black man into a rapist: low-grade liquor and the suggestive and obscene labels that adorned it.

Prohibitionists targeted black saloons. The liquor commonly sold in the "low dives" that catered to a black clientele was alleged to be of a particularly low grade.[144] Corrigan explained that owing to fierce competition within the distilling industry, many manufacturers were producing "low-grade, 'mean' liquor" that had flooded into the black saloons in Georgia.[145] An investigative article by Will Irwin alleged that the bottles of gin sold at "every low Negro dive of the South" did not contain "what their labels imply; chemical analysis shows that the mixture is only cheap, blended gin, with a slight infusion, in some cases, of a sweetening which might be Benedictine."[146] Thus, the impact on the men who consumed it was believed to be even more destructive to their sense of morality and self-restraint than ordinary liquor was. "Inflamed by cheap liquor, which is sold at every cross-roads in the South," wrote Alabama Baptist B. F. Riley in his book *The White Man's Burden*, "the Negro was more easily manipulated against the white race."[147] The manipulation to which Riley referred was the suggestive labeling found on these bottles of cheap liquor.

Lewd Labels

In 1907 these obscene liquor labels became the core of prohibition propaganda, providing tangible evidence of the link between saloons and black sexual aggression. Vague yet titillating descriptions of the words and images on these labels were increasingly referenced by evangelical prohibitionists. Their descriptions had to be vague, of course, because standards of decency forbade full disclosure in a public forum. Horace DuBose, a Tennessee Methodist bishop, claimed that some of the labels were "so vile that if they were even described in these columns the paper would be excluded from the United States mail." DuBose explained that "the labels bear pictures of naked white females in positions, and with printed insinuations, too vile to be even thought upon."[148] The Reverend E. C. Atkins brought up the topic of obscene labels while speaking at a WCTU-sponsored rally in Nashville, but "to describe them in the presence of ladies would be a gross violation of common decency," he said.[149] The labels contained images that bordered on pornography, as well as slogans laden with sexual innuendo and suggestions that the liquor contained aphrodisiacs.

For southern prohibitionists, the labels constituted the smoking gun proving a direct connection between liquor and rape. The labels were blamed for instigating both the rape crisis and the lynchings and riots that had plagued southern society in recent years. Evangelicals rarely missed an opportunity to point out when such bottles were found in the possession of an accused black rapist. The *Nashville Tennessean* cited the example of Ed Johnson in Chattanooga, who had been accused of raping a young white girl. The paper charged that, when arrested, Johnson had "three bottles of the obscenely labeled gin in his possession." After several failed attempts to lynch Johnson, a mob was finally successful.[150] W. B. Crumpton likewise noted the discovery of such a bottle on a black man who had raped a white woman outside of Birmingham. DuBose connected the labels with the Atlanta riots, charging that afterward, "thousands of bottles of this elixir from hell were found in the low saloons and Negro dives." He attacked the Model Saloon License League, an organization representing liquor makers and dealers, charging that Lucifer himself could not have devised a more diabolical scheme than that hatched by white distillers when they marketed impure liquor with evocative labels to blacks. DuBose argued that the gin and its inflammatory label "has made more black rape fiends, and has procured the outrage of more white women in the South, than all other agencies combined."[151] Evangelical prohibitionists made it clear: so long as cheap, debilitating liquor in titillating packaging was available to black men, the white women of the South were unsafe. Atkins warned his Nashville audience that so long as this "aphrodisiacal gin" was being sold in the city, none of the young women in the audience was safe from sexual assault at the hands of a black man.[152]

For evangelical prohibitionists, the cause-and-effect relationship between liquor and lynching was clear. Southern black men were already reverting to their inherent barbaric nature, they believed. In addition, whatever inhibitions and sensibilities they did possess were being crippled by the cheap, impure liquor sold in black saloons. Even more impure were the mental images supplied by the liquor labels, encouraging inebriated black men to claim possession of that which was denied them: sexual liaisons with white women. Thus, black men emerged from these saloons as black beasts, bent on ravaging the first white females they encountered. Their subsequent brutal execution at the hands of white mobs was simply the culmination of a series of events launched from a simple source: the saloon. Eradicate these "deep, dark, damnable dens of degradation," prohibitionists promised, and the twin tragedies of rape and lynching would wither and disappear.[153]

In a series of articles for *Colliers* that were subsequently reprinted and widely quoted in the southern press and in religious newspapers, northern writer Will Irwin investigated the southern epidemic of rape and racial conflict. He too concluded that saloons selling liquor with suggestive labels to blacks were to blame for much of the region's turmoil. Irwin explained that the "obscene labels advertise by suggestion and double meaning, that these compounds contain a drug to stimulate the low passions which have made the race problem such a dreadful thing in the South."[154] Irwin also noted that the lewd suggestions and innuendos on these labels "are apparent only to one who knows southern Negro slang; the suggestions in their advertising cards and posters are only a little more open."[155] A 1909 editorial in the *Alabama Christian Advocate* pointed out the inflammatory and offensive nature of such posters and advertisements: "When the distillers placed the pictures of nude white women upon whiskey bottles and put them on sale in the low Negro dives of Alabama, thereby sowing seed which ripened into nameless outrages upon Alabama women, decent people thought the depth had been reached, but recent events have demonstrated that the worst was yet to come." Cartoons were also being circulated by liquor company representatives among patrons at black saloons, the paper reported. It described one that pictured "a pretty young white woman marching to the marriage altar leaning on the arm of a big black Negro." Such advertisements serve as "an incentive to the commission of outrage by vicious blacks," argued the Methodist editor.[156]

Regardless of whether the suggestive labels actually inflamed the baser passions of African American drinkers, they certainly inflamed white passion against the liquor industry. Many wets threw their support behind prohibition after viewing the vile bottles. At a Nashville rally, local attorney J. R. Aust stated that seeing one of these obscene bottles "had caused him to become a prohibitionist." A bottle had been passed around the rally for attendees to view, and the paper reported a general agreement "that this picture to a large extent was responsible for their attitude towards prohibition."[157] Evangelical prohibitionists recognized that these bottles served as effective propaganda for their cause. The bottles were frequently employed to outrage white voters and garner support for prohibition legislation.

In the summer of 1908, E. E. Folk used an obscenely labeled gin bottle as a campaign prop. Edward Carmack was engaged in a bitter political challenge against sitting Democratic governor of Tennessee Malcolm Patterson at the time. Folk had become an outspoken supporter of Carmack, lobbying tirelessly to urge Patterson Democrats to throw their support behind the dry alternative. A key weapon in his arsenal was a bottle of gin marketed primarily to African Americans. W. T. Crotzer, a Patterson supporter, wrote to the *Nashville American* about a recent encounter he had had with Folk. According to Crotzer, Folk had approached him and announced, "Brother Crotzer, I have a thing in my pocket which, if you will let me show you, you will go home a Carmack man and for statewide prohibition." Crotzer consented to view the mystery object, and Folk produced a gin bottle "upon which was a partially nude female holding in her right hand over her head a black rooster. Beneath the picture of the female were the words in clear, bold type, 'The Game Cock of Democracy.'" Crotzer continued: "By placing his hand in some way over or about the picture, he showed its vile lewdness, a thing that did not otherwise appear." According to Crotzer's account, Folk went on to explain that this was the same brand of gin sold to the black man accused of raping and murdering a white woman named Margaret Lears in Shreveport, Louisiana, and he blamed the Democratic Party and Governor Patterson for allowing it to still be sold in Tennessee.[158] Although Folk failed to convert Crotzer to the cause, he apparently continued to use the gin bottle as an object lesson in support of Carmack and statewide prohibition.

Crumpton also recounted the role that the contemptible labels played in the prohibition campaign in Birmingham. He recalled that a particular brand of gin, called Come Back Gin, was sold only in black saloons. "In all the barrooms, exposed to view in the show windows," said Crumpton, "were flasks on which was the picture of a beautiful white woman in bed, with the curtains drawn aside." Crumpton praised the work of Connie Austin, a Birmingham resident who was so incensed by the labels that he took to the streets to publicize the vile bottles. Austin had come into possession of a bottle that had allegedly been found on a black man accused of assaulting a white woman outside of Birmingham. As Crumpton explained:

> He stood on the side-walk and exhibited it to the passers by, explaining the incident which led to its discovery. Of course the crowds increased. Connie was arrested for obstructing the side-walks, but he continued at another corner and was again arrested—bond was easily made. . . . His speech was about this: "Men, we are working people in this district. Here is liquor sold only to Negroes, to inflame their minds and under its devilish influence the drinker is liable to do any thing that is mean. How do you know when you are away at your work, some brute of a Negro will not go into your house and ruin your home?"[159]

For evangelicals campaigning for prohibition, these labels presented a clear threat to the wives and daughters of white southerners. Crumpton credited Austin's use of the bottle of Come Back Gin, with its alleged ability to unleash the brutish nature of black men through both its contents and its packaging, with swaying many votes into the dry column when Birmingham voted for prohibition in 1907. The message about what was being sold to African Americans in their saloons became a favorite tool of prohibitionists. As Crumpton wrote, "The preachers took it up in their pulpits and when the time came to vote on the question, it hit the liquorites like a cyclone and their greatest stronghold fell."[160]

An Alternative Solution

The panic surrounding the black beast provided southern prohibitionists with a valuable tool in their push for statewide legislation. But southern prohibitionists were also offering an alternative response to the perceived danger posed by blacks to white women and to society in general, and they were doing so at a time when most responses to this threat involved ropes or bullets. Southern evangelical prohibitionists agreed with the popular notion that blacks were degenerating into beasts and preying on virtuous white women. But they claimed that these assaults could be reduced by eliminating their fuel—cheap liquor in evocative packaging—as opposed to the increasingly popular solution to the problem: swift, brutal, merciless punishment at the hands of a white mob. Instead of stringing up every black man accused of, suspected of, or in any way associated with an alleged rape, prohibitionists suggested that the source of the crime be attacked instead. And the individuals standing at that source were white, not black. The evangelical response was aimed at punishing and eradicating the white distillers that produced the cheap whiskey and the white-owned saloons that sold it to African Americans. Evangelicals tried to disperse the culpability by arguing that the white saloon owners and distillers were partially to blame for the heinous crimes committed by blacks, whose minds and bodies had been poisoned by foul liquor and arousing labels. Obviously, this served the grander purpose of cutting off the sale of liquor altogether. Also, it was easier to eliminate the supply of whiskey than to reform the morals of blacks. Indeed, evangelicals had come to believe that such moral uplift might not be possible within the African American community. Prohibitionists began to place less emphasis on the "black beast" and more on the distillers and retailers that created him.

By offering this solution to the perceived "rape crisis," evangelicals were embracing and perpetuating racist stereotypes. At the same time, it was certainly a more just and reasonable response than that urged by individuals such as Georgia newspaper publisher John Temple Graves or Populist leader Rebecca Latimer Felton. The former publicly offered a $1,000 reward for the successful lynching of a black rapist, while the latter declared, "I say lynch; a thousand times a week if it becomes necessary" to protect white women from drunken black men.[161] Though tainted with racism and the basest form of paternalism, the evangelical solution offered a course of action that served as a corrective to the dominant societal impulses of the time. It was also more suitable to the evangelicals' sense of biblical morality and to their long-standing desire to see prohibition enacted in the South.

In 1908 Thornwell Jacobs, a Presbyterian clergyman and later president of Oglethorpe University in Atlanta, wrote *The Law of the White Circle* after visiting Atlanta following the 1906 riots. The novella deals with the race problem in the South and the factors that led to the racial discord in Atlanta. Jacobs advances the evangelical argument that instead of the reactionary approach to black atrocities that most southern whites embraced—lynching—the South should take a proactive approach by cutting off the fuel that creates and drives the "black beast." In the book, an Atlanta newspaper editor named Henry Webster receives news that a white woman has been killed on the outskirts of town by a black man. The "wild beast" assaulted and killed her while she was innocently picking flowers in a field in broad daylight. Webster runs the story, and over it the headline: "Clean Out the Dives! Close Up the Saloons! The Present Crisis Cannot Last Much Longer! Above All, Keep Cool!" Visiting the newspaper's office that day is Mr. Elliston, a northerner who has come south to study the race problem. Webster explains the headline to him, saying, "There are my sentiments, Elliston. I didn't add, 'Shoot down the wild beast at sight.' I hope to my God I will never say it."[162] Jacobs's message, and the message of many evangelical prohibitionists, was that prohibition could solve both the epidemic of rape and the epidemic of mob retaliation.

Jacobs aims the brunt of his critique not at the bestial nature of African American men but at the whites who facilitated their retrogression. He notes that most observers of the southern race conflict had spent "too large a part of their time in expostulations concerning Negro inferiority and too little in arraignment of our white lepers who have converted a disaster into dynamite." Jacobs suggests: "What is the Negro problem? Rakes and rum—white rakes, white men's rum." Many evangelicals shared Jacobs's view of the problem. A Nashville prohibitionist wrote to the *Tennessean* in 1908 arguing that "the man who makes whisky and rum, the man who sells whisky and rum, is just as much to blame for the results of the vile stuff as the person who drinks and commits the deed." White distillers and saloon keepers help "make a brute and demon of the already brutish Negro, and cause him to commit outrages on our noble womanhood." These whites, he argued, "should meet the same fate as the Negro who commits the deed."[163]

It should be noted that evangelicals did not try to impose prohibition on African Americans alone. The Reverend John White of

Atlanta argued that even people who had never been teetotalers were now recognizing a "sense of moral obligation" to cut off the flow of alcohol to the black population, even if it meant renouncing it themselves.[164] McKelway likewise argued that "the moderate drinker in the South is willing to forego his privileges in order to protect the Negro from the unlimited sale of liquor."[165] In 1912 Leonard Scott Blakey, a professor at Dickinson College in Pennsylvania, conducted a county-by-county study of the growth of local option efforts in the South. The economist and early cliometrician concluded that "the hypothesis that the purpose of the prohibitory movement in the South was to make intoxicating liquors inaccessible to the Negro without taking them away from the more resourceful white man would be difficult to defend."[166] When an Atlanta judge proposed, in the aftermath of the riots, to "put any man in stripes who sells or gives liquor to a Negro," Georgia Methodists responded by urging, "But, Judge, let's go further and 'put in stripes any man who sells or gives liquor' as a beverage to any man in the state." The editor of the *Wesleyan Christian Advocate* urged that the state close not only the saloons for blacks and poor whites but also the "gilded saloon" catering to more respectable whites.[167]

Prohibition did not, of course, spell the end of lynching in the South. In the decade following the passage of statewide prohibition in Georgia, the number of lynchings actually increased. However, whereas accusations of rape or attempted rape had precipitated more than 40 percent of the lynchings between 1898 and 1907, in the decade after the passage of statewide prohibition, such charges accounted for only 15 percent of lynchings.[168] The marketing of prohibition as a vital step in the elimination of the black threat had been successful.

Prohibition and the "New Negro"

In 1964 African American novelist Ralph Ellison wrote an essay in which he attacked the view (popular among many white historians at the time) that segregation had created an absolute separation of the races in the South. "Whatever the efficiency of segregation as a socio-political arrangement," Ellison observed, "it has been far from absolute on the level of culture. Southern whites cannot walk, talk, sing, conceive of laws or justice, think of sex, love, the family or freedom without responding to the presence of Negroes."[169] Ellison's point should not be taken lightly, and it would be a mistake to assume that white evangelicals formed their prohibition stance in a vacuum and that this stance guided their attitudes toward blacks. Although the prohibition sentiment of southern white evangelicals certainly influenced their attitude toward African Americans between 1880 and 1915, it is clear that the relationship worked the other way as well. The evangelicals' embrace of prohibition in this period was driven largely by their growing discomfort with the actions and attitudes of the black community. Especially after 1890, there emerged a new generation of African Americans who were born after emancipation and less reticent about demanding respect and equality from whites. This played out on multiple levels. On a public and national level, it manifested in 1903 when W. E. B. DuBois made a very public break with Booker T. Washington over the latter's strategy of accommodation and deference toward the white man. DuBois advocated a more proactive attitude among blacks, urging them to agitate for equality instead of waiting passively for white America to give it to them. On a more personal and everyday level—quite literally the man on the street—young African Americans increasingly refused to behave according to long-established patterns of public submissiveness.

Southern whites became concerned about the way young blacks acted in public spaces, especially the sidewalks. As Jane Dailey's examination of an 1883 race riot in Danville, Virginia, reveals, altercations over sidewalk space became a growing source of tension between the races. The Danville riot started when a black man bumped into a white man as the two passed on the sidewalk. It was fueled by the abundance of concealed weapons among the white crowd that soon gathered and led to the deaths of four black men. According to Dailey, "The appropriation of public space was an important way for African Americans in this period to assert their humanity." Sidewalks were an area particularly ripe for confrontation between the races. In the late nineteenth century, young black men and women participated in what was called "projecting," or refusing to yield to whites who were approaching them on crowded sidewalks, forcing the whites to step off the sidewalk into the gutter. This represented more than mere rudeness; it was an outright rejection of the attitude of deference and obeisance that previous generations of southern blacks had shown to whites.[170]

In 1898 another race riot broke out in Wilmington, North Carolina. Much of the blame for this outbreak of white-on-black violence was laid on Alex Manly, the editor of a local African American newspaper. Writing about the rising number of rape allegations made by white women against black men, Manly suggested that in most cases the white women had been willing participants in the sexual encounter. These provocative editorials were used to justify the subsequent destruction of the newspaper's printing press and office by a white mob, which in turn led to armed conflict between black and white mobs. McKelway defended the actions of the white citizenry of Wilmington and also revealed that Manly's inflammatory editorials had not been the only provocation for the whites to riot. Decrying the increasingly impudent attitude of the town's black population, McKelway noted, "They demanded the whole of the sidewalk as a matter of right, white women learning soon, for fear of insult, to step out into the street to avoid collision." Manly's editorials, it turned out, were just the final straw in demonstrating that blacks in Wilmington had forgotten their proper place.[171] Such acts of insolence and disrespect became ingrained in the white mind and immortalized in works of fiction by Thomas Dixon and Margaret Mitchell. Refusal to yield sidewalk space was just a symptom of a larger change of attitude taking place among blacks at the turn of the century.

In 1905 a woman in South Carolina noted in her diary, "A Negro who moved out into the gutter to let us pass was in our eyes a 'good darkey.'"[172] But by that date, most whites believed that such persons were increasingly hard to find. In the minds of southern whites, the African American population had been transformed from quiet, subservient "good darkies" who knew their proper, inferior place to "uppity blacks" who refused to play the role of subordinates and demanded respectful treatment from whites. This generation of blacks became known as the "New Negro." Born in the aftermath of the Civil War, these nineteenth-century baby boomers had no memory of what life had been like under slavery. They were not content with the attitude of deference and accommodation exhibited by their parents and grandparents. The downcast eyes, sheepish grin, and shuffling feet—modes of behavior practiced by African Americans for generations because they appeased and comforted whites—were being replaced by a new air of confidence, pride, and assertiveness. The most comprehensive examination of the rise of the New Negro generation is Leon Litwack's *Trouble in Mind*. As he observes, "When whites talked about a New Negro, and they did so with increasing regularity, more often than not they were acknowledging problems in containing the ambitions and controlling the behavior of a new generation of black southerners." Southern whites were shocked to find that the New Negro had the audacity to believe that he had just as much right to the sidewalk as did white pedestrians.[173]

White evangelicals were deeply concerned about the new generation of black men who had grown up in a free South and had not experienced the "civilizing" and uplifting effects of slavery. Haygood expressed anxiety about the younger generation of southern blacks in 1893. "Nearly all crimes of violence by the Negroes are committed by those who were children in 1865 or have been born since that time," Haygood argued. He still held a positive view of older African Americans, lauding them as "the best citizens and as well as the best laborers today." But blacks under the age of thirty-five had developed "a spirit of insubordination to the social order" and were the prime perpetrators of the kind of crimes that incited whites to mob justice.[174] Furthermore, whites saw urbanization and industrialization as contributing to the degeneration of southern blacks. As more and more African Americans left their rural farms in search of higher wages in cities, mining towns, and railroad camps, they were "out from under the influence of the whites and of their own best people." The editor of the *Alabama Christian Advocate* explained that once blacks arrived in these places, they were "congregated into Negro camps and settlements, a prey to every hellish influence, with little uplift to restrain them."[175]

According to Litwack and others, this increasing fear of young, insubordinate African Americans was largely responsible for whites' changing racial attitude between 1880 and World War I. The more threatening that blacks became in the white mind, the more whites sought to rein in black rights through both legal (disfranchisement and Jim Crow laws) and extralegal (lynching) means. But Litwack pays scant attention to the concurrent rise of prohibition sentiment among whites at this time, despite the fact that prohibition factored into this whole process and, in the end, benefited from it. Liquor became tied to popular white conceptions about the declining morals and behavior of black men, and prohibition correspondingly rose in popularity among white voters. In a way, prohibition offers a window into the process of the declining white attitude toward and rhetoric about blacks between 1880 and 1915, with a particular focus on the declining racial attitudes of white evangelical Christians. It suggests that some of the deeper motives for evangelicals' support of prohibition after 1880 were darker than merely trying to improve the morals and well-being of society.

For many evangelicals, prohibition was a means by which they could address the perceived breakdown in the social order caused by the decline of the black race. The optimistic paternalism of evangelical prohibitionists in the 1880s reflected the white conception of southern blacks as a generally submissive and compliant lot. With proper instruction and training, New South prohibitionists believed, black voters would come to embrace the views of their white betters. But by the mid-1890s, a number of factors—including recognition that the new generation of African Americans might not be so malleable— soured that optimism. Like other southern whites, evangelicals began to embrace the idea that allowing blacks to vote was a dangerous idea, and they approved of the process of circumscribing their rights. After the turn of the century, whites became increasingly disconcerted by the behavior of the New Negro. And during the course of those years, white evangelical prohibitionists embraced some of the darkest racial attitudes of the period, often to the advantage of their prohibition cause.

Prohibitionists achieved their victory in the South at great detriment to race relations. Playing on the racist stereotype of the black beast and the rape panic among southern whites was essential to the ultimate success of prohibition in Georgia, as well as the subsequent domino effect of prohibition victories in the South after 1907. Evangelical prohibitionists finally achieved victory in their long battle against the demon rum. In the process, however, a metamorphosis of white evangelical racial views took place. The racial rhetoric of white evangelicals trended far from the optimism and geniality of the 1880s. In those early days of the southern prohibition push, evangelicals had embraced an optimistic attitude toward their "brothers in black," who they saw as imminently capable of self-improvement and progress. By the time prohibition victory was achieved at the end of the first decade of the twentieth century, some evangelicals had incorporated the vilest of racial stereotypes into their quest to eradicate liquor. The evangelical churches in the South participated in the deteriorating racial trends occurring in the larger white society, even though they tried to focus the public's attention on the perceived source of black misbehavior—liquor with provocative labeling—rather than on violent retribution through mob justice.

Chapter Five

"Let the Cowards Vote as They Will, I'm for Prohibition Still"

Prohibition and the Southern Cult of Honor

WHEN EDWARD WARD CARMACK left his office at the *Nashville Tennessean* on the afternoon of November 9, 1908, he was only moments away from changing the course of the Tennessee prohibition movement and Tennessee politics in general. Unfortunately, he was also only moments away from his death. Carmack had been at the helm of Nashville's leading newspaper for only three months, yet his fiery editorials during that brief tenure had earned him many enemies. One of those enemies, Colonel Duncan B. Cooper, had once been a close friend and colleague of Carmack's. Both men were long-time loyal Tennessee Democrats. In recent years, however, the issue of prohibition had destroyed the men's relationship, much as it had bitterly divided the Democratic Party as a whole in the state.

In the spring of 1908, Carmack had lost his bid to unseat incumbent Malcolm R. Patterson as the Democratic Party's gubernatorial nominee. During his first term as governor, Patterson had proved himself to be an enemy of the state's prohibition forces, and prohibition leaders convinced Carmack to mount a campaign against Patterson. The two had a political rivalry dating back to 1896, when Carmack had defeated Patterson's father, Colonel Josiah Patterson, in the congressional race for Tennessee's Tenth District. Colonel Patterson, who had held the seat for three terms, challenged the results, and the election had to be decided by the House of Representatives, which ultimately decided against the incumbent.[1] Patterson's son, who had served as his father's campaign manager in 1896, regained the congressional seat for the family in 1900, when Carmack vacated it after being elected to the U.S. Senate. In 1906 Patterson resigned from the House to become Tennessee's governor. In Carmack's race against the elder Patterson, the debate over gold versus silver had been the primary campaign issue, but his challenge of the younger Patterson was primarily a contest over statewide prohibition. In a primary election fraught with corruption on the part of Patterson Democrats, Carmack lost.

For Tennessee drys, the cause was not lost. Evangelical prohibitionists such as E. E. Folk and the Anti-Saloon League endorsed Patterson's Republican challenger in the general election. For his part, Carmack accepted the position of editor at the *Tennessean* and used its influential editorial page to lambaste the Patterson administration. When Patterson won reelection in the fall, Carmack pressed forward with his vitriolic editorials. Colonel Cooper, one of Patterson's closest advisers, received the lion's share of these attacks. Carmack accused Patterson of involvement in unethical deals with the liquor industry and named Cooper as a corrupting and evil influence in the administration. The editor's attacks were often as personal as they were political; Carmack referred to Cooper as "a little bald-headed angel of hell" and further insulted Cooper by referring to him as "Major," implying that some of his wartime promotions had been undeserved.[2] In response, Cooper warned Carmack to back off, telling him that Nashville was not big enough for the two of them. But Carmack refused to desist, and on November 9, Cooper reached his breaking point. As Carmack was leaving his downtown office, Colonel Cooper and his son, Robin, approached the editor, and a gunfight ensued that shocked the state.

In many ways, the Cooper-Carmack shoot-out constituted a continuation of the antebellum southern tradition of the duel. Cooper's defenders even justified his actions by calling the incident a simple "street duel." Carmack had publicly impugned Colonel Cooper's character and disrespected him, and the antebellum code of honor demanded that Cooper respond by squaring off against Carmack in a duel. Thus, Cooper sought out Carmack and made clear his intention to settle the matter. He taunted Carmack and called his honor into question, accusing him of being a coward and hiding behind a woman. The woman was an innocent passerby who had stopped to talk to Carmack on the street and found herself caught between him and the approaching Coopers. Carmack's defenders insisted that he was merely trying to move the woman out of harm's way— "courteous, considerate gentleman that he was to the last."[3] Cooper's violent and brash response to Carmack's insults harked back to a tradition that, in earlier times, had dominated the southern mind and behavior, whereas the reaction to Cooper's attack on Carmack reflected how southern ideas about honor had changed in the New South, the role that evangelicals played in redefining honor, and the centrality of prohibition to these changes taking place in southern culture.

Dueling and Honor in the Antebellum South

The Cooper-Carmack confrontation was far from a textbook antebellum gentlemen's duel; rather, it was a two-against-one shoot-out. Cooper and his son issued no challenge beforehand and caught Carmack unawares; they had come prepared to shoot him regardless of whether he was armed to defend himself. In the end, however, the effect was the same: the aggrieved man faced off against the one who had insulted him, exchanged shots with him, and thereby vindicated his honor.

In antebellum duels, whether one killed one's opponent or was killed oneself was irrelevant; the fact that a man bravely faced death was enough to restore his status as a man of honor. This idea that honor was not contingent on victory served southerners well in the aftermath of the Civil War, allowing them to feel confident that by standing bravely and fighting against overwhelming forces they had successfully maintained their own honor and the honor of the South.[4] Cooper's attack on Carmack was a relic of the South's mythical past, when gentlemen from the planter aristocracy would face off on a magnolia-lined field of battle to resolve disputes and avenge insults by firing pistols at each other. But dueling in the antebellum South was no myth. It was an accepted and common occurrence between upper-class white males. In the Old South, the duel was a structured and organized event. By the 1830s, dueling guidebooks and even dueling coaches existed, such as former South Carolina governor John Lyde Wilson's *The Code of Honor: Or Rules for the Government of Principals and Seconds in Dueling*. This work became the standard text on the proper procedure for challenging someone to duel, responding to a challenge, and conducting a duel. If a southern gentleman received an insult or affront from another gentleman, he would issue a challenge, usually in writing.[5] Each man would choose a second, and the seconds would confer with one another to designate a time and place for the duel. The seconds were in charge of conducting the duel on the appointed day.

These *affaires d'honneur* took place only between men of high social standing; a gentleman would not deign to duel with a man from a lower social class. Thus, a duel between a white man and a black man was unthinkable. The practice of caning was reserved for such situations. If an upper-class white man felt insulted by a lower-class white man, he would publicly assault him with either a cane or a horse whip. This action not only defended the man's honor but also indicated that he did not recognize his opponent as his social equal. The significance and meaning of such southern practices often escaped outside observers.[6] But among southerners, the practice of violent recourse following even the slightest perceived affront was a well-known fact of life.

In the minds of southern gentlemen, the function of the code duello was twofold: it both defended personal honor and imposed order on society. As Jack Williams has noted, dueling among the upper class served to "hold in place the lower orders."[7] Southerners believed that the code of the duel gave structure and security to society, ingraining a strong sense of accountability, respect, and deference among men of all social classes. They argued that dueling resulted in a more courteous and refined society because individuals were well aware that they would be held accountable for their words and deeds and for any lack of courtesy or respect.

Dueling was only one aspect of a larger matrix of activities, customs, and codes of behavior in antebellum southern culture that is collectively referred to as the code of honor. Honor was of paramount importance, but an examination of honor is a difficult undertaking precisely because the concept was so deeply ingrained in southern culture that it rarely required blatant elucidation. As Edward Ayers has noted, honor was "simultaneously potent and elusive."[8] The infamous duel was the most blatant expression of the underlying code, but honor manifested itself in a multitude of ways in day-to-day life in the South and impacted all levels of society. The code was evident in the way a wealthy white man would challenge another to a gunfight for even the slightest affront or show of disrespect; in the way a white man would remove his hat when entering the home of a white family, but keep it on when entering an African American home; in the way southern gentlemen disliked the game of baseball because it required one to be chased around the bases by one's opponent; in the way the words of a white man of honor were unquestioned—even if blatantly false—unless one was prepared to engage in a duel; in the way that testimony from an African American against a white man in court was not accepted, since a black man was inherently without honor and therefore assumed to be a liar; in the way parents emphasized their lineage by giving children distinguished family surnames rather than traditional Christian names; in the way men regarded the nose as the most important part of their body because it was the most visible, making the pulling of another man's nose the highest personal insult; in the way parents discouraged sons from pursuing effeminate interests such as playing the piano; in the way an adult white female was referred to as a "lady" but an adult black female was referred to as a "woman"; in the way that the giving of a gift could be a means of insulting someone; and in the tradition of boundless hospitality offered to guests in southern white homes.[9] This complex of attitudes, beliefs, and behavior sharply differentiated southern society from that of the North in the antebellum years. Although practices such as dueling had existed in both the North and the South during the eighteenth century, the sections took significantly different routes after 1800. In the North, the duel became extinct, while in the South, the number of duels actually increased during the decades leading up to the Civil War.[10]

The cult of honor, defined by Ayers as "the overwhelming concern with the opinions of others," placed the greatest emphasis on how a man was perceived by those around him.[11] It was a complex ordering force within southern society, often intangible and elusive, yet universally accepted and understood by southerners. Honor depended entirely on how one was regarded by others; if the community did not have a good opinion of a man, he could not have honor. Thus the southern cult of honor valued external appearance and public perception above all else. The disorderly, unpredictable nature of life in the antebellum South—a wilder, frontier-like region where the constraints of law enforcement were much looser than in the North—led to a pessimistic and backward-looking mentality among its denizens. Lacking much of the security that afforded their northern neighbors the luxury of a more optimistic and forward-looking mind-set, southerners shared more in common with their ancestors in Old Europe than they did with their fellow Americans. The code of honor, Bertram Wyatt-Brown argues, helped make the South a more predictable and orderly place by establishing standards of appropriate conduct. By making public opinion "the dominant force in public life," the code of honor quashed individualism.[12] In so doing, it reduced the threat of insurrection and unruliness posed by both slaves and lower-class whites.

The concept of honor was one that southerners inherited from their Old World ancestors. In particular, Grady McWhiney argues, it came from the Celtic heritage that was the predominant shaper of southern culture.[13] C. Vann Woodward has argued that what made the South so distinctive was the extent of its commonalities with the Old World, which contrasted sharply with the truly aberrant and unique American North.[14] Wyatt-Brown argues that honor lay at the heart of the United States' sectional division and its civil conflict. While northerners became increasingly guided by an internalized sense of right and wrong, southerners continued to be guided primarily by the externally focused code of honor, under which one's actions were governed more by the opinions and expectations of society than by one's conscience.[15] Wyatt-Brown believes that old ideas of honor may have lingered among some northerners, which explains why some antebellum Yankees continued to be more accepting of southern slavery. McWhiney agrees that the code of honor was the driving force behind not only the South's defense of its peculiar institution but also its attitude toward and conduct of the Civil War. He cites historian Bell I. Wiley, who declared, "No people ever went to war with greater enthusiasm than did Confederates in 1861." Given that they were products of a distinctly Celtic culture that clung to Old World ideas of honor, McWhiney argues that southerners could not have been expected to do otherwise.[16]

Although southerners owed much of their affection for the code of honor to their Old World ancestors, the region's peculiar institution no doubt contributed to the important role played by the system of honor. It is noteworthy that a society whose economy was built on the enslavement of Africans by whites should place so much emphasis on external appearance. The dark-skinned slaves were, by their mere complexion, completely locked out of the system by which one gained social acceptance, respect, and rights in the South. The code of honor clearly delineated the social superiority of the planter aristocracy over the middle class, and in turn, the superiority of the middle class over the plebian yeomanry; it also clarified the social superiority of even the poorest white man over any African American. Thus, even the lowliest white man had a claim to honor, as well as to the pride and sense of social rank that accompanied it. This imbued poor southern whites with a vested interest in maintaining the existing social order, lest they lose what little status they possessed.[17]

Honor had to be consciously and carefully maintained, so southern white men—especially those of the upper class, who had the most honor and therefore the most to lose—remained ever vigilant in defending it, often taking it to an absurd level.[18] This explains the hypersensitivity to insults and disrespect that developed among the antebellum upper crust. Even the slightest affront demanded a full and uncompromising defense, lest one's public image be harmed. Always concerned about the opinion of others, southern men believed that losing face meant losing honor, and losing honor meant losing social standing and prestige. Young men of the upper class learned early in life that the only acceptable retort to any perceived insult was one that was swift and violent. To resort to legal remedies was considered a sign of weakness. President Andrew Jackson recalled that as a young man in Tennessee his mother had admonished him, "Never sue anybody for slander or assault and battery. Always settle them cases yourself."[19] Jackson went on to earn a reputation as an expert duelist.[20] Young men in the antebellum South were not expected to complete their education without exchanging shots with a classmate or two along the way[21]—or, in some cases, with their teachers. For instance, one teacher from the North who had taken a position at a school in antebellum Tennessee was shocked when, after reprimanding some misbehaving boys in his class, they produced guns and threatened to kill him. Likewise, at the University of Alabama, a student assaulted some professors with a weapon after they punished him for having liquor in his dormitory room. In 1853 a math professor at the University of Georgia accused a student of cheating, whereupon the student's brother challenged the teacher to a duel. The professor, himself a self-respecting southerner, accepted the young man's challenge, though ultimately, the duel was averted.[22]

The embrace of violence was essential if a southern man was to defend his honor and that of his family. As John William De Forest, a northerner, observed when he traveled through the South just after the Civil War, "Self-respect, as the southerners understand it, has always demanded much fighting."[23] While white women were responsible for maintaining the home and raising the children, white men were charged with defending the honor of a widening circle of entities: a man had to defend his own honor, as well as that of his wife, his family, his community, his state, and his region. Southerners had an acute sense of place and heritage and were deeply loyal to their home states. This love of their home states motivated many men who fought for the Confederacy on a deeper level than did their love for the Confederate cause itself. As one southern woman admonished her cousin, who was serving on the front lines with the Confederate army, "In the God of battle trust, and die for old Virginia."[24]

In addition to violence, other manly activities were highly esteemed in the honor-centric culture of the antebellum South, including drinking, gambling, hunting, smoking, and cursing. Alcohol played an important role both in hospitality—a prerequisite for being an honorable gentleman—and in the process of male bonding.[25] In keeping with the idea that the word of a man of honor was always true, southern men enjoyed gambling and considered it a respectable pastime. Because the act of gambling hinges on a man making some statement about the future (such as which horse will win a race, which rooster will win a fight, or how good a hand of cards he will be dealt) and then having those words proved accurate and truthful, men of honor considered gambling an attractive and tempting leisure-time activity. Thus, a man of honor was willing and able to engage in violence, considered the consumption of alcohol an indispensable element of hospitality and manly camaraderie, and enjoyed leisure activities such as gambling. So it is not difficult to understand how the code of honor in the South ran afoul of the region's growing evangelical movement during the antebellum era. The code tolerated and indeed encouraged gambling, drinking, dueling, and sexual license among white males, behavior that contravened the principles of self-restraint and strict biblical morality promoted by evangelicals.

Ayers notes that "from its earliest days, southern evangelicalism defined itself in opposition to the culture of honor."[26] Membership in antebellum evangelical churches was predominantly female. Men did join, but this often made them outsiders in terms of the prevailing culture of masculinity and honor. Southern evangelicalism existed in the antebellum period as an alternative to this culture, and evangelicals targeted many of its features—including drinking and dueling—as unchristian and immoral. For a southern white male, becoming an evangelical in the prewar South generally meant abandoning any claim to what the larger society called "honor" and embracing instead a lifestyle modeled on the figure of Christ and the teachings of the Bible. This lifestyle mandated such things as turning the other cheek when assaulted or insulted, forgiving and loving one's enemies, not caring about the opinions of others, shunning the cares and values of the world, embracing an egalitarian ethic that rejected social distinctions (save race), and abiding by moral strictures against such sinful activities as drinking, gambling, and sexual licentiousness. These doctrines rendered evangelicalism inherently incompatible with the core elements of the antebellum system of honor. An article in the *Christian Advocate* of Nashville in 1850 highlighted the disjunction between the evangelical ethic and the code of honor. The author rejected the right of a Christian man to retaliate against not only insults but also physical attacks. The Christian should respond to such assaults with kindness and "nonresistance," the Tennessee Methodist argued. He explained that "the doctrine of non-resistance is a Bible doctrine" to which Christians are still bound, regardless of what the prevailing "modern doctrine" of honor teaches.[27]

Thus, it was no surprise that evangelicals were appalled when Duncan and Robin Cooper, in their latter-day version of the once-honored southern tradition of the duel, shot and killed Edward Carmack. By the time of Carmack's death, however, the attitude of southerners regarding dueling and the code of honor in general had changed significantly. Evangelicals were no longer an indignant minority wringing their hands about the deteriorating mores of the prevailing culture. In antebellum Tennessee, public consensus would have declared Cooper justified in his actions, and more importantly, he would have regained his status as a man of honor. Times had changed, however, as had ideas about what constituted honor and how one went about achieving and maintaining it. When eulogies of the fallen prohibition leader began to pour forth, a consistent theme was Carmack's position as a man of honor, in contrast to the dishonorable and cowardly Coopers. Folk reflected on Carmack as "the ablest, purest, noblest man that has appeared in public life in Tennessee in two generations" and lauded him as a "brave" and "knightly" martyr for the cause of prohibition.[28] Carmack was added to the list of valiant and honorable men who had died for the cause of prohibition, including Roderick Dhu Gambrell in Mississippi and John R. Moffett in Virginia.[29]

Prohibitionists also used the tragedy as an opportunity to disparage not only the Coopers but also all anti-prohibitionists as dishonorable. The *Baptist and Reflector* declared the Coopers to be "cowardly" assassins.[30] The Alabama Conference of the MECS likewise extolled the honor of the "chivalrous, consistent, and Christian Carmack," who had been "slain by the assassin's bullet." The conference predicted that Christian men who were truly honorable would take up the fight for prohibition where Carmack had left off, proclaiming, "to the music of Carmack's memory a mighty multitude of manly men march to conquer the foul foe by which he fell."[31]

Governor Patterson's pardon of the Coopers ended his political career and led to the rupture of the state's Democratic Party, a large portion of which fused with the Republicans to form a majority coalition. More important, the aftermath of the shooting highlights how southern perceptions of what made a man honorable had been reshaped, largely in terms dictated by southern evangelicals.

A New Code for the New South

The practice of dueling had persisted during the Civil War, with Confederate officers occasionally taking time off from fighting Yankees to shoot at one another.[32] After the war, however, the practice faced increasing public disapproval. Most southern states had enacted antidueling measures early in the nineteenth century, but only after the Civil War were they strictly enforced, and the practice began to wane.[33] In part, postwar antidueling sentiment emerged as an element of the Populist animosity toward the old planter elite. Romanticized ideas about dueling and the old aristocracy had been greatly diminished by the devastation of war.[34] In Virginia, Bourbon Democrats argued that the state must pay off its massive debt accumulated during the war and Reconstruction as a matter of honor. "Honor won't buy breakfast," was the response from the Populist Readjuster movement, which sought to repudiate the state's debts and allocate the money to improving education and meeting other needs of the people. When the Readjusters gained control of the state government in 1879, a law against dueling was one of the first reforms instituted.[35]

The postwar era also found evangelicals reenergized in their crusade against dueling and other aspects of the old code of honor. The Civil War provided evangelicals and the rest of southern society with a new model for manliness and honor in the figures of Robert E. Lee and Stonewall Jackson, both of whom rejected the practice of dueling.[36] In the years following the war, these men became increasingly ensconced at the heights of the cult of the Lost Cause, presenting evangelicals with vibrant examples of how a man could be both a pious Christian and a true man of honor. One of the earliest articles to employ the term *New South* to describe this emerging impulse appeared in the northern *American Missionary*, which expressed the hope and expectation that a new code of honor would emerge in the South. In the New South, the editor wrote, "a Christian conscience will displace a false code of honor among the people as a rule of conduct, and methods more civilized than the pistol and bowie-knife will be resorted to in adjusting misunderstandings among neighbors."[37] Southern evangelicals had already begun to embrace this theme of true versus false honor. In 1878 the editor of the *Alabama Baptist* gleefully announced that "the days of 'the code' are pretty nearly ended." In 1881 the editor of the *Holston Methodist* declared that "dueling must be made odious," and those who participate in duels should be treated like any other murderer. That same year, the editor of the *Alabama Baptist* decried the "spurious honor of the code" and proclaimed that "nothing but the hempen cord can exorcise the thin-skinned, bloodthirsty demon of the code."[38]

The efforts to eliminate dueling, however, were part of a larger pattern that emerged after the Civil War as evangelicals attempted to redefine the code of honor in the South. During this period they began to restate what it meant to be a man of honor—and a manly man—along more Christian lines. It was a definition of honor that was couched in evangelical, Victorian, middle-class terms. Evangelicals sought to establish two points: first, that living a Christian lifestyle was wholly compatible with being a man of honor, and second, that standing up for the cause of prohibition was an honorable and manly undertaking. By extension, opposing prohibition was painted as dishonorable.

Some historians have argued that post-Reconstruction southern evangelicals continued to position themselves entirely in opposition to the concept of honor. Wyatt-Brown maintains that in the postwar era, neither evangelicalism nor the old code of honor achieved victory over the other. Instead, he argues, the South increasingly possessed a "divided soul," torn between honor and piety. This cognitive dissonance, Wyatt-Brown contends, continued to haunt the region throughout much of the twentieth century.[39] Ted Ownby presents a similar explanation of how the inherent conflict between the two modes of thinking was resolved. In his view, the legacy of the old code of honor was the hedonistic masculine world of fighting, gambling, and drinking, whereas evangelical culture was feminine and centered on the home. This masculine-feminine dichotomy, however, paints with too broad a brush. The feminine culture of evangelicalism, Ownby argues, was intent on quashing the recreational pursuits of the secular, masculine culture. The manly pastimes of fighting, gambling, drinking, and hunting constitute Ownby's definition of southern honor, and he argues that they were targeted by evangelicals in an attempt to bring men closer to the temperament of women.[40]

In Ownby's New South, evangelicalism was composed almost entirely of women. He characterizes those men who filled the numerous positions as pastors, denominational leaders, and editors as effeminate dandies who shunned manly pursuits and engaged in activities that were more acceptable to feminine sensibilities. Ownby also offers a psychoanalysis of evangelical male behavior. Men attending evangelical church services sat separately from the women, arrived late, and chewed tobacco during church, he believes, as a means of demonstrating that "they were not fully comfortable with church life and evangelical sentiment."[41] But this masculinity versus femininity explanation tends to oversimplify some of the issues underlying evangelical opposition to leisure-time activities. Instead of noting the biblical reasons behind evangelical objections to drinking, gambling, and fighting, it portrays evangelicals simply as killjoys intent on imposing their quiet, boring, feminine pastimes on the fun-loving male population. Ownby ignores the fact that the crusade against drinking, gambling, and violence was such a powerful force in southern politics and society because the evangelical camp included a large number of males; he also fails to recognize that these evangelical males were trying to lay claim to the code of honor that continued to permeate southern culture. It was not a struggle between the cult of honor and evangelicalism, as Ownby argues, but rather a struggle between two groups of white males that transcended class boundaries. One group's vision of honor was shaped primarily by their evangelical mores and Victorian ideals about the need for structure and orderliness in society and a reliance on laws. The other group was less likely to be part of the evangelical community, and its version of honor reflected more traditional southern ideas about violence, extralegal means of responding to insults, and participation in such pastimes as drinking and gambling.

Among southern evangelicals in the late nineteenth century, Ownby's suggestion that Christian ministers were less manly than men outside the church undoubtedly would have been fighting words. Southern evangelicals were, in fact, quite adamant that they were a manly lot. "There are some 'miss cissys' in every profession," the editor of the *Alabama Baptist* opined, "but take them all in all we do not know of a manlier set than can be found in the ministry."[42] Evangelicals refused to concede the title of honor and the trait of manliness to the unchurched. As one Baptist put it, "The enemies of God are not to have a monopoly on the stirring watchwords of the world, nor are they to be considered the only ones who can appeal to that which is strong and manly in men." The writer encouraged Christian men to embrace manliness. "Have manliness, certainly, but let it be Christ-like manliness," he explained, noting that Christians should exude a "manliness mellowed and irradiated" by the principles of Jesus Christ. The editor maintained that the bravery and manliness of Christian men should be regarded as second to none.[43]

Another evangelical made a distinction between "manliness" and "mannishness." The latter consisted of the frivolities and vices displayed by the rougher elements of society, such as smoking, chewing tobacco, drinking, swearing, and fighting. Manliness, in contrast, was a characteristic that all Christian men and boys should strive for, and it included not only physical strength but also an ethic of hard work and diligence, the ability to write and speak correctly, and morally uprightness.[44] What the author offered was, in fact, an evangelical redefinition of the word *manliness*. Echoing this sentiment that Christ was the ultimate exemplar of manliness and honor, an editorial in the Georgia Baptist newspaper the *Christian Index* proclaimed that "Jesus Christ is the one true standard for a noble manhood."[45] Georgia Baptist C. H. Wetherbe declared in 1900 that "the gospel of Christ is designed to not only save men from their sins, but also to make them manly Christians." He continued by pointing out, "The strongest and most influential Christians are they who are governed by manly honor and stalwart Christian principle."[46]

The movement to give Christianity a more rugged and masculine makeover was by no means unique to the South. Mid-nineteenth-century England had witnessed the emergence of efforts to infuse the Christian faith with manliness through the work of Thomas Hughes and others. This was a reaction to the widely held perception that Christianity had become too "feminized." As the famous English Baptist preacher Charles Haddon Spurgeon put it, people had come to believe that in order to join the church, "you must sink your manliness and turn milksop."[47] In the northern United States, this same perception that Christianity had become too effeminate and centered on emotion produced a movement of "muscular Christianity" between 1880 and 1920. Its supporters came from both the Social Gospel and the conservative evangelical ranks, and it promoted health, exercise, sports, and manliness.[48]

In the South, however, evangelical rhetoric about manliness reflected more than a simple attempt to repair the image of a church deemed to be too feminized; it was part of an effort to lay claim to the title of honor. It was also about competing with a version of masculinity and honor that emphasized violence and drunkenness. Contrary to Ownby's suggestion, honor was not the sole property of the rowdy, unchurched menfolk in the cities and towns. In reality, honor was an entity being contested by two different groups of southern white men who sought to lay claim to it. Both groups—evangelical males and unchurched males—vied for the title of honor because it would justify their actions. In the midst of an epidemic of lynchings, by which mobs of white men sought to reaffirm white supremacy and black subservience, poor whites claimed that they were acting out of duty to the code of honor. Lynching was routinely justified on the grounds that honor demanded that southern white women be protected against the threat of black rapists. This, they believed, justified the gruesomeness and lawlessness of their actions. Stephen West notes that after the Civil War, many upper-class men abandoned some of the more violent aspects of the old code of personal honor, while lower-class white men clung to "traditional notions of honor as a bulwark against social and economic changes that undermined the traditional prerogatives of white manhood." Thus, violence in the name of honor increasingly became the domain of the lower class, manifesting itself in lynchings, pistol carrying, gunfights, brawling, night-riding terrorism of both blacks and whites, and, of course, drinking, gambling, and cursing.[49]

At the same time, southern evangelicals, in their attempt to reform and remake southern society in their own image, sought to wrap their efforts in the mantle of honor. Although not all southern evangelicals hailed from the middle class, evangelicalism was becoming increasingly aligned with middle-class values and Victorian mores. Because evangelicalism cut across class lines, however, the controversy cannot be labeled as a simple class conflict.[50] The sides in this clash were drawn along the lines of those who allowed their evangelical morality to define their concept of honor, manliness, and bravery versus those who defined such issues in more traditional terms of physical conflict and raucous leisure activities.[51] Evangelicals largely embraced middle-class, bourgeois, Victorian values and mores and viewed them as normative for all social classes, not just the middle class.[52] After the Civil War, shifts in the makeup and social position of southern evangelicalism took place. The middle and upper classes of white males increasingly joined Methodist and Baptist churches and began to discard some of the more offensive accoutrements of the southern code of honor, such as drinking, gambling, and dueling.[53] At the same time, socially displaced poor white males increasingly clung to the traditional code of honor—including drinking, fighting, pistol carrying, and racial violence—in an attempt to define and defend their place in an increasingly complex social and economic order.[54]

Now that upper-class men were abandoning many of the more unchristian aspects of honor, evangelicals were able to mount a more extensive and effective campaign against these practices. In the antebellum period, attacking such aspects of honor and manhood as dueling or even drinking would have pitted evangelicals against the planter aristocracy, resulting in a strained relationship between evangelicalism and the cult of honor. In the New South, however, the upper class was less resistant to such attacks. It was much less dangerous for evangelical ministers to attack gambling, drinking, brawling, and even lynching when the participants were mainly from the rougher, lower-class elements of society.

Beginning in the 1880s and increasing in the years following, evangelicals emphasized that being a true and steadfast Christian was synonymous with being a "manly man" and a man of honor. Along with a New South, evangelicals after Reconstruction began to promote what can be called a "New Honor." They attacked the violent aspects of the old code. For example, West observes that after the war, the carrying of small, inexpensive "pocket pistols" increasingly became a social marker of lower-class white men, distinguishing them from the middle and upper classes.[55] An article in the *Holston Methodist* in 1879 claimed that liquor and pistols were "the twin agents of crime" and declared that there was no excuse for carrying a pistol "in this civilized age." The writer went so far as to turn the tables on those who carried pistols, calling it an act of cowardice. A brave and true man, he suggested, would rely on the law for protection.[56]

Such attacks on the violent aspects of the South's culture of honor were not new to evangelicals. But instead of just stating what honor was not—such as fighting, drinking, gambling, and lynching—evangelicals were now attempting to redefine what constituted honorable behavior. The *Alabama Baptist* lamented the fact that "in church relations men are constantly manifesting a want of manhood." The problem, according to the paper, was that men in the church were too concerned with the opinion of others and often neglected their Christian duty as a result. What the church needed was men who were honorable and stalwart, willing "to do conscientiously their duty, without regard to the actions and opinions of others."[57] From the evangelical perspective, a man could lay claim to honor not by being overly concerned about how he was perceived by the public—the guiding principle of the old code of honor—but rather by following his Christian principles regardless of what others thought or said. J. B. Hawthorne, pastor of Atlanta's First Baptist Church, argued in a prohibition sermon that "the brave, progressive, and manly man is never afraid to express what he feels."[58] During the Kelley controversy in Tennessee in 1890, Folk called B. F. Haynes—one of Kelley's staunchest supporters against the Methodist hierarchy—a true man because he had the courage to stand by his prohibition convictions in the face of stiff opposition from his superiors.[59] Folk likewise attacked the actions of the bishop opposed to Kelley's prohibition politicking—as well as the Methodists' episcopacy system as a whole—as not only "anti-American, anti-scriptural and anti-Christian" but also "anti-manly."[60] One evangelical writer in the *Alabama Baptist* explained that the elements of Christian manliness and honor included a desire to know and obey the truth at any cost; strength to stand alone with God, regardless of opposition; and a gentle spirit even in the face of defeat or insult.[61] According to evangelicals, standing firmly for one's Christian principles, even if it invited ridicule from one's social and business associates, was the mark of true courage and honor.

Evangelicals in the New South worked to shift the emphasis from the exterior focus of the antebellum code of honor to an interior focus that valued a man for what was in his heart. Among the traits that evangelicals highlighted as central to the new conception of honorable manhood were a rejection of the violent aspects of the old code, including dueling, fighting, and pistol carrying; an embrace of morally upright personal behavior, including the total rejection of alcohol, cursing, and gambling; support of law and order administered by government officials, as opposed to the use of mob action to settle disputes and mete out justice; a close correlation between one's private values and one's public duty, meaning that one should vote in strict accordance with one's religious beliefs and that public officials should vote and legislate in accordance with their religious views; self-sacrifice on the part of the weaker elements of society, including drunkards and African Americans; and adherence to one's moral convictions regardless of any public ridicule it might engender, rather than putting on a "public face" that does not necessarily reflect one's private thoughts and convictions but merely conforms to popular social values. West describes this as a shift from honor to dignity, with honor being a "social personality that made a man sensitive to insults" and dignity being primarily an internal "conviction of self-worth" unswayed by public sentiment.[62] Although this clearly describes the new ethic promoted by evangelicals, it does not reflect the language they employed. Southern evangelicals spoke not of dignity and integrity but of honor and manliness. By invoking the time-honored southern language of honor, evangelicals sought to redefine these terms along new lines and contested the ownership of honor with those who still adhered to the old code's more violent aspects.

Some historians have begun to recognize a pattern that can be called the "democratization of honor" taking place in the South following the Civil War. Frank Stewart has examined the function and variety of concepts of honor, primarily in the European context, and distinguished between "vertical honor" and "horizontal honor." The former aligned men vertically and distributed honor likewise. Those at the top of the social hierarchy were in a certain honor group, bound by a mutually understood code or set of rules by which they maintained their honor status. These codes existed to establish the superiority of one social group over another. (The antebellum South exhibited this type of honor system, distinguishing the planter aristocracy from other white men below it.) In horizontal honor, honor was equally available across a demographic group. Thus, all white men enjoyed the same potential to achieve the status of honor, regardless of their social or economic position. Stewart maintains that after the Renaissance in Europe, the meaning of honor shifted from its medieval and external emphasis to a more "modern and internal" locus.[63]

Building on Stewart's work, Richard Hamm has suggested that a similar expansion of honor from the vertical to the horizontal transpired in the South after the Civil War. Honor became something to which white men of all social ranks could lay claim; it became something obtainable by all white men.[64] Southern evangelicals recognized this shift in southern culture and engaged in a struggle with lower-class, nonevangelical white males over the new definition of honor. The debate centered largely around how much of the old, violent definition should persist in the New South. Although evangelicals had long wanted to jettison the violent aspects of honor, they found themselves in a precarious position. Especially in the 1890s and after, lower-class white men argued that they obtained and defended their honor by lynching African Americans to protect white womanhood. The rape fears that flourished around the turn of the century functioned to provide lower-class white men with an opportunity to demonstrate that they were honorable. In a way, the epidemic of rape allegations and the affiliated epidemic of lynchings gave certain white men a sense of meaning and self-worth.

The question of how far to go in rejecting this definition of honor was a vexing one for evangelicals. Although they strongly advocated law and order and denounced extralegal punishment, they recognized the powerful claim to honor made by mob defenders. Going too far risked being accused of condoning the actions of "black brutes." In the minds of southern white masses at the end of the nineteenth century, honor came to mean, above all else, protecting white women from assaults by black men, and southerners were frequently reminded that honor demanded a violent response. A letter to the *Nashville Tennessean* asked, "How can any newspaper condemn men for lynching the Negro demons when they insult our white women?"[65] Indeed, most secular papers that denounced lynching made a clear exception for cases in which the assault of a white woman was involved.[66] The letter in the *Tennessean* continued, "Our noble women MUST BE—AND SHALL BE—protected from these accursed hell hounds and their accomplices in crime."[67] In the *Birmingham Times*, an editorial opined, "The heart of every male in this state who deserves the name of man should burn with indignation that such wanton insults are being heaped upon the women—those gentle creatures in whose hearts and minds are born the tenderest, holiest and most sacred impulses the world can ever know, and who are entitled to the protection of the manhood of the state."[68]

By and large, evangelical prohibitionists tried to embrace this core aspect of honor—defending women—without condoning the most popular means of doing so—lynching. They sought to persuade the public that prohibition was honorable and manly in part because it provided a more effective means of defending women from blacks who were turned into beasts by liquor. Thus, during the 1908 Democratic primary campaign in Tennessee, the Reverend J. A. Witherspoon used a play on words to tell an audience that Carmack's attempt to unseat Governor Patterson was "a fight for their wives." Alabama Baptist B. F. Riley declared that lynchings were carried out under "the guise of a false chivalry" and observed that a truly chivalrous and honorable southern man recognized his duty to protect not only the white women of the South but also the lesser men (blacks) from injustice. "No genuinely chivalrous man," he said, "would suffer a Negro to be openly robbed before his eyes on the street, nor would he without protest witness undue advantage taken openly of an ignorant Negro in the purchase of goods."[69] In a similar vein, E. E. Hoss called the mob execution of an accused but untried man "murder of the most cowardly sort."[70] In this way, evangelicals negotiated the fine line between upholding an evangelical standard of honor and being "soft" on African American criminals. They touted the evangelical approach as honorable and manly, and they rejected the violent, extralegal approach as dishonorable and cowardly.

Honor and Prohibition

Southern evangelicals sought to demonstrate that they were the true heirs to the tradition of honorable southern manhood, not the pistol-toting, liquor-drinking, card-playing, low-class hooligans running around in lawless mobs. Their purpose was not simply to lay claim to a designation long denied them but to undergird their reform efforts and legitimize them as authentic southern movements that were wholly compatible with honor and manliness. Prohibition, in particular, required special efforts to recast it as an honorable and genuinely southern position. In addition to being opposed to an activity long associated with manliness, the prohibition movement still suffered in the South because of its Yankee heritage. Opponents continued to try to discredit the movement by pointing out that it had been imported from the North. Jefferson Davis, for example, accused the movement of being composed entirely of "Yankees, Cranks, and Negroes, with a few recreant Confederates."[71] Booker T. Washington reported that similar charges were leveled during the campaign for prohibition in Alabama. A particularly easy target there was the state's Anti-Saloon League superintendent, the Reverend Brooks Lawrence, who was a native of Ohio. "One of the charges brought against him during the campaign was that he was a carpetbagger," Washington recalled, "and that the prohibition movement was an attempt 'to dump northern ideas' upon the South, where they did not fit condition[s]."[72] In his recent study of the prohibition movement in Texas, James Ivy observes, "Whatever the nativity of its proponents, prohibition was a northern reform, akin to abolitionism, racial egalitarianism, or congressional Reconstruction. However well meaning its proponents may be, prohibition was a decidedly un-southern idea."[73] Southern evangelicals knew that for prohibition and other evangelical causes to be widely embraced by southern voters, popular conceptions of honor had to be remade so that they were compatible with prohibition.

The temperance report of the North Georgia Conference of the MECS in 1889 informed its churches that, when it came to drinking, popular and traditional notions of what constituted honor must be changed. "Young people must be made to feel that it is more manly to decline than to accept an invitation to drink," the conference instructed.[74] Two years later the conference argued that support of prohibition was the duty of every "soldier of Christ." To ignore the issue, the temperance committee declared, "is such cowardice as justifies his dismissal from service; and to defend [saloon licensing], by word or ballot, is a betrayal of the home and treachery to the cause of the Son of God."[75] Baptist minister E. K. Cox of Nashville warned the parents in his congregation that in the saloons "your sons are sacrificing honor and manhood on the altars of lust."[76] An editorial in a Georgia Methodist paper assured readers that a gospel message against the dangers of alcohol, if "preached by manly men who are less concerned about popularity and newspaper notoriety than they are for the salvation of the world," would quickly see results.[77]

Evangelical writers often equated manliness with patriotism and devotion to law and order. The Reverend W. L. Pickard declared, "God never made a true minister without making him first a true man!"[78] After the passage of statewide prohibition in Georgia, evangelicals emphasized the importance of upholding and enforcing the law. To fail to do so, one writer remarked, "is cowardice."[79] Evangelicals also praised characteristics such as pulling oneself up by one's bootstraps. One editorial, describing a young preacher who had come from poverty but worked hard to get an education and become a minister, declared, "Here is manliness and grit."[80]

William J. Albert of Atlanta attacked Methodist ministers for not taking a stronger stance against members of their congregations who supported the liquor trade by their actions and their votes. He accused ministers who failed to do so of being guilty of "moral cowardice."[81] In Alabama, W. B. Crumpton called on those men who were "brave enough" to start petitions to counter any efforts to repeal local option laws.[82] In a tract on the benefits of the Adams prohibition law, Folk included this poem:

Oh, who would not a hero be,
In this the noblest chivalry?
For there be those who ache to see
The day dawn of our victory.

Work, brothers, work,
Work hand and brain.
Let's win a better day again.
We will, we will true heroes be.
In this the grandest chivalry.[83]

For evangelical prohibitionists, their cause was the "noblest chivalry" that a southern white man could pursue, and those who advocated prohibition were the "true heroes" of the South. This language echoes an 1885 prohibition speech by Georgia Baptist J. B. Hawthorne, who called those who labored for prohibition "heroes of the greatest chivalry the world ever saw."[84] In the new evangelical definition of honor and manhood, living a moral life and standing boldly for causes such as prohibition were the key ingredients, not violent and rowdy behavior. One prohibitionist wrote to Folk that "not one noble impulse or manly principle" could be found in the motives of those who opposed prohibition, while another praised Folk's own "brave, manly fight" for the cause.[85] Voting for prohibition candidates was touted as true manliness, as a broadside published in Durham, North Carolina, in 1886 affirmed. Urging voters to cast their ballots for a list of dry candidates in the city's upcoming election, the poster exclaimed: "ASSERT YOUR MANHOOD . . . VOTE LIKE MEN!"[86]

The language of honor and manhood is likewise found in the political debates over prohibition. The Reverend Pickard of Birmingham called on those Democrats in the state legislature who opposed prohibition to prove their manliness. "If whiskey is such a boon and blessing to a community, certainly those who think so are willing for their names to be published in the papers with the application for license," wrote Pickard in 1891. "As a citizen and Democrat I see no objection to this manly procedure on the part of a 'majority' of the Democrats."[87] Job Harral of Tennessee called the honor of both Democrats and Republicans into question when making the case for a third party, saying, "if the great political parties are too cowardly, or too corrupt, to range themselves on the side of the best interests of man, on the side of sobriety and decency, on the side of law and order, we can organize separately and support men and measures looking to the good of the land."[88] Carmack himself had invoked the language of honor in one of his first editorials for the *Nashville Tennessean*. To the great pleasure of Tennessee evangelicals, Carmack wrote: "The duty which a Democrat owes to his party should never be separated in his thought from the duty he owes to his country; and he is either faithless or a coward who will see his party made the harlot of a corrupt machine and lift no hand to save it from dishonor. The real friend of the Democrat party is he who would keep it pure and honest, true to its principles."[89]

Evangelical women also participated in the effort to redefine honor, especially as it related to drinking and prohibition. In 1880 a young lady from Alabama warned young men to abstain from alcohol consumption because it "destroys all that is lovely and good and pure and noble in man," and promised that those of her sex "will admire and honor you for it."[90] When Emory professor Henry Scomp was fired for his prohibition politics, Mrs. W. C. Sibley of the Georgia WCTU defended him as a man of true honor, writing, "All honor to Professor Scomp, the man who refuses to sacrifice principle and self-respect for position!"[91] In Alabama, Julia Tutwiler was an active social reformer and widely known temperance activist. As a member of the Alabama WCTU, she penned a rally song for prohibition workers that deftly communicated the evangelical message of the honorableness of the prohibition cause and the cowardice of those who opposed it:

Where's the man who fears opinion?
He is not the friend for me.
Let him cringe to ruin's dominion,
Sister, you and I are free.
So, let the cowards vote as they will,
I'm for prohibition still.
Prohibition, prohibition,
I'm for prohibition still.[92]

Like their male counterparts, evangelical women equated support for prohibition with manliness and honor, while those who opposed prohibition were labeled cowards and had their honor called into question.

Evangelicals recognized the powerful force of the concept of honor in southern culture, and at the end of the nineteenth century, they increasingly sought to appropriate the designation of honorable men and to redefine what it meant to have honor. This was a significant change from their antebellum position as outsiders to the cult of honor. In the antebellum years, southern evangelicals could only offer an alternative to the southern cult of honor; in the New South, they were in a position to redefine honor in a way that allowed them to claim honor without forsaking their evangelical principles. Prohibition was a central element in this movement, as were evangelical efforts to end pistol carrying, gambling, and other forms of lawlessness. The attempt to reclaim honor was important because it gave prohibition legitimacy as a truly southern reform effort, despite what ex-Confederates such as Jefferson Davis said about the movement. It also put them in an advantageous position in terms of being able to label their opponents both dishonorable and unchristian.

Chapter Six

"Some of Our Best Preachers Part Their Hair in the Middle"

Prohibition and Gender

WOMEN PLAYED A CENTRAL ROLE in the way that southern evangelicals made their case for prohibition in the late nineteenth and early twentieth centuries. Women were viewed as the most vulnerable victims of intemperance and as the key justification for prohibitory legislation. The idea that white women were endangered by alcohol underpinned most evangelical arguments for prohibition. From the drunkard's wife who was left impoverished, abused, and unable to properly rear her children to the white woman who was exposed to liquor-crazed black rapists every time she stepped outdoors, women were portrayed as victims of the saloons and as the central rallying cry for prohibition. Both Victorian gender ideals and the ideology of the Lost Cause worked to elevate women in the New South to unprecedented levels. Male evangelical prohibitionists capitalized on this by making the threat posed by liquor to southern white womanhood a central element of the campaign. And the core of the argument appealed to the very heart of the southern sense of honor across all social and religious strata.

But women were not merely passive participants in the crusade for southern prohibition, vulnerable objects of pity utilized to manipulate the passions of the male electorate. Women were also important actors in the southern campaign for prohibition. The WCTU, in particular, benefited both the prohibition cause and the campaign for women's rights in the South. Female agitation for prohibition helped sway public opinion, and women's presence at the polls on election day helped secure victory for prohibition measures. At the same time, the WCTU gave southern women an opportunity to expand their public voice and involvement in public affairs. However, women's participation in the prohibition movement also raised deep concerns among southern white men, especially in relation to women's suffrage and women's leadership in the church. Although many southern evangelical men welcomed the contribution made by women's activism to the prohibition cause, the WCTU eventually met with stiff criticism and sometimes outright opposition from the male evangelical leadership of the South. This chapter focuses on both the activities of southern women to promote prohibition and other social reforms and the harsh reaction against such labors by their male counterparts.[1]

The Woman's Christian Temperance Union

The primary agency through which women participated actively in the prohibition movement was the Woman's Christian Temperance Union. The organization originated in the North, and the southern states always lagged behind in terms of membership and number of chapters. Nevertheless, the union was central to southern women's involvement in the prohibition effort. Formed in 1874, the WCTU presented itself as a "sober second thought" to the more spontaneous and emotional outpouring of female temperance activity known as the Women's Temperance Crusade of 1873–1874. The crusade was sparked in Hillsboro, Ohio, in December 1873 and spread across the Midwest during the following months. Women in the community of Hillsboro left a prayer meeting at the local Presbyterian church en masse and descended upon local saloons, where they stayed day after day conducting nonviolent protests. The women sang, prayed, argued with saloon keepers, pleaded with saloon patrons, and generally created enough of a nuisance that many barkeeps, druggists, and hotel owners relented and pledged not to sell alcohol.[2]

The victory in Hillsboro was widely reported, and the campaign was mimicked by women in other towns and even in the cities of Dayton and Cleveland. When the emotional outpouring of that winter subsided, there remained a strong desire among several Ohio women to establish a temperance organization. During the summer of 1874, these women gathered at Chautauqua to discuss the need for such an organization, and in the fall they formed the WCTU in Cleveland. Annie Wittenmyer served as the union's first president, and during her five-year tenure, the WCTU experienced remarkable growth. By 1875, twenty-one state unions had been organized, and at the end of the 1870s, the WCTU had become the largest organization of women in the world, boasting nearly twelve hundred local unions with a membership of twenty-seven thousand women.[3]

The WCTU successfully tapped into women's strong desire to become involved in the world outside the traditional sphere of the home. This yearning had its roots in the recent necessities of wartime. Northern and southern women had been called on to serve the needs of soldiers, and that experience had led many of them to recognize the untapped potential of American women to work for the nation outside the home. Wittenmyer considered her wartime service a transformative experience, and after the war, she and other women "perceived other 'emergencies' that were calling them from their home into the world." In 1868 she established the Ladies and Pastors Christian Union to facilitate women's religious work in the cities.[4] Such awakenings were experienced by women in both the North and the South. In the South, men's absence from the farms and plantations created new responsibilities for women, as did the need to care for wounded soldiers. After the war, the male population in the South was greatly depleted, meaning that women had to continue to pick up the slack and assume new responsibilities outside the home.[5] In 1861 an Alabama Methodist laywoman wrote to Bishop Andrew regarding the war work being done by herself and other southern women. Noting that these women loved their God even more than they loved the Confederacy, she suggested that women could be more actively and effectively engaged in the church's work if the church would only identify specific tasks for them.[6] When the WCTU emerged in the mid-1870s, it created an opportunity for women to mobilize on behalf of a respectable social cause.

The WCTU had a particularly strong organization at the grassroots level. Local unions focused primarily on getting individuals to sign pledges of abstinence and creating clubs for boys and girls to inculcate the principles of temperance in the young. During the 1870s the union was also on the leading edge of the movement to replace wine with grape juice in communion services, embracing the two-wine theory in its publications. The WCTU's motto, "For God and home and native land," summed up the idea that by taking on these new roles in society, women were doing God's work, and they were doing so not for their own aggrandizement but to protect home and hearth as well as the Republic itself. The WCTU emphasized that women were exercising guardianship over an arena—the home—that men conceded was their proper domain. By 1878, the WCTU had firmly committed itself to statewide prohibition. Under Wittenmyer, the union argued that both men and women should have a voice in prohibition politics, the former via the ballot and the latter by means of petitions to state legislatures and Congress. The petition was the primary means by which women sought a political voice in the 1870s, and the WCTU delivered massive stacks of signed petitions to Congress each year.[7]

In 1879 Frances Willard became president of the national WCTU and instituted a dramatic shift in the organization's goals and tactics. The tenacious Methodist laywoman advocated a "do everything" agenda that involved educational reform, prison reform, and urban ministries, in addition to the union's emphasis on temperance. Willard also politicized the WCTU and instigated its embrace of the controversial issue of women's suffrage. Under Willard, the union first endorsed the Republican Party but soon became disillusioned by its reluctance to embrace prohibition. Willard helped create the Home Protection Party, which in 1882 merged with the national Prohibition Party. In the early 1890s Willard embraced the Populist Party as well, and she launched an ultimately unsuccessful effort to merge the Prohibition and Populist parties.[8] During this period Willard became increasingly radical politically, being introduced to socialism while traveling in England.[9] Under Wittenmyer's leadership, the WCTU had clung to Victorian gender ideals that relegated women to a separate and distinct sphere and viewed women as fundamentally different from men in nature. With Willard at the helm, however, the national organization increasingly rejected this definition of womanhood in favor of a proto-feminist ethic of gender equality. The national WCTU had not taken a stance on suffrage with Wittenmyer as its president, although some state unions did embrace it. The suffrage issue was a key aspect of Willard's ideology, however. The success of reform movements depended on what she called the "home protection ballot"—the inclusion of women in the political process.[10]

When Willard died in 1898, the WCTU came under the leadership of Lillian Stevens, who redirected the organization along a more conservative path. Stevens did not advocate women's suffrage, and in 1899 the WCTU withdrew its endorsement of the Prohibition Party and disengaged from direct involvement in party politics. The union also resumed a more narrow focus, eschewing the "do everything" philosophy and focusing all its energies on prohibition.[11] In her inaugural address, Stevens made no reference to any reforms other than temperance and prohibition. She made no mention of the many causes that had become so central to the national WCTU during her predecessor's term: suffrage, labor problems, educational reform, women's rights, poverty, and prostitution. Stevens personally believed in women's suffrage but was not a radical advocate of it and did not want the issue to cloud the vision and purpose of the WCTU.[12]

The development of the WCTU in the South was slower than in the North, but it met with significant success nonetheless. Supporters of the WCTU encountered resistance in the South during the 1870s because of religious objections to women doing such work in public. In 1876 a Tennessee woman told the national WCTU that she and her colleagues faced particularly strong opposition from southern ministers. "They quote St. Paul, and tell us we are wonderfully out of our places," she reported.[13] In 1881 Frances Willard made a lecture tour of the southland, visiting every southern state over the course of fourteen weeks and establishing local unions across the region. She repeated the tour in 1882 and 1883. Along with Willard, Sallie Chapin of South Carolina was influential in establishing local temperance unions in the South. Like so many other WCTU workers, she had first entered the realm of public service during the Civil War, and beginning in 1881, she tirelessly traveled back and forth across the South, working for the cause.[14]

The women's movement of the winter of 1874 was not limited to Ohio; it spread into the South as well. In the east Tennessee town of Greeneville, a group of women laid siege to the town's three saloons in February. Two of the bars were closed, at least temporarily, and a shelter was built outside the remaining saloon (owned and operated, coincidentally, by a woman) where the women could seek protection from the weather as they gathered daily to pray, sing, and harangue the obstinate saloon keeper and her patrons.[15] Elizabeth Fisher Johnson of Memphis attended the national WCTU's first convention in 1875 and was responsible for establishing a union in Memphis in 1876. By 1878, the Memphis chapter had collected six thousand abstinence pledges, but membership began to flag until it was revived by Willard's visit to the city in 1881.[16] In 1882 Johnson worked with women from the newly created Nashville union to form a Tennessee WCTU. Johnson served as president of the state union initially, but it experienced its greatest growth after 1889, when Silena Moore became state president. Between 1894 and 1898, the number of unions in Tennessee grew from thirty-three to fifty-nine.[17]

Georgia's first WCTU was founded in Atlanta in 1880 in the basement of the Trinity Methodist Church. More unions were formed when Willard visited the state the following year, and by 1883, enough local chapters existed to establish the Georgia Woman's Christian Temperance Union.[18] The state WCTU elected Jane Sibley of Augusta as its first president, and she served in that capacity until 1900. Georgia women embraced the petition movement, and over a three-month period they collected thirty-seven thousand signatures in support of local option laws.[19] Two leading women of the Georgia WCTU were the Latimer sisters. Rebecca Latimer Felton was an active WCTU member and worked to eradicate the convict lease system. She argued that the work of saving sons and husbands, and of protecting the home and the family, "was preeminently God's work for women to do."[20] Younger sister Mary Latimer McLendon was one of the founders of the Atlanta chapter of the WCTU and a strong advocate of women's suffrage. Known as the "mother of woman suffrage in Georgia," McLendon also served as president of the Georgia Woman Suffrage Association for decades.[21]

The first WCTU chapter in Alabama was organized in 1881 in Mobile, during Willard's visit that year. Over the next two years, eighteen more unions sprang up across the state, and the Alabama WCTU was formed in 1884.[22] Julia Tutwiler became one of the Alabama WCTU's most well-known leaders. Like so many other women of her generation, Tutwiler's desire to employ her skills and intelligence outside the home emerged during the sectional conflict. She longed to help in the war effort and even wrote a poem about how duty called her to aid her bleeding and wounded countrymen, but her father would not allow it. Nevertheless, the impulse to influence the course of events remained with Tutwiler and eventually found an outlet through the WCTU, where she served as vice president of the Alabama union and as chairperson of prison and jail work.[23] Tutwiler studied at Vassar and then in Paris and Germany. President Grover Cleveland once called her "the brainiest woman I ever met." In Germany, Tutwiler was introduced to innovative approaches to both education and incarceration. After returning to Alabama, Tutwiler devoted her life to reforming these two institutions in the South. She created the state's first kindergarten and introduced the reformatory model to the state's prison system.[24]

Women's Prohibition Activities

Anne Firor Scott has observed that immediately after the Civil War, women became engaged with the world outside the home in unprecedented ways. During the antebellum period, there had been a dearth of female benevolence societies in the South. Although female-run mission and abolition societies had flourished in the antebellum North, the movement had largely bypassed the South.[25] When they had participated in temperance activities, southern women had done so only in mixed-sex groups.[26] Female mission societies had existed in the antebellum South, but not until the 1870s did women's involvement in such organizations explode. Scott notes that the benevolent activities of southern women went through three phases after the war: mission society membership grew rapidly in the 1870s, temperance societies—primarily the WCTU—boomed in the 1880s, and women's clubs emerged in the South in the 1890s. Each wave "stemmed from the same impulse"—women's desire to engage in the world around them—and each widened their sphere of activity and influence.[27]

By and large, the push for temperance and prohibition by southern women and southern men progressed along similar lines. They participated in debates about the use of wine in communion, they used similar lines of argumentation on behalf of temperance, and they even shared the same declining views of African Americans in the late 1880s. Regarding the use of unfermented grape juice for communion, the WCTU was particularly devoted to the spread of this practice. The organization declared in 1875 that it would marshal all its power to stop the use of fermented wine in communion services, and for the next two decades, it used tracts, newspaper articles, Sunday school lessons, and pleas to every level of ecclesiastical hierarchy—from local pastors to denominational gatherings—to purify the church's communion practice. Union publications provided recipes for unfermented grape juice so that women could provide it free to their churches. One such recipe was accompanied by the following poem describing why strict adherence to Jesus's example of using wine was unacceptable:

> Our savior took the cup and blessed,
> "Drink this rememb'ring me."
> It was His last and fond request,
> His dying legacy.
> And we, His faithful followers, still,
> 'Tho' Christ be risen from the dead,
> Glad to obey His dying will
> Still drink the wine and break the bread.
> But dare we pass the sacred cup
> Filled with a poison to the brim,
> To yonder youth, that he may sup
> That which contains a curse to him?
> You cannot know what fiends you raise
> When to his tried and tempted lips
> You press with sacred songs of praise
> The deadly poison that he sips.[28]

Some union members publicly refused to receive communion if fermented wine was being served. By 1892, the WCTU was proud to announce that two-thirds of the churches in the United States used unfermented wine at the communion table.[29] Others, however, were less willing to embrace this alternative for fear that it would alienate traditionalists. In 1884 the Georgia Baptist Conference admonished the WCTU to tone down its opposition to the use of wine in the Lord's Supper, believing that the majority of Georgia Baptists were unprepared to embrace such a change. "Any reference made by them to the use of wine at the Lord's Supper," the convention explained, "will, to some extent, alienate from them the sympathies of ninety-nine in a hundred of all the Christian people in the country."[30] The convention accused the WCTU of doing more harm than good. Women's commitment to ridding the nation's communion tables of fermented wine, however, never wavered.

Like white evangelical men, southern WCTU members had a shift in attitude toward African Americans between the 1880s and the 1890s. Early WCTU leaders in the South, such as Sallie Chapin, encouraged southern unions to work closely with the black population. Addressing a state WCTU meeting in 1884, she challenged the women present regarding their black neighbors: "You must educate them as you would any other class to think right about temperance and prohibition. . . . If you do not teach them, someone else will." Her rationale for incorporating blacks into the movement was not simply a pragmatic attempt to sway their votes; it was based on the more positive view of southern blacks typical of 1880s New Southites.[31] "They are your laboring class, living in your midst, with unalienable rights and privileges," she explained to her audience of female prohibitionists.[32] Many southern WC-TUs did work with African American women to organize black unions in the mid-1880s, and some even created a Department of Colored Work for that purpose.[33] But when prohibition efforts failed in 1887, southern women blamed black voters. In response to Tennessee's 1887 election, WCTU women in Alabama reported to their members that "the election was lost by the solid Negro votes in the large cities."[34]

Women argued for prohibition using the same kinds of emotional appeals and citing the same social costs of alcohol abuse as their male counterparts. Tales of personal destruction and family abandonment were a mainstay of prohibition advocates both male and female. However, using the example of women becoming the victims of drunken men led to an irony: while the WCTU was strengthening women's public voice and in many ways providing a gateway to greater equality with men, southern WCTU leaders also embraced their identity as the "weaker sex" to advance their cause. In an appeal to male voters and legislators, the Alabama WCTU adopted the stereotype of men as the protectors of southern womanhood. "Men of Alabama!—you who have ever stood gallant for your wives, your home, and your children, you who are strong and brave and bold," the resolution read, "we have no power to prevent this great evil." The plea went on to lament to the state's men: "Do you hear the cry of the women . . . listen to the wailing."[35]

Thus, the southern WCTU sometimes presented two opposing images: woman as weak and in need of male protection, and woman as aggressively taking on evils that men were unable or unwilling to conquer. In the latter vein, southern temperance women, like those in the North, frequently evoked the image of the crusading woman, harking back to the crusade of the 1870s that had launched women's active role in the temperance struggle. In 1903 the Alabama WCTU, for example, resolved that "today, as in Crusader days," the women of America were being called by God to free the country from the tyranny of liquor, and it encouraged women to rely on the "crusader spirit" of those who had gone before them.[36] Holly Berkley recently examined how the WCTU maintained the icon of the crusading woman throughout the early twentieth century, and she finds in this image a key method by which women took the role of defenseless victim and transformed it into a means of empowerment.[37]

By expressing their public activities on behalf of prohibition in terms of protecting the home and safeguarding their proper sphere, southern women were able to slowly expand their realm of influence. Although southern female temperance advocates often sought to distance themselves from the more controversial aspects of the "do everything" approach, they took on many social issues beyond the cause of prohibition. Southern WCTUs engaged in myriad causes, including hospital work, child labor issues, and antinarcotic campaigns; they helped create schools in prisons, urged the establishment of reform schools for young criminals, crusaded against the convict lease system, and advocated raising the age of consent (in Alabama the age of consent was ten years, and the WCTU lobbied to change it to eighteen).[38] Southern WCTU women may have denied that they were seeking greater political rights, but they did use the organization to broaden their impact on society. They also lauded the impact of the national WCTU on expanding women's opportunities in society. The Alabama WCTU noted that "they have made it possible for 2,000,000 women in America to earn their own living and still be respected, they have made it possible for them to demand reasonable pay for their work."[39]

Just as male evangelical prohibition advocates became deeply involved in political campaigns for prohibition legislation, evangelical women participated in those campaigns as well. Although they were not allowed to vote themselves, women worked the polls on election day, encouraging men to vote in favor of prohibition and discouraging agents of the liquor industry from convincing voters to support wet candidates or to oppose local option measures. Sometimes, women even tried to keep wet voters from the polls. Booker T. Washington noted that "prohibition in the South is to a certain extent a woman's movement," because it was the women who "stood all day at the polls to see that their husbands, sons, and fathers voted 'right.'"[40] The WCTU organized a parade of women in Birmingham in 1909 to encourage men to vote for the prohibition amendment in the upcoming election. The women marched and held placards reading "Vote for Us" and "God Wills It."[41]

In 1908 the Nashville WCTU was committed to helping Edward Carmack unseat Democratic governor Malcolm Patterson, and the organization set aside the Friday before the primary election as a special day of prayer and fasting.[42] On election day, the union's forces were fully mobilized and working the polls across the state. Nannie Curtis, a leader of the Texas WCTU, traveled to Memphis to motivate Christian women. She urged them to take an active role in election day activities, in defiance of their husbands, if necessary. Meeting at the city's Second Methodist Church, WCTU leaders laid plans to have women and children parade at polling places carrying banners and singing prohibition songs such as "Give Us Prohibition," sung to the tune of "Old Time Religion." The WCTU arranged for women to be present at polling stations from the time they opened in the morning until they closed, praying, singing, and serving lunch to the poll workers. This guaranteed that at no time during the day would Carmack supporters be absent from the polls. It also organized parades of children who waved prohibition flags and wore banners proclaiming: "Tremble King Alcohol, for We Shall Grow Up!" Recognizing that many immigrants and working-class whites did not know how to vote, the WCTU made sure that members were there to help those individuals understand the ballot and "to see that they voted for the right ticket—Carmack and prohibition."[43]

Women also made their presence known in the state legislatures. During the 1907 drive for statewide prohibition in Georgia, the women of the WCTU worked tirelessly at the polls to help elect legislators who favored the measure and then focused their energy on holding the legislators' feet to the fire once they were in office. During the weeks when the prohibition bill was being debated, women gathered at the capitol daily. The WCTU organized sunrise prayer meetings at the church of John E. White in Atlanta, just across the street from the capitol building. These services were designed to get prohibition supporters to the statehouse early and pack the gallery before the liquor interests could bring in their people. Every day, men and women supporting statewide prohibition filled the stiflingly hot gallery, sometimes applauding speeches by dry legislators, sometimes hissing at wet speakers or those who tried to filibuster the proceedings, sometimes breaking into song (usually "Georgia's Going Dry," sung to the tune of "Bringing in the Sheaves"),[44] and always wearing the white ribbons and waving the prohibition flags provided by the WCTU.[45]

Political involvement, especially election day activities, became a mainstay of women's efforts on behalf of prohibition in the South, but not all women approved of such behavior. Lida B. Robertson of Mobile thought that such undertakings were unbecoming for a Christian lady. In her day, Robertson explained, it was considered bold for a lady to even go into town on election day. "And I can not now in my gray hairs appear at the polls to serve Tom, Dick, and Harry refreshments," she chided. Robertson viewed intemperance as a problem for men to deal with and found it distasteful for women "to commonize themselves to the level of men lobbying at the poles [sic] to influence votes and serve coffee and sandwiches to ungodly strange men and political toughs."[46] Similar sentiments were expressed by a Methodist laywoman in Georgia who wrote to the *Wesleyan Christian Advocate* to reprove women for taking up men's work. "Never was there a more serious mistake," she warned, than for a woman to "thrust herself from the pure atmosphere" of the domestic sphere, which was "hers by divine right." She maintained that it was against women's nature to venture into "the impure, unwholesome, fetid, poisonous, political air which men breathe so often until body and soul become asphyxiated by moral contagion."[47]

Men, too, sometimes criticized the efforts of union women to influence elections. Following Carmack's disappointing defeat by incumbent governor Patterson in the Tennessee primary of 1908, the *Christian Advocate* of Nashville placed some of the blame on the

WCTU. "The activity of the Woman's Christian Temperance Union in holding public meetings addressed by ladies, in organizing parades, and especially in having ladies present at the voting places was of very little service, perhaps even in some ways a disadvantage, to the cause which these ladies advocated," the editor explained. He conceded that the ladies' motives were pure, but their activities were misguided. The editor continued, "Ladies at the polling places, singing and offering audible prayers, dispensing lemonade, sandwiches, etc., on the occasion of a contest between two prominent politicians for a purely political advantage seemed to most men out of place." The reason was clear to the editor: southerners did not like to see ladies involved in political matters, even if the cause was godly. "Such is the distaste in the South for public speaking and political activity upon the part of women that in our opinion about as many votes would have been lost as won by such methods," he concluded.[48]

For the most part, however, evangelicals warmly embraced women's activities in support of prohibition during the 1880s. Male prohibitionists realized early on the powerful influence that women could have in shaping public opinion regarding liquor and in getting something done about it. As early as 1880, a Baptist from Alabama expressed his confidence that women would lead the prohibition cause to victory. He explained that in his county, petitions were being circulated to secure local prohibition for the town of Fort Deposit. Volunteers disseminated the petitions around the countryside, including several women, "two of whom rode many miles in the country, although the roads were bad and the day a very cold and bleak one, and ended their day's work saying they would ride a week if necessary." The commitment of these women made the writer optimistic about the prospect of instituting prohibition across the state. He wrote, "Rest assured if the ladies will take the matter in hand we will meet with success."[49] W. B. Crumpton argued in 1884 that women were the "worst sufferers from the effects of liquor, and they have a right to be heard on this question, and work in the front ranks of this movement."[50] Crumpton, like other prohibitionists, recognized that women could effect change in ways that men could not. When towns were faced with possible repeal of local option measures, Crumpton advised them to circulate counterpetitions. "Let every woman in the county sign a petition against the repeal. The Legislature will not put the saloon on any county where the *women* will exert their influence against it."[51]

Following the 1887 defeat of a prohibition amendment in Tennessee, the *Christian Advocate* of Nashville praised the valiant efforts by women on behalf of the amendment. "They came with prayer, with song, with persuasion, with a zeal that nothing could quench," the editor noted. "It was a new thing in Tennessee, but it was a good thing in every way."[52] L. L. Gwaltney of Prattville, Alabama, also praised the campaign efforts of women. At the polls, "where the last battle is to be fought," women "line up as soldiers of the cross, and sing the songs of Zion, and bring over many a vote which would have otherwise been corrupted with tainted money." In addition to encouraging many voters to cast their ballots against the saloon, Gwaltney believed that these women "kept back many of the opposition from voting at all."[53] The editor of Georgia's *Wesleyan Christian Advocate* reassured his readers in 1888 that women participating in the state's WCTU were not radicals. After attending the state WCTU convention in Atlanta, he observed, "These women are not short-haired women, but the first women in the churches and communities in which they lived." He further noted that the delegates showed little interest in obtaining suffrage rights. "The women of the convention, so far as I could hear and judge by their applause of Mrs. Chapin, are opposed to women voting."[54]

During the mid-1880s, denominational endorsements of the WCTU became ubiquitous in evangelical temperance reports. In 1884 the Georgia Baptist Convention lauded the WCTU as "noble women in a noble cause." In 1886 the Tennessee Baptist Convention resolved to "give our sympathy and cooperation to the Women's Christian Temperance Union and all other temperance organizations in every prudent and scriptural measure they may adopt in their efforts to suppress the liquor traffic." That same year, the Tennessee Conference of the MECS declared that the WCTU was "a potent factor in the creation of the growing sentiment for prohibition in this country," and the Holston Conference pledged its "moral support" to the union, which it deemed "worthy of all praise."[55]

Through the WCTU, southern women played a significant role in changing public opinion about prohibition and in accomplishing electoral and legislative victories for the movement. Furthermore, the WCTU was a profoundly important institution for women, offering them their first opportunity to speak out boldly on an issue that was becoming as political in nature as it was moral and religious. Especially during the 1880s, active participation in the prohibition cause under the auspices of the WCTU allowed women to "pursue their own development and social reform without drastically offending the prevailing views of the community about ladylike behavior."[56] As the national WCTU became increasingly radicalized and politicized under Willard in the 1890s, however, the activities of southern unionists became offensive to southern evangelical males and were opposed by them.

Women's Suffrage and Prohibition

Despite the broad support the WCTU received from southern evangelicals during the 1880s, the direction in which Frances Willard was taking the national organization had unfortunate consequences for southern unions during the 1890s. An examination of denominational temperance reports during this era demonstrates declining support for the WCTU during the years of Willard's leadership. Such reports reveal a recurring pattern in terms of denominational endorsement of the union. Between the late 1880s and about 1905, southern evangelical denominational bodies were consistently silent about the WCTU. The Alabama Conference of the MECS was typical of other Methodist conferences, expressing its support for the WCTU in 1886 and then falling into a long silence regarding the organization throughout the 1890s; the conference did not mention the WCTU again until 1904. WCTU endorsements were likewise absent from the temperance reports of the North Georgia Conference, which mentioned the women's organization in 1891 and was then silent about it until 1908. The Tennessee Conference praised the WCTU in 1886, and then made no mention of the group for more than two decades, next endorsing the union in 1908. The Holston Conference never mentioned the WCTU at all until 1905. The WCTU took a similar hiatus from the temperance reports of state Baptist conventions. The Georgia Baptists embraced the organization in 1884, and then waited until 1907 to express any further support for the group. The Tennessee Baptist Convention's first endorsement of the WCTU came in 1886, and its second came in 1908. Alabama Baptists endorsed the WCTU and its work in 1885, and then ignored the organization in its temperance reports until 1915. This pattern strongly suggests more than mere oversight. The absence of denominational support for the

WCTU reflects the frigid relationship that existed between the union and southern evangelical leadership during the turbulent decade of the 1890s—a relationship that thawed only after Willard's influence over the national WCTU ended and the organization resumed a less threatening agenda.

It is not surprising that southern evangelical men found the WCTU more palatable in the years before and after Willard's tenure. Concern about the more radical objectives of the union began in the late 1880s but became more acute during the 1890s. The prospect of women seeking enfranchisement was disconcerting enough to southern men, but when the WCTU threw its support behind third-party political movements in the 1890s, male opposition to the organization—especially among Bourbon evangelicals—became vehement. Leslie Kathrin Dunlap has noted that the period from 1896 to 1910 marks the "doldrums" of both the women's suffrage movement and the WCTU in the South. This downturn in their fortunes, she maintains, reflects a larger backlash against such movements by advocates of a more muscular, masculine Christianity.[57] But the hiatus of evangelical endorsement and support for the WCTU seems to reflect a change in attitude specific to the WCTU and its actions. By embracing both a radical feminist social agenda and a radical Populist political agenda, the national WCTU caused a long period of male discontent with the organization. Once a change in leadership and direction took place, relations between female prohibitionists and their male evangelical counterparts began to improve. Within a few years of Stevens's ascension to the presidency of the WCTU, and her determination that the organization should focus solely on prohibition, the WCTU regained its respected place as a valued coworker in the prohibition cause.

The WCTU entered the political arena fully in 1884 when the Prohibition Party chose Kansas governor John St. John as its presidential nominee. Frances Willard served on the nominating committee, and she spoke at the party's convention in Pittsburgh. Initially, this connection with the Prohibition Party was most controversial because of its position in favor of women's suffrage. The union's support of the Prohibition Party became even more divisive during the 1890s, when the hegemony of the Democratic Party in the South was threatened by such third parties chipping away at its base. Southern evangelicals called Willard's involvement with the party "a serious blunder," saying that it "carries with it the idea of determined inseparableness, in some minds at least, of prohibition and woman suffrage." The *Alabama Baptist* knew that the suffrage issue would drive a wedge between southern voters and prohibition. "If this great temperance movement is made to embrace or endorse the suffrage of women, then the South cannot be relied upon for support," wrote the editor.[58] Another editorial in the same paper lamented, "We are greatly, earnestly, and vehemently in favor of prohibition, but pray deliver us from woman suffrage."[59] In 1888 T. R. McCarty, an Alabama Methodist, observed that the Prohibition Party "evidently prefers protective tariff and woman suffrage to prohibition." McCarty despaired that intemperance was destroying the nation but nevertheless declared that any solution that included women's suffrage was not welcomed.[60]

The *Alabama Christian Advocate* admitted that its support for the union had cooled in recent years. The editors explained the change in their attitude toward the WCTU, saying:

We wanted to help them because it was right, and we did so just as long as they held on to the one work to which God seemed to have called them; but when they allowed a few such women as old Sister Cady Stanton and her sort to put into the movement woman suffrage, they put the thing beyond our reach. We want to work for temperance, but if we can not do it without helping forward woman suffrage, then we shall simply rest until the temperance cause appears under a form that we can work for it.[61]

The paper suggested that southern WCTUs should break off from the national organization and create a separate southern union "from which woman suffrage will be eliminated and over which the Cady Stanton's of the North will have no jurisdiction."[62] In another editorial, the paper went on to criticize the WCTU for its "complications and alliances that render it distasteful to many of the best people of the country."[63]

Many southern unions began to distance themselves from the national leadership in a bid to squelch opposition from male evangelicals and the larger community. By dissociating themselves from the more radical stance of the national union and eschewing any desire for the ballot, southern WCTU leaders demonstrated that they were what William O'Neill has called "social feminists." These women were deeply committed to moral reform work and to impacting the world around them, but they did not embrace (at least not publicly) the agenda of women's suffrage and equality espoused by suffragists such as Frances Willard and Susan B. Anthony.[64] Social feminists greatly outnumbered their more radial sisters into the early twentieth century, and a large movement of women opposed to suffrage emerged in both the South and the North.[65] Many of these women found empowerment in the "separate spheres" model and feared that its demise would mean a significant loss of influence.[66]

The Alabama WCTU addressed the issue of the ties between local unions and the national WCTU in 1888. Esther Pugh of Chicago was present at the annual meeting and was asked for clarification on a question: "Should it be regarded as an evidence of disloyalty if a state or local Union should not endorse every position taken by the National WCTU?" Pugh's answer was "No, emphatically—No." She explained that the national organization demanded only two things of its members: the signing of a total abstinence pledge and the payment of dues. Individuals were not bound by all the utterances of the national body, she assured the women, and each state was free to "take the lines of work suited to its environment." The state WCTU found Pugh's answer satisfactory and resolved that it was a "sufficient guarantee for the future." The women also passed a resolution distancing themselves from the more extreme positions of Willard, saying that they "differ with, and cannot endorse every line of work adopted by the National WCTU," yet praising her "loving leadership" and reaffirming their loyalty to her.[67] By taking such a position, women in the South often succeeded in mollifying some of the union's critics. The *Alabama Christian Advocate* commended the work done by the Alabama WCTU and the way it clearly delineated its position from that of the national WCTU. The paper happily reported that the Alabama WCTU had passed a resolution embracing Pugh's remarks and affirming that her sentiments regarding the relationship between the Alabama chapter and the national WCTU was representative of the entire Alabama union. Satisfied, the editors noted that the paper "will most cheerfully give them our support just as long as they confine themselves to this one work, and leave politics and woman suffrage to be taken care of by the politicians, and this we believe they will do."[68] It was not until 1914 that the Alabama WCTU changed course and endorsed women's suffrage.[69]

Unfortunately, no such détente could be reached between the Georgia WCTU and the Methodist leadership in that state, where Warren A. Candler was the most strident and influential opponent of the WCTU. After the national WCTU embraced women's suffrage and began to endorse third-party politicians, southern white evangelical men, especially Bourbon evangelicals like Candler, turned on the union. They waged an unrelenting war on state and local unions in the South, fearing that they were in fact fronts for propagating the radical views of the national leadership. Candler's row with the WCTU was intertwined with his controversial dismissal of professor Henry Scomp in 1894, but it actually began several years prior to that. Scomp's wife was president of the Oxford, Georgia, WCTU, the chapter to which Candler's wife, Nettie, belonged. After 1890, both Candler and his wife became alarmed at the growing support for suffrage and party politics in the local union. In 1891 Professor Scomp introduced a resolution at the State Temperance Alliance Convention in Atlanta calling on the convention to "indorse woman's work upon the platform, and wherever else God might call her." Evangelicals like Candler feared that the "wherever else" might include the pulpit or the voting booth and accused the Georgia WCTU of embracing the national WCTU's suffrage agenda.

In 1890 Jane Sibley, president of the state WCTU in Georgia, gained some notoriety when she found herself defending Frances Willard and the WCTU against attacks from one of Georgia's leading Baptists. Henry McDonald, editor of the *Christian Index*, the state Baptist paper, accused Willard of being a socialist who sought to lead women out of their proper sphere and into the gospel ministry. "Subversion of the relations of women as taught by the Word of God," claimed McDonald in an editorial, "is a prime article of her creed." He alleged that under Willard's leadership, the national WCTU "contemplates the most thorough and radical revolution of ancient or modern times."[70] Sibley came to Willard's defense, although she had a difficult time finding a forum for her rebuttals to McDonald. The *Christian Index* refused to publish her responses, and the *Atlanta Constitution* printed only summaries of them. Only the temperance paper the *Advance* would agree to run her letters in full. Sibley argued that Willard and the WCTU sought only to "glorify womanhood and create pure homes." Although she claimed to disagree with Willard regarding the ordination of women to the ministry, Sibley nevertheless affirmed her unity with the national WCTU on the "essentials of the organization—that of rescuing humanity from the drink curse and saving souls."[71]

Sibley's conflict with Candler began in 1892. In the summer of that year she wrote a letter to him asking for his support and for permission to use quotations from one of his earlier temperance tracts. She also invited Candler and his wife to attend the WCTU convention and offered him an opportunity to advise the state WCTU on how to deal with such controversial issues as suffrage and involvement in party politics. The Georgia union's position on the suffrage issue thus far, she assured him, had been "hands off." Yet she alluded to the fact that the tide might be turning in the South. "I have been holding off all these years from the pressure through the National [organization]," she explained to Candler. But because the state legislature had failed to act aggressively against the liquor threat, Sibley was beginning to wonder whether greater female involvement in the political process might be the only recourse. "I have been driven to desperation" by legislative inaction, she lamented, and she had begun to question whether women's suffrage was contrary to God's law after all. Sibley promised Candler that she would try to keep the Georgia WCTU from following the national leadership on the suffrage issue, saying, "If I can I will hold the question at bay still longer and try to keep them out of our work." But she placed the onus on Candler to facilitate greater support in Georgia for the WCTU's work there. The deal (and the thinly veiled threat) was clear: if he and other church leaders would adopt a more supportive attitude toward the union and help its members achieve legislative victories in the state, the women of Georgia would continue to staunchly resist the controversial example set by Frances Willard.[72]

In a terse response to Sibley, Candler hardened his position against the state WCTU. He stated that the Methodist Church in Georgia "will not cooperate with the WCTU until this suffrage business is stopped." Candler declared that he viewed the suffrage issue as a grave threat to the Methodist Church and that he would not allow the church to support the WCTU on any level—local, state, or national—so long as suffrage was part of the national organization's agenda. "If woman's suffrage were adopted," Candler warned, "it would adjourn prohibition over fifty years in the South if not forever." He distrusted the approach of supporting the national WCTU without embracing its women's suffrage plank. "It is a Trojan horse method to gain this doctrine such standing and then seek to allay the opposition to it in the South by saying it will not be mentioned in the state conventions," Candler warned. "It is firing on us with a masked battery." The martial imagery used by Candler reflected his view that women's suffrage was part of a war being waged against southern values. "We have been slow to fire back but are getting to the point where we will fire back in earnest," wrote Candler. Part of that "firing back" included his efforts to divorce the North Georgia Conference from any support for the state or local WCTU. He explained to Sibley that the church is "not willing to furnish churches for meeting places, give pulpit support to an organization which has already rent the northern church and will sooner or later divide ours if not resisted in its suffrage ideas. Besides we believe the whole basis of the woman's suffrage movement unscriptural and sinful."[73]

Candler made good on his threat to cut off the WCTU's access to Methodist meeting places and to stifle any Methodist support for the organization. Since its inception, the MECS had been the WCTU's greatest source of support in the South. Georgia's first union had been formed at a Methodist church, and Methodist churches had been the primary venues for Willard during her early tours of the South. Bishop Atticus Haygood had personally invited Willard to visit Oxford, whereupon the local union had been founded. But when the North Georgia Conference met a few months after Candler's correspondence with Sibley, the future bishop saw to it that the conference disowned the WCTU. Apparently not privy to Candler's intentions, the chairman of the conference's temperance committee, the Reverend W. W. Bays of Rome, Georgia, included in the temperance report a resolution endorsing the WCTU. Candler spoke in opposition to the resolution, arguing that because the Georgia WCTU was affiliated with the national WCTU, and the national WCTU advocated women's suffrage, the conference could not endorse the state union. Candler was successful in challenging the resolution, which was ultimately dropped from the report. He went on to urge pastors of Methodist churches in northern Georgia not to allow local WCTUs to use their facilities for meetings. Until the Georgia WCTU broke from the national WCTU, Candler vowed, it would receive no support from the Methodist churches of Georgia.[74]

The impact of Candler's war against the state WCTU was devastating to the organization. Attendance at the union's state convention fell off by 50 percent. Sibley addressed the controversy at the 1893 Georgia WCTU convention, saying that she was confident that the North Georgia Conference would soon recognize its mistake. Candler had recently reiterated his demand that the Georgia WCTU secede from the national organization because of that body's tainting by the suffrage issue. In her address to the convention, Sibley said that such an action "is not to be thought of for a moment." Regarding the issue of women's suffrage, she tried to turn the tables on Candler by blaming him for bringing it to the fore. "We have hitherto shunned the very idea" of embracing the suffrage position of the national WCTU, she declared. But because of Candler, the issue had been "thrust upon us for discussion and decision." The convention discussed both the topic of suffrage and its connection with the national WCTU, but the women refused to embrace suffrage. Ultimately, the Georgia WCTU passed resolutions reaffirming its loyalty to the national WCTU but rejecting women's suffrage as not being "conducive to the best interests of our cause in Georgia."[75]

Over the next two years, outspokenness on the part of Georgia WCTU leaders and their supporters continued to grow. In 1893 another leading voice within the Georgia WCTU, Rebecca Felton, responded to attacks by Atlanta preacher J. B. Hawthorne against Willard and the national WCTU. She defended Willard and, in a move that alienated many male evangelicals, demanded women's full participation in the conferences of the MECS.[76] For Candler and others, these ominous signs indicated growing support for women's suffrage in Georgia. In 1894 the National American Woman Suffrage Association held its annual convention outside of Washington, D.C., for the first time, and it chose Atlanta as the location for its national meeting.[77] Atlanta was selected in part, the association explained, because a suffrage speaker had found a receptive audience there the previous year. Meanwhile, a work entitled *Prominent Georgia Men in Favor of Woman Suffrage* had been published, listing men in the state who endorsed the movement.[78] Jane Sibley's husband, Augusta businessman William C. Sibley, was included in the tract, and rumors were circulating that Mrs. Sibley had expressed support for women's suffrage at the national WCTU convention.[79]

Such developments hardened the opposition of Candler and other Georgia evangelicals to the WCTU and its political affiliate, the Prohibition Party. In the *Wesleyan Christian Advocate*, Candler warned that he knew of a dozen suffragists who were members of local WCTUs just within the North Georgia Conference. And in the big city, things were even worse. "Nearly every woman in the unions in Atlanta is a suffragist at heart," he revealed. He qualified this statement by noting that some women advocated only "municipal suffrage," which would allow women to vote on local issues such as local option laws. Nevertheless, the danger such women posed was clear and present.[80] The conflict came to the fore again in 1894, when Candler forced Scomp from his position at Emory University. Scomp used Candler's well-known antagonism toward the WCTU as evidence of his hostility to the prohibition movement in general. He called Candler a "hater" of the WCTU and claimed that his attacks on that body had "gone beyond the bounds of all decency and quiet sufferance." According to Scomp, Candler had single-handedly led the effort to reverse the North Georgia Conference's stance in support of the union. Scomp also viewed Candler's attack on the Oxford WCTU as a direct personal assault on his wife, the chapter's president.[81] In public statements defending Scomp, Jane Sibley alleged that Candler's hostility toward the WCTU "knew no bounds." According to Sibley, Candler had denounced WCTU women as "short-haired female agitators," "platform screamers," "Jezebels," and other disdainful terms, even "going so far as to utter the unchristian and murderous wish that the world's grand leader of the temperance cause, Miss Willard, might be taken from the scene of agitation and action with the grip." Sibley also charged that Candler had said that "he would prefer to have a saloon upon every other fence-corner and bawdy-houses between" than permit women to vote.[82] Candler denied making this statement and sought to defend his status as a staunch prohibitionist. He had supposedly made the comment during a conversation with Scomp and Dr. W. W. Evans, a physician, so Candler wrote to Evans and asked about his recollection of the conversation. Evans replied, "You spoke of bawdy houses as being 'one of the channells through which woman's suffrage would work in the lower grades of society,' but as to saying that 'you would rather have saloons and bawdy houses all over the land than to have woman's suffrage' I do not remember any such remark."[83]

Whether or not Candler actually made the remark, the WCTU and party prohibitionists hoped that demonstrating Candler's hostility toward the WCTU would allow them to paint him and other Bourbon evangelicals as weak on prohibition, allowing third-party prohibitionists to claim sole possession of the cause. But the entanglement of the suffrage issue in both the Prohibition Party and the WCTU tainted those organizations in the eyes of many southern evangelicals. The Prohibition Party already faced an almost impossible task in trying to gain adherents in a region where the Democratic Party had a powerful hold on the white population and the Populist Party was drawing in the vast majority of those who dared to oppose the dominant party. As noted earlier, it was only within the ranks of southern evangelicalism that the Prohibition Party had any significant hope of making inroads in the South. But by embracing the women's suffrage plank, the party alienated itself from the southern constituency. J. William Jones of Atlanta stated that he would oppose the Prohibition Party until it ceased to support women's suffrage.[84] A. B. Cabaniss declared that the Prohibition Party "is digging its political grave" by insisting on women's suffrage as part of its party platform.[85] One minister noted that the Prohibition Party, though small, contained a large proportion of "demagogues in trousers and in skirts."[86]

The southern evangelical leadership strongly and almost universally opposed women's suffrage. For southern evangelical men, placing women on a pedestal and confining them to the domestic sphere were essential to the maintenance of a Christian, morally superior culture in the South. As Marjorie Wheeler explains, a key element of southern society was "a dualistic conception of the natures and responsibilities of the sexes that precluded the participation of women in politics and cast 'the southern Lady' in the role of guardian and symbol of southern virtue."[87] The editor of the *Alabama Christian Advocate* expressed it thusly: "The manhood of any race is great and noble only in proportion as the womanhood of that race is clothed with that reverent regard and marked by that purity, virtue, and modesty that belongs to the wife and mother in the American home." He warned of the danger of discarding this view that bifurcated the world into masculine and feminine realms, saying, "When American womanhood shall voluntarily surrender this for the glitter of political power, then shall the splendid fabric of our civilization crumble to ruin and Ichabod may be written upon the shattered walls of its fallen greatness."[88] In Georgia, one evangelical argued that Christ himself had instituted the separate sphere of influence for women and that only within that sphere could women be an "unmixed blessing to mankind."[89]

Under the guise of "protecting" women's traditional role as caretaker of the home, evangelical men sought to rein in what they viewed as the dangerous growth of women's activity outside the home sphere. They often maintained that they were doing women a favor by withholding the ballot from them. "In our southland," explained the editor of Georgia's *Wesleyan Christian Advocate* in 1891, "women are so ensconced in the esteem and affections of man, that it does seem a pity to disturb their happy place." He argued that women "ought to be freed from the petty annoyances and confused thoughts that come from the busy, contending, wrangling world outside." His condescending justification for denying women full political rights continued: "It looks like dethronement to talk, even, of sending her out on the platform, or down in the hustings, or away to the dirty polls."[90] A. J. Dickinson was an Alabama Baptist who was unusually progressive for a southern evangelical, embracing higher criticism and defending the liberal theology of the University of Chicago from his pulpit in Birmingham's First Baptist Church. But he too felt that women "ought not to be burdened with the ballot."[91] G. P. Keyes wrote that he did not doubt that women were better than men, full of more faith and integrity than their male counterparts, and for that reason should not be "polluted by the environment of the polls."[92] Just as the doctrine of the spirituality of the church demanded that the church keep itself pure by steering clear of the secular political realm, some evangelicals advocated what amounted to a doctrine of the spirituality of women. Participation in the carnal realm of politics would contaminate their pure and elevated nature. As the editor of the *Alabama Christian Advocate* explained, the paper "holds firm to the doctrine that the church and the women have a higher calling than the discussion of political questions, and can not, without soiling themselves, descend into the mire of partisan strife. Woman was placed here to mould the character of the men who vote." In short, women, like the church, had no business in the political sphere. As many evangelical prohibitionists did with the doctrine of the spirituality of the church, however, the editor went on to argue that prohibition was a moral issue, not purely a political one. Thus it was acceptable for women to work for the cause of prohibition, so long as they did not seek to gain political power as a means of addressing the issue.[93] The editor of the *Wesleyan Christian Advocate* no doubt expressed the opinion shared by many evangelical men in the South when he pleaded, "Will somebody please stop the whole thing, and let us feel once more that we can have homes to go to, and can settle down to work and happy life again?"[94]

A recurring theme among evangelical men who opposed the WCTU because of the suffrage issue was that by moving outside the domestic sphere, women were becoming less womanly. One Alabama Baptist lamented the decline of femininity in women who embraced suffrage. "By some occult process known only to Susan B. Anthony and her school," wrote J. W. Willis, "the old time woman has been evoluted [*sic*] into the 'new woman,' and it will take but one step more to evolve the 'wo' and leave the 'new man.'"[95] Alabama Methodist W. A. McCarty stated that if there were equality between the sexes, a woman would no longer be "queen of the home circle . . . she no longer maintains the delicacy of her sex."[96] In the *Christian Index*, the editor pondered women's attempts to gain both ecclesial and political equality and asked, "How far may a woman go in these new avenues before she ceases to be womanly?"[97]

Traditional southern reverence for women and their elevated sphere of influence was not the only reason that southern evangelical men objected to the idea of women's suffrage. As always, the race issue lay just below the surface. In private correspondence, Candler expressed his concern that suffrage would allow more "bad" women to vote than good women. "The Negro women, and bad women not cumbered with cares of maternity would have every advantage and the good women would be at the greatest disadvantage," he explained.[98] Publicly, he complained in the state's Methodist paper, "We have suffered enough from Negro suffrage already without bringing in the Negro women."[99] Job Harral contended that women's suffrage was a scheme devised by the devil to defeat the prohibition cause. He wrote in the *Tennessee Baptist*, "But now Satan is pursuing his old policy. He is doing all in his power to connect it, prohibition, with woman's suffrage, in the hope that both will be rejected together." Should that strategy fail, Harral argued, the devil's backup plan was to give African American women the right to vote. "The enfranchisement of two or three millions of Negro women will give him the victory, as he can lead them to the polls to vote for whiskey," he wrote.[100]

The fear was widespread among male prohibitionists that women's suffrage would bring more voters into the wet ranks. But leading southern suffragists such as Belle Kearney of Mississippi argued that allowing white women to vote would help cancel out the black male vote in the South.[101] Following the defeat of statewide prohibition in Texas in 1887, some suggested that if women had been allowed to vote, the amendment would have passed. Keyes made the same claim about the failure of the prohibition amendment in Tennessee that same year. He pointed to the positive results in Wyoming and Washington, where women were enfranchised. It was unfair for a woman to be barred from the polls, he argued, while "the tramp and the colored troop and the abandoned profligate march to the polls and decide for her what policy shall prevail and what licenses shall blight the happiness of her family and make desolate her home forever."[102] But most evangelical men remained unconvinced of the potential upside of women's suffrage. McCarty argued that the thirty thousand African American men and the sixty thousand German men who had voted wet in the Texas election "would likely have carried their women with them" to the polls and canceled out the vote of evangelical women.[103] Like Candler, he feared that allowing white women to vote would also mean allowing black women to vote, and he assumed that their influence on southern politics would be anything but uplifting. As the *Alabama Christian Advocate* concluded, if women's voting rights are part of prohibitionism, then "surely the remedy is worse than the malady."[104]

Ecclesial Equality

Underlying the women's suffrage issue was another threat that was equally unnerving to southern evangelical men: expanded roles and rights for women within the church. As calls for women's equality in the public sphere became increasingly commonplace, more and more women began to expect it in the ecclesial realm as well. Some evangelical men, such as the *Alabama Christian Advocate*'s W. A. McCarty, tried to remain hopeful that women's political equality would not have spiritual consequences. Although he was resigned to the fact that women's suffrage would likely become a reality, McCarty remained "confident that the pulpit will stand in sublime onliness [*sic*], the sole witness to the world, that God made them 'male and female.'"[105] Most men, however, were less optimistic that the church would be insulated from the winds of change impacting the secular world. For southern evangelical men, the late 1880s and early 1890s were marked by distressing signs of change in American denominational life. The northern Methodist Church in 1888 voted to grant lay privileges to its female members. Southern evangelical men saw this as the work of suffragists within the denomination, and they pointed to developments in the North as an omen of the danger posed by radical women. "They have already made a fissure in the northern Methodist church and they will make a similar fissure in the southern Methodist church if not resisted at once," warned Candler.[106] In 1892 the Cumberland Presbyterian Church, based in Tennessee, ordained its first female minister. That same year, the *Christian Index* in Georgia ruefully observed that the MEC had struck the word *obey* from its marriage ceremony.[107] The following year the southern Presbyterians decreed that every session must "absolutely enforce the injunction of scripture forbidding women to speak in churches" and generally adhere to the biblical teaching of women's subordination.[108] Evangelicals were particularly worried that southern women might try to enter the pulpit. One lady in Alabama, known simply as "Mrs. Perry," was bold enough to do so. She began preaching in rural churches, and when one pastor refused her request to preach at his church, his congregation split over the issue.[109]

Evangelicals feared that increased ecclesial rights for women would only further their efforts to gain the franchise. James Anderson, a Tennessee editor whose father had been a prominent Methodist minister in Nashville, explained in a letter to the General Conference of the MECS that granting women lay privileges in the church would "give them a stronger foothold in their efforts to get political privileges."[110] The *Alabama Christian Advocate* likewise thought that granting women voting rights within the church would be a big step toward granting them voting rights outside the church as well. When the MEC did give such rights to its laywomen, the editors of the paper said of women's suffrage: "It is done, the matter is practically settled." The editors also doubted women's capacity to take on such serious responsibilities within the church. The right to vote meant the right to legislate for the church and sit on juries in ecclesial trials. Concerned that women would not be up to the challenge, the paper condescendingly observed, "To legislate for the church . . . is not like running a sewing bee, or managing a neighborhood picnic, or teaching a Sunday School class, or conducting a small auxiliary of the Woman's Missionary Society, etc."[111] Such complaints about women's judgment did not fade quickly among southern evangelical men. In 1910, when the MECS was debating granting the same ecclesial rights to women that the MEC had granted in 1888, the *Alabama Christian Advocate* received a letter from a layman who likewise questioned women's ability to be trusted with such important decisions. He wrote, "The only objection I can see to giving the women the rights of the laity is that women are not good judges of men. Women judge a man superficially, by the cut of his clothes, the depth of his bow, the condition of his fingernails. They do not look beneath the surface and find a true nobleman hidden by a shabby exterior. They do not like a man who parts his hair in the middle, for that is a prerogative women arrogate to themselves, yet some of our best preachers part their hair in the middle." Women's preoccupation with a man's hairstyle was merely a symptom of their inability to judge what really matters, the reader argued. If women were granted the right to vote on bishops, he explained, "they shall vote for a man for bishop who is a lady's man, not a man's man. We will have our episcopacy filled with effeminates instead of stalwarts."[112]

E. E. Hoss expressed his frustration at women who sought ecclesial and political equality and at the men who supported their cause, saying, "I have no sympathy with the masculine women who insist on carrying on a chronic quarrel against God for not having made them men, nor for the lady-like men who are aiding them in their fight."[113] The editor of the *Alabama Christian Advocate* contrasted the "fanatical" women of the North, who sought greater ecclesial and political rights, with the "true women" of the South, who were too "wise and conservative" to embrace the "revolutionary spirit" that pervaded the women of the MEC.[114] Fear of a "revolutionary spirit" overtaking the women of the South led many evangelicals to oppose the WCTU. Their dedication to eradicating liquor from the southland was trumped by their concern about the degradation of southern womanhood through the breakdown of their dearly held views of proper gender roles and spheres of influence.

Male prohibitionists preferred to use women in the campaign as objects of pity or as beings in need of protection. Images of women and children were frequently used in prohibition campaign material and in posters promoting the cause. The religious press ran portraits of innocent children above large captions such as "Please Protect Us," or cradled in the arms of their angelic white mother, who pleaded, "Help Keep Him Pure. Please vote against the sale of liquors."[115] Evangelical prohibitionists portrayed a vote for prohibition as a vote for the purity and sanctity of the South's women and children. Both women and children were presented as innocent, defenseless victims of the liquor trade who needed the protection of the white male electorate. Through the WCTU, southern women embraced a more active role for themselves in the crusade against the saloon. This opened up opportunities that had not previously existed in southern culture, giving women a chance to have their voices heard in the public sphere. Because this was done in the name of protecting the domestic realm, over which they had responsibility, women's foray into the public sphere was initially accepted and even encouraged by southern white evangelical men. Yet despite their early backing of the WCTU and their shared objectives, southern denominations eventually found that the threat posed by increasing public roles for women made their continued support of the WCTU untenable.

In the conflation of Victorian mores and Lost Cause sentimentality that came to define southern culture at the end of the nineteenth century, the purity and sanctity of white womanhood symbolized the purity and sanctity of the southland itself. From the 1870s until well into the twentieth century, southern white womanhood became, in the words of one historian, a "hostage to the Lost Cause." Marjorie Wheeler explains that for southern white males, maintaining traditional gender roles became an aspect of maintaining the South's perceived cultural and moral superiority over the North. Both New Southites and advocates of the Lost Cause saw the strict distinctions between male and female spheres of influence crumbling in northern culture, and they were equally committed to preventing such transformations from taking place in the South.[116] Women's elevated status was what made appeals to protect them such a powerful weapon in the arsenal of southern prohibitionists. It is also what made the active involvement of women in the movement a much more complex issue in the South than it was in the North. Most male evangelicals in the South supported the vital role that women played in the movement, but it became a two-edged sword in the eyes of many when it threatened to bring reforms such as women's suffrage, female preaching, and increased ecclesiastical rights for women.

Women's participation in the prohibition movement both reinforced and challenged the structured gender roles of the region.
Involvement in prohibition work through the WCTU created unprecedented opportunities for women. One of Georgia's most outspoken WCTU leaders, Rebecca Latimer Felton, went on to become
the first woman to serve in the U.S. Senate when she was appointed
to the position following the death of her husband in 1922. Yet under
the leadership of Frances Willard, the WCTU moved in a direction
that made most southern evangelical men uneasy and that cost unions
in the South much of their support from denominational leadership.
Wary that the organization would serve as a front for the radical
feminist agenda of the WCTU's national leadership, and disgruntled
by the union's endorsement of third-party political alternatives during the turbulent 1890s, some evangelical men distanced themselves
from the organization, while others forthrightly attacked it. While
the southern WCTU languished without evangelical support from
1890 to 1905, another organization emerged that captivated the attention and backing of the southern evangelical denominations: the
Anti-Saloon League. The ASL's effectiveness in securing prohibition
legislation, along with its nonpartisan approach to the politics of prohibition, won it the hardy support of evangelical men in the South and
overshadowed the WCTU. Even after the establishment of statewide
and then nationwide prohibition, however, the WCTU continued to
thrive in the southland as an organization that allowed women to participate more fully and effectively in the public sphere.

Conclusion

PROHIBITION, LIKE MOST REFORM initiatives of the Progressive Era, did not originate in the South. Both Ted Ownby and Dewey Grantham have argued that few reforms can be called "distinctively southern."[1] Nevertheless, it seems clear that in some ways prohibition is an exception to this rule. Though birthed far north of the Mason-Dixon Line, prohibition was southernized in the years following the Civil War, transformed into a movement with a distinctly southern accent. Postwar efforts to reform the morals of Americans were in no way limited to the Southeast. Evangelicals in the Northeast and Midwest also sought to impose prohibition on the general populace. A recent study by Gaines Foster demonstrates that an active Christian lobby developed in Washington after the war, seeking to convince the federal government to expand its moral powers and make the nation more righteous through legislation aimed not only at eradicating alcohol but also at eliminating gambling, lotteries, polygamy, obscenity, pornography, prostitution, prizefighting, cigarettes, divorce, and Sunday mail delivery.[2] But the crown jewel of the moral reform movement—prohibition—found its greatest success in the region that had long offered the stiffest opposition to it: the South.

Southern evangelicals—primarily Baptists and Methodists—led the way in taking this Yankee reform movement, which had never fully lodged in the hearts and minds of the southern populace during the antebellum period, and conforming it to the peculiarities of southern culture. By doing so, they made prohibition the leading and by far the most successful social reform effort in the South between 1880 and 1915. Although prohibition never gained the level of widespread support in the North necessary to achieve statewide prohibition laws,

231

in the South, prohibition became the law of the land a full decade before nationwide prohibition was ratified. By 1908, Atlanta Baptist minister John E. White could rightfully proclaim that the southern states served as the "main-spring" of prohibition sentiment in the United States.[3] The legislative victories that evangelical southerners achieved, first on the local level and then at the statewide level, were owed in large part to the way prohibitionists conformed their message to the needs of their unique cultural surroundings. Evangelical leaders accommodated their message to the distinctive southern culture and convincingly marketed prohibition as an effective solution to the problems and stresses facing southern society. By attaching prohibition to the needs of the South at the turn of the century, southern evangelicals effectively convinced the majority of white southern voters that prohibition was the best course of action.

Numerous obstacles faced those southern evangelicals who were intent on drying up the southland. Long-held theological and political beliefs both inside and outside southern evangelical circles had to be challenged and reinterpreted. The doctrine of the spirituality of the church, which disallowed ministers from bringing political matters into the pulpit, had been integral to the identity and self-justification of southern denominations since before the Civil War. Nevertheless, evangelical prohibitionists reinterpreted the doctrine to allow for unabashed political involvement on the part of Christian ministers and denominational leaders. Activism on behalf of prohibition often conflicted with other political priorities of southerners, mainly the preservation of Democratic hegemony in the region. Yet a crop of evangelical ministers arose during the 1880s that made the spread of prohibition sentiment a central aspect of their ministry, and they worked tirelessly to sway public opinion in favor of prohibition.

One of the most vexing issues with which postwar southern whites struggled was the presence of a transformed African American population—once their bondsmen, now their fellow citizens. In reality, the specter of racism and race relations overarches and embraces every aspect of the story of southern prohibitionism. From political turmoil to concepts of honor to attitudes toward women, every aspect of life in the South was shaped by whites "responding to the presence of Negroes," as Ralph Ellison noted. White evangelical prohibitionists clearly underwent a transformation in racial attitude between 1880 and 1915. Reflecting the optimism and excitement of the New South movement that flourished in the 1880s, evangelical prohibitionists initially looked on black voters as a potential boon to their cause. This optimism soon faded to paternalism and disfranchisement, however, and after the turn of the century, some of the harshest racial stereotypes were embraced by evangelical prohibitionists and used to promote their cause.

Equally important for understanding southern evangelicalism is the recognition of just how much southern evangelicals' attitudes toward alcohol and its legal proscription were driven by fear and apprehension about the new social arrangement in the South. The transformation in their stance toward legal prohibition—resisting it before the war but ardently advocating it afterward—coincides with the dramatic shift of the race paradigm in the region. Drunkenness in the antebellum era, limited to white men, posed a threat primarily to the moral fiber of society. Most evangelicals, though understandably concerned about correcting such behavior, did not perceive it as a crisis that warranted the use of the state. In the era of free black men, however, southern evangelicals began to see drunkenness as something much more sinister and dangerous. It was now perceived as a threat to the white race and to the entire social order. The presence of a large population of free African Americans, and especially the emergence of a generation determined to shake off the yoke of subservience, are key to understanding several important aspects of southern prohibition: why southern white evangelicals embraced prohibition so fervently after 1880, why they wanted to impose sobriety on society at large rather than only on those within the church, and why the South led the way in the nation's prohibition experiment.

In addition to the race issue, the concept of honor permeated all of southern culture. Buoyed by their growing status in postwar southern society, evangelicals sought to appropriate honor for themselves, whereas in the antebellum period, this designation had been viewed as largely incompatible with evangelical piety. As evangelicals reinterpreted the traditional concept of honor in evangelical terms, prohibition became a standard by which a man's honor was measured in the New South. By doing so, southern evangelicals were able to establish prohibition as a movement that was not only genuinely southern, despite its northern roots, but also honorable and manly. Those who opposed prohibition, by contrast, were labeled cowards and had no claim to the title of honor in the New South.

Finally, the issue of gender required careful negotiation by southerners who advocated prohibition. No other movement in American history so effectively broadened women's participation in public and political discourse. Through the Woman's Christian Temperance Union, women in the South were able to expand their spheres of influence beyond the domestic realm, where both Victorian values and the Lost Cause ideology conspired to keep them. Women played a vital role in swaying public sentiment in favor of prohibition, and evangelical men recognized this. Yet the southern male fear of women gaining political or ecclesial equality led them to rescind their initial backing for the WCTU. While the South led the nation on its course toward the Eighteenth Amendment, it remained resistant to the growing impulse that would culminate in the Nineteenth Amendment. Prohibition provided one of the only "respectable" outlets for women to explore the public sphere in the turn-of-the-century South. But because Victorian gender values were so entrenched in southern culture, the male evangelical leadership put up stiff opposition when it deemed women's involvement in the prohibition cause too threatening to the social order.

Prior to the Civil War, the South had been known as "the land of Dixie and whiskey," and its inhabitants were well known to have a cultural predisposition toward consuming strong drink and doing so frequently. Yet by the end of the first decade of the twentieth century, more than seventeen million of the twenty million denizens of the former Confederacy found themselves living under some form of prohibitory legislation.[4] Southern evangelicals had worked tirelessly to expand the reach of local prohibition laws throughout the 1880s and 1890s. With Georgia's passage of statewide prohibition in 1907, the South cleared the path for nationwide prohibition. Even after the repeal of national prohibition by the Twenty-first Amendment in 1933, statewide prohibition lingered in the South, and many counties in the southland remain dry today.[5]

Historians often point to the downfall of national prohibition as a signal of evangelicalism's declining influence in American culture. Jean Schmidt, for instance, states, "In a sense, the repeal of the Eighteenth Amendment in 1933 was symbolic of the end of rural Protestantism's dominance in the United States."[6] In a similar vein, Mark Noll has observed that the prohibition movement "could be considered the last gasp of Protestant hegemony" in America.[7] Although such an assessment might be true of traditional Protestant hegemony over the nation as a whole, it does not reflect the reality in the South. The rise and success of prohibition in the South between 1880 and 1915 correspond with the waxing influence of evangelical Christianity in the region, not with its decline. And when the Eighteenth Amendment went into effect on January 16, 1920, it marked not the last gasp of Protestantism in the South but rather its arrival as the primary arbiter of southern cultural mores. The passage of statewide prohibition legislation throughout the South prior to the enactment of national prohibition was the culmination of a process that had begun just after the American Revolution, when evangelicalism began to take firm root in the region, and grew rapidly after 1800.

The success of prohibition cemented the South's role as a region marked by its religiosity and conservatism. A few years later, the nation's attention—and that of subsequent generations of historians—would be captured by another event in the South: the Scopes trial in Dayton, Tennessee. That well-known case, in which state law became a vehicle for evangelical Christianity to spread its moral teachings, remains a favorite example that historians cite as evidence of the captivity of southern culture to evangelical fundamentalism. As Jeanette Keith has observed, "The Tennessee Monkey trial is one of the great set-pieces of twentieth-century American history, a story told in every textbook, with an agreed-upon symbolic meaning."[8] What the trial symbolized was the conflict between two movements—forward-looking modernism and backward-looking fundamentalism. It was, in the words of George Marsden, "the clash of two worlds."[9] Although the Scopes trial garners the lion's share of historians' attention, prohibition is an immensely important and regularly overlooked window into understanding the process that led to the South becoming a place where such laws could be passed.[10] The prohibition movement predated the evangelical influence on the education legislation that resulted in the Scopes trial and, more importantly, laid the necessary groundwork for the church's influence in the region's secular culture.[11]

The rise of prohibition sentiment within the general population serves as a more reliable gauge of the expanding role of the evangelical church in southern society than does legislation against the teaching of evolution in the 1920s. The evangelical crusade against Darwinism was secondary to the crusade against the demon rum. Indeed, the space dedicated to attacking evolution in the evangelical religious press of Tennessee, Alabama, and Georgia between 1880 and 1915 was dwarfed by that devoted to antialcohol writings.[12] During a relatively brief period between the end of the First World War and 1925, southern evangelicals became increasingly concerned about the teaching of evolution in public schools, and state legislatures quickly passed laws banning such teaching.[13] The passage of antievolution laws in southern statehouses—Tennessee was the third to do so—was not the result of evangelical fundamentalists suddenly taking over the apparatus of the state. Rather, these laws owed their existence to the political prowess and capital that southern evangelicals had garnered over the previous four decades in their effort to pass prohibition. Ever since the antebellum period, evangelicalism had dominated the religious scene in the South. But with the decline of the cultural dominance of the planter aristocracy after the Civil War, evangelicals not only continued to grow in number but also played a greater role in shaping southern culture. The central element of the evangelical vision of a truly redeemed South was prohibition, and its growth and success paralleled the rising influence of evangelicals on the culture of the region. Restrictions on the teaching of evolution were easily passed in southern states only because evangelicals had established their presence in the southern political realm through decades of prohibition activism.

Prohibition has long been disparaged as a reactionary and priggish impulse—a "pseudo-reform, a pinched, parochial substitute for reform," Richard Hofstadter has called it, spread via "the rural-evangelical virus."[14] Southern evangelicals at the end of the nineteenth century, however, viewed it quite differently. Liquor, they maintained, lay at the heart of the region's many social, economic, and moral problems: widespread poverty, lack of industrial development, black attacks on whites, white lynchings of African Americans, violence and immorality among lower-class whites, lack of quality education, and political corruption.[15] For evangelicals, prohibition was a means of addressing the problems associated with the increased urbanization and industrialization of the New South; it was in tune with their focus on individual salvation and responsibility, yet it did not call into question the larger economic structure of the new economy. It was a complex movement whose leaders were, by and large, sincere individuals driven by a deep sense that their course was in the best interest of both society and the church. Many of their achievements were, in turn, laudable attempts to address complicated and troubling issues at a deeply challenging time in the nation's history. Nevertheless, it was also a movement full of many contradictions that yielded some ignominious results. While attempting on some level to resolve racial animosity and the epidemic of lynching via more ethical and lawful means, prohibitionists embraced some of the worst elements of southern white racism. While attempting to rid the old southern code of honor of its most violent and damaging aspects, prohibitionists endorsed those elements of the code that undergirded extralegal mob activity by southern white males. And while affording unprecedented opportunities for southern white women to participate in society, prohibition retrenched southern resistance to full equality for women.

The story of how Dixie came to not only embrace prohibition but also lead the nation in legislating against alcohol is one that centers on evangelical Christians and their ability to adapt the prohibition message to the idiosyncrasies of southern culture. Evangelicals had expanded their sphere of influence by breaking free from self-imposed boundaries that limited them to the spiritual realm. Issues such as race, honor, and gender made the prohibition message of southern evangelicals unique, and they also help explain why prohibition enjoyed such success between 1880 and 1915. By meshing their prohibition message with the unique southern culture in which it was being advocated, white southern evangelicals were able to achieve at least symbolic victory over liquor within the land of the Lost Cause. More important, they entered the twentieth century with substantial sway over the region's culture and politics, which would prove to be even more lasting and significant than their victory over the demon rum.

Notes

Introduction

1. Lula Barnes Ansley, *History of the Georgia Woman's Christian Temperance Union: From Its Organization, 1883–1907* (Columbus, Ga.: Gilbert Printing, 1914), 239.

2. Rayford W. Logan, *The Negro in American Life and Thought: The Nadir, 1877–1901* (New York: Dial Press, 1954).

3. Thomas J. Little, "The Origins of Southern Evangelicalism: Revivalism in South Carolina, 1700–1740," *Church History* 75 (December 2006): 768–808, offers an overview of the recent historiography of southern evangelicalism as well as a challenge to the growing consensus that evangelical Christianity arrived relatively late to the southland.

4. Mark A. Noll, *The Old Religion in a New World: The History of North American Christianity* (Grand Rapids, Mich.: Eerdmans, 2002), 53.

5. Rhys Isaac, *The Transformation of Virginia, 1740–1790* (Chapel Hill: University of North Carolina Press, 1982), 163–64.

6. Philip N. Mulder, *A Controversial Spirit: Evangelical Awakenings in the South* (Oxford: Oxford University Press, 2002), 13, 37, 66–67. John Boles notes that Presbyterians were not prepared "to cope with expansions in the southern backcountry, but the Baptists and Methodists seemed ideally suited for the kind of accommodation to frontier and semi-frontier realities that had stymied the Anglican Church." John B. Boles, "Evangelical Protestantism in the Old South: From Religious Dissent to Cultural Dominance," in *Religion in the South*, ed. John B. Boles (Jackson: University Press of Mississippi, 1985), 16.

7. Frederick A. Bode, "The Formation of Evangelical Communities in Middle Georgia: Twiggs County, 1820–1861," *Journal of Southern Religion* 60 (November 1994): 716.

8. David R. Goldfield, *Still Fighting the Civil War: The American South and Southern History* (Baton Rouge: Louisiana State University Press, 2002), 45.

9. Mitchell Snay, *Gospel of Disunion: Religion and Separatism in the Antebellum South* (Cambridge: Cambridge University Press, 1993), 127–35.

10. C. Vann Woodward, *Origins of the New South 1877–1913*, vol. 10 of *A History of the South*, ed. Wendell Holmes Stephenson and E. Merton Coulter (n.p.: Louisiana State University Press, 1951), 170.

11. See Daniel W. Stowell, *Rebuilding Zion: The Religious Reconstruction of the South, 1863–1877* (New York: Oxford University Press, 1998).

12. William L. Barney's *The Secessionist Impulse: Alabama and Mississippi in 1860* (Princeton, N.J.: Princeton University Press, 1974), 135, 273, finds a direct correlation between the rate of slaveholding and support for secession in Alabama. In Black Belt counties where slaveholder density was greatest, secessionist sentiment was strongest; support for secession was weakest in the northeastern hill country, where slaveholder density was very low.

13. Carl N. Degler, *The Other South: Southern Dissenters in the Nineteenth Century* (New York: Harper and Row, 1974), 170. Unlike eastern Tennessee, western Virginia, and other upper South bastions of Unionism, the northern portions of Alabama and Georgia had been overwhelmingly Democratic during the antebellum period.

14. Carl V. Harris, "Reforms in Government Control of Negroes in Birmingham, Alabama, 1890–1920," *Journal of Southern History* 38 (November 1972): 569.

15. Wayne Mixon, "Georgia," in *Religion in the Southern States: A Historical Study*, ed. Samuel S. Hill (Macon, Ga.: Mercer University Press, 1983), 83–84.

16. J. Wayne Flynt, "Alabama," in Hill, *Religion in the Southern States*, 9.

17. David E. Harrell Jr., "Tennessee," in Hill, *Religion in the Southern States*, 294–96.

18. Ibid., 303; J. Wayne Flynt, *Alabama Baptists: Southern Baptists in the Heart of Dixie* (Tuscaloosa: University of Alabama Press, 1998), 255; Christopher H. Owen, *The Sacred Flame of Love: Methodism and Society in Nineteenth-Century Georgia* (Athens: University of Georgia Press, 1998), 189–90.

19. See Goldfield, *Still Fighting the Civil War*, 29.

20. Donald G. Mathews, "'Christianizing the South'—Sketching a Synthesis," in *New Directions in American Religious History*, ed. Harry S. Stout and D. G. Hart (New York: Oxford University Press, 1997), 84.

21. John B. Boles, *The Irony of Southern Religion* (New York: Peter Lang, 1994), 3.

22. Samuel S. Hill, "The South's Two Cultures," in *Religion and the Solid South*, ed. Samuel S. Hill (Nashville: Abingdon, 1972), 34–36. In his landmark study of southern religion, Hill utilized Ernst Troeltsch's classification of two types of religious institutions: the church type, which "accepts the social order and is at peace with it," and the sect type, which is "at odds with the prevailing order and isolates itself from it." Although Baptists and Methodists by nature tend to exist as sect-type movements, in the South they became the dominant religious force and thus assumed a church-type form. Thus the evangelical church in the South became identified with the surrounding culture and functioned largely to affirm and sustain it. Samuel S. Hill, *Southern Churches in Crisis* (New York: Holt, Rinehart and Winston, 1966), 139–40, 150–59.

23. Presbyterians, Heyrman points out, were slower to assault the Anglican hierarchy and quicker to accept and defend the practice of slavery. Christine Leigh Heyrman, *Southern Cross: The Beginnings of the Bible Belt* (New York: Knopf, 1997), 15.

24. Heyrman's work expands on a similar thesis put forward by Robert M. Calhoon in *Evangelicals and Conservatives in the Early South, 1740–1861* (Co-

lumbia: University of South Carolina Press, 1988). Calhoon argues that when evangelicals first charged into the southern backcountry, they were not conservative guardians of the larger social order of the South. Rather, southern evangelicalism in its youth had been in conflict with prevailing southern social views. After the Revolution, however, the movement became more comfortable in its new environs and began to absorb and reflect the conservatism of the region.

Chapter One. "Distilled Damnation"

1. Heman Humphrey, *Intemperance: An Address to the Churches and Congregations of the Western District of Fairfield County* (New Haven, Conn.: Eli Hudson, 1813). Although Humphrey's work appears to be the earliest extant temperance tract published in the United States, it was not the first published in the New World. In 1730 Josiah Smith had published *Solomon's Caution against the Cup: A Sermon Delivered at Cainhoy, in the Province of South-Carolina* (Boston: D. Henchman, 1730). It would be safe to say that Smith, a Presbyterian minister and the first native South Carolinian to graduate from college, was the first southern minister to preach a temperance sermon.

2. Various interpretations of what drove such reform efforts have been offered over the years, including the desire for social control; the millennial expectations of the New Divinity theology; the political frustration of the Federalists, whose political power was waning; and the need to impose order on a westward-expanding society. For these and other analyses of the movement, see Charles I. Foster, *An Errand of Mercy: The Evangelical United Front, 1790–1837* (Chapel Hill: University of North Carolina Press, 1960), 122; Dietrich Buss, "The Millennial Vision as Motive for Religious Benevolence and Reform: Timothy Dwight and the New England Evangelicals Reconsidered," *Fides et Historia* 16 (fall–winter 1983): 18–34; John W. Quist, "Slaveholding Operatives of the Benevolent Empire: Bible, Tract, and Sunday School Societies in Antebellum Tuscaloosa County, Alabama," *Journal of Southern History* 62 (August 1996): 525–26; John W. Kuykendall, *Southern Enterprize: The Work of National Evangelical Societies in the Antebellum South* (Westport, Conn.: Greenwood Press, 1982), 5–20; and Robert H. Wiebe, *The Opening of American Society: From the Adoption of the Constitution to the Eve of Disunion* (New York: Knopf, 1984), 229–32.

3. W. J. Rorabaugh, "Estimated U.S. Alcoholic Beverage Consumption, 1790–1860," *Journal of Studies on Alcohol* 37 (March 1976): 360–61.

4. Charles Sellers, *The Market Revolution: Jacksonian America 1815–1846* (New York: Oxford University Press, 1991), 259–60. In 1979 Rorabaugh noted that the current per capita level of liquor consumption in the United States was about one-third of the 1830 level. W. J. Rorabaugh, *The Alcoholic Republic: An American Tradition* (New York: Oxford University Press, 1979), 189. Ian Tyrrell argues that early temperance support came primarily from those areas hardest hit by the economic crisis following the War of 1812, which may account for the large number of individuals drowning their sorrows in liquor. Ian

R. Tyrrell, *Sobering Up: From Temperance to Prohibition in Antebellum America, 1800–1860* (Westport, Conn.: Greenwood Press, 1979), 34–35.

5. Humphrey, *Intemperance*, 31.

6. Tyrrell, *Sobering Up*, 70.

7. Quoted in Rorabaugh, *The Alcoholic Republic*, 30.

8. Carl A. L. Binger, *Revolutionary Doctor: Benjamin Rush, 1746–1813* (New York: Norton, 1966), 126.

9. Norman H. Clark, *Deliver Us from Evil: An Interpretation of American Prohibition* (New York: Norton, 1976), 22; Sellers, *The Market Revolution*, 261; John E. White, "Social Movements in the South," in *The South in the Building of the Nation: A History of the Southern States Designed to Record the South's Part in the Making of the American Nation; to Portray the Character and Genius, to Chronicle the Achievements and Progress and to Illustrate the Life and Traditions of the Southern People*, vol. 10 (Richmond, Va.: Southern Historical Publication Society, 1909), 570.

10. In 1812 Humphrey's own Consociation of the Western District of Fairfield County had resolved to no longer use ardent spirits at its meetings. Humphrey, *Intemperance*, [ii].

11. Joseph R. Gusfield, *Symbolic Crusade: Status Politics and the American Temperance Movement*, 2nd ed. (Urbana: University of Illinois Press, 1986); John R. Rumbarger, *Profits, Power, and Prohibition: Alcohol Reform and the Industrialization of America, 1800–1930* (Albany: State University of New York Press, 1989); William Breitenbach, "Sons of the Fathers: Temperance Reformers and the Legacy of the American Revolution," *Journal of the Early Republic* 3 (spring 1983): 75–76; Tyrell, *Sobering Up*, 34, 36, 46–48; Lois W. Banner, "Religious Benevolence as Social Control: A Critique of an Interpretation," *Journal of American History* 60 (June 1973): 23–41.

12. Jack S. Blocker Jr., *American Temperance Movements: Cycles of Reform* (Boston: Twayne, 1989), 11; Humphrey, *Intemperance*.

13. In his landmark study of revivalism in Rochester, New York, during this period, Paul Johnson likewise found that the city's wealthy and influential men took the lead in the temperance effort, seeking to reform the morals of lesser men of the community by starting at the top. See Paul E. Johnson, *A Shopkeeper's Millennium: Society and Revivals in Rochester, New York, 1815–1832* (New York: Hill and Wang, 2004), 80–83. Catherine Gilbert Murdock briefly discusses how industrialists sought to end the consumption of alcohol during the workday, which eventually led to greater productivity and shorter workdays; however, it also led to drinking becoming a deeply entrenched element of leisure time. See Catherine Gilbert Murdock, *Domesticating Drink: Women, Men, and Alcohol in America, 1870–1940* (Baltimore: Johns Hopkins University Press, 1998), 14–15.

14. James H. Rohrer, "The Origins of the Temperance Movement: A Reinterpretation," *Journal of American Studies* 24 (August 1990): 228–35, challenges the dominant theory of the New England origins of the temperance movement, arguing that the push for abstinence appeared in remote areas such as Kentucky and Ohio in the decade prior to 1815.

15. According to Tyrrell (*Sobering Up*, 135), the term *teetotalism* comes from a stuttering English temperance advocate who condemned partial abstinence in favor or "tee-tee-total" abstinence.

16. Ibid., 163–82.

17. Tyrrell refutes the accusation made by historians such as Joseph Gusfield that the Maine law movement of the 1850s was a nativistic reaction to the increased Irish immigration that began in the mid-1840s. Tyrrell instead sees Maine laws as the logical development of the earlier no-license approach to prohibition. See ibid., 253, 290, 307.

18. Ian Tyrrell, "Drink and Temperance in the Antebellum South: An Overview and Interpretation," *Journal of Southern History* 48 (November 1982): 485–86, 491.

19. John M. Kloos, *A Sense of Deity: The Republican Spirituality of Dr. Benjamin Rush* (Brooklyn, N.Y.: Carlson, 1991), 6, 88.

20. Herbert Aptheker, "John Brown and Heman Humphrey: An Unpublished Letter," *Journal of Negro History* 52 (July 1967): 220.

21. Heman Humphrey, *Parallel between Intemperance and the Slave Trade: An Address Delivered at Amherst College, July 4, 1828* (Amherst, Mass.: J. S. and C. Adams, 1828), 8, 22. For a similar pecking order of evil as argued by southern Presbyterian John Holt Rice in the late 1820s, see Ernest Trice Thompson, "Continuity and Change in the Presbyterian Church in the United States," *Austin Seminary Bulletin: Faculty Edition* 85 (April 1970): 26.

22. Ann-Marie E. Szymanski, *Pathways to Prohibition: Radicals, Moderates, and Social Movement Outcomes* (Durham, N.C.: Duke University Press, 2003), 30–31.

23. C. C. Pearson and J. Edwin Hendricks, *Liquor and Anti-Liquor in Virginia, 1619–1919* (Durham, N.C.: Duke University Press, 1967), 88 n57.

24. See, for example, Rorabaugh, *The Alcoholic Republic*, 214; Pearson and Hendricks, *Liquor and Anti-Liquor in Virginia*, 88–90; Gusfield, *Symbolic Crusade*, 54; Szymanski, *Pathways to Prohibition*, 30–31.

25. Tyrrell "Drink and Temperance in the Antebellum South," 486–87.

26. Sellers, *The Market Revolution*, 20.

27. Tyrrell, "Drink and Temperance in the Antebellum South," 489. Tyrrell notes that many planters who supported the movement did so out of concern about the rising problem of slaves drinking alcohol.

28. Rufus B. Spain, *At Ease in Zion: Social History of Southern Baptists, 1865–1900* (Nashville: Vanderbilt University Press, 1967), 176.

29. Stephen A. West, "From Yeoman to Redneck in Upstate South Carolina, 1850–1915" (Ph.D. diss., Columbia University, 1998), 223–24; Tyrrell, *Sobering Up*, 258.

30. Bertram Wyatt-Brown, *The Shaping of Southern Culture: Honor, Grace, and War 1760s–1880s* (Chapel Hill: University of North Carolina Press, 2001), 98.

31. Blocker, *American Temperance Movements*, 26.

32. Douglas Carlson, "Temperance Reform in the Cotton Kingdom" (Ph.D. diss., University of Illinois at Urbana-Champaign, 1982), 12–13.

33. Douglas W. Carlson, "'Drinks He to His Own Undoing': Temperance Ideology in the Deep South," *Journal of the Early Republic* 18 (winter 1998): 665.

34. Carlson, "Temperance Reform," 143.

35. Ibid., 18, 154; Carlson, "'Drinks He to His Own Undoing,'" 687.

36. Carlson, "Temperance Reform," 303.

37. Carlson, "'Drinks He to His Own Undoing,'" 670.

38. Tyrrell, "Drink and Temperance in the Antebellum South," 488.

39. Anne C. Loveland, *Southern Evangelicals and the Social Order 1800–1860* (Baton Rouge: Louisiana State University Press, 1980), 130; Guion Griffis Johnson, *Ante-Bellum North Carolina: A Social History* (Chapel Hill: University of North Carolina Press, 1937), 169.

40. In 1886 G. J. Davis of Cave Springs, Georgia, wrote to the *Christian Index* that a temperance society had existed in Jackson County, Georgia, as early as 1824, although no records of such an organization can confirm this. See Henry A. Scomp, *King Alcohol in the Realm of King Cotton: Or, A History of the Liquor Traffic and of the Temperance Movement in Georgia from 1733 to 1887* (n.p.: Blakely Printing, 1888), 241.

41. Charles Dutton Mallary, *Memoirs of Elder Jesse Mercer* (New York: John Gray, 1844), 225–27.

42. Scomp, *King Alcohol in the Realm of King Cotton*, 289.

43. Lula Barnes Ansley, *History of the Georgia Woman's Christian Temperance Union: From Its Organization, 1883–1907* (Columbus, Ga.: Gilbert Printing, 1914), 27.

44. B. D. Ragsdale, *Story of Georgia Baptists: The Convention, Its Principles and Policies, Its Allies and Agencies, Its Aims and Its Achievements*, vol. 3 (Atlanta: Executive Committee of the Georgia Baptist Convention, 1938), 83–87; Carlson, "Temperance Reform," 13.

45. Holcombe was a leading temperance advocate in antebellum Alabama and was also opposed to slavery. He inherited some slaves in about 1820 but was not free to emancipate them, so he gave them to his half brother. J. Wayne Flynt, *Alabama Baptists: Southern Baptists in the Heart of Dixie* (Tuscaloosa: University of Alabama Press, 1998), 43.

46. James Benson Sellers, *The Prohibition Movement in Alabama, 1702 to 1943* (Chapel Hill: University of North Carolina, 1943), 28, 32.

47. Oscar Penn Fitzgerald, *John B. McFerrin: Biography* (Nashville: Publishing House of the Methodist Episcopal Church, South, 1888), 219.

48. John Abernathy Smith, *Cross and Flame: Two Centuries of United Methodism in Middle Tennessee* (Nashville: Parthenon Press, 1984), 230.

49. E. Merton Coulter, *William G. Brownlow: Fighting Parson of the Southern Highlands* (Knoxville: University of Tennessee Press, 1937), 120.

50. Paul E. Isaac, *Prohibition and Politics: Turbulent Decades in Tennessee 1885–1920* (Knoxville: University of Tennessee Press, 1965), 6–8.

51. Hosea Holcombe, *A History of the Rise and Progress of the Baptists in Alabama: With a Miniature History of the Denominations from the Apostolic Age down to the Present Time* (Philadelphia: King and Baird, 1840), 344.

52. John G. Crowley, *Primitive Baptists of the Wiregrass South: 1815 to the Present* (Gainesville: University Presses of Florida, 1998), 47–48. For more on primitive Baptist attitudes toward temperance, see James R. Mathis, *The Making of the Primitive Baptists: A Cultural and Intellectual History of the Antimission Movement, 1800–1840* (New York: Routledge, 2004), 95–97.

53. Scomp, *King Alcohol in the Realm of King Cotton*, 286–87.

54. William Birney, *James G. Birney and His Times: The Genesis of the Republican Party with Some Account of Abolition Movements in the South before 1828* (New York: D. Appleton, 1890), 48.

55. Byron Cecil Lambert, *The Rise of the Anti-Mission Baptists: Sources and Leaders, 1800–1840* (New York: Arno Press, 1980), 410–13.

56. Primitive Baptists formed associations, but they were fiercely democratic and rejected the idea of establishing any type of centralized authority or having matters of the church controlled by boards or conventions. Lawrence Edwards, *The Baptists of Tennessee, with Particular Attention to the Primitive Baptists of East Tennessee* (n.p., 1940), 41–42.

57. See Wyatt-Brown, *The Shaping of Southern Culture*, 98; Ragsdale, *Story of Georgia Baptists*, 86.

58. Quoted in Holcombe, *A History of the Rise and Progress*, 210, 282, 290.

59. Scomp, *King Alcohol in the Realm of King Cotton*, 287.

60. James O. Farmer, *The Metaphysical Confederacy: James Henley Thornwell and the Synthesis of Southern Values* (Macon, Ga.: Mercer University Press, 1986), 185–86.

61. Loveland, *Southern Evangelicals and the Social Order*, 141.

62. Robert Franklin Bunting, "'To Lay Anew the Foundations of a Mighty Church': Robert Franklin Bunting Reports the First and Second General Assemblies of the Presbyterian Church in the Confederate States," ed. Thomas W. Cutrer, *Journal of Southern Religion* 6 (2003): n21, archived copy available from http://jsr.as.wvu.edu/2003/Cutrer.htm (accessed July 18, 2007); Eugene D. Genovese, *The Southern Front: History and Politics in the Cultural War* (Columbia: University of Missouri Press, 1995), 12, 34; Edward L. Ayers, *Vengeance and Justice: Crime and Punishment in the Nineteenth-Century American South* (New York: Oxford University Press, 1984), 118; Holcombe, *A History of the Rise and Progress*, 350.

63. Flynt, *Alabama Baptists*, 94.

64. Scomp, *King Alcohol in the Realm of King Cotton*, 5.

65. William Warren Rogers, Robert David Ward, et al., *Alabama: The History of a Deep South State* (Tuscaloosa: University of Alabama Press, 1994), 370; William A. Link, *The Paradox of Southern Progressivism, 1880–1930* (Chapel Hill: University of North Carolina Press, 1992), 35; Isaac, *Prohibition and Politics*, 54.

66. Henry Wheeler, *Methodism and the Temperance Reformation* (Cincinnati: Walden and Stowe, 1882), 110.

67. Carlson, "Temperance Reform," 68–69. Carlson notes that southern Methodists had favored a strong episcopacy as early as 1820, although Christopher Owen argues that Georgia Methodists showed no such concern until

the issue came to the fore in 1844, when Georgia bishop James O. Andrew was deposed for owning slaves. Christopher H. Owen, *The Sacred Flame of Love: Methodism and Society in Nineteenth-Century Georgia* (Athens: University of Georgia Press, 1998), 55.

68. Mitchell Snay, *Gospel of Disunion: Religion and Separatism in the Antebellum South* (Cambridge: Cambridge University Press, 1993), 127.

69. Allen P. Tankersley, "Basil Hallam Overby: Champion of Prohibition in Ante Bellum Georgia," *Georgia Historical Quarterly* 31 (March 1947): 14–16.

70. Ansley (*History of the Georgia Woman's Christian Temperance Union*, 30) recalls that when whiskey was in short supply during the war, people distilled "their grain, fruits, and vegetables into whiskey."

71. William M. Robinson Jr., "Prohibition in the Confederacy," *American Historical Journal* 37 (October 1931): 50.

72. Rogers, Ward, et al., *Alabama*, 371; Avery Hamilton Reed, *Baptists in Alabama: Their Organization and Witness* (Montgomery: Alabama Baptist State Convention, 1967), 136; Thomas R. Pegram, *Battling Demon Rum: The Struggle for a Dry America, 1800–1933* (Chicago: Ivan R. Dee, 1988), 124.

73. Physician, *Liquor and Lincoln* (n.p., n.d.), 3–4.

74. Quoted in Smith, *Cross and Flame*, 231. General Thomas J. "Stonewall" Jackson also recognized the ruinous effects of alcohol on the southern army's fortunes. An officer serving under Jackson later recounted that just before the Second Battle of Manassas they came upon a warehouse full of whiskey. Jackson ordered every drop destroyed, saying, "I fear that liquor more than General Pope's army." See "Stonewall Jackson's 'Most Dreaded Foe,'" *Southern Historical Society Papers* 23 (1895): 334.

75. For the Civil War's impact on the southern economy, infrastructure, and social order, see Eric Foner, *A Short History of Reconstruction, 1863–1877* (New York: Harper and Row, 1990), 55–56, and David Herbert Donald, Jean H. Baker, and Michael F. Holt, *The Civil War and Reconstruction* (New York: Norton, 2001), 498–500. For a contrasting opinion, see Robert S. Cotterill, "The Old South and the New," in *Myth and Southern History*, ed. Patrick Gerster and Nicholas Cords (Chicago: Rand McNally, 1974), 171–76, who argues that the devastation of the Old South's economic order has been overstated by historians.

76. Sidney Lanier, "The Raven Days," in *Poems of Sidney Lanier*, new ed. (New York: Charles Scribner's Sons, 1899), 221.

77. Edward L. Ayers, *The Promise of the New South: Life after Reconstruction* (New York: Oxford University Press, 1992), 178; Hunter Dickinson Farish, *The Circuit Rider Dismounts: A Social History of Southern Methodism, 1865–1900* (Richmond, Va.: Dietz Press, 1938), 306; Reed, *Baptists in Alabama*, 136.

78. Smith, *Cross and Flame*, 229.

79. Job Harral, "When Is a Man Drunk?" *Tennessee Baptist*, March 27, 1886, 4.

80. Ibid.

81. "Report on Temperance," in *Minutes of the Forty-seventh Anniversary of the Georgia Baptist State Convention, Held at Cuthbert, April 23d, 24th, & 26th, 1869* (Atlanta: Franklin Printing House, 1869), 10–11.

82. "Report on Temperance," in *Minutes of the Forty-eighth Anniversary of the Georgia Baptist State Convention, Held at Newnan, April 22d, 23d, and 25th, 1870* (Atlanta: Franklin Steam Printing House, 1870), 13.

83. *The Holston Annual, 1875. No. 3. Semi-Centennial Number. Minutes of the First and Fifty-second Sessions of the Holston Annual Conference, Methodist Episcopal Church, South*, ed. J. R. Payne (Knoxville, Tenn.: Press and Herald Job Dept., 1875), 42.

84. See Farish, *The Circuit Rider Dismounts*, 312–14.

85. "Report of the Committee on Temperance," in *Minutes of the Forty-ninth Anniversary of the Georgia Baptist State Convention, Held at Cartersville, April 21st, 22d, & 24th, 1871* (Atlanta: Franklin Steam Printing House, 1871), 11.

86. "Report of the Committee on Temperance," in *Minutes of the Fifty-second Anniversary of the Baptist Convention of the State of Georgia, Held at Americus, April 23d, 24th, 25th, & 27th, 1874* (Atlanta: Franklin Steam Print House, 1874), 16.

Chapter Two. "It Is Not Enough That the Church Should Be Sober"

1. Benjamin Franklin Riley, *A Memorial History of the Baptists of Alabama: Being an Account of the Struggles and Achievements of the Denomination from 1808 to 1923* (Philadelphia: Judson Press, 1923), 211.

2. Joseph Shackelford, "How to Get Rid of It," *Alabama Baptist*, February 9, 1882, 2.

3. "Committee on Temperance," in *Year Book and Minutes of the Twenty-fifth Session of the North Georgia Conference Methodist Episcopal Church, South, Held in Methodist Church, Cartersville, Ga., from December 9th to 15th, 1891*, ed. Ellison R. Cook (Macon, Ga.: J. W. Burke, 1891), 36.

4. Such recipes can be found as late as 1883 in Georgia; see, for example, "Making Apple Wine," *Christian Index*, December 6, 1883, 14.

5. *Minutes of the Fifty-sixth Anniversary of the Baptist Convention of the State of Georgia, Held at LaGrange, April 25, 26, 27 and 29, 1878* (Atlanta: James P. Harrison, 1878), 20.

6. J. G. Mundine, "The Evils of Intemperance," *Alabama Baptist*, October 26, 1876, 3.

7. Editorial, "Inconsistencies of Temperance Men," *Holston Methodist*, May 3, 1879, 2.

8. "Temperance," in *Minutes of the Fifty-fourth Assembling of the East Tennessee Association of Baptists, Held with Newport Church, Commencing, Thursday, Sept. 22, 1892* (Morristown, Tenn.: Morristown Medicine, 1892), 9.

9. *Tennessee Baptist Convention: 20th Session, Held in Edgefield Baptist Church, Nashville, October 17–20, 1894* (Memphis: Wills and Crumpton, n.d.), 41.

10. I. O. Rust, "The Temperance Movement," *Baptist and Reflector*, April 10, 1902, 2.

11. *Minutes of the Eighty-fifth Anniversary of the Baptist Convention of the State of Georgia: Held in Cartersville, November 20–22, 1906* (Atlanta: Foote and Davies, 1906), 36.

12. William Garrott Brown, "The South and the Saloon," *Century Magazine* 76 (July 1908): 465.

13. Temperance advocates in the North had evolved from favoring moderation in the consumption of alcohol to demanding total abstinence during the antebellum years; thus, the southern "all-or-nothing" approach was not original. Indeed, one of the earliest extant temperance tracts—Heman Humphrey's from 1813—skipped the "moderation" stage (unusual for its time) and demanded "total abstinence from the use of all intoxicating liquors," believing that it was impossible for men to "reform by degrees." Heman Humphrey, *Intemperance: An Address to the Churches and Congregations of the Western District of Fairfield County* (New Haven, Conn.: Eli Hudson, 1813), 25.

14. Brown, "The South and the Saloon," 465; Walter Hines Page, "The Prohibition Wave over the South," *World's Work* 14 (September 1907): 9278.

15. Brown, "The South and the Saloon," 465.

16. When the English Puritan settlers arrived in the colonies aboard the *Arabella* in 1630, they brought with them ten thousand barrels of beer but only twelve gallons of distilled alcohol. Jack S. Blocker Jr., *American Temperance Movements: Cycles of Reform* (Boston: Twayne, 1989), 3.

17. Grady McWhiney, *Cracker Culture: Celtic Ways in the Old South* (University, Ala.: University of Alabama Press, 1988), xiii, 92. The "Celtic thesis," as it has come to be called, was first put forth by McWhiney and Forrest McDonald, primarily in their jointly authored articles "The Antebellum Southern Herdsman: A Reinterpretation," *Journal of Southern History* 41 (May 1975): 147–66, and "The Celtic South," *History Today* 30 (July 1980): 11–15. The Celtic argument proved to be somewhat controversial, and several historians have rejected it. Its most vociferous critic has been Rowland Berthoff, who attacked McWhiney and McDonald's definition of *Celtic* as too broad and accused them of "free-floating logic and dubious scholarship." McWhiney and McDonald retorted that Berthoff's objections were driven primarily by the fact that his Scottish wife detested the idea of being lumped ethnically with the Irish. That said, they have also further documented the connection between Celtic (broadly defined) folkways and culture and that of the American South, and the thesis has enjoyed widespread acceptance. See Rowland Berthoff, "Celtic Mist over the South," *Journal of Southern History* 52 (November 1986): 523–46; Forrest McDonald and Grady McWhiney, "[Celtic Mist over the South]: A Response," *Journal of Southern History* 52 (November 1986): 547–48; Rowland Berthoff, "[Celtic Mist over the South]: A Rejoinder," *Journal of Southern History* 52 (November 1986): 548–50; Rowland Berthoff, Forrest McDonald, Grady McWhiney, et al., "Comparative History in Theory and Practice: A Discussion," *American Historical Review* 87 (February 1982): 131–37; Bertram Wyatt-Brown, *Southern Honor: Ethics and Behavior in the Old South* (New York: Oxford University Press, 1982), 37.

Like McWhiney and McDonald, David Hackett Fischer, *Albion's Seed: Four British Folkways in America* (New York: Oxford University Press, 1989), 606–34, argues that the culture of the American backcountry—especially the southern Appalachian highlands—was distinctly shaped by the culture and customs brought by the immigrants from Scotland, northern Ireland, and northern England who flooded the area during the eighteenth century. Most recently, the Celtic thesis has served as the centerpiece of such works as James Webb's *Born Fighting: How the Scots-Irish Shaped America* (New York: Broadway Books, 2004) and Michael Fry's *How the Scots Made America* (New York: Thomas Dunne Books, 2005).

18. Stephen A. West, "From Yeoman to Redneck in Upstate South Carolina, 1850–1915" (Ph.D. diss., Columbia University, 1998), 184, 196; McWhiney, *Cracker Culture*, xiii, 92. The important role of drinking in the process of male bonding, especially in Euro-American cultures, is also discussed in Lionel Tiger, *Men in Groups* (New York: Random House, 1969), 152–55.

19. Kenneth M. Stampp, *The Peculiar Institution: Slavery in the Ante-Bellum South* (New York: Knopf, 1956), 370–71; Eugene D. Genovese, *Roll, Jordan, Roll: The World the Slaves Made* (New York: Pantheon Books, 1974), 644–46.

20. Ian Tyrrell, "Drink and Temperance in the Antebellum South: An Overview and Interpretation," *Journal of Southern History* 48 (November 1982): 501; Douglas W. Carlson, "'Drinks He to His Own Undoing': Temperance Ideology in the Deep South," *Journal of the Early Republic* 18 (winter 1998): 689. In 1808 Georgia prohibited the sale of liquor to slaves without the permission of their owners. In 1822 Alabama passed a law making it illegal for free blacks to sell liquor, and in 1838 it prohibited the sale of alcohol to slaves by anyone. Tennessee passed a similar law barring the sale of liquor to slaves in 1845. Henry A. Scomp, *King Alcohol in the Realm of King Cotton: Or, A History of the Liquor Traffic and of the Temperance Movement in Georgia from 1733 to 1887* (n.p.: Blakely Printing, 1888), 187; James Benson Sellers, *The Prohibition Movement in Alabama, 1702 to 1943* (Chapel Hill: University of North Carolina, 1943), 29; Eric Russell Lacy, "Tennessee Teetotalism: Social Forces and the Politics of Progressivism," *Tennessee Historical Quarterly* 24 (fall 1965): 220.

21. Sellers, *The Prohibition Movement in Alabama*, 25–26.

22. Wyatt-Brown, *Southern Honor*, 90, 279; Tyrrell, "Drink and Temperance in the Antebellum South," 503. Genovese (*Roll, Jordan, Roll*, 645) also notes that, among the upper class, it was customary to consume a mint julep prior to breakfast, and lower- and middle-class southerners often kept a bottle of whisky on the dinner table instead of a bottle of wine.

23. For an excellent overview of these interpretations, see Harvey H. Jackson, "The Middle-Class Democracy Victorious: The Mitcham War of Clarke County, Alabama, 1893," *Journal of Southern History* 57 (August 1991): 454–55; McWhiney, *Cracker Culture*, 149–51.

24. A. C. Dixon, "The First Drunkard," *Baptist and Reflector*, January 15, 1891, 2.

25. G. W. Garner, "Origin of Inebrates [*sic*]," *Christian Index*, June 16, 1892, 2.

26. Editorial, "Temperance," *Alabama Baptist*, August 4, 1881, 2.

27. *The Holston Annual, 1875. No. 3. Semi-Centennial Number. Minutes of the First and Fifty-second Sessions of the Holston Annual Conference, Methodist Episcopal Church, South*, ed. J. R. Payne (Knoxville, Tenn.: Press and Herald Job Dept., 1875), 42.

28. *The Holston Annual, 1880—No. 8. Official Record of the Holston Annual Conference, Methodist Episcopal Church, South, Fifty-seventh Session Held at Morristown, Tenn., Oct., 1880,* ed. J. R. Payne (Knoxville, Tenn.: Whig and Chronicle, 1880), 25.

29. *The Holston Annual, for 1883—No. 11. Official Record of the Holston Annual Conference, Methodist Episcopal Church, South, Sixtieth Session, Held at Chattanooga, Tenn., October, 1883,* ed. J. R. Payne (Knoxville, Tenn.: Ogden Bros. and Rule, 1883), 42.

30. Rufus B. Spain, *At Ease in Zion: Social History of Southern Baptists, 1865–1900* (Nashville: Vanderbilt University Press, 1967), 192.

31. William A. Link, *The Paradox of Southern Progressivism, 1880–1930* (Chapel Hill: University of North Carolina Press, 1992), 45.

32. "Supplement.—Reports Adopted. IX.—Temperance," in *Journal of the Seventy-sixth Session of the Tennessee Annual Conference of the Methodist Episcopal Church, South: Held at Murfreesboro, Tenn., October 9–14, 1889* (Nashville: Publishing House of the Methodist Episcopal Church, South, 1889), 31–32.

33. W. H. Burton, "Temperance," *Alabama Baptist,* March 3, 1881, 1.

34. According to Robert C. Fuller, *Religion and Wine: A Cultural History of Wine Drinking in the United States* (Knoxville: University of Tennessee Press, 1996), 77, the practice of treating in American politics dates back at least to the Revolution.

35. Editorial, "Whisky in Politics," *Christian Index,* December 5, 1878, 5.

36. *Minutes of the Fifty-ninth Anniversary of the Baptist Convention of the State of Georgia: Held at Athens, April 21, 22, 23 and 25, 1881* (Atlanta: Jas. P. Harrison, 1881), 20.

37. Ibid., 28.

38. *Minutes of the Sixty-seventh Anniversary of the Baptist Convention of the State of Georgia: Held at Marietta, April 25th, 26th, 27th and 29th, 1889* (Macon: Georgia Baptist Publishing, 1889), 29.

39. *Minutes of the Sixty-eighth Anniversary of the Baptist Convention of the State of Georgia* [remainder of title page missing; 1891], 33.

40. *Minutes of the Seventy-eighth Anniversary of the Baptist Convention of the State of Georgia: Held in Griffin, March 29–April 1, 1900* (Atlanta: Foote and Davies, 1900), 51.

41. Henry H. Tucker, "Editorial," *Christian Index,* August 22, 1889, 1.

42. Editorial, "Reforms," *Alabama Christian Advocate,* November 21, 1889, 4.

43. "Tennessee Baptist Convention," *Baptist and Reflector,* October 19, 1899, 9.

44. "On Temperance," in *Minutes of the North Georgia Conference, Held in Milledgeville, Ga. 1888,* ed. H. L. Crumley (Atlanta: Constitution Publishing, n.d.), 13.

45. *Minutes of the Eighty-second Anniversary of the Baptist Convention of the State of Georgia: Held in Athens, November 19–22, 1903* (Atlanta: Foote and Davies, 1903), 33.

46. Washington Bryan Crumpton, *A Book of Memories 1842–1920* (Montgomery, Ala.: Baptist Mission Board, 1921), 199.

47. Ibid., 191.

48. J. Wayne Flynt, "Dissent in Zion: Alabama Baptists and Social Issues, 1900–1914," *Journal of Southern History* 35 (November 1969): 525.

49. Crumpton, *A Book of Memories*, 192.

50. Washington Bryan Crumpton, *A Story: How Alabama Became Dry* (Montgomery, Ala.: Paragon Press, 1925), 12.

51. A biographer said of Crumpton, "he was never governor, but he could have been." In 1912, when Congressman Oscar W. Underwood of Birmingham sought the Democratic nomination for president, Crumpton's endorsement of him (despite their differing views on prohibition) proved crucial. With Crumpton's support, Underwood (an Episcopalian) received his home state's votes at the Democratic convention. James Chapman, "Alabama Baptist Biographies, 1910–1925," James Chapman Papers, Southern Baptist Historical Library and Archives, Nashville, Tenn. (hereafter, SBHLA).

52. Benjamin Franklin Riley, *The White Man's Burden: A Discussion of the Interracial Question with Special Reference to the Responsibility of the White Race to the Negro Problem* (Birmingham, Ala.: for the author, 1910), 44–48.

53. Benjamin Franklin Riley, "The Negro Prohibition Movement," *Alabama Baptist*, April 21, 1909, 6.

54. Paul E. Isaac, *Prohibition and Politics: Turbulent Decades in Tennessee 1885–1920* (Knoxville: University of Tennessee Press, 1965), 102; John Abernathy Smith, *Cross and Flame: Two Centuries of United Methodism in Middle Tennessee* (Nashville: Parthenon Press, 1984), 238.

55. Haygood's primary biographer, Harold Mann, observes that Haygood's prohibition activity ended abruptly in 1887, after which he "did not make a single appearance . . . on behalf of the prohibitionist movement." Mann cites Haygood's opposition to the WCTU and his disappointment over the controversy between Bishop Galloway and Jefferson Davis (discussed in chapter 3) as the primary reasons for Haygood's disaffection with the prohibition cause after 1887. The political implications of prohibitionists' support for Bourbon Democrats such as Haygood (also discussed in chapter 3) could well be added to Mann's list. See Harold W. Mann, *Atticus Greene Haygood: Methodist Bishop, Editor, and Educator* (Athens: University of Georgia Press, 1965), 158–60.

56. Mark K. Bauman, *Warren A. Candler: The Conservative as Idealist* (Metuchen, N.J.: Scarecrow Press, 1981), 177. Candler was known for other indulgences as well, such as playing cards with his grandchildren and—perhaps not surprisingly for a bishop who had been assigned to oversee the missionary conference in Cuba on twenty different occasions—chain-smoking fine cigars. Alfred M. Pierce, *Giant against the Sky: The Life of Bishop Warren A. Candler* (New York: Abingdon-Cokesbury Press, 1948), 90.

57. Kathleen Minnix, *Laughter in the Amen Corner: The Life of Evangelist Sam Jones* (Athens: University of Georgia Press, 1993), 71, 103.

58. Ibid., 167–68, 173.

59. Kathleen Minnix, "'That Memorable Meeting': Sam Jones and the Nashville Revival of 1885," *Tennessee Historical Quarterly* 48 (fall 1989): 155–57; David B. Parker, "'Quit Your Meanness': Sam Jones's Theology for the New South," *Georgia Historical Quarterly* 77 (winter 1993): 716.

60. Small recounts his conversion experience in Samuel W. Small, *"From Bar-Room to Pulpit": Lectures Delivered by Samuel W. Small, at Stokes Hall, Monday Evening, May 4th, 1888* (Durham, N.C.: W. Whitker, 1888), 12–15.

61. Minnix, *Laughter in the Amen Corner*, 92–93.

62. W. B. Crumpton, [no title], *Alabama Baptist*, September 25, 1884, 1.

63. These proscriptive texts include Leviticus 10:9, Proverbs 31:4, and Luke 1:15.

64. See John 2:1–10; Matthew 16:27–29.

65. For an overview of the early development of the two-wine theory, see John L. Merrill, "The Bible and the American Temperance Movement: Text, Context, and Pretext," *Harvard Theological Review* 81 (April 1988): 153–66.

66. Genesis 9:21; Proverbs 23:20, 29–31.

67. Psalms 104:15; 1 Timothy 5:23.

68. Dixon, "The First Drunkard," 2.

69. Jennie L. Hayzlett, "Temperance Column," *Alabama Baptist*, February 19, 1885, 1.

70. Daniel Sack, *Whitebread Protestants: Food and Religion in American Culture* (New York: St. Martin's Press, 2000), 17–19.

71. "The Two-Wine Theory," *Baptist* (Memphis), May 19, 1888, 4.

72. Mark Gstohl and Michael Homan, "Jesus the Teetotaler: How Dr. Welch Put the Lord on the Wagon," *Bible Review* 18 (April 2002): 29.

73. Ibid.

74. William Chazanof, *Welch's Grape Juice: From Corporation to Co-operative* (Syracuse, N.Y.: Syracuse University Press, 1977), 31–32.

75. Hayzlett, "Temperance Column," 1.

76. Hunter Dickinson Farish, *The Circuit Rider Dismounts: A Social History of Southern Methodism, 1865–1900* (Richmond, Va.: Dietz Press, 1938), 314.

77. Gstohl and Homan, "Jesus the Teetotaler," 29.

78. *Year Book and Minutes of the Thirty-fourth Session of the North Georgia Conference, M. E. Church, South: Held at Trinity Church, Atlanta, GA. November 21st to 26th, 1900*, ed. John W. Heidt (Rome, Ga.: Fletcher Smith, n.d.), 49.

79. "Report of Committee on Temperance," in *Year Book and Minutes of the Forty-first Session of the North Georgia Conference, M. E. Church, South, Held at Cartersville, Georgia, November the Twentieth to the Twenty-fifth, Nineteen Hundred and Seven*, ed. John W. Heidt (Atlanta: Converse and Wing, n.d.), 40.

80. Editorial, "Communion Wine," *Alabama Baptist*, May 17, 1900, 4.

81. Editorial, "Whisky in Politics," 5.

82. J. W. Slaten, "The Twin Evils of the World," *Baptist and Reflector*, July 6, 1905, 3.

83. Charles H. White, "The Nickel behind the Bar," *Baptist and Reflector*, July 30, 1908, 3.

84. Editorial, "Letter from a Wife," *Baptist and Reflector*, May 11, 1905, 8.

85. "Suicide Winds up Period of Drinking," *Nashville Tennessean*, June 18, 1908, 1. Isaac (*Prohibition and Politics*, 148) notes that the *Tennessean* became "practically a prohibition organ."

86. Editorial, "Temperance," 2.

87. G. W. Garner, "Why I Favor State Prohibition," *Christian Index*, July 12, 1900, 1.

88. J. Wayne Flynt, *Alabama Baptists: Southern Baptists in the Heart of Dixie* (Tuscaloosa: University of Alabama Press, 1998), 211.

89. Editorial, "Rum's Ruin," *Alabama Baptist*, September 6, 1894, 2.

90. Cyrus Stebbins, "The Liquor Business," *Baptist and Reflector*, July 2, 1908, 3; Editorial, "Saloons and Crime," *Baptist and Reflector*, December 17, 1908, 8.

91. Editorial, "Man Shot—Who Is Responsible?" *Baptist and Reflector*, June 1, 1905, 9.

92. Atticus G. Haygood, *Save Our Homes: A Prohibition Sermon* (Macon, Ga.: J. W. Burke, 1884), 13–14.

93. "Supplement.—Reports Adopted. IX.—Temperance," 31.

94. *Thirtieth Anniversary of the Tennessee Baptist Convention: Held with the Centennial Baptist Church, Knoxville, October 13–15, 1904* (Nashville: n.p., 1904), 32–33.

95. "The Fruit of the Saloon," *Knoxville Journal and Tribune*, February 11, 1907, 10.

96. See Roger Dale Posey, "Anti-Alcohol City: Social, Economic, and Political Aspects of Knoxville, Tennessee, 1870–1907" (master's thesis, University of Tennessee, 1982), 39.

97. "Loss of Revenue Easily Repaid," *Knoxville Journal and Tribune*, February 11, 1907, 10.

98. Editorial, "Business and Prohibition," *Baptist and Reflector*, July 23, 1908, 8.

99. Editorial, "The Methodist and Politics," *Holston Methodist*, November 11, 1882, 2.

100. *The Holston Annual 1911. Official Record of the Holston Annual Conference, Methodist Episcopal Church, South, Eighty-eighth Session Held at Morristown, Tenn., October 4–10, 1911*, ed. J. A. Burrow (n.p.: n.d.), 55.

101. *Thirtieth Anniversary of the Tennessee Baptist Convention*, 34.

102. Quoted in R. L. Watts, "A Great League Convention," *Epworthian* (Knoxville) 1 (January 1893): 89.

103. *The Holston Annual 1904. Official Record of the Holston Annual Conference, Methodist Episcopal Church, South, Eighty-first Session, Held at Abingdon, Virginia, October 1904*, ed. J. A. Burrow (n.p.: n.d.), 56.

104. E. E. Folk, "Vote as You Pray," *Baptist and Reflector*, April 6, 1905, 8.

105. A. T. W. Lytle, "Who Is Responsible?" *Wesleyan Christian Advocate* (Atlanta), May 25, 1892, 3.

106. William J. Albert, "Church and Politics," *Wesleyan Christian Advocate* (Atlanta), June 15, 1892.

107. George A. Brewer, "Christian Voters of 1884," *Alabama Baptist*, January 17, 1884, 1.

108. James D. Dickson, "Our Duty to the Temperance Cause," *Alabama Baptist*, May 22, 1884, 3.

109. J. C. Wright, *Autobiography of Rev. A. B. Wright, of the Holston Conference, M. E. Church* (Cincinnati: Cranston and Curtis, 1896), 261.

110. Flynt, *Alabama Baptists*, 222.

111. Pictured in Link, *The Paradox of Southern Progressivism*, 107.

112. Editorial, "Duty Concerning Prohibition," *Baptist* (Memphis), September 17, 1887, 6.

113. G. L. Ellis, "Prohibition Scriptural," *Baptist* (Memphis), February 18, 1888, 2.

114. "The Fruit of the Saloon," 10.

115. Washington B. Crumpton, "To the Friends of Temperance in Alabama," *Alabama Baptist*, December 16, 1880, 2.

116. D. P. G., "Prohibition in Alabama," *Alabama Baptist*, December 23, 1880, 1; J. M. Fortune, "The Liquor Business—What to Do," *Alabama Baptist*, March 31, 1881, 1.

117. "Tennessee Baptist State Convention," *Baptist and Reflector,* October 19, 1893, 5.

118. *Tennessee Baptist Convention: 22d Anniversary, Held with Paris Baptist Church, October 14–16, 1896* (Memphis: Wills and Crumpton, n.d.), 31.

119. "The General Convention of Baptists of North America," *Alabama Baptist*, June 5, 1907, 12.

120. The legislators did not share the former Methodist minister's animosity toward the burgeoning Tennessee liquor industry. In 1870 two attempts to insert a local option clause into the state's new constitution were defeated. Local option legislation was also defeated in both 1870 and 1871 and barely passed the legislature in 1873, only to be vetoed by the state's new Democrat governor. Isaac, *Prohibition and Politics*, 8–10.

121. *The Holston Annual 1885. Official Record of the Holston Annual Conference, Methodist Episcopal Church, South, Sixty-second Session, Held at Cleveland, Tenn., October 1885*, ed. W. C. Carden (Morristown, Tenn.: Gazette Book and Job Office, 1885), 49.

122. "Supplement.—Reports Adopted. II.—Temperance," in *Journal of the Seventy-fourth Session of the Tennessee Annual Conference of the Methodist Episcopal Church, South: Held at Gallatin, Tenn., October 12–18, 1887* (Nashville: Southern Methodist Publishing House, 1887), 21.

123. "Sam Small," *Knoxville Daily Journal*, July 22, 1887, 5.

124. Brewer, "Christian Voters of 1884," 1.

125. Job Harral, "Prohibition War," *Baptist and Reflector,* November 21, 1889, 2.

126. *The Holston Annual 1889. Official Record of the Holston Annual Conference, Methodist Episcopal Church, South, Sixty-sixth Session, Held at Morristown, Tenn., October, 1889*, ed. W. C. Carden (Morristown, Tenn.: Morristown Medicine, n.d.), 47.

127. "Committee on Temperance," in *Year Book and Minutes of Twenty-fifth Session of North Georgia Conference, 1891*, 36.

128. *Minutes of the Seventy-fifth Anniversary of the Baptist Convention of the State of Georgia: Held at Gainesville, April 2–5, 1897* (Atlanta: Franklin Printing and Publishing, 1897), 41.

129. Editorial, *Christian Index*, January 24, 1889, 1.

130. W. B. Crumpton, "Reply to the Above," *Alabama Baptist,* January 10, 1895, 2.

131. Farish, *The Circuit Rider Dismounts,* 324.

132. Editorial, "The Saloon in the South," *Outlook,* March 14, 1908, 581.

133. Birmingham prohibitionists, led by the Birmingham Pastors' Union, fought to dry up the city by means of local option rather than the high-license approach they had once endorsed. In 1907 they were able to get local prohibition enacted by rallying the rural population surrounding the city to make the entire county dry. See Carl V. Harris, "Reforms in Government Control of Negroes in Birmingham, Alabama, 1890–1920," *Journal of Southern History* 38 (November 1972): 575.

134. John Dittmer, *Black Georgia in the Progressive Era, 1900–1920* (Urbana: University of Illinois Press, 1977), 111.

135. While maintaining that "the most appropriate remedy for intemperance is moral suasion," the convention resolved that "the best legislation on this subject is that which is known as local option." *Minutes of the Sixty-seventh Anniversary of the Baptist Convention of the State of Georgia,* 29.

136. Editorial, "Danger to Prohibition," *Wesleyan Christian Advocate* (Macon, Ga.), January 27, 1886, 1.

137. Bauman, *Warren A. Candler,* 172–73.

138. Minnix, *Laughter in the Amen Corner,* 174.

139. "Temperance," in *Year Book and Minutes of the Thirty-ninth Session of the North Georgia Conference, M. E. Church, South, Held at Newnan, Georgia, November the Twenty-second to the Twenty-seventh, Nineteen Hundred and Five,* ed. John W. Heidt (Atlanta: Blosser, 1906), 33.

140. Alexander J. McKelway, "Local Option and State Prohibition in the South," *Charities and the Commons,* January 25, 1908, 1452.

141. Quoted in Sellers, *The Prohibition Movement in Alabama,* 177.

142. Isaac, *Prohibition and Politics,* 9.

143. Smith, *Cross and Flame,* 231.

144. E. E. Folk, "The Adams Law vs. Local Option," *Baptist and Reflector,* November 1, 1906, 8.

145. "Supplement.—Reports Adopted. III.—Temperance," in *Journal of the Seventy-third Session of the Tennessee Annual Conference of the Methodist Episcopal Church, South: Held at Clarksville, Tenn., October 6–12, 1886* (Nashville: Southern Methodist Publishing House, n.d.), 24.

146. *Tennessee Baptist Convention: Fifteenth Annual Session, Held with the Baptist Church at Humboldt, Tennessee, October 17, 18, 19, 1889* (Nashville: Board of Missions and Sunday-Schools, n.d.), 43.

147. *Tennessee Baptist Convention: 22d Anniversary,* 31.

148. Quoted in Isaac, *Prohibition and Politics,* 79.

149. E. E. Folk, "The Tidal Wave of Temperance," *Baptist and Reflector,* February 12, 1903, 8.

150. *Thirty-first Anniversary of the Tennessee Baptist Convention: Held with the First Baptist Church, Jackson, October 12–14, 1905* (Nashville: Keelin-Williams, 1905), 36–37.

151. *The Holston Annual 1905. Official Record of the Holston Annual Conference, Methodist Episcopal Church, South, Eighty-second Session, Held at Bristol, Tenn.-Va., October 11–17, 1905*, ed. J. A. Burrow (n.p.: n.d.), 58.

152. "Supplement.—Reports Adopted. VI.—Temperance," in *Journal of the Ninety-second Session of the Tennessee Annual Conference of the Methodist Episcopal Church, South: Held at Nashville, Tenn., October 25–30, 1905* (Nashville: Publishing House of the Methodist Episcopal Church, South, n.d.), 43.

153. "Temperance Report," *Baptist and Reflector,* October 22, 1908, 5.

154. Editorial, "The Legislature and Temperance," *Baptist and Reflector,* April 20, 1905, 8.

155. E. E. Folk, "State-Wide Prohibition," *Baptist and Reflector,* October 29, 1908, 4.

156. Thomas R. Pegram, "Temperance Politics and Regional Political Culture: The Anti-Saloon League in Maryland and the South, 1907–1915," *Journal of Southern History* 63 (February 1997): 78.

157. *Thirty-third Anniversary of the Tennessee Baptist Convention: Held with the Baptist Churches of Knoxville, Tenn. October 18–21, 1907* (Nashville: Folk-Keelin, 1907), 46.

158. Folk, "State-Wide Prohibition," 4.

159. See "Committee on Temperance," in *Year Book and Minutes of the Twenty-fifth Session of the North Georgia Conference, 1891,* 36; "Committee on Temperance," in *Year Book and Minutes of the Twenty-seventh Session of the North Georgia Conference, Methodist Episcopal Church, South, Held in County Court House, Gainesville, Ga., from Nov. 29th to Dec. 5th, 1893,* ed. Ellison R. Cook and Joel T. Davies Jr. (Atlanta: Foote and Davies, 1893), 24; Warren A. Candler, "Temperance Legislation in Georgia," *Christian Advocate* (Nashville), February 8, 1894, 1.

160. W. B. Crumpton, "A Chapter of Temperance History," *Alabama Baptist,* December 13, 1900, 3.

161. Richard F. Hamm, *Shaping the Eighteenth Amendment: Temperance Reform, Legal Culture, and the Polity, 1880–1920* (Chapel Hill: University of North Carolina Press, 1995), 128.

162. David Leigh Colvin, *Prohibition in the United States: A History of the Prohibition Party, and of the Prohibition Movement* (New York: George H. Doran, 1926), 293.

163. West, "From Yeoman to Redneck," 534.

164. John Evans Eubanks, *Ben Tillman's Baby: The Dispensary System of South Carolina 1892–1915* (n.p.: 1950), 59.

165. William Warren Rogers, Robert David Ward, et al., *Alabama: History of a Deep South State* (Tuscaloosa: University of Alabama Press, 1994), 373; Sellers, *The Prohibition Movement in Alabama,* 87.

166. S. O. Y. Ray, "Prohibition for Alabama," *Southern and Alabama Baptist,* April 23, 1902, 10; O. C. Doster, "Against Dispensary," *Alabama Baptist,* March 1, 1900, 3; Lida B. Robertson, "The Dispensary," *Alabama Baptist,* May 25, 1900, 5.

167. Sheldon Hackney, *Populism to Progressivism in Alabama* (Princeton, N.J.: Princeton University Press, 1969), 303.

168. In South Carolina, allegations of kickbacks, bribery, embezzlement, and the mislabeling of low-grade whiskey in order to sell it as high-grade plagued administrators of the dispensary. Eubanks, *Ben Tillman's Baby*, 137.

169. See Flynt, *Alabama Baptists*, 271.

170. John Kobler, *Ardent Spirits: The Rise and Fall of Prohibition* (New York: G. P. Putnam's Sons, 1973), 170–71.

171. K. Austin Kerr, *Organized for Prohibition: A New History of the Anti-Saloon League* (New Haven, Conn.: Yale University Press, 1985), 77–81.

172. Pegram, "Temperance Politics and Regional Political Culture," 65.

173. Ibid., 81, 124.

174. For an exhaustive account of the causes and aftermath of the riot, see Gregory L. Mixon, "The Atlanta Riot of 1906" (Ph.D. diss., University of Cincinnati, 1989).

175. Mark Bauerlein, *Negrophobia: A Race Riot in Atlanta, 1906* (San Francisco: Encounter Books, 2001), 218. It was widely speculated that many more blacks had been killed during the riots and that their bodies had been disposed of in the countryside.

176. Booker T. Washington, "Prohibition and the Negro," *Outlook* 88 (March 14, 1908): 587.

177. Editorial, "Effects of Prohibition," *Baptist and Reflector*, July 23, 1908, 9.

178. M. M. Welch, "Prohibition in Atlanta," *Our Home Field* 19 (March 1908): 240.

179. Editorial, "Georgia's Example to the Nation," *Independent* 64 (January 16, 1908): 162.

180. Pegram, "Temperance Politics and Regional Political Culture," 78.

181. William R. Majors, *Editorial Wild Oats: Edward Ward Carmack and Tennessee Politics* (Macon, Ga.: Mercer University Press, 1984), 134.

182. Isaac, *Prohibition and Politics*, 138.

183. Dewey W. Grantham, *Southern Progressivism: The Reconciliation of Progress and Tradition* (Knoxville: University of Tennessee Press, 1983), 81; William R. Majors, *Change and Continuity: Tennessee Politics since the Civil War* (Macon, Ga.: Mercer University Press, 1986), 44.

184. Edgar E. Folk, "Senator Edward Ward Carmack," Edgar Estes Folk Collection, SBHLA.

185. Ibid.

186. Grantham, *Southern Progressivism*, 166.

187. Quoted in Joe Michael Shahan, "Reform and Politics in Tennessee: 1906–1914" (Ph.D. diss., Vanderbilt University, 1981), 180.

188. Majors, *Change and Continuity*, 45.

189. J. B. Gambrell to E. E. Folk, January 15, [1909?], E. E. Folk Collection, SBHLA. At the age of twenty-three, Roderick Dhu Gambrell had become editor of the *Sword and Shield*, a prohibition paper in Jackson, Mississippi, and he launched an editorial campaign against liquor interests in the state. Three previous attempts had been made on his life before he was finally killed by a drunken foe. See "Roderick Dhu Gambrell," *Texas Baptist and Herald*, June

8, 1887, 4, and David M. Gardner, "J. B. Gambrell," *Baptist Training Union Magazine*, March 1945, 6.

190. A. J. Holt to E. E. Folk, January 14, 1909, E. E. Folk Collection, SBHLA.

191. Margaret E. Ward, "The Early Churches and Pastors," in *Early Days of Birmingham* (Birmingham, Ala.: Birmingham Publishing, 1937), 31.

192. Hackney, *Populism to Progressivism in Alabama*, 315–17; Sellers, *The Prohibition Movement in Alabama*, 167, 173.

193. Quoted in John Samuel Ezell, *The South since 1865* (New York: Macmillan, 1963), 400.

194. In 1918 Texas and Florida passed statewide prohibition, leaving Louisiana as the only Confederate state not to enact statewide legislation prior to the passage of the Eighteenth Amendment.

195. Peter H. Odegard, *Pressure Politics: The Story of the Anti-Saloon League* (New York: Columbia University Press, 1928), 130.

196. Richard F. Hamm, "Southerners and the Shaping of the Eighteenth Amendment, 1914–1917," *Georgia Journal of Southern Legal History* 1 (spring–summer 1991): 99.

197. *Report of the Alabama Woman's Christian Temperance Union Twenty-third Annual Convention: Held in Dexter Avenue M. E. Church, South, Montgomery, Alabama, October 16th, 17th, and 18th, 1907* (Montgomery, Ala.: Paragon Press, n.d.), 18.

Chapter Three. "Why Don't He Give His Attention to Saving Sinners?"

1. See William A. Link, *The Paradox of Southern Progressivism, 1880–1930* (Chapel Hill: University of North Carolina Press, 1992), 38–41, and Thomas R. Pegram, "Temperance Politics and Regional Political Culture: The Anti-Saloon League in Maryland and the South, 1907–1915," *Journal of Southern History* 63 (February 1997): 63.

2. Jesse M. Littleton, "Extract from Speech of Hon. Jesse M. Littleton Delivered at Rutledge, Tenn., July 4, 1904," E. E. Folk Collection, Southern Baptist Historical Library and Archives, Nashville, Tenn.

3. R. A., "Preachers in Politics," *Christian Advocate* (Nashville), October 8, 1887, 7.

4. J. B. Hawthorne, "Separation of Church and State," *Baptist and Reflector*, December 18, 1890, 3.

5. Quoted in Warren A. Candler, *Bishop Charles Betts Galloway: A Prince of Preachers and a Christian Statesman* (Nashville: Cokesbury Press, 1927), 217.

6. Quoted in Hudson Strode, *Jefferson Davis: Tragic Hero, the Last Twenty-five Years, 1864–1889* (New York: Harcourt, Brace, and World, 1964), 490.

7. William Larkin Duren, *Charles Betts Galloway: Orator, Preacher, and "Prince of Christian Chivalry"* (Atlanta: Emory University, Banner Press, 1932), 243–45.

8. However, Galloway defended Davis when the latter was attacked by New York Methodists. Reporting on the conflict between Davis and Galloway,

the *Christian Advocate* of New York assailed the former Confederate president as a traitor. Bishop Galloway responded by harshly criticizing the paper for its attack on Davis's character and political history. See Duren, *Charles Betts Galloway*, 243.

9. Job Harral, "Prohibition War," *Baptist and Reflector*, November 21, 1889, 2.

10. W. A. McCarty, "Jefferson Davis versus Prohibition," *Alabama Christian Advocate*, January 26, 1888, 1. McCarty also took the opportunity to attack Davis for his recent self-promotion tour across the southland, traveling by train and stopping along the way so that people could come to see him. McCarty complained that Davis conducted these stops on Sundays, "thereby drawing inconsiderate young people, and older ones as well, from the Sunday-schools and churches to gaze on him on the Sabbath day." Finally, McCarty subtly reminded his readers of Davis's humiliating capture by Union soldiers at the end of the war. In an unsuccessful effort to evade the enemy, Davis had dressed as woman—an act that was widely heralded by the northern press and brought a great deal of disgrace to Davis in both the North and the South. See Kenneth S. Greenberg, *Honor and Slavery: Lies, Duels, Noses, Masks, Dressing as a Woman, Gifts, Strangers, Humanitarianism, Death, Slave Rebellions, the Proslavery Argument, Baseball, Hunting, and Gambling in the Old South* (Princeton, N.J.: Princeton University Press, 1996), 31.

11. Editorial, "The Spectator," *Christian Advocate* (Nashville), October 8, 1887, 1.

12. Quoted in Candler, *Bishop Charles Betts Galloway*, 230, 239–40.

13. John Nelson Norwood, *The Schism in the Methodist Episcopal Church, 1844: A Study of Slavery and Ecclesiastical Politics* (Philadelphia: Porcupine Press, 1976), 60–61.

14. See Frederick A. Norwood, *The Story of American Methodism: A History of the United Methodists and Their Relations* (Nashville: Abingdon Press, 1974), 197–99; H. Shelton Smith, *In His Image, But: Racism in Southern Religion, 1780–1910* (Durham, N.C.: Duke University Press, 1972), 108; Mitchell Snay, *Gospel of Disunion: Religion and Separatism in the Antebellum South* (Cambridge: Cambridge University Press, 1993), 128–29, 131.

15. See H. Leon McBeth, *The Baptist Heritage: Four Centuries of Baptist Witness* (Nashville: Broadman Press, 1987), 385–89; Bill J. Leonard, *Baptist Ways: A History* (Valley Forge, Pa.: Judson Press, 2003), 188–89; Smith, *In His Image*, 125–27.

16. Ernest Trice Thompson, "Continuity and Change in the Presbyterian Church in the United States," *Austin Seminary Bulletin: Faculty Edition* 85 (April 1970): 28. Although he does not follow it through to the 1845 resolution, Mitchell Snay hints at the origins of the doctrine of the spirituality of the church when discussing the New School–Old School split of 1837. Northern Old Schoolers, including Princetonians such as Charles Hodge, needed the allegiance of the southern Presbyterians against the New Schoolers and agreed in 1836 to remain silent on the issue of slavery "as a means of courting this crucial southern support." See Snay, *Gospel of Disunion*, 116–17. Northern Old

Schoolers thus laid the groundwork for the 1845 enunciation of the doctrine of spirituality. This doctrine not only pleased the southern half of the denomination but also provided a doctrinal framework wherein northern Old Schoolers could justify keeping their 1836 promise to the southerners.

17. Southerners represented only about 10 percent of the New School Presbyterian Church in 1857 and organized the Southern New School Presbyterian Church in that year. See Harold M. Parker Jr., *The United Synod of the South: The Southern New School Presbyterian Church* (Westport, Conn.: Greenwood Press, 1988), 291.

18. James Henley Thornwell, "Speech on African Colonization," in *The Collected Writings of James Henley Thornwell*, ed. John B. Adger and John L. Girardeau (Richmond, Va.: Presbyterian Committee of Publication, 1873), 4:473; see also Joe L. Coker, "The Sinnott Case of 1910: The Changing Views of Southern Presbyterians on Temperance, Prohibition, and the Spirituality of the Church," *Journal of Presbyterian History* 77 (winter 1999): 248–49.

19. Thompson, "Continuity and Change," 26.

20. Frederick A. Bode, "Religion and Class Hegemony: A Populist Critique in North Carolina," *Journal of Southern History* 37 (August 1971): 417.

21. Quoted in Christopher H. Owen, "Sanctity, Slavery, and Segregation: Methodists and Society in Nineteenth-Century Georgia" (Ph.D. diss., Emory University, 1991), 208 n11, 233. Bishop Andrew appears to have been one of the most consistent opponents of church-state intermingling among antebellum southern Methodists. Following the secession of South Carolina in December 1860, Baptists in Alabama declared that they backed Alabama's right to secede and pledged their support to the independent state. A group of Alabama Methodists met in Montgomery in December 1860 and also declared themselves in favor of secession. The Alabama Conference of the MECS, however, declined to make any formal statement in support of secession, largely because Bishop Andrew "wanted a non-political church" and thwarted efforts to have the conference issue an opinion on the issue. See Walter L. Fleming, *The Churches of Alabama during the Civil War and Reconstruction* (Montgomery, Ala.: W. M. Rogers, 1902), 5. Another influential southern bishop who opposed political declarations by the church was Joshua Soule, the head bishop of the MECS. Soule had opposed the MEC's resolution against Bishop Andrew in 1844 because of its political nature and moved from Maine to take a leadership role in the nascent MECS the following year.

22. Snay, *Gospel of Disunion*, 137.

23. "The Southern Baptist Convention," *Southern Recorder* (Milledgeville, Ga.), May 27, 1845, 2.

24. See A. H. Redford, *History of the Organization of the Methodist Episcopal Church, South* (Nashville: n.p., 1871), appendix B; D. R. Manally, *Life and Times of Rev. S. Patton, D.D., and Annals of the Holston Conference* (St. Louis: Methodist Book Depository, 1859), 254–59.

25. Antebellum Baptists also began to recognize the implications of the spiritual nature of the church in terms of other issues, such as temperance. In 1853 an Alabama Baptist paper noted that although it stood for temperance

principles, it would "eschew all connection with politics, and shall carefully avoid all interference with elections." Editorial, "The Temperance Cause," *South Western Baptist*, April 1, 1853, 2.

26. Ernest Trice Thompson, *The Spirituality of the Church: A Distinctive Doctrine of the Presbyterian Church in the United States* (Richmond, Va.: John Knox Press, 1961), 28.

27. Benjamin M. Palmer, "Sermon, Preached in the First Presbyterian Church, Augusta, Ga., December 4th, 1861, at the Opening of the First General Assembly of the Presbyterian Church in the Confederate States of America," in *Minutes of the General Assembly of the Presbyterian Church in the Confederate States of America* 1 (1861): 71.

28. James Henley Thornwell, "Address by the General Assembly to All the Churches of Jesus Christ throughout the Earth," in *Minutes of the General Assembly of the Presbyterian Church in the Confederate States of America* 1 (1861): 53.

29. Jack P. Maddex, "From Theocracy to Spirituality: The Southern Presbyterian Reversal on Church and State," *Journal of Presbyterian History* 54 (winter 1976): 438.

30. E. Brooks Holifield, *The Gentlemen Theologians: American Theology in Southern Culture 1795–1860* (Durham, N.C.: Duke University Press, 1978), 154.

31. Lewis G. Vander Velde, *The Presbyterian Churches and the Federal Union 1861–1869* (Cambridge, Mass.: Harvard University Press, 1932), 42–43. Likewise, Maddex, "From Theocracy to Spirituality," 446, claims that it was "not in the Confederacy, but in the border slave states of the Union that the 'spirituality of the church' idea flourished during the war." This raises the possibility that the border-state representatives were somewhat sincere in their desire to maintain ecclesiastical union despite political disunion, based on their belief in the doctrine of spirituality. The Presbyterians of the Deep South, in contrast, seem to have decided later, after the schism, that they too would have maintained denominational union with the North had it not violated the doctrine of spirituality.

32. Thompson, *The Spirituality of the Church*, 29.

33. Ernest Trice Thompson, *Presbyterians in the South*, vol. 3, *1890–1972* (Richmond, Va.: John Knox Press, 1973), 260.

34. Alfred Jones, "Thoughts on the Relations of Church and State," *Presbyterian Quarterly* 4 (April 1890): 216.

35. W. C. Clark, "Church and State," *Presbyterian Quarterly* 14 (January 1900): 117.

36. Samuel Spahr Laws, *Reasons for the Organization and for the Perpetuation of the Southern Presbyterian Church* (n.p.: [1910?]), 22, 31.

37. W. H. Frazer, "The Origin, Doctrines, and History of the Presbyterian Church in the United States," *Presbyterian of the South*, May 17, 1911, 3.

38. "Methodists in Missouri Declare Southern Church Will Reorganize and Continue," in *The Methodist Experience in America: A Sourcebook*, vol. 2, ed. Russell E. Richey, Kenneth E. Rowe, and Jean Miller Schmidt (Nashville: Abingdon Press, 2000), 337–38.

39. As early as 1784, at the famed "Christmas Conference" in Baltimore, American Methodists rejected the Anglican model of church-state entanglement. Preaching at the Christmas Conference, Thomas Coke pronounced the old pattern deceased, and American Methodists adopted the idea of separation of church and state as part of their identity. See Dee E. Andrews, *The Methodists and Revolutionary America, 1760–1800: The Shaping of an Evangelical Culture* (Princeton, N.J.: Princeton University Press, 2000), 71–72.

40. In *Cross and Flame: Two Centuries of United Methodism in Middle Tennessee* (Nashville: Parthenon Press, 1984), 231, John Abernathy Smith argues that Tennessee Methodists embraced the principle of spirituality in the years following the Civil War in response to the actions of northern Methodists during the Reconstruction period. In Knoxville, for example, the Church Street Methodist Church, an MECS congregation, was commandeered by Federal troops during the war and used as a stable for Union horses, only to be seized again by an MEC congregation after the war. The northern Methodists, led by William G. Brownlow, held the property for eight years, after which a court ordered that it be returned to its MECS congregation. *Our Heritage and Our Hope: Church Street Church, 1816–1966* (n.p.: n.d.), 9–10.

41. Quoted in Walter L. Fleming, *Civil War and Reconstruction in Alabama* (New York: Columbia University Press, 1905), 637.

42. Early Baptist leaders who staunchly opposed the state establishment of religion, especially those in North America, never embraced the idea that ministers should refrain from involvement in secular politics. Roger Williams founded and served as governor of the Rhode Island colony, and John Leland served as a lobbyist to the Virginia General Assembly and ran against James Madison for a position as a delegate to the Virginia Ratification Convention. See Joe L. Coker, "Sweet Harmony vs. Strict Separation: Recognizing the Distinctions between Isaac Backus and John Leland," *American Baptist Quarterly* 16 (September 1997): 245.

43. J. B. Jones, "The Political Canvass—The Duty of Christian Voters," *Baptist Beacon* (Knoxville, Tenn.), August 5, 1880, 2.

44. Editorial, "The Distinctive Doctrines of Baptists," *Baptist Expositor*, March 15, 1891, 1.

45. John Patrick Daly, *When Slavery Was Called Freedom: Evangelicalism, Proslavery, and the Causes of the Civil War* (Lexington: University Press of Kentucky, 2002), 136.

46. "Methodists in Missouri Declare Southern Church Will Reorganize and Continue," 338.

47. Editorial, "Dr. Kelley and the Liquor Dealers," *Christian Advocate* (Nashville), January 25, 1873, 1. In his sermon, Kelley acknowledged that "the laws of his church forbade the discussion of politics in the pulpit."

48. C. W. Miller, "Organic Union—Disruption and Fraternity," *Quarterly Review of the Methodist Episcopal Church, South* 3 (October 1881): 588, 591, 601. See also Frederick A. Bode, *Protestantism and the New South: North Carolina Baptists and Methodists in Political Crisis, 1894–1903* (Charlottesville: University of Virginia Press, 1975), 13–14.

49. David C. Kelley, "Fraternity—Another View," *Quarterly Review of the Methodist Episcopal Church, South* 4 (January 1882): 95–96, 102–3.

50. Ibid.

51. David C. Kelley, *Prohibition, the Amendment: A Reply to the Attack of the Liquor-Dealers' Attaches [sic] on the Bible, the Churches, the Women and the Democrat Party* (Nashville: Southern Methodist Publishing House, 1887), 4, 10.

52. Quoted in Kathleen Minnix, *Laughter in the Amen Corner: The Life of Evangelist Sam Jones* (Athens: University of Georgia Press, 1993), 165, and Isaac Patton Martin, *Methodism in Holston* (Nashville: Parthenon Press, 1945), 142.

53. Editorial, "The Temperance Reform," *Alabama Baptist*, May 1, 1884, 2.

54. John C. Orr, "Politics and Religion," *Alabama Baptist*, November 6, 1884, 2.

55. T. S. Eastes, "Relations between Temperance and Prohibition," *Baptist and Reflector*, July 31, 1890, 2.

56. J. B. Downing, "Preachers and Politics," *Alabama Baptist*, October 27, 1892, 1.

57. Quoted in "Supplement.—Reports Adopted. VI.—Temperance," in *Journal of the Eighty-third Session of the Tennessee Annual Conference of the Methodist Episcopal Church, South: Held at Nashville, Tenn., October 21–27, 1896* (Nashville: Publishing House of the Methodist Episcopal Church, South, n.d.), 35.

58. C. K. Henderson, "Religion and Politics Are the Two Sides of the Same Thing," *Alabama Baptist*, July 28, 1892, 1.

59. Editorial, "Non-Political," *Holston Methodist*, December 27, 1879, 2.

60. Rufus B. Spain, *At Ease in Zion: Social History of Southern Baptists, 1865–1900* (Nashville: Vanderbilt University Press, 1967), 197n. Barnes argues that the convention's vote was related more to its respect for the aged and ailing Boyce than to its agreement with his use of the doctrine of spirituality to block prohibition resolutions. See William Wright Barnes, *The Southern Baptist Convention 1845–1953* (Nashville: Broadman, 1954), 246n.

61. *The Holston Annual 1888. Official Record of the Holston Annual Conference, Methodist Episcopal Church, South, Sixty-fifth Session, Held at Asheville, N.C., October 1888*, ed. W. C. Carden (Morristown, Tenn.: Gazette Book and Job Office, 1888), 37.

62. Quoted in Kenneth K. Bailey, "Southern White Protestantism at the Turn of the Century," *American Historical Review* 68 (April 1963): 630.

63. John Lee Eighmy, *Churches in Cultural Captivity: A History of the Social Attitudes of Southern Baptists*, rev. ed. (Knoxville: University of Tennessee Press, 1987), 52.

64. M. J. Webb, "Wrong and Dangerous," *Christian Index*, December 8, 1892, 1.

65. "Preachers in Politics: An Eminent Presbyterian Divine on the Question," *Nashville Daily American*, August 25, 1887.

66. W. C. McCoy, "Prohibition and Its Relation to Other Questions," *Alabama Christian Advocate*, August 2, 1888, 4.

67. L. O. Dawson, "Preachers and Politics," *Alabama Baptist*, March 19, 1896, 1. Dawson's role as a Bourbon Democrat was perhaps inescapable, being the son of Andrew Jackson Dawson and Marie Antoinette Dawson.

68. Editorial, "Preachers and Politics," *Christian Advocate* (Nashville), April 7, 1892, 8.

69. S. P. Richardson, "Preachers and Politics," *Wesleyan Christian Advocate* (Atlanta), May 4, 1892, 2.

70. S. P. Richardson, "Preachers and Politics," *Wesleyan Christian Advocate* (Atlanta), August 24, 1892, 3.

71. David C. Kelley, "Rev. Sam Jones," *Southern Bivouac*, n.s., 1 (January 1886): 503–4 (emphasis in original).

72. Minnix, *Laughter in the Amen Corner*, 165.

73. William G. McLoughlin, *Modern Revivalism: Charles Grandison Finney to Billy Graham* (New York: Ronald Press, 1959), 294.

74. See William G. McLoughlin, "Jones vs. Jones," *American Heritage* 12 (April 1961): 56.

75. Sam P. Jones, *Thunderbolts: Comprising Most Earnest Reasonings, Delightful Narratives, Poetic and Pathetic Incidents, Caustic and Unmerciful Flagellation of Sin, Together with Irresistible Appeals to the Higher Sensibilities of Man to Quit His Meanness and Do Right* (Nashville: Jones and Haynes, 1895), 389–92, 418.

76. "Sam Small," *Knoxville Daily Journal*, July 22, 1887, 5.

77. Quoted in Minnix, *Laughter in the Amen Corner*, 167–68.

78. Christopher H. Owen, *The Sacred Flame of Love: Methodism and Society in Nineteenth-Century Georgia* (Athens: University of Georgia Press, 1998), 151.

79. Parker adds, "While Jones had little use for the doctrinal aspects of Holiness, he certainly approved of its emphasis on Christian perfectibility and proper behavior." David B. Parker, "'Quit Your Meanness': Sam Jones's Theology for the New South," *Georgia Historical Quarterly* 77 (winter 1993): 719.

80. Owen, *The Sacred Flame of Love*, 163–64.

81. Roger L. Hart, *Redeemers, Bourbons, and Populists: Tennessee 1870–1896* (Baton Rouge: Louisiana State University Press, 1975), 58.

82. J. Wayne Flynt, *Alabama in the Twentieth Century* (Tuscaloosa: University of Alabama Press, 2004), 7–8.

83. Primitive Baptists were located primarily in the Appalachian and rural upcountry areas and represented only a small segment of the Baptist population. Paul Harvey, *Redeeming the South: Religious Cultures and Racial Identities among Southern Baptists, 1865–1925* (Chapel Hill: University of North Carolina Press, 1997), 86. Landmarkism, though it shared the antebellum antimissionary movement's disdain for denominational hierarchies and auxiliary structures, was not antithetical to prohibition support. Alabama Baptist J. J. D. Renfroe wrote *Trail of Blood*–style articles for the *Alabama Baptist* tracing the genealogy of the Baptists back through the Petrobrusians, the Waldenses, and the Anabaptists, but he was nevertheless an outspoken supporter of prohibition and of the right of Christian ministers to engage in the political struggle to abolish the liquor trade. J. Wayne Flynt, *Alabama Baptists: Southern Baptists in the Heart of Dixie* (Tuscaloosa: University of Alabama Press, 1998), 161–62; J. J. D. Renfroe, "Want of a History," *Alabama Baptist*, February 17, 1876, 2; J. J. D. Renfroe, "Pike on Baptist Succession, Number 1," *Alabama Baptist*, April

20, 1876, 2; J. J. D. Renfroe, "Pike on Baptist Succession, Number 2," *Alabama Baptist*, April 27, 1876, 2.

84. Quoted in Owen, *The Sacred Flame of Love*, 182. Jones never officially joined the Populist Party, choosing instead to take a more ambiguous political position. In 1898 he launched a campaign for governor of Georgia and garnered significant media attention, but within five days he withdrew from the race without ever affiliating with a party.

85. C. Vann Woodward, *Origins of the New South 1877–1913*, vol. 10 of *A History of the South*, ed. Wendell Holmes Stephenson and E. Merton Coulter (n.p.: Louisiana State University Press, 1951), 189.

86. See Lawrence Goodwyn, *Democratic Promise: The Populist Moment in America* (New York: Oxford University Press, 1976), 58; Gene Clanton, *Populism: The Humane Preference in America, 1890–1900* (Boston: Twayne Publishers, 1991), 6; Linda Wilke-Long, "Populists, Politics, and Prohibition," *Nebraska Lawyer* (May 1999): 12–13; Stanley B. Parsons, *The Populist Context: Rural versus Urban Power on a Great Plains Frontier* (Westport, Conn.: Greenwood Press, 1978), 22–23, 27; Bruce Palmer, *"Man over Money": The Southern Populist Critique of American Capitalism* (Chapel Hill: University of North Carolina Press, 1980), xiii; Alex Mathews Arnett, *The Populist Movement in Georgia: A View of the "Agrarian Crusade" in the Light of Solid-South Politics* (New York: Longmans, Green, 1922), 49–73; Michael R. Hyman, *The Anti-Redeemers: Hill-Country Political Dissenters in the Lower South from Redemption to Populism* (Baton Rouge: Louisiana State University Press, 1990), 202.

87. Parsons, *The Populist Context*, 147. Rather than simply idealizing an agrarian past and mourning its demise, many Populists, such as William Mahone of Virginia, advocated the economic development of the South in a new, modern direction. Carl N. Degler, *The Other South: Southern Dissenters in the Nineteenth Century* (New York: Harper and Row, 1974), 274–75. Both Stephen Hahn and Samuel L. Webb have noted that the strength of populism in the upcountry regions of Georgia and Alabama in the 1890s derived less from economic hardship than from discontent with the elite urban and Black Belt leadership of the Democratic Party. Opposition to "ring rule" and political "bossism" ran high in the less fertile upcountry of north Alabama, north Georgia, and east Tennessee. Populism received little support in the Tennessee Valley or in the Black Belt region of Alabama and Georgia—areas densely populated with African Americans who sharecropped land still owned by the conservative planter elite. Samuel L. Webb, "From Independents to Populists to Progressive Republicans: The Case of Chilton County, AL, 1880–1920," *Journal of Southern History* 59 (November 1993): 713; Steven Hahn, *The Roots of Southern Populism: Yeoman Farmers and the Transformation of the Georgia Upcountry, 1850–1890* (New York: Oxford University Press, 1983), 270–71.

88. William A. Peffer, *Populism: Its Rise and Fall* (Lawrence: University Press of Kansas, 1992), 48; Arthur S. Link, "The Progressive Movement in the South, 1870–1914," in *Myth and Southern History: The New South*, ed. Patrick Gerster and Nicholas Cords (Chicago: Rand McNally, 1974), 69.

89. A congressional investigation revealed that "Negroes who had been dead for years and others who had long since left the county," as well as men who never even existed, somehow managed to vote for the Democratic candidate. Quoted in Edward L. Ayers, *The Promise of the New South: Life after Reconstruction* (New York: Oxford University Press, 1992), 276. Kolb won thirty-seven counties but carried only five counties in the Black Belt, an area where, Flynt notes, "vote stealing was white Democratic tradition." J. Wayne Flynt, "Introduction to the 1901 Alabama Constitution," http://accr.constitutionalreform.org/symposium/1901flint.html (accessed July 18, 2007).

90. Michael Perman, *Struggle for Mastery: Disfranchisement in the South, 1888–1908* (Chapel Hill: University of North Carolina Press, 2001), 174; John B. Clark, *Populism in Alabama* (Auburn, Ala.: Auburn Printing, 1927), 158–59.

91. Woodward, *Origins of the New South*, 203.

92. Overall, Populist success was less impressive in Tennessee than in Alabama and Georgia. This fits with the larger pattern of Populists doing more poorly in the upper South than in the Deep South. See Ayers, *The Promise of the New South*, 275.

93. David Leigh Colvin, *Prohibition in the United States: A History of the Prohibition Party, and of the Prohibition Movement* (New York: George H. Doran, 1926), 65–69.

94. K. Austin Kerr, *Organized for Prohibition: A New History of the Anti-Saloon League* (New Haven, Conn.: Yale University Press, 1985), 41–44; Andrew Sinclair, *Prohibition: The Era of Excess* (Boston: Little, Brown, 1962), 84; Ann-Marie E. Szymanski, *Pathways to Prohibition: Radicals, Moderates, and Social Movement Outcomes* (Durham, N.C.: Duke University Press, 2003), 134.

95. R. A. Moseley Sr., "Christianity and the Prohibition Party," *Alabama Baptist*, March 11, 1886, 2.

96. Flynt, *Alabama Baptists*, 221; Jack S. Blocker Jr. *Retreat from Reform: The Prohibition Movement in the United States 1890–1913* (Westport, Conn.: Greenwood Press, 1976), 100; Allen Johnston Going, *Bourbon Democracy in Alabama, 1874–1890* (Tuscaloosa: University of Alabama Press, 1992), 59–60.

97. Barton C. Shaw, *The Wool-Hat Boys: Georgia's Populist Party* (Baton Rouge: Louisiana State University Press, 1984), 59, 66, 152, 191.

98. See William Warren Rogers, *The One-Gallused Rebellion: Agrarianism in Alabama, 1865–1896* (Baton Rouge: Louisiana State University Press, 1970), viii–ix.

99. Degler, *The Other South*, 337–42. Watson even went so far as to suggest that racial animosity was deliberately created and encouraged by the dominant political class for its own gain.

100. Robert Saunders, "Southern Populists and the Negro," in *Populism: The Critical Issues*, ed. Sheldon Hackney (Boston: Little, Brown, 1971), 53, 63.

101. Paul M. Pruitt, "Joseph C. Manning, Alabama Populist: A Rebel against the Solid South" (Ph.D. diss., College of William and Mary, 1980), 67; Arnett, *The Populist Movement in Georgia*, 153. Historians beginning with Woodward have often viewed the Populist movement as the high-water mark of race relations in the postbellum South. Woodward observed that "never

before or since have the two races in the South come as close together as they did during the Populist struggles." C. Vann Woodward, *Tom Watson: Agrarian Rebel* (New York: Macmillan, 1938), 222. Later scholars such as Herbert Shapiro, "The Populists and the Negro: A Reconsideration," in *The Making of Black America: Essays in Negro Life and History*, vol. 2, ed. August Meier and Elliott Rudwick (New York: Atheneum, 1969), 27–36, suggested that Populists were, in general, just as racist as their Democratic foes. When a group of black Birmingham ministers endorsed Democrat William Oates over Populist Reuben Kolb, one of Kolb's prominent supporters was quoted as advocating "shooting every God damned one [of the black voters] who goes to the polls to cast his ballot." Quoted in Saunders, "Southern Populists and the Negro, 65.

102. Henry C. Ferrell Jr., "Prohibition, Reform, and Politics in Virginia, 1895–1916," in *Studies in the History of the South, 1875–1922* (Greenville, N.C.: East Carolina College, 1966), 177.

103. Quoted in Richard F. Hamm, *Murder, Honor, and Law: Four Virginia Homicides from Reconstruction to the Great Depression* (Charlottesville: University of Virginia Press, 2003), 70–73. For more on the murder of Moffett, who was killed by a member of his own congregation, see Richard F. Hamm, "The Killing of John R. Moffett and the Trial of J. T. Clark: Race, Prohibition, and Politics in Danville, 1887–1893," *Virginia Magazine of History and Biography* 101 (July 1993): 375.

104. Job Harral, "Prohibition the Safety of the People," *Baptist* (Memphis), April 14, 1888, 4.

105. L. C. Coulson, "Bro. Coulson Is Not Satisfied with the Democrat Party," *Alabama Baptist*, March 17, 1887, 1; L. C. Coulson, "Bro. Coulson a Political Party Prohibitionist," *Alabama Baptist*, January 26, 1888, 1.

106. Flynt, *Alabama Baptists*, 218.

107. Editorial, "Prohibition and Its Relation to Other Questions," *Alabama Christian Advocate*, August 2, 1888, 4; "Prohibition and Its Relation to Other Questions," *Alabama Baptist*, September 6, 1888, 1.

108. Editorial, "Limiting the Atonement," *Wesleyan Christian Advocate* (Atlanta), May 4, 1892, 1.

109. Editorial, "Prohibition and Religion," *Alabama Baptist*, January 8, 1885, 2.

110. S. Henderson, "A Word to the Wise," *Alabama Baptist*, February 11, 1886, 2.

111. Editorial, "A Word on Prohibition," *Alabama Baptist*, April 8, 1886, 2.

112. Orr, "Politics and Religion," 2.

113. E. T. Smyth, "My Prohibition Platform," *Alabama Baptist*, June 3, 1886, 3.

114. Editorial, "To Prohibitionists," *Alabama Baptist*, February 18, 1886, 2.

115. D. I. Purser, "The Prohibition Convention," *Alabama Baptist*, July 15, 1886, 2.

116. A. S. Worrell, "Prohibition and Politics," *Alabama Baptist*, March 11, 1886, 2.

117. J. J. D. Renfroe, "Keep It out of Politics," *Alabama Baptist*, February 18, 1886, 1.

118. M. J. Turnley, "Keep It out of Politics," *Alabama Baptist*, April 1, 1886, 1.

119. J. D. Smith, "Should There Be a Political Party Advocating the Aboli-tion of the Licensed Liquor Traffic; and if so, What Should Be the Attitude of Christian Voters towards It?" *Tennessee Methodist*, May 25, 1893, 7.

120. J. T. Millican, "Should There Be a Political Party Advocating the Abo-lition of the Licensed Liquor Traffic; and if so, What Should Be the Attitude of Christian Voters towards It?" *Tennessee Methodist*, June 15, 1893, 1.

121. J. D. Smith, "Should There Be a Political Party Advocating the Aboli-tion of the Licensed Liquor Traffic; and if so, What Should Be the Attitude of Christian Voters towards It?" *Tennessee Methodist*, June 29, 1893, 7.

122. Horace Merritt, "The Smith-Millican Controversy," *Tennessee Meth-odist*, July 6, 1893, 7.

123. J. T. Millican, "Should There Be a Political Party Advocating the Abo-lition of the Licensed Liquor Traffic; and if so, What Should Be the Attitude of Christian Voters towards It?" *Tennessee Methodist*, July 13, 1893, 7.

124. J. T. Millican, "The Smith-Millican-Merritt Controversy," *Tennessee Methodist*, June 20, 1893, 7.

125. Hunter Dickinson Farish, *The Circuit Rider Dismounts: A Social History of Southern Methodism, 1865–1900* (Richmond, Va.: Dietz Press, 1938), 321.

126. E. E. Folk, "B. F. Haynes vs. R. K. Hargrove," *Baptist and Reflector*, December 11, 1890, 8.

127. Smith, *Cross and Flame*, 237. Smith speculates that Hargrove's deter-mination to punish Kelley may have been driven primarily by a desire to make an example of him and thus deter the growing number of holiness-influenced Methodist ministers who might follow Kelley's lead and abandon their duties for evangelistic work.

128. Editorial, "The Kelley Case," *Baptist and Reflector*, October 16, 1890, 8. Baptists soon moved beyond attacking Hargrove and presented the entire epi-sode as an indictment of Methodist ecclesiology. E. E. Folk wrote that "while we have had a good deal to say about bishop Hargrove, we have been using him only as illustrating a policy. Bishop Hargrove, as an individual, is nothing to us comparatively . . . we have been shooting at far higher game—the episcopacy, which he represents, and which we believe to be unscriptural, unjust, radically wrong, and pregnant with danger. In this claim of bishop Hargrove we have illustrated the evil of the Episcopal office in its highest degree." In another editorial he commented, "How a man can remain a preacher in the Methodist conference subject to an irresponsible master we can not see. How an Ameri-can citizen with all of his glorious ideas about liberty can do so, passes our understanding." Folk, "B. F. Haynes vs. R. K. Hargrove," 8; Editorial, "The Kelley Case Again," *Baptist and Reflector*, October 23, 1890, 8.

129. Quoted in editorial, "The Methodist Church and Politics," *Alabama Christian Advocate*, December 25, 1890, 4.

130. "The State Convention," *Baptist and Reflector*, October 23, 1890, 5; "The Report on Temperance," *Baptist and Reflector*, October 30, 1890, 4.

131. *Tennessee Baptist Convention: Sixteenth Annual Session, Held with the First Baptist Church, at Chattanooga, Tenn., October 16, 17, 18, 1890* (Chattanooga: MacGowan and Cooke, 1890), 40.

132. H. B. Folk, "That Report on Temperance," *Baptist and Reflector,* October 23, 1890, 5.

133. S. E. Jones, "Remarks on the Report," *Baptist and Reflector,* October 30, 1890, 4.

134. For a brief overview of Landmarkism, see Harvey, *Redeeming the South,* 88–91, and Timothy George, "Southern Baptist Ghosts," *First Things* 93 (May 1999): 21. For the strong influence of Landmarkism in Tennessee, see James E. Tull, *A History of Southern Baptist Landmarkism in the Light of Historical Baptist Ecclesiology* (New York: Arno Press, 1980), 130.

135. George A. Lofton, "That Report on Temperance," *Baptist and Reflector,* November 6, 1890, 1.

136. William Huff, "The Report on Temperance—Is It Right?" *Baptist and Reflector,* November 13, 1890, 1.

137. W. P. Maury, "Brother Huff vs. Brother Jones," *Baptist and Reflector,* November 27, 1890, 3.

138. S. E. Jones, "That Temperance Report Again—Reply to Dr. Lofton," *Baptist and Reflector,* November 13, 1890, 4.

139. S. E. Jones, "That Temperance Report Again—Reply to Brother G. A. Lofton's Last," *Baptist and Reflector,* December 25, 1890, 2. Jones found precedent for Baptist conventions in the fifteenth chapter of Acts, where Christians cooperated using messengers, or delegates.

140. George A. Lofton, "That Temperance Report Once More—Reply to Rev. S. E. Jones," *Baptist and Reflector,* January 1, 1891, 4.

141. J. William Jones's 1887 *Christ in the Camp: Or, Religion in Lee's Army,* played a significant role in shaping the cult of the Lost Cause. Called the "supreme exponent" of the religion of the Lost Cause by Wilson, Jones helped ingrain in the southern mind the conviction that the Confederacy, though defeated on the battlefield, was nonetheless morally and religiously superior to the Union victors. And his 1874 biography of Robert E. Lee secured the general's beatification as a saint in the South. See Charles Reagan Wilson, *Baptized in Blood: The Religion of the Lost Cause 1865–1920* (Athens: University of Georgia Press, 1980), 119–23.

142. J. William Jones, "Does 'Prohibition' Necessarily Mean 'Third Party'?" *Baptist and Reflector,* December 18, 1890, 4.

143. *Baptist State Convention of Tennessee: Seventeenth Annual Session, Held with the First Baptist Church, Clarksville, Tenn., October 15, 16, 17, 1891* (Knoxville: S. B. Newman, 1891), 41.

144. "The State Convention," *Baptist and Reflector,* October 22, 1891, 4.

145. Atticus G. Haygood, introduction to Henry A. Scomp, *Alcohol in the Realm of King Cotton: Or, A History of the Liquor Traffic and of the Temperance Movement in Georgia from 1733 to 1887* (n.p.: Blakely Printing, 1888), 33.

146. "On Temperance," in *Minutes of the North Georgia Conference, Held in Milledgeville, Ga. 1888,* ed. H. L. Crumley (Atlanta: Constitution Publishing, n.d.), 13.

147. Henry A. Scomp, "A Card from Professor Scomp, He Replies to a Recent Communication from Bishop Haygood," clipping from unnamed newspaper, box 110:2, Warren A. Candler Collection, Emory University, Atlanta.

148. Ibid.

149. Warren A. Candler to T. Y. Ramsey, April 11, 1895, Candler Collection.

150. S. E. Sibley, "Candler Persecuted Scomp," undated *Voice* newspaper clipping, box 110:2, Candler Collection.

151. Editorial, "Says He's a Prohibitionist," *Daily Advance* (Harriman, Tenn.), July 13, 1894.

152. Ibid. Candler sought testimony to support his position that he had long considered Scomp an incompetent teacher. He wrote to a Judge Hines reminding him of an Emory board of trustees meeting in 1893, after which Hines had asked Candler his opinion of Scomp as a professor. Candler asked the judge to "write me the occasion and nature of those questions as you remember them, and the character of my reply." It is unclear whether Hines responded. See Warren A. Candler to "Judge Hines," July 19, 1894, Candler Collection.

153. Editorial response to "A Georgia Correspondent Speaks up for Dr. Candler and Bishop Haygood," undated *Voice* newspaper clipping, box 110:2, Candler Collection.

154. John W. Akin to Warren A. Candler, June 7, 1894, Candler Collection.

155. Mark K. Bauman, "Prohibition and Politics: Warren Candler and Al Smith's 1928 Campaign," *Mississippi Quarterly* 31 (winter 1977–1978): 113.

156. Mark K. Bauman, *Warren A. Candler: The Conservative as Idealist* (Metuchen, N.J.: Scarecrow Press, 1981), 172–73.

157. Owen, *The Sacred Flame of Love*, 183; Bauman, "Prohibition and Politics," 111. Candler's equivocation on the issue of the spirituality of the church continued for the rest of his career. In 1914 the General Conference asked him to pen the Episcopal address, which was entitled "The Church of God." In it Candler maintained that "the spirituality of the church" was "the most fundamental element of her existence." In 1928 he wrote two articles for the *Wesleyan Christian Advocate:* "No Dissent from the Position of My Church" and "Position of the Church Unchanged." In both, he sought to reconcile the 1926 resolution that all government officials should support and enforce national prohibition with earlier statements by the MECS, such as its 1894 resolution and his own 1914 address. During the 1928 presidential campaign, many evangelical prohibitionists, such as Methodist bishop James Cannon of Virginia, worked feverishly to defeat Democratic nominee Alfred E. Smith, who was a Roman Catholic and had vowed to work to overturn the Eighteenth Amendment if elected. Candler refused to offer an opinion on the election or to speak out against the Democratic candidate, citing the church's tradition of political noninvolvement. Cannon and others argued that Candler's silence served the Smith cause in that historic election, in which the South refused to fall in line behind the Democratic candidate: Tennessee, North Carolina, and Cannon's Virginia all voted Republican. See Bauman, *Warren A. Candler,* 174–75; Bartlett C. Jones, "Prohibition and Christianity, 1920–1933," *Journal of Religious Thought* 19 (1962–1963): 52–54.

158. Quoted in Owen, *The Sacred Flame of Love*, 183. Upon his return to Georgia from California in 1893, Haygood proudly stated that he "has vot-

ed always the 'regular Democratic ticket.'" Atticus G. Haygood, "The Black Shadow in the South," *Forum* 16 (October 1893): 170.

159. Quoted in editorial, "Danger to Prohibition," *Wesleyan Christian Advocate* (Macon, Ga.), January 27, 1886, 1.

160. Frank Eakes to Warren A. Candler, July 20, 1894, Candler Collection.

161. Quoted in Owen, *The Sacred Flame of Love*, 176.

162. Ibid., 183.

163. C. Vann Woodward, *The Burden of Southern History*, rev. ed. (New York: Mentor, 1968), 23.

164. Dewey W. Grantham, "The Contours of Southern Progressivism," *American Historical Review* 86 (December 1981): 1041.

165. Len Broughton, "The Men We Need," *Georgia Baptist*, June 12, 1902.

166. Editorial, "The Preacher and Politics," *Alabama Baptist*, November 8, 1905, 8.

167. W. B. Rutledge, "Religion and Politics," *Baptist and Reflector*, November 5, 1908, 2.

168. Barnes notes that although there was a sea change in the southern Baptist attitude toward using the arm of the state to address moral questions, the convention refused to address questions involving issues of "social relationships within the secular sphere." Baptists wanted to change the mores and behavior of society, but they almost never addressed questions of social and economic inequality or injustice. Barnes, *The Southern Baptist Convention*, 246.

169. A. J. Dickinson, "The Church and Politics," *Alabama Baptist*, August 7, 1907, 2.

170. E. K. Cox, "The Church and the Liquor Traffic," *Baptist and Reflector*, October 22, 1908, 2.

171. "Temperance Report," *Baptist and Reflector*, October 22, 1908, 5.

172. W. B. Crumpton, "Dr. Crumpton Replies," *Alabama Christian Advocate*, February 25, 1909, 2.

173. Quoted in Paul E. Isaac, *Prohibition and Politics: Turbulent Decades in Tennessee 1885–1920* (Knoxville: University of Tennessee Press, 1965), 163.

174. The reticence of the PCUS to officially endorse prohibition legislation was probably due as much to the weak prohibition sentiment among its membership, relative to other southern evangelicals, as to the southern church's long devotion to the doctrine of spirituality.

175. Leslie Frank, "How Presbytery of North Alabama Endorsed the Constitutional Amendment," *Alabama Christian Advocate*, November 4, 1909, 9; see also Coker, "The Sinnott Case of 1910," 254–55.

Chapter Four. "But What Seek Those Dark Ballots?"

1. Rayford Logan, *The Negro in American Life and Thought: The Nadir, 1877–1901* (New York: Dial Press, 1954).

2. Henry W. Grady, "The New South," in *The New South: Writings and Speeches of Henry Grady* (Savannah, Ga.: Beehive Press, 1971), 11.

3. The term had also been used by the editor of the *American Missionary*

in October 1880, who praised the improvements in the South since the war in an editorial called "A New South, Not a New England in the South," *American Missionary* 34 (October 1880): 294–95, and then by Atticus Haygood in a sermon the following month.

4. Paul M. Gaston, *The New South Creed: A Study in Southern Mythmaking* (New York: Knopf, 1970), 32–35.

5. Atticus Greene Haygood, "The New South: Gratitude, Amendment, Hope (a Thanksgiving Sermon)," in *Sermons*, vol. 1 (Nashville: Publishing House of the Methodist Episcopal Church, South, 1895), 116–17 (emphasis in original).

6. Ibid., 117–18, 121, 124. It was said that Haygood's "new light" resulted from an encounter with a black janitor while he was president of Emory University. Haygood supposedly lost his temper and gave the janitor a harsh tongue-lashing but then felt deeply remorseful and went to the janitor in the middle of the night to apologize. Following that incident, he resolved to follow a new path of action and attitude toward blacks. See Joel Williamson, *The Crucible of Race: Black-White Relations in the American South since Emancipation* (New York: Oxford University Press, 1984), 90.

7. Quoted in Robert R. Mathisen, "Conflicting Southern Cultures, Social Christianity, and Samuel Porter Jones," *Fides et Historia* 25 (fall 1993): 72.

8. Northerners were enthralled with the reconciliatory tone of New Southites. The day after Grady's famous 1886 speech, the New York newspapers praised him and his message lavishly. See Ferald J. Bryan, *Henry Grady or Tom Watson: The Rhetorical Struggle for the New South, 1880–1890* (Macon, Ga.: Mercer University Press, 1994), 47.

9. Kathleen Minnix, *Laughter in the Amen Corner: The Life of Evangelist Sam Jones* (Athens: University of Georgia Press, 1993), 91.

10. Samuel W. Small, "Deliverance from Bondage: A Temperance Sermon," in *Sam Jones' Own Book: A Series of Sermons*, ed. Sam Jones (Cincinnati: Cranston and Stowe, 1886), 532–33.

11. David C. Kelley, "Fraternity—Another View," *Quarterly Review of the Methodist Episcopal Church, South* 4 (January 1882): 95–96, 103.

12. A. B. Cabaniss, "Dr. J. M. Pendleton's Prophecy," *Baptist and Reflector*, October 9, 1890, 6.

13. Dan R. Frost, *Thinking Confederates: Academia and the Idea of Progress in the New South* (Knoxville: University of Tennessee Press, 2000), 51–52.

14. Quoted in J. Wayne Flynt, *Alabama Baptists: Southern Baptists in the Heart of Dixie* (Tuscaloosa: University of Alabama Press, 1998), 193.

15. Quoted in Frost, *Thinking Confederates*, 50.

16. Quoted in Minnix, *Laughter in the Amen Corner*, 99. Grady praised General Sherman, although he noted that many in Georgia still considered him to be "a kind of careless man about fire." Grady, "The New South," 7.

17. Henry W. Grady, "The Race Problem in the South," in *The New South: Writings and Speeches of Henry Grady*, 95.

18. Atticus G. Haygood, *Our Brother in Black: His Freedom and His Future* (New York: Phillips and Hunt, 1881), 24, 129, 134–36.

19. President Hayes and his wife, known as "Lemonade Lucy" for her refusal to serve alcoholic beverages at the White House, shared Haygood's devotion to the temperance cause. One disgruntled guest of the Hayeses commented, "At the White House, water flows like champagne." Eric Burns, *The Spirits of America: A Social History of Alcohol* (Philadelphia: Temple University Press, 2004), 123.

20. Atticus G. Haygood, "Slater Fund Beginnings: Letters from General Agent Atticus G. Haygood to Rutherford B. Hayes," ed. Curtis W. Garrison, *Journal of Southern History* 5 (May 1939): 232, 233–34.

21. Glenn T. Eskew, "Black Elitism and the Failure of Paternalism in Postbellum Georgia: The Case of Bishop Lucius Henry Holsey," *Journal of Southern History* 58 (November 1992): 649.

22. Haygood, "Slater Fund Beginnings," 238. Haygood worked tirelessly throughout the 1880s promoting these causes. One month he reported that "in 25 days I made 27 speeches, average two hours, and preached 4 sermons . . . I believe I spoke and preached to 60,000 people" (ibid., 239).

23. Quoted in Gaston, *The New South Creed*, 104.

24. Editorial, "Temperance Text-Books in Our Schools," *American Missionary* 36 (August 1882): 230.

25. Edward L. Ayers, *The Promise of the New South: Life after Reconstruction* (New York: Oxford University Press, 1992), 180; John Hammond Moore, "The Negro and Prohibition in Atlanta, 1885–1887," *South Atlantic Quarterly* 69 (winter 1970): 38.

26. James A. Morone, *Hellfire Nation: The Politics of Sin in American History* (New Haven, Conn.: Yale University Press, 2003), 297. Historians have long been divided over the nature of racism in the years after Reconstruction. C. Vann Woodward first argued that there was a brief period of positive racial relations—the soon-to-be "forgotten alternatives" for black-white relations in the South—in the 1870s and 1880s. Others, such as John Cell and Joel Williamson, retorted that there was a continuity of racism from the antebellum to the postwar eras and that de facto segregation existed in the South for decades before Jim Crow. The evidence from southern white evangelicals, especially those involved in the prohibition campaign and the New South movement, supports the contention of Woodward and others such as Carl Degler, who note a brief respite in the 1880s from the racist sentiment that characterized the South later in the nineteenth century and for much of the twentieth. See C. Vann Woodward, *Origins of the New South 1877–1913*, vol. 10 of *A History of the South*, ed. Wendell Holmes Stephenson and E. Merton Coulter (n.p.: Louisiana State University Press, 1951), 210, 351; C. Vann Woodward, *The Strange Career of Jim Crow*, 3rd ed. (New York: Oxford University Press, 1974), 35–44; John N. Degler, "Dawn without Noon: The Myths of Reconstruction," in *Myth and Southern History*, ed. Patrick Gerster and Nicholas Cords (Chicago: Rand McNally, 1974), 166–67; John W. Cell, *The Highest Stage of White Supremacy: The Origins of Segregation in South Africa and the American South* (Cambridge: Cambridge University Press, 1982), 90; August Meier and Elliott Rudwick, "A Strange Chapter in the Career of Jim Crow," in *The Mak-*

ing of Black America: Essays in Negro Life and History, vol. 2, ed. August Meier and Elliott Rudwick (New York: Atheneum, 1969), 14–18. The tendency to collapse the four or five decades following Appomattox into one consistently racist period, ignoring changes in white racial attitudes over the course of time, persists. A recent example can be found in Natalie N. Ogle, "Brother against Brother: Baptists and Race in the Aftermath of the Civil War," *American Baptist Quarterly* 23 (June 2004): 137–54.

27. Roger Dale Posey, "Anti-Alcohol City: Social, Economic, and Political Aspects of Knoxville, Tennessee, 1870–1907" (master's thesis, University of Tennessee, 1982), 40–41.

28. Editorial, "The Tennessee Election," *Christian Advocate* (Nashville), October 8, 1887, 8.

29. Andrew Sinclair, *Prohibition: The Era of Excess* (Boston: Little, Brown, 1962), 30.

30. Moore, "The Negro and Prohibition in Atlanta," 40. Harold Paul Thompson's recent dissertation thoroughly explores the role of black voters in Atlanta's prohibition elections of 1885 and 1887. He notes that black elites worked closely with white New South prohibitionists in the 1885 election and successfully delivered a large number of black votes for the local option cause. But following the election, broken promises on the part of white prohibitionists and uneven implementation of prohibition led to great resentment within the black community, so that by 1887, those who had voted dry in 1885 were eager to vote down the city's experiment with prohibition. See Harold Paul Thompson, "Race, Temperance, and Prohibition in the Postbellum South: Black Atlanta, 1865–1890" (Ph.D. diss., Emory University, 2005), 230–86.

31. Charles Reagan Wilson, *Baptized in Blood: The Religion of the Lost Cause 1865–1920* (Athens: University of Georgia Press, 1980), 11; Charles Reagan Wilson, "The Religion of the Lost Cause: Ritual and Organization of the Southern Civil Religion, 1865–1920," *Journal of Southern History* 46 (May 1980): 232–34.

32. Wilson, *Baptized in Blood,* 100.

33. Mathisen, "Conflicting Southern Cultures," 69.

34. Frost, *Thinking Confederates,* 109; Woodward, *Origins of the New South,* 154–55.

35. Woodward, *Origins of the New South,* 155.

36. Paul M. Gaston, "The New South Creed: A Study in Southern Myth-making," in *Myth and Southern History: The New South,* ed. Patrick Gerster and Nicholas Cords (Chicago: Rand McNally, 1974), 193.

37. Williamson, *The Crucible of Race,* 100.

38. Grady, "The New South," 7.

39. J. J. D. Renfroe, "A Star of the First Magnitude—The Death of General Robert E. Lee," J. J. D. Renfroe Papers, Samford University, Birmingham, Ala.

40. As Gaines Foster points out, public ceremonies such as veterans' reunions, monument unveilings, and Memorial Day celebrations provided important opportunities to indoctrinate the lower classes in the revised historical

interpretation of the Civil War, since most of them were unlikely to read the new account set forth in the numerous books coming out. Gaines M. Foster, *Ghosts of the Confederacy: Defeat, the Lost Cause, and the Emergence of the New South, 1865–1913* (New York: Oxford University Press, 1987), 127, 144. See also Wilson, *Baptized in Blood*, 43–51.

41. Woodward, *Origins of the New South*, 157; Gaston, "The New South Creed," 199–201.

42. Bertram Wyatt-Brown, *The Shaping of Southern Culture: Honor, Grace, and War 1760s–1880s* (Chapel Hill: University of North Carolina Press, 2001), 270, mistakenly credits Georgia Populist Thomas E. Watson with writing this poem, which was actually penned in England in 1865 by Sir Henry Houghton. Houghton wrote it in response to the popular poem "The Conquered Banner" by Father Abram Ryan, a Catholic priest in Knoxville, Tennessee. Father Ryan's poem embodied the disillusionment and crestfallenness that so many southerners felt after Appomattox. Houghton's poem praised the fallen Confederacy and expressed remorse for England's failure to support the South's cause.

43. Gaston, "The New South Creed," 190.

44. Minnix, *Laughter in the Amen Corner*, 91. In his landmark 1944 study of race relations in the American South, Gunnar Myrdal noted that northerners long harbored a fondness for the cavalier myth of the Old South. Myrdal reasoned that because the North had no vestiges of feudalism, northerners were enchanted and captivated by those found in the South. Gunnar Myrdal, *An American Dilemma: The Negro Problem and Modern Democracy* (New York: Harper and Brothers, 1944), 1375 n3.

45. Gaston, "The New South Creed," 52; see also Joyce Appleby, "Reconciliation and the Northern Novelist, 1865–1880, *Civil War History* 10 (June 1964): 119–21.

46. Woodward, *Origins of the New South*, 167. For the role of Julia Ward Howe's "Battle Hymn of the Republic" in the Civil War, see James H. Moorhead, *American Apocalypse: Yankee Protestants and the Civil War 1860–1869* (New Haven, Conn.: Yale University Press, 1978), 79.

47. Francis Pendleton Gaines, *The Southern Plantation: A Study in the Development and the Accuracy of a Tradition* (Gloucester, Mass.: Peter Smith, 1962), 62–63, 80.

48. Lawrence J. Friedman, *The White Savage: Racial Fantasies in the Postbellum South* (Englewood Cliffs, N.J.: Prentice-Hall, 1970), 59–60.

49. See Haygood, "Slater Fund Beginnings," 244.

50. Michael Perman, *Struggle for Mastery: Disfranchisement in the South, 1888–1908* (Chapel Hill: University of North Carolina Press, 2001), 50.

51. E. E. Hoss, "Our Brother in Black," *Christian Advocate* (Nashville), September 13, 1890, 1.

52. S. A. Steel, "The Race Problem," *Nashville Daily American*, July 29, 1890, 5. Steel's reference to the son of Noah reflected a revival of antebellum evangelists' use of the Hamitic curse to justify the institution of slavery. For more on the antebellum use of the Hamitic myth, see Stephen R. Haynes,

Noah's Curse: The Biblical Justification of American Slavery (New York: Oxford University Press, 2002), 65–86.

53. O. P. Fitzgerald, "The Southern Race Problem," *Christian Advocate* (Nashville), April 19, 1890, 2; Hoss, "Our Brother in Black," 1; W. C. McCoy, "The Negro in the South," *Alabama Christian Advocate*, September 25, 1890, 4; Atticus G. Haygood, "The Black Shadow in the South," *Forum* 16 (October 1893): 172.

54. Steel, "The Race Problem," 5; Fitzgerald, "The Southern Race Problem," 2.

55. Steel, "The Race Problem," 5.

56. McCoy, "The Negro in the South," 4. Henry Grady echoed this claim about the preference for white jurors in an 1887 address, claiming that black jurors were commonly dismissed by a black defendant so "that white men may judge his case." Grady, "The Race Problem in the South," 95.

57. Warren A. Candler likewise wrote, "The southern people are unwilling to have Negroes exercise authority over them," but he explained that "the negro is not denied any right by the refusal of the southern people to submit to his exercising authority over them." Warren A. Candler, "The Color Line, North and South," box 84:12, Warren A. Candler Papers, Emory University, Atlanta.

58. McCoy, "The Negro in the South," 4.

59. Ibid.; Steel, "The Race Problem," 5; Fitzgerald, "The Southern Race Problem," 3.

60. Steel, "The Race Problem," 5.

61. Ibid.; McCoy, "The Negro in the South," 4.

62. Fitzgerald, "The Southern Race Problem," 2–3.

63. Editorial, "The Negro Problem," *Alabama Baptist*, January 30, 1890, 2.

64. Editorial, "Prohibition the Better Way," *Alabama Baptist*, April 3, 1890, 2.

65. For example, in an 1884 prohibition sermon, Haygood had argued for prohibition on economic, moral, and religious grounds but made no mention of race. This is a significant omission for a man who believed that his calling from God was to uplift the black race in the South. Instead, he emphasized how alcohol made men idle, inefficient workers and how it led to pauperism and damaged their ability to get credit at stores. Atticus G. Haygood, *Save Our Homes: A Prohibition Sermon* (Macon, Ga.: J. W. Burke, 1884), 13–14.

66. According to John Blassingame, Sambo was "the most pervasive and long-lasting of the literary stereotypes of the slave in antebellum southern novels, plays, and essays." John W. Blassingame, "Sambos and Rebels: The Character of the Southern Slave," in *Historical Judgments Reconsidered: Selected Howard University Lectures in Honor of Rayford W. Logan*, ed. Genna Rae McNeil and Michael R. Winston (Washington, D.C.: Howard University Press, 1988), 57. Whites played up the image of the "congenitally docile" Sambo, Blassingame asserts, because it relieved the "anxiety of thinking about slaves as men," made the institution of slavery look less harsh, and quelled their ever-present fear that their own slaves were plotting to revolt. John W. Blassingame, *The Slave Community: Plantation Life in the Antebellum South*, rev. ed. (New York: Oxford University Press, 1979), 225, 230–33.

67. Williamson, *The Crucible of Race*, 22–23.

68. Stanley M. Elkins, *Slavery: A Problem in American Institutional and Intellectual Life*, 3rd ed., (Chicago: University of Chicago Press, 1976), 82. Former Confederate chaplain James Battle Avirett likewise described the slaves who inhabited the plantation where he grew up as "overgrown children." Quoted in David R. Goldfield, *Still Fighting the Civil War: The American South and Southern History* (Baton Rouge: Louisiana State University Press, 2002), 21. James McPherson has examined postbellum northern missionaries' role in perpetuating the Sambo image in the South. The descriptions of freedmen that these missionaries sent back north painted them as "psychologically crippled" by slavery and possessing a childlike need for moral as well as economic and educational uplift. See James M. McPherson, *The Abolitionist Legacy: From Reconstruction to the NAACP* (Princeton, N.J.: Princeton University Press, 1975), 64–66.

69. Editorial, "The Race Conference," *Alabama Baptist*, May 17, 1900, 4.

70. Clericus Civio [A. J. Dickinson], "Christian Civics—No. 3," *Alabama Baptist*, April 27, 1899, 3; John Howard Burrows, "The Great Disturber: The Social Philosophy of Alfred James Dickinson" (master's thesis, Samford University, 1970), 86. North Carolina Baptist Thomas Dixon Jr. also used the phrase in the subtitle of his 1902 novel *The Leopard's Spots: A Romance of the White Man's Burden, 1865–1900*. Alabama Baptist B. F. Riley continued the application of this imagery to the southern race problem in his book *The White Man's Burden: A Discussion of the Interracial Question with Special Reference to the Responsibility of the White Race to the Negro Problem* (Birmingham, Ala.: for the author, 1910).

71. George Fredrickson calls this view of African Americans as childlike "liberal paternalism," in contrast to the emerging popular conception of blacks as barbaric and less than human. See George M. Fredrickson, *The Black Image in the White Mind: The Debate on Afro-American Character and Destiny, 1817–1914* (New York: Harper and Row, 1971), 283–88, 297. I have used the less forgiving adjective *sinister* to describe the paternalism of 1890s evangelicals who advanced the Sambo image, in contrast to the more optimistic and positive paternalism that dominated the 1880s. Also, this reemergence of the Sambo image took place, at least among the evangelicals I examined, just prior to the real explosion of "black beast" rhetoric after 1900.

72. John E. White, "Prohibition: The New Task and Opportunity of the South," *South Atlantic Quarterly* 7 (April 1908): 136.

73. Herbert J. Doherty Jr., "Voices of Protest from the New South, 1875–1910," *Mississippi Valley Historical Review* 42 (June 1955): 56.

74. Quoted in Joseph H. Cartwright, *The Triumph of Jim Crow: Tennessee Race Relations in the 1880s* (Knoxville: University of Tennessee Press, 1976), 204.

75. Gaston, *The New South Creed*, 129–30.

76. Henry A. Scomp, "Can the Race Problem Be Solved?" *Forum* (December 1889): 366–68.

77. Dickinson, "Christian Civics—No. 3," 3. Dickinson likewise lamented

the negative impact of the Fourteenth Amendment on southern race relations. Burrows, "The Great Disturber," 86 n20.

78. J. Morgan Kousser, *The Shaping of Southern Politics: Suffrage Restrictions and the Establishment of the One-Party South, 1880–1910* (New Haven, Conn.: Yale University Press, 1974), 110–14, 134–36. Exceptions were made to minimize the disfranchisement of uneducated whites, such as the Dortch law provision that voters who were eligible to vote in 1857 could have assistance in the voting booth.

79. J. Wayne Flynt, *Alabama in the Twentieth Century* (Tuscaloosa: University of Alabama Press, 2004), 14, 214–23.

80. Henry C. Vedder, "A Calm View of the Southern Question," *Baptist Quarterly Review* 12 (April 1890): 235–38.

81. Editorial, "The New South and the Old South," *American Missionary* 46 (May 1892): 142.

82. See Woodward, *The Strange Career of Jim Crow*, 71.

83. Malcolm Cook McMillan, *Constitutional Development in Alabama, 1798–1901: A Study in Politics, the Negro, and Sectionalism* (Chapel Hill: University of North Carolina Press, 1955), 229.

84. Alexander J. McKelway, "The Race Problem in the South: 1—The North Carolina Revolution Justified," *Outlook* 60 (December 31, 1898): 1058. For a more extensive examination of McKelway's views of race and social reform, see Jack Temple Kirby, *Darkness at the Dawning: Race and Reform in the Progressive South* (Philadelphia: Lippincott, 1972), 74–80.

85. Editorial, *Alabama Baptist*, April 11, 1901, 4.

86. Mathisen, "Conflicting Southern Cultures," 74.

87. Quoted in William G. McLoughlin Jr., *Modern Revivalism: Charles Grandison Finney to Billy Graham* (New York: Ronald Press, 1959), 306.

88. Quoted in Flynt, *Alabama Baptists*, 303.

89. W. L. Pickard, "The Temperance Bill," *Alabama Baptist*, January 22, 1891, 2.

90. See Moore, "The Negro and Prohibition in Atlanta," 53.

91. Cartwright, *The Triumph of Jim Crow*, 207.

92. Editorial, "The Tennessee Election," *Christian Advocate* (Nashville), October 8, 1887, 8.

93. Alexander J. McKelway, "The North Carolina Suffrage Amendment," *Independent* 52 (August 16, 1900): 1957. McKelway also offered the circular reasoning that African Americans had proved their political incapacity and unfitness for suffrage by their inability to stop the removal of their voting rights.

94. S. O. Y. Ray, "Prohibition for Alabama," *Southern and Alabama Baptist*, April 23, 1902, 10. Presumably, "others like them" referred to poor, illiterate whites, whom prohibitionists also considered pawns of the liquor interest. See also Flynt, *Alabama Baptists*, 271.

95. Bertram Wyatt-Brown, *Southern Honor: Ethics and Behavior in the Old South* (New York: Oxford University Press, 1982), 436.

96. Figures are based on tables in Walter White, *Rope and Faggot: A Biography of Judge Lynch* (New York: Arno Press, 1969), 254–58. As mentioned, not

all mob violence was directed at blacks. Amid the economic depression and cultural and political changes of the early and mid-1890s, lower-class whites sometimes banded together to fight the forces of change around them. Such mobs participated in night-riding (often known as whitecapping)—campaigns of terror and violence modeled on Ku Klux Klan activities of the Reconstruction era.

In northern Georgia, rural whites whose livelihood increasingly relied on moonshining conducted a campaign of terror in 1893 and 1894 against federal liquor revenuers and their informants, along with anyone—both white and black—they considered immoral or against whom they held some grudge. A similar outbreak of violence took place in southern Alabama when rural white bootleggers squared off against middle-class townspeople in a conflict that became known as the Mitcham War of Clarke County. It began when night-riding rural whites shot a local white merchant to death in his home and ended with martial action by the townspeople against the rural element. Another outbreak of white-on-white mob violence erupted in northwestern Tennessee when Nashville capitalists bought a lake and all the surrounding property, planning to develop it as a resort. Local whites who had squatted on the property for generations retaliated against the entrepreneurial activities that threatened their traditional lifestyle and livelihood by means of a whitecapping campaign of terrorism, arson, lynchings, and even the murder of two of the most prominent attorneys in the state. See William F. Holmes, "Moonshining and Collective Violence: Georgia, 1889–1895," *American History* 67 (December 1980): 589–611; Harvey H. Jackson, "The Middle-Class Democracy Victorious: The Mitcham War of Clarke County, Alabama, 1893," *Journal of Southern History* 57 (August 1991): 453–78; Paul J. Vanderwood, *Night Riders of Reelfoot Lake* (Tuscaloosa: Alabama University Press, 2003).

97. According to Paul E. Isaac, *Prohibition and Politics: Turbulent Decades in Tennessee 1885–1920* (Knoxville: University of Tennessee Press, 1965), 149, by 1907, the majority of lynchings in the nation took place in just three states: Alabama, Georgia, and Mississippi. A study by sociologists Richard E. Nisbett and Dov Cohen, *Culture of Honor: The Psychology of Violence in the South* (Boulder, Colo.: Westview Press, 1996), suggests that the South's legacy of violence lives on. They compared violence in the South to that in the rest of the nation by looking at factors such as homicides, gun control legislation, laws concerning self-defense, use of the death penalty, corporal punishment in schools, and domestic violence statistics. They found that the level of violence in the South is far greater than that in the North or West, especially "in matters where honor is concerned" (57).

98. White, *Rope and Faggot*, 40.

99. Minnix, *Laugher in the Amen Corner*, 200.

100. Hugh C. Bailey, *Liberalism in the New South: Southern Social Reformers and the Progressive Movement* (Coral Gables, Fla.: University of Miami Press, 1969), 56.

101. Editorial, *Christian Index*, June 16, 1892, 1.

102. Quoted in Kenneth K. Bailey, "Southern White Protestantism at the

Turn of the Century," *American Historical Review* 68 (April 1963): 629n. It should be noted that the Southern Baptist Convention resolution came about in response to a report forwarded from the Georgia Baptist Convention that condemned the practice of lynching in even stronger terms. The GBC resolution asserted that the body "deeply deplores the great and decrying evil [of lynching] . . . and insist[s] on reforms in the criminal law until both the criminal and the lyncher can see before him nothing but the inevitable doom which the state will visit upon all who trample on her majesty by violating her laws." Editorial, "Crimes and Lynching," *Baptist and Reflector*, May 10, 1906, 4.

103. Editorial, "The Palmetto Incident," *Christian Index*, March 23, 1899, 6.

104. Editorial, *Alabama Baptist*, January 24, 1889, 2.

105. A. J. Preston, "The Enforcement of the Law," *Alabama Baptist*, November 8, 1905, 2–3.

106. Editorial, *Alabama Baptist*, March 13, 1890, 2.

107. John W. Stewart, "Opposed to the Mob," *Alabama Baptist*, February 23, 1893, 1.

108. Editorial, "Shall Lynchings Go On?" *Alabama Baptist*, February 22, 1894, 2; Terry Lawrence Jones, "Attitudes of Alabama Baptists toward Negroes, 1890–1914" (master's thesis, Samford University, 1968), 88.

109. Ralph E. Luker, *The Social Gospel in Black and White: American Racial Reform, 1885–1912* (Chapel Hill: University of North Carolina Press, 1991), 100; Haygood, "The Black Shadow in the South," 167, 174–75; Eskew, "Black Elitism and the Failure of Paternalism," 649n.

110. Stephen A. West, "From Yeoman to Redneck in Upstate South Carolina, 1850–1915" (Ph.D. diss., Columbia University, 1998), 413.

111. Some of the primary historians who have studied the Sledd affair have misinterpreted Sledd's article by incorrectly conflating two separate events: Sledd's own experience on a train and the murder of Sam Hose. Both Ralph Reed and Terry Matthews assert that "Andrew Sledd was traveling by train when the conductor stopped to allow passengers to view the lynching of Sam Hose." Sledd's experience with lynch mobs meeting his train was a distinct event from the Hose lynching, and Sledd does not purport to have witnessed the latter. Sledd describes his trip aboard a train believed to be carrying an unnamed black man accused of murder and then segues to the Hose incident by writing: "Take another instance. The burning of Sam Hose took place on a Sabbath day." See Terry Lee Matthews, "The Voice of a Prophet: Andrew Sledd Revisited," *Journal of Southern Religion* 6 (2003): 5, available from http://jsr.as.wvu.edu/2003/Matthews.pdf (accessed July 18, 2007); Ralph E. Reed Jr., "Emory College and the Sledd Affair of 1902: A Case Study in Southern Honor and Racial Attitudes," *Georgia Historical Quarterly* 72 (fall 1988): 468; Andrew Sledd, "The Negro: Another View," *Atlantic Monthly* 90 (July 1902): 71.

112. Sledd, "The Negro," 70–71. Brundage uncovers the role played by the popular press in arousing the public's passion against accused blacks such as Hose. Sam Hose had gotten into an argument with his employer, who drew a pistol and threatened to kill Hose. Hose grabbed an ax and hit the other man once, killing him. While Hose was on the run, the press embellished the

story to the point that newspapers had Hose sneaking up on his victim while he was eating dinner, hacking him repeatedly with an ax, raping the victim's wife multiple times, and mortally wounding his infant child. By the time Hose was caught, the popular press had credited him with perpetrating almost every unsolved murder, rape, and theft in northern Georgia. The wantonness of mobs such as the one witnessed by Sledd was fomented in large part by the carelessness and sensationalism of the secular press. See W. Fitzhugh Brundage, *Lynching in the New South: Georgia and Virginia, 1880–1930* (Urbana: University of Illinois Press, 1993), 82–84. Even some modern historians continue to perpetuate the exaggerated and sensationalized version of Hose's misdeeds. For example, see Williamson, *The Crucible of Race*, 204.

113. Sledd, "The Negro," 71.

114. Henry Y. Warnock, "Andrew Sledd, Southern Methodists, and the Negro: A Case History," *Journal of Southern History* 31 (August 1965): 252.

115. Reed, "Emory College and the Sledd Affair," 486–90.

116. Terry Lee Matthews, "The Emergence of a Prophet: Andrew Sledd and the 'Sledd Affair' of 1902" (Ph.D. diss., Duke University, 1989), 163.

117. Mark K. Bauman, *Warren A. Candler: The Conservative as Idealist* (Metuchen, N.J.: Scarecrow Press, 1981), 157. Matthews, "The Voice of a Prophet," 2-3, 10–11, has uncovered some incidents prior to the 1902 controversy that may have predisposed Candler and Emory president Dickey to be less than supportive of Sledd and his right to academic free speech. For instance, before becoming president, Dickey had been nominated to receive an honorary doctorate from Emory. Sledd, however, single-handedly led a successful campaign to stop the conferring of such degrees just for the sake of flattering influential individuals, and Dickey was denied that honor. In an unfortunate case of instant karma for Sledd, the college's president resigned just weeks later, and Dickey was elected to replace him. Furthermore, Dickey's predecessor had been forced from his position because of the perceived "liberality of his views and the progressiveness of his policies." Sledd also enjoyed a cool relationship with his wife's father, in part due to Sledd's successful fight to eliminate Emory's law school in the name of educational reform. Sledd viewed the small program as a sham and a disgrace to the college. For Candler, however, it was part of his legacy as president of Emory, and the lone law professor whose job was eliminated as a result of the school's closing was John S. Candler, the bishop's brother. Taken together, none of these incidents inclined Dickey or Candler to make a bold stance in defense of Sledd when his inflammatory article appeared. Warnock, "Andrew Sledd," 262, notes that Warren Candler's brothers were among the most ardent advocates of firing Sledd after the controversy broke.

118. Wyatt-Brown, *The Shaping of Southern Culture*, 288; Edward L. Ayers, *Vengeance and Justice: Crime and Punishment in the Nineteenth-Century American South* (New York: Oxford University Press, 1984), 247.

119. Roberta Senechal de la Roche, "The Sociogenesis of Lynching," in *Under Sentence of Death: Lynching in the South*, ed. W. Fitzhugh Brundage (Chapel Hill: University of North Carolina Press, 1997), 49. Bailey, *Liberalism in the*

New South, 56, claims that only 16.7 percent of lynchings were the result of a rape accusation, and another 6.7 percent resulted from charges of attempted rape.

120. Fredrickson, *The Black Image in the White Mind*, 258, notes that the rise of Darwinism, and the idea that different classes of the same species can experience dissimilar rates of evolutionary development, played an important role in the view "that the black community was retrogressing instead of advancing."

121. Mark Bauerlein, *Negrophobia: A Race Riot in Atlanta, 1906* (San Francisco: Encounter Books, 2001), 58.

122. Editorial, "Prohibition in the South," *Alabama Christian Advocate*, September 3, 1903, 1.

123. A. J. Dickinson, "The Negro Problem Can Not Now Be Solved," *Alabama Baptist*, September 6, 1905, 6.

124. Haygood, "The Black Shadow in the South," 168, 172.

125. Alexander J. McKelway, "The Atlanta Riots: I—A Southern White Point of View," *Outlook* 84 (November 3, 1906): 562.

126. Ayers, *Vengeance and Justice*, 243.

127. Williamson, *The Crucible of Race*, 306–8, 318. Brundage, *Lynching in the New South*, 70–72, also examines the relationship among the fear of the black rapist, the changing economic order of the South, and the shifting role of women in the region. According to Brundage, the lynching of blacks for rape functioned not only to reaffirm white superiority over blacks but also to buttress weakening white male control of white females. More recently, Donald Mathews has explored this theme and examined how southern white evangelicals constructed the idea that blacks were dangerous. "People at the cultural margins are always dangerous," he points out, and whites further marginalized blacks through disfranchisement and fear of black sexual assault on white women in an effort to purify and revive the South. See Donald G. Mathews, "Lynching Is Part of the Religion of Our People: Faith in the Christian South," in *Religion in the American South: Protestants and Others in History and Culture*, ed. Beth Barton Schweiger and Donald G. Mathews (Chapel Hill: University of North Carolina Press, 2004), 162–63.

128. W. Fitzhugh Brundage, introduction to *Under Sentence of Death: Lynching in the South*, ed. W. Fitzhugh Brundage (Chapel Hill: University of North Carolina Press, 1997), 8.

129. Wilbur J. Cash, *The Mind of the South* (New York: Vintage Books, 1941), 118–19.

130. Whites also became increasingly convinced that the black community aided and abetted accused rapists. This sentiment contributed to the justification of indiscriminate mob violence against the entire black population, such as Atlanta's race riots in 1906. In defense of the white mob in Atlanta, McKelway noted that "there was the universal suspicion that the criminals were known to the Negroes, and there was never the slightest effort on the part of any Negro to bring any of them to justice." McKelway, "The Atlanta Riots," 559.

131. Will Irwin, "Who Killed Margaret Lear?" *Nashville Tennessean*, June 26, 1908, 1.

132. Morone, *Hellfire Nation*, 295–97.

133. The veracity of rape allegations by white women against black men was rarely questioned. In one remarkably aberrant case, the press discovered and reported that a woman had recanted her earlier charge that a black man had assaulted her. In March 1906 it was discovered that Mae Dupree had lied about the attack to mask a failed suicide attempt. Bauerlein, *Negrophobia*, 69.

134. Ibid., 218. See also Gregory L. Mixon, "The Atlanta Riot of 1906" (Ph.D. diss., University of Cincinnati, 1989).

135. John Corrigan, "The Prohibition Wave in the South," *American Review of Reviews* 36 (September 1907): 330.

136. Editorial, "After Our Trouble," *Wesleyan Christian Advocate*, October 4, 1906, 4.

137. Editorial, "'Dry' Atlanta," *Wesleyan Christian Advocate*, October 4, 1906, 4.

138. "Prohibition to Come to Atlanta," *Wesleyan Christian Advocate*, October 11, 1906, 2.

139. McKelway, "The Atlanta Riots," 559.

140. Alexander J. McKelway, "Local Option and State Prohibition in the South," *Charities and the Commons* 19 (January 25, 1908): 1452.

141. Dewey W. Grantham, *Hoke Smith and the Politics of the New South* (Baton Rouge: Louisiana State University Press, 1958), 190.

142. Although popular support for prohibition rose after the race riots of 1906, the unusual apportionment system in Georgia's state legislature also aided the cause. Each district was composed of several counties, and the right to appoint that district's senator rotated from one county to another every two years. When the legislature met in June 1907, most of the large cities in Georgia were not represented because it was not their turn to select the district's senator. Thus, only four of the fifteen largest cities in the state had a senator that year. This virtually assured the passage of prohibition legislation in the senate, where such legislation had repeatedly died in previous years. Frank Foxcroft, "Prohibition in the South," *Atlantic Monthly* 101 (May 1908): 627–28.

143. Editorial, "Prohibition in the South," *Alabama Christian Advocate*, September 3, 1903, 1.

144. Alexander J. McKelway, "State Prohibition in Georgia and the South," *Outlook* 86 (August 31, 1907): 947.

145. Corrigan, "The Prohibition Wave in the South," 330.

146. Irwin, "Who Killed Margaret Lear?" 1.

147. Riley, *The White Man's Burden*, 19.

148. Horace DuBose, "The Model Saloon License League," *Nashville Tennessean*, June 14, 1908, 4.

149. "Liquor Traffic Strongly Denounced," *Nashville Tennessean*, June 19, 1908, 2.

150. Editorial, "To the Manhood of Tennessee," *Nashville Tennessean*, June 16, 1908, 1. A recent study of the Johnson lynching does not mention any such discovery, although Johnson's alibi was that he was working in a Chattanooga saloon when the murder happened. This neither convinced Johnson's accusers

of his innocence nor garnered any sympathy for him among the white mob outside the courthouse. See Mark Curriden and Leroy Phillips Jr., *Contempt of Court: The Turn-of-the-Century Lynching That Launched a Hundred Years of Federalism* (New York: Faber and Faber, 1999), 94.

151. DuBose, "The Model Saloon License League," 4.

152. "Liquor Traffic Strongly Denounced," 2. Fear about allowing white women to go out unsupervised was a key component of the turn-of-the-century rape scare. Julia Tutwiler, an Alabama WCTU leader and education reformer, created boarding schools for girls because she thought it was too dangerous for them to walk to and from school each day. Bailey, *Liberalism in the New South*, 56. See also Charles Carroll, *The Negro a Beast: Or, In the Image of God* (Miami: Mnemosyne Publishing, 1969), 292. Warning young white girls never to venture out without white male protection was an important aspect of how the black rape and lynching matrix dealt with changing gender roles and reinforced the traditional sexual hierarchy. Brundage, *Lynching in the New South*, 70–72.

153. Quoted from the *Birmingham News-Herald* in Carl V. Harris, "Reforms in Government Control of Negroes in Birmingham, Alabama, 1890–1920," *Journal of Southern History* 38 (November 1972): 572.

154. Quoted in editorial, "Why the South Demands Prohibition," *Alabama Christian Advocate*, January 23, 1913, 1.

155. Irwin, "Who Killed Margaret Lear?" 1.

156. "A Gross Insult," *Alabama Christian Advocate*, November 4, 1909, 13.

157. "Prominent Citizens Speak in 17th Ward," *Nashville Tennessean*, June 18, 1908, 7.

158. "Dr. E. E. Folk Issues Card," *Commercial Appeal* (Memphis), June 25, 1908, 5. Whether the label actually included the slogan "The Game Cock of Democracy" is unclear. Crotzer submitted his account after the *Nashville American* had published an editorial suggesting that Folk had doctored the label. In response, Folk filed a libel suit against the paper, charging that the bottle's label did not include the "Game Cock" slogan. According to Folk, the picture on the label and its suggestive nature (which apparently became even more suggestive if certain parts were obscured) were all he used to try to sway Patterson supporters such as Crotzer.

159. Washington Bryan Crumpton, *A Story: How Alabama Became Dry* (Montgomery, Ala.: Paragon Press, 1925), 30.

160. Ibid.

161. Bailey, *Liberalism in the New South*, 61; Williamson, *The Crucible of Race*, 128.

162. Thornwell Jacobs, *The Law of the White Circle* (Nashville: Taylor-Trotwood, 1908), 130–34.

163. Quoted in F. W. Barnett, "The Law of the White Circle," *Alabama Baptist*, March 24, 1909; William Henry Kerlen, "Fight for the Glorious Cause of Our Noble Women," *Nashville Tennessean*, June 18, 1908, 3.

164. White, "Prohibition," 134–35.

165. McKelway, "Local Option," 1453.

166. Leonard Scott Blakey, *The Sale of Liquor in the South: The History of the Development of a Normal Social Restraint in Southern Commonwealths* (1912; reprint, New York: AMS Press, 1969), 26.

167. Editorial, "'Dry' Atlanta," 4.

168. Figures are based on data in appendix A of Brundage, *Lynching in the New South*, 273–78. Brundage recognizes a decline in sexual offenses as the basis for mob justice after 1910. He attributes this to both a reduction in the occurrence of sexual transgressions by blacks and alterations in the male code of honor, but he offers no explanation for why these shifts took place precisely when they did. See ibid., 67–72.

169. Ralph Ellison, "The World and the Jug," in *Shadow and Act* (New York: Random House, 1964), 116.

170. Jane Dailey, "Deference and Violence in the Postbellum Urban South: Manners and Massacres in Danville, Virginia," *Journal of Southern History* 63 (August 1997): 558–59.

171. McKelway, "The Race Problem in the South," 1058.

172. Quoted in Dailey, "Deference and Violence in the Postbellum Urban South," 589.

173. Leon F. Litwack, *Trouble in Mind: Black Southerners in the Age of Jim Crow* (New York: Knopf, 1998), 184, 198–201.

174. Haygood, "The Black Shadow in the South," 173–74.

175. Editorial, "Prohibition in the South," *Alabama Christian Advocate*, September 3, 1903, 1.

Chapter Five. "Let the Cowards Vote as They Will"

1. See Clyde J. Faries, "Carmack vs. Patterson: The Genesis of a Political Feud," *Tennessee Historical Quarterly* 38 (fall 1979): 332–37.

2. William R. Majors, *Editorial Wild Oats: Edward Ward Carmack and Tennessee Politics* (Macon, Ga.: Mercer University Press, 1984), 142; William R. Majors, *Change and Continuity: Tennessee Politics since the Civil War* (Macon, Ga.: Mercer University Press, 1986), 45.

3. Edgar E. Folk, "Senator Edward Ward Carmack," Edgar Estes Folk Collection, Southern Baptist Historical Library and Archives, Nashville, Tenn. (hereafter SBHLA).

4. See Kenneth S. Greenberg, *Honor and Slavery: Lies, Duels, Noses, Masks, Dressing as a Woman, Gifts, Strangers, Humanitarianism, Death, Slave Rebellions, the Proslavery Argument, Baseball, Hunting, and Gambling in the Old South* (Princeton, N.J.: Princeton University Press, 1996), 74; Elliott J. Gorn, "'Gouge and Bite, Pull Hair and Scratch': The Social Significance of Fighting in the Southern Backcountry," *American Historical Review* 90 (February 1985): 36. Southern duels were, however, quite deadly affairs, and they resulted in the death of one or both participants more frequently than did duels elsewhere. Frederick Marryat, an Englishman visiting the antebellum South, observed that duels there were more likely to result in death than in his homeland. In England, he noted, men exchanged shots to satisfy honor but made little effort

to actually hit their opponents. In the South, however, he found that duelers actually practiced beforehand and went to the field determined to kill. In some cases, duels in the antebellum South were conducted with shotguns rather than pistols, which generally resulted in the death of both participants. See Jack K. Williams, *Dueling in the Old South: Vignettes of Social History* (College Station: Texas A&M University Press, 1980), 41–50.

5. The issuance of a letter challenging a man to a duel made the affair more contractual and dispassionate in nature, and it also had the effect of making the challenge more public and difficult to ignore. If a man refused to accept a challenge, he would likely be "posted" via a poster or newspaper ad proclaiming his cowardice to the community. Williams, *Dueling in the Old South*, 75–76. Evangelicals frequently complained that some men used the duel to bully those they disliked into a fight. This tendency persisted into the postbellum period, when one infamous dueler from South Carolina was quoted as saying, "I can make a dog fight, if I write a letter or two." E. T. Winkler, "An Affair of Honor," *Alabama Baptist*, March 17, 1881, 2.

Typical of the antebellum written challenges was the note sent by Alabama congressman William Yancey to fellow congressman Thomas Clingman of North Carolina in 1845, which simply stated, "Having failed in all my efforts of an amicable adjustment of the difficulty between us, nothing remains for me, but to *demand* of you the satisfaction usual among gentlemen." William L. Yancey, *Memoranda of the Late Affair of Honor between Hon. T. L. Clingman, of North Carolina, and Hon. William L. Yancey of Alabama* (n.p., 1845), 6–7. Yancey and Clingman settled their dispute in a manner known as the "Irish Code," which demanded that shots be fired by both men; then, if neither was killed, one could honorably apologize for or explain his offending remark. After Yancey and Clingman each fired a shot at the other and missed, Clingman clarified his initial remarks that had spurred such a heated retort from Yancey, and the latter then retracted his statements. Under a stricter interpretation of the Irish Code, only after each man had fired two shots was one permitted to offer an apology, and after three shots, the men could either offer an "explanation" of their remarks or just keep firing until someone was hit. See George W. Hooper, *Down the River: Or, Practical Lessons under the Code Duello* (New York: E. J. Hale and Sons, 1874), 262.

6. In May 1856 the caning of Senator Charles Sumner of Massachusetts by Representative Preston Brooks on the floor of the U.S. Senate shocked the sensibilities of the North. Brooks attacked Sumner because the senator had maligned Brooks's uncle, South Carolina senator Andrew Pickens Butler, in a speech three days earlier. The violence was intended to defend the honor of Senator Butler, but Brooks's decision to attack Sumner with a cane rather than challenging him to a duel was a clear (to southerners, at least) message that he did not consider Sumner to be a gentleman or his own social equal.

7. Williams, *Dueling in the Old South*, 72.

8. Edward L. Ayers, *Vengeance and Justice: Crime and Punishment in the Nineteenth-Century American South* (New York: Oxford University Press, 1984), 19.

9. Dailey notes that whites' refusal to use honorific titles for African Americans continued well into the New South era, so one black Mississippi couple christened their newborn daughter "Misjulia," thus forcing whites to address her as "Miss." Jane Dailey, "Deference and Violence in the Postbellum Urban South: Manners and Massacres in Danville, Virginia," *Journal of Southern History* 63 (August 1997): 572.

10. William Oliver Stevens, *Pistols at Ten Paces: The Story of the Code of Honor in America* (Boston: Houghton Mifflin, 1940), 246–47.

11. Ayers, *Vengeance and Justice*, 19.

12. Bertram Wyatt-Brown, *Southern Honor: Ethics and Behavior in the Old South* (New York: Oxford University Press, 1982), 29, 364.

13. See Grady McWhiney, *Cracker Culture: Celtic Ways in the Old South* (University, Ala.: University of Alabama Press, 1988).

14. The South's experience was actually very "un-American," Woodward argues. Unlike those in the North, southerners did not embrace the view that history was, in the words of Arnold Toynbee, "something unpleasant that happens to other people." Beginning with the overthrow of colonial rule and continuing throughout the nineteenth century, northerners had enjoyed a legacy of success and abundance in which southerners had never fully participated. See C. Vann Woodward, *The Burden of Southern History*, rev. ed. (New York: Mentor, 1968), 25–26, 135–37. James McBride Dabbs, *Haunted by God: The Cultural and Religious Experience of the South* (Richmond, Va.: John Knox Press, 1972), 76, likewise sees the South as inhabiting an "intermediate position between past and future," between Europe and the American North.

15. James McPherson expresses some doubt about this difference between northerners and southerners. "A substratum of truth underlies the stereotype of the old South as a society with a profound sense of honor while Yankees were driven by conscience. Like all stereotypes, however, it oversimplifies a complex reality," writes McPherson in *For Cause and Comrades: Why Men Fought in the Civil War* (New York: Oxford University Press, 1997), 24. He finds that some wartime letters from Union soldiers contained references to honor and shame, just as southern letters did.

16. McWhiney, *Cracker Culture*, 269–70.

17. It is noteworthy that when a new social and economic order was forced on the South, the region's lowest classes went to the most violent extremes to try to recapture the clear sense of social superiority they had enjoyed during the antebellum period. Antebellum southern aristocrats were correct in their belief that the code of honor served to maintain social stability and safeguard their hegemony over the poor white population. These poor white men did the greatest share of dying during the Civil War to preserve the old economic order, despite the fact that the slave economy benefited them very little. Much more than economic interest, honor was the main impetus for poor whites to fight for the Confederacy and maintain the old slavocracy. The cult of honor had instilled in them a deep sense of loyalty and a desire to protect their region from northern aggression; in addition, the old order for which they fought guaranteed them a more secure social standing than what they could expect under the threatened free-labor system.

18. Greenberg describes an amusing incident of a southern gentleman who invited guests to dine with him but then forgot about the invitation. When the guests arrived for dinner, the unprepared gentleman met them at the gate and announced, "I am not here." The guests accepted the man's words as true and departed in peace rather than call his blatant lie into question, which would have maligned his honor and necessitated his armed defense of it. Greenberg, *Honor and Slavery*, 11.

19. McWhiney, *Cracker Culture*, 169–70. Edward Crowther notes that Jackson "embodied the very essence of the violent tenor of the Old South and its code of honor," despite the fact that Jackson claimed to read three chapters of scripture each day. Edward R. Crowther, "Holy Honor: Sacred and Secular in the Old South," *Journal of Southern History* 58 (November 1992): 625.

20. In 1806 Jackson's reputation was tarnished when, during a duel with Charles Dickinson, Jackson's gun misfired. Instead of counting the misfire as his shot, as the rules of dueling demanded, Jackson fired his pistol again and killed Dickinson.

21. William Stevens recounts the story of a young man who, upon hearing the news of southern secession and the outbreak of civil war, abandoned his studies in Europe to return home to fight for the South. While traveling home he met up with his brother, who had withdrawn from the U.S. Naval Academy to serve the Confederacy. Before continuing their journey, the brother from Europe insisted that he must first carry out a duel with his best friend, with whom he had had a disagreement. The young men dueled, and the brother was killed. Stevens, *Pistols at Ten Paces*, 246.

22. McWhiney, *Cracker Culture*, 169–70, 204; Williams, *Dueling in the Old South*, 28.

23. Quoted in Clement Eaton, *The Waning of the Old South Civilization, 1860–1880s* (Athens: University of Georgia Press, 1968), 31. For more on the rough-and-tumble environment of the southern backcountry, primarily as observed by northerners and Englishmen traveling in the antebellum South, see Gorn, "Gouge and Bite," 18–43.

24. Mary M. "Mollie" Houser to James Houser, April 5, 1864, John F. Houser Papers, Special Collections Department, Duke University Library, Durham, N.C.; available from http://etext.lib.virginia.edu/etcbin/civwarlett-browse?id=A6152 (accessed July 18, 2007).

25. For more on the important role of drinking in male bonding, especially within Euro-American cultures, see Lionel Tiger, *Men in Groups* (New York: Random House, 1969), 152–55.

26. Ayers, *Vengeance and Justice*, 28. See also Anne C. Loveland, *Southern Evangelicals and the Social Order 1800–1860* (Baton Rouge: Louisiana State University Press, 1980), 180.

27. Carvosso [pseudonym], "But I Say unto You that Ye Resist Not Evil," *Christian Advocate* (Nashville), March, 1, 1850, 1. Interestingly, the author's argument relies heavily on the prevailing code of honor. He argues that because the code declares it to be dishonorable for a man to attack someone who cannot or will not defend himself, the embrace of nonresistance by Christian

men renders them free from attack by others. If a Christian is attacked, it is proof that he has not exhibited kindness and the ethic of Christian nonviolence toward that individual in the past and is therefore guilty of sin and has no right to retaliate physically against the individual.

28. Folk, "Senator Edward Ward Carmack."

29. Eulogizing Gambrell in 1887, one newspaper described "the cowardly assassination of the brave and chivalrous young Gambrell" by an anti-prohibitionist. "Roderick Dhu Gambrell," *Texas Baptist and Herald,* June 8, 1887, 4.

30. Editorial, "Personal and Practical," *Baptist and Reflector,* November 19, 1908, 1.

31. "Report of the Committee on Temperance," *Minutes of the Alabama Conference of the Methodist Episcopal Church, South (Seventy-sixth Session) Held at Greensboro, Ala., Dec .9–14, 1908* (n.p.: n.d.), 41.

32. For examples of wartime duels, see Stevens, *Pistols at Ten Paces,* 245–50.

33. Stephen A. West, "From Yeoman to Redneck in Upstate South Carolina, 1850–1915" (Ph.D. diss., Columbia University, 1998), 376.

34. C. A. Harwell Wells, "The End of the Affair? Anti-Dueling Laws and Social Norms in Antebellum America," *Vanderbilt Law Review* 54 (May 2001): 1838–39. Ayers, *Vengeance and Justice,* 271, notes that dueling diminished after the war even though violent overreaction to personal insults did not, and he argues that it was the "calculating aspect of dueling"—that is, the fact that the event took place not in the heat of passion but after several days of rumination and careful planning—that made it so distasteful to southerners after the war.

35. Quoted in Carl N. Degler, *The Other South: Southern Dissenters in the Nineteenth Century* (New York: Harper and Row, 1974), 275. Wells, "The End of the Affair?" 1840–41, observes that the conflict between Readjusters and the Bourbon "Funders" produced ten challenges and six duels between 1879 and 1883. Most notable about these cases was the increasing ability of southern politicians, attorneys, and newspaper editors to refuse a challenge without facing public humiliation. Not all Populists in the New South were opposed to the practice of dueling, however. In his days as an attorney, Georgia Populist leader Tom Watson shot a fellow lawyer who had "invaded his sensibilities" during the course of a trial. Bertram Wyatt-Brown, *The Shaping of Southern Culture: Honor, Grace, and War 1760s–1880s* (Chapel Hill: University of North Carolina Press, 2001), 263.

36. Richard F. Hamm, *Murder, Honor, and Law: Four Virginia Homicides from Reconstruction to the Great Depression* (Charlottesville: University of Virginia Press, 2003), 60.

37. Editorial, "A New South, Not a New England in the South," *American Missionary* 34 (October 1880): 295.

38. Editorial, "Dueling," *Alabama Baptist,* September 5, 1878, 2; Editorial, "Dueling," *Holston Methodist,* March 5, 1881, 2; Winkler, "An Affair of Honor," 2.

39. Wyatt-Brown, *Shaping of Southern Culture,* 104–5.

40. Ted Ownby, *Subduing Satan: Religion, Recreation, and Manhood in the Rural South, 1865–1920* (Chapel Hill: University of North Carolina Press,

1990), 12–14. Ownby pays particular attention to hunting in the South and the propensity for "binge killing." Although he argues that evangelicals sought to impose restrictions on hunting, I found no mention of this issue in any of the evangelical sources from Alabama, Georgia, or Tennessee.

41. Ibid., 133.

42. Editorial, "A Manly Preacher," *Alabama Baptist*, October 9, 1912, 8.

43. Vox [pseudonym], "Christian Manliness," *Alabama Baptist*, December 22, 1881, 1.

44. Roy Robbins, "Manishness [*sic*] and Manliness," *Alabama Baptist*, October 7, 1880, 4.

45. Editorial, "The White Life of Pure Manhood," *Christian Index and South-Western Baptist*, May 10, 1900, 2.

46. C. H. Wetherbe, "Christian Manliness," *Christian Index and South-Western Baptist*, February 15, 1900, 3.

47. Quoted in Sean Gill, "How Muscular Was Victorian Christianity: Thomas Hughes and the Cult of Christian Manliness Reconsidered," in *Gender and Christian Religion: Papers Read at the 1996 Summer Meeting and the 1997 Winter Meeting of the Ecclesiological History Society*, ed. R. N. Swanson (n.p.: Boydell Press, 1998), 424.

48. One of the most well-known manifestations of muscular Christianity was the Men and Religion Forward Movement, a nationwide effort to bring more males into the church and more manliness into Christianity. The muscular Christianity impulse was centered in the North, although the Men and Religion Forward Movement did have a successful chapter in Atlanta in the early 1910s. Primarily, however, it appealed to middle- and upper-class northerners who held white-collar jobs. The growth of professionalism, with its sedentary, office-based work environment, spurred concerns that Christian men were becoming soft and that the hard-laboring, lower-class immigrants might overthrow the elites. Clifford Putney, *Muscular Christianity: Manhood and Sports in Protestant America, 1880–1920* (Cambridge, Mass.: Harvard University Press, 2001), 2–4, 53; Gail Bederman, "'The Women Have Had Charge of the Church Work Long Enough': The Men and Religion Forward Movement of 1911–1912 and the Masculinization of Middle-Class Protestantism," *American Quarterly* 41 (September 1989): 432–35, 455–56. A recent study by Martin Summers, *Manliness and Its Discontents: The Black Middle Class and the Transformation of Masculinity, 1900–1930* (Chapel Hill: University of North Carolina Press, 2004), explores how ideas about manhood and material success played out within the African American community during this period, although the focus is primarily on blacks in the North.

49. West, "From Yeoman to Redneck," 356.

50. Catherine Murdock has suggested that perhaps "respectable" is a more useful designation than "middle class" when talking about supporters of temperance and prohibition, since it hinges less on economic status than on the ideas and attitudes that linked evangelicals across class lines. Catherine Gilbert Murdock, *Domesticating Drink: Women, Men, and Alcohol in America, 1870–1940* (Baltimore: Johns Hopkins University Press, 1998), 6.

51. Stephen West oversimplifies, it seems, when he characterizes the conflict as primarily one between lower-class and middle-class whites. The latter, he argues, were primarily New Southites worried about how lynching and other forms of lawlessness hurt the image of the South and jeopardized the flow of capital from the North. In doing so, West ignores the moral and religious components of the different definitions of honor in the New South, which affected white men of all classes and impacted their attitude toward violence, lawlessness, and drunkenness. See "From Yeoman to Redneck," 406–12.

52. Both Hunter Farish and Paul Harvey examine how the Baptist and Methodist leadership, which had a modernized and centralized vision, sought to "enforce bourgeois codes on evangelicals." This included combating theological movements within the denominations that conflicted with their progressive vision, especially holiness doctrine and Landmarkism. The MECS leadership took action to bring holiness evangelists, who were seen as extremists promulgating not only unsound doctrine but also uncouth worship practices, under stricter control of the church. Harvey examines how Baptist leaders sought to establish uniformity, structure, and principles of efficiency across the denomination, even though the majority of the Southern Baptist Conference constituency was rural based. Like the Methodists, Baptist leaders tried to rein in noisy and passionate revivalism. The denomination also succeeded in bringing order and homogeneity to southern Baptist churches by infusing urban worship practices, such as the use of hymnals, into rural churches. Traditional, unstructured, plain-folk hymnody was replaced by sentimental Victorian hymns presented in a structured and uniform format. See Hunter Dickinson Farish, *The Circuit Rider Dismounts: A Social History of Southern Methodism, 1865–1900* (Richmond, Va.: Dietz Press, 1938), 74–75; Paul Harvey, *Redeeming the South: Religious Cultures and Racial Identities among Southern Baptists, 1865–1925* (Chapel Hill: University of North Carolina Press, 1997), 86–102.

53. For more on the growing affluence of the MECS, see Farish, *The Circuit Rider Dismounts*, 77. He examines the rise in the value of the denomination's buildings and property, which climbed rapidly in the postwar era even though property values in general were declining. The value of MECS church buildings and property grew from $13.3 million in 1883 to $35 million in 1898.

54. West, "From Yeoman to Redneck," 356.

55. Ibid., 390–94. After Carmack's death, those close to him reported that he had strongly resisted the idea of carrying a pistol but had been goaded into it by some friends who were concerned about the threats from Colonel Cooper. Folk, "Senator Edward Ward Carmack."

56. W. W. Stringfield, "Whisky and Pistols," *Holston Methodist*, May 3, 1879, 1. As they did with alcohol, evangelical papers were quick to point to cases in which pistol carrying led to tragedy. For example, the *Alabama Baptist* noted how a quarrel between two Alabama teenagers over a dog had escalated into a gunfight because of "a ready pistol," leaving one of the boys and his father dead. Editorial, "Pistol—Death," *Alabama Baptist*, August 23, 1894, 2.

57. "Wanted—Manhood," *Alabama Baptist*, February 18, 1886, 2.

58. J. B. Hawthorne, "Separation of Church and State," *Baptist and Reflector,* December 18, 1890, 3.

59. E. E. Folk, "B. F. Haynes vs. R. K. Hargrove," *Baptist and Reflector,* December 11, 1890, 8.

60. Editorial, "The Kelley Case," *Baptist and Reflector,* October 16, 1890, 8.

61. A. E. Waffle, "Manliness in the Ministry," *Alabama Baptist,* September 1, 1881, 1.

62. West, "From Yeoman to Redneck," 382. Ethicist Peter Berger has examined the impact of modernity and industrialization on the role of honor and dignity in a society. Honor, he notes, depends on having relatively stable and intact institutions that provide institutional roles. Modernity tends to destroy such stable institutions and replace them with institutions that oppress individuality. In such a setting, Berger argues, honor is replaced by dignity as a rule of social behavior, because the latter is "essentially independent of institutional roles." See Peter L. Berger, Brigitte Berger, and Hansfried Kellner, *The Homeless Mind: Modernization and Consciousness* (New York: Vintage Books, 1973), 90–96. The market revolution that finally reached the South after the Civil War, it might be argued, contributed to the redefinition of honor that took place there toward the end of the century.

63. Frank H. Stewart, *Honor* (Chicago: University of Chicago Press, 1995), 41, 54–59.

64. Hamm, *Murder, Honor, and Law,* 62.

65. William Henry Kerlen, "Fight for the Glorious Cause of Our Noble Women," *Nashville Tennessean,* June 18, 1908, 3.

66. Joseph Charles Kiger, "Social Thought as Voiced in Rural Middle Tennessee Newspapers, 1878–1898" (Ph.D. diss., Vanderbilt University, 1950).

67. Kerlen, "Fight for the Glorious Cause of Our Noble Women," 3.

68. Quoted in editorial, *Alabama Christian Advocate,* November 4, 1909, 13.

69. B. F. Riley, *The White Man's Burden: A Discussion of the Interracial Question with Special Reference to the Responsibility of the White Race to the Negro Problem* (Birmingham, Ala.: for the author, 1910), 41–42, 207.

70. E. E. Hoss, *Christian Advocate* (Nashville), March 24, 1892, 1.

71. Quoted in Christopher H. Owen, *The Sacred Flame of Love: Methodism and Society in Nineteenth-Century Georgia* (Athens: University of Georgia Press, 1998), 181.

72. Booker T. Washington, "Prohibition and the Negro," *Outlook* 88 (March 14, 1908): 589.

73. James D. Ivy, *No Saloon in the Valley: The Southern Strategy of Texas Prohibitionists in the 1880s* (Waco, Tex.: Baylor University Press, 2003), 72.

74. "Temperance," in *Minutes of the North Georgia Conference, Held in Cedartown, Ga. 1889,* ed. H. L. Crumley (Atlanta: Constitution Publishing, n.d.), 15.

75. "Committee on Temperance," in *Year Book and Minutes of the Twenty-fifth Session of the North Georgia Conference Methodist Episcopal Church, South, Held in Methodist Church, Cartersville, Ga., from December 9th to 15th, 1891,* ed. Ellison R. Cook (Macon, Ga.: J. W. Burke, 1891), 37.

76. E. K. Cox, "The Church and the Liquor Traffic," *Baptist and Reflector*, October 22, 1908, 3.

77. Editorial, "Limiting the Atonement," *Wesleyan Christian Advocate* (Atlanta), May 4, 1892, 1.

78. W. L. Pickard, "The Preacher-Citizen," *Christian Index*, January 28, 1909, 2.

79. Ibid.

80. Editorial, "A Manly Preacher," 8.

81. William J. Albert, "Church and Politics," *Wesleyan Christian Advocate* (Atlanta), June 15, 1892.

82. W. B. Crumpton, "Reply to the Above," *Alabama Baptist*, January 10, 1895, 2.

83. E. E. Folk, *The Adams Law, How It Operates: Testimonies from Twenty-six Towns* (Nashville: Bowder Printing, 1904), 50.

84. J. B. Hawthorne, "Dr. Hawthorne's Great Temperance Speech," *Alabama Baptist*, November 19, 1885, 1.

85. Rutherford Brett to E. E. Folk, January 14, 1909, and Sharp to Folk, March 11, 1909, E. E. Folk Collection, SBHLA.

86. "Voters of Durham!" broadside produced by the Prohibition Committee of Durham, N.C., 1886.

87. W. L. Pickard, "The Temperance Bill," *Alabama Baptist*, January 22, 1891, 2.

88. Job Harral, "Prohibition the Safety of the People," *Baptist* (Memphis), April 14, 1888, 4.

89. Quoted in editorial, "Editor Carmack," *Baptist and Reflector*, September 3, 1908, 8.

90. Hattie May, "By an Alabama Young Lady," *Alabama Baptist*, March 18, 1880, 1.

91. S. E. Sibley, "Candler Persecuted Scomp," undated *Voice* newspaper clipping, box 110:2, Warren A. Candler Collection, Emory University, Atlanta.

92. Quoted in Anne Gary Pannell, *Julia S. Tutwiler and Social Progress in Alabama* (University, Ala.: University of Alabama Press, 1961), 119. Another of Tutwiler's poems later became the state poem of Alabama.

Chapter Six. "Some of Our Best Preachers Part Their Hair in the Middle"

1. As noted in the introduction, the majority of the extant sources relating to women's involvement in the prohibition movement in the South are filtered through the male-dominated press and denominational organs, obscuring the voices of southern women. Anne Firor Scott has rightly observed that historians of the South tend to write "as if the word southerner was a masculine noun." While attempting to avoid this erroneous approach, this chapter is concerned with both the activities of southern women in the prohibition campaign and how those actions divided and antagonized the male evangelical prohibitionists

who have figured so prominently in this study thus far. Anne Firor Scott, "A Different View of Southern History," in *Unheard Voices: The First Historians of Southern Women,* ed. Anne Firor Scott (Charlottesville: University of Virginia Press, 1993), 1.

2. Susan Hill Lindley, *"You Have Stept out of Your Place": A History of Women and Religion in America* (Louisville, Ky.: Westminster John Knox Press, 1996), 100–101.

3. Ruth Bordin, *Woman and Temperance: The Quest for Power and Liberty, 1873–1900* (New Brunswick, N.J.: Rutgers University Press, 1990), 15–25, 34–42, 51–52, 72; Barbara Leslie Epstein, *The Politics of Domesticity: Women, Evangelism, and Temperance in Nineteenth-Century America* (Middletown, Conn.: Wesleyan University Press, 1981), 90–96.

4. Carolyn DeSwarte Gifford, "For God and Home and Native Land: The WCTU's Image of Woman in the Late Nineteenth Century," in *Women in New Worlds: Historical Perspectives on the Wesleyan Tradition,* ed. Hilah F. Thomas and Rosemary Skinner Keller (Nashville: Abingdon Press, 1981), 312–13.

5. John Patrick McDowell, *The Social Gospel in the South: The Women's Home Mission Movement in the Methodist Episcopal Church, South, 1886–1939* (Baton Rouge: Louisiana State University Press, 1982), 10.

6. Anne Firor Scott, *The Southern Lady: From Pedestal to Politics, 1830–1930* (Chicago: University of Chicago Press, 1970), 136.

7. Bordin, *Woman and Temperance,* 51–55.

8. For more on Willard's unsuccessful bid to merge the two parties, see Ruth Bordin, "Frances Willard and the Practice of Political Influence," *Hayes Historical Journal* 5 (1985): 18–28.

9. Epstein, *The Politics of Domesticity,* 116–42; Gifford, "For God and Home and Native Land," 315–17.

10. Bordin, *Woman and Temperance,* 59.

11. Epstein, *The Politics of Domesticity,* 145; Janet Zollinger Giele, *Two Paths to Women's Equality: Temperance, Suffrage, and the Origins of Modern Feminism* (New York: Twayne Publishers, 1995), 63–67; Lindley, *"You Have Stept out of Your Place,"* 106.

12. Bordin, *Woman and Temperance,* 152–55.

13. Quoted in ibid., 52.

14. Ibid., 76–81.

15. Grace Leab, "Tennessee Temperance Activities, 1870–1899," *East Tennessee Historical Society's Publications* 21 (1949): 56.

16. Marsha Wedell, *Elite Women and the Reform Impulse in Memphis, 1875–1915* (Knoxville: University of Tennessee Press, 1991), 57–58.

17. Leab, "Tennessee Temperance Activities," 61.

18. Lula Barnes Ansley, *History of the Georgia Woman's Christian Temperance Union: From Its Organization, 1883–1907* (Columbus, Ga.: Gilbert Printing, 1914), 42.

19. Diana Cummings, "Peculiar Feminism: The Georgia Woman's Temperance Union," available at http://www.sip.armstrong.edu/WCTU/essay.html (accessed July 18, 2007).

20. Quoted in editorial, "WCTU in Atlanta," *Wesleyan Christian Advocate* (Atlanta), June 13, 1888.

21. A. Elizabeth Taylor, "Revival and Development of the Woman Suffrage Movement in Georgia," *Georgia Historical Quarterly* 42 (December 1958): 339.

22. Avery Hamilton Reed, *Baptists in Alabama: Their Organization and Witness* (Montgomery: Alabama Baptist State Convention, 1967), 136; Mrs. S. T. Slaton, "Fifty Years," in *The Story of the Alabama Woman's Christian Temperance Union: 1884–1959* (n.p.: 1959), 5.

23. Anne Gary Pannell, *Julia S. Tutwiler and Social Progress in Alabama* (University, Ala.: University of Alabama Press, 1961), 13, 111; Slaton, "Fifty Years," 23.

24. Valeria Gennaro Lerda, "The Woman's Christian Temperance Union Reform Movement in the South in the Late Nineteenth Century," in *Religious and Secular Reform in America: Ideas, Beliefs, and Social Change*, ed. David K. Adams and Cornelis A. Van Minnen (Edinburgh: Edinburgh University Press, 1999), 165–66; Ralph M. Lyon, *Julia Tutwiler* (Livingston, Ala.: Alabama-Tombigbee Rivers Regional Planning and Development Commission, 1976), 43.

25. Bordin, *Woman and Temperance*, 81.

26. Douglas W. Carlson, "'Drinks He to His Own Undoing': Temperance Ideology in the Deep South," *Journal of the Early Republic* 18 (winter 1998): 682. The Good Templars, founded in Georgia by English émigré James G. Thrower in 1867, was the first temperance organization in the South to admit women as equal members with men. Ansley, *History of the Georgia Woman's Christian Temperance Union*, 31. One of the most extensive examinations of the Good Templar movement is David N. Fahey, *Temperance and Racism: John Bull, Johnny Reb, and the Good Templars* (Lexington: University Press of Kentucky, 1996).

27. Scott, *The Southern Lady*, 136. Jean Friedman, *The Enclosed Garden: Women and Community in the Evangelical South, 1830–1900* (Chapel Hill: University of North Carolina Press, 1985), 119, speculates that southern women were slower to join the WCTU because the South's economy did not begin to recover from the war until the 1880s, only then generating enough middle- and upper-class women with sufficient leisure time to pursue extracurricular activities such as participating in reform organizations.

28. *Report of the Fifth Annual Convention of the Woman's Christian Temperance Union of the State of Alabama: Held in Mobile, Alabama, December 1st and 2d, 188[7]* (Selma, Ala.: Mail Book and Job Print, 1888), 59–60.

29. Daniel Sack, *Whitebread Protestants: Food and Religion in American Culture* (New York: St. Martin's Press, 2000), 24–27.

30. *Minutes of the Sixty-second Anniversary of the Baptist Convention of the State of Georgia: Held at Atlanta, April 24, 25, 26 and 28, 1884* (Atlanta: Jas. P. Harrison, 1884), 29.

31. Holly Berkley observes, however, that Chapin's language was not entirely free of the paternalistic defense of the institution of slavery. Addressing the national WCTU, she lamented the decline of morality in the African

American community since the end of slavery, when Christian owners had "protected" their slaves from temptations such as alcohol. Holly Berkley, "From Self-Made Men to Crusading Women: The Gendered Evolution of the American Temperance Movement in the Nineteenth Century" (Ph.D. diss., University of Oklahoma, 2004), 196–97.

32. *Minutes of the Second Annual Convention of the Alabama Woman's Christian Temperance Union: Held in Selma, Alabama, November 13th and 14th, 1884* (Selma, Ala.: Selma Printing, 1884), 22.

33. Mary Martha Thomas, *The New Woman in Alabama: Social Reforms and Suffrage, 1890–1920* (Tuscaloosa: University of Alabama Press, 1992), 19.

34. Ellen C. Bryce, "President's Address," in *Report of the Fifth Annual Convention of the Woman's Christian Temperance Union of the State of Alabama*, 23. It is worth noting, however, that Alabama WCTU records after the turn of the century are free from the language of "black beasts" and rape scares that became so common in the male-dominated press and denominational reports.

35. *Minutes of the Alabama Woman's Christian Temperance Union: At the Fourth Annual Meeting in Montgomery, November 17th and 18th . . . 1886* (Selma, Ala.: Selma Printing, 1887), 23–24.

36. *Minutes of the Alabama Woman's Christian Temperance Union: Held in Tuscaloosa, Alabama, December 3–6, 1903* (n.p.: n.d.), 18.

37. See Berkley, "From Self-Made Men to Crusading Women," 169–206.

38. Wedell, *Elite Women and the Reform Impulse in Memphis*, 73; Anastasia Sims, *The Power of Femininity in the New South: Women's Organizations and Politics in North Carolina, 1880–1930* (Columbia: University of South Carolina Press, 1997), 70–71.

39. *Minutes of the Alabama Woman's Christian Temperance Union at the Tenth Annual Meeting: Selma, Alabama, December 1st to 3d, 1893* (Selma, Ala.: Selma Printing, n.d.), 39.

40. Booker T. Washington, "Prohibition and the Negro," *Outlook* 88 (March 14, 1908): 589.

41. Dewey W. Grantham, *Southern Progressivism: The Reconciliation of Progress and Tradition* (Knoxville: University of Tennessee Press, 1983), 170.

42. "W.C.T.U. Will Work with Renewed Energy," *Nashville Tennessean*, June 17, 1908.

43. "Women Attend Carmack Rally: Twenty Men Are Present," *Commercial Appeal* (Memphis), June 25, 1908, 5; Ansley, *History of the Georgia Woman's Christian Temperance Union*, 224–26.

44. This tune was a favorite at WCTU rallies and was easily adapted to different settings; ladies at a Birmingham rally sang "Jefferson's Going Dry," referring to the county where Birmingham is located, and at a rally in Montgomery they sang "Montgomery's Going Dry."

45. Ansley, *History of the Georgia Woman's Christian Temperance Union*, 230–36.

46. Lida B. Robertson, "When We Christians Really Want Temperance God Is Going to Give It to Us," *Alabama Baptist*, August 17, 1910, 5.

47. Mrs. S. C. S., "Woman's Responsibility," *Wesleyan Christian Advocate*, August 20, 1890, 2.

48. Editorial, "Politics in Tennessee," *Christian Advocate* (Nashville), July 10, 1908, 1.

49. D. P. G., "Prohibition in Alabama," *Alabama Baptist*, December 23, 1880, 1.

50. Washington Bryan Crumpton, *Alabama Baptist*, September 25, 1884, 1.

51. W. B. Crumpton, "Reply to the Above," *Alabama Baptist*, January 10, 1895, 2 (emphasis in original).

52. Editorial, "The Tennessee Election," *Christian Advocate* (Nashville), October 8, 1887, 8.

53. L. L. Gwaltney, "A Review of the Prohibition Status as Seen by a Delegate," *Alabama Baptist*, March 24, 1909, 2–3. In later years, Gwaltney embraced women's suffrage and supported the Nineteenth Amendment, only to later regret enfranchising women because he blamed the further decline of the home on the expansion of women's opportunities. See Robert F. Crider, "The Social Philosophy of L. L. Gwaltney, 1919–1950" (master's thesis, Samford University, 1969), 41.

54. Editorial, "WCTU in Atlanta."

55. *Minutes of the Sixty-second Anniversary of the Baptist Convention of the State of Georgia*, 29; *Baptist State Convention of Tennessee, Twelfth Annual Session Held with the Central Baptist Church, Nashville, Tenn., October 14, 15, 16, 1886* (Chattanooga: Baptist Publishing, 1886), 25; "Supplement.—Reports Adopted. III.—Temperance," in *Journal of the Seventy-third Session of the Tennessee Annual Conference of the Methodist Episcopal Church, South: Held at Clarksville, Tenn., October 6–12, 1886* (Nashville: Southern Methodist Publishing House, n.d.), 24; "Report on Temperance," in *The Holston Annual 1886. Official Record of the Holston Annual Conference, Methodist Episcopal Church, South. Sixty-third Session, Held at Knoxville, Tenn., October 1886*, ed. W. C. Carden (Morristown, Tenn.: Gazette Book and Job Office, 1886), 37.

56. Scott, *The Southern Lady*, 147.

57. Leslie Kathrin Dunlap, "In the Name of the Home: Temperance Women and Southern Grass-Roots Politics, 1873–1933" (Ph.D. diss., Northwestern University, 2001), 13.

58. Editorial, "Woman Suffrage and Temperance," *Alabama Baptist*, August 28, 1884, 2.

59. Editorial, *Alabama Baptist*, August 28, 1884, 2.

60. T. R. McCarty, "The Prohibition Party," *Alabama Christian Advocate*, July 12, 1888, 1.

61. Editorial, "The WCTU," *Alabama Christian Advocate*, August 9, 1888, 4.

62. Ibid.

63. Editorial, "Temperance in Alabama," *Alabama Christian Advocate*, August 9, 1888, 4.

64. William L. O'Neill, *Everyone Was Brave: The Rise and Fall of Feminism in America* (Chicago: Quadrangle Books, 1969), 51. More recently, Giele's *Two Paths to Women's Equality* has contrasted "domestic feminists," whose activism focused on moral reform and benevolence activities, with "equal rights feminists," who sought to improve women's lives by increasing their legal and social equality with men.

65. Jane Camhi, *Women against Women: American Anti-Suffragism, 1880–1920* (New York: Carlson, 1994), documents the not-so-silent majority of women who opposed the suffrage movement, often overlooked by historians. The women's "antisuffrage resistance" emerged in the 1880s and was embodied in a national organization that established associations in more than twenty-five states across the nation.

66. Elna Green, "'Ideals of Government, of Home, and of Women': The Ideology of Southern White Antisuffragism," in *Hidden Histories of Women in the New South*, ed. Virginia Bernhard, Elizabeth Fox-Genovese, et al. (Columbia: University of Missouri Press, 1994), 103–9, demonstrates that many southern women cherished "the nineteenth-century ideals of separate spheres and republican motherhood" because they viewed the existence of their distinct home sphere as "a guaranteed area of power and influence."

67. *Report of the Sixth Annual Convention of the Woman's Christian Temperance Union of the State of Alabama: Held in Gadsden, Alabama, November 29th and 30th, 1888* (Selma, Ala.: Mail Book and Job Print, 1888), 12, 14, 16.

68. Editorial, "The WCTU in Alabama," *Alabama Christian Advocate*, February 18, 1889, 4.

69. Thomas, *The New Woman in Alabama*, 18.

70. Henry McDonald, "W.C.T.U.," *Christian Index*, December 4, 1890, 8.

71. Ansley, *History of the Georgia Woman's Christian Temperance Union*, 140–41.

72. Jane Elizabeth (Mrs. W. C.) Sibley to Warren A. Candler, April 29, 1892, Warren A. Candler Collection, Emory University, Altanta.

73. Warren A. Candler to Jane Elizabeth (Mrs. W. C.) Sibley, May 2, 1892, Candler Collection.

74. Ansley, *History of the Georgia Woman's Christian Temperance Union*, 141–42; Nancy A. Hardesty, "'The Best Temperance Organization in the Land': Southern Methodists and the WCTU in Georgia," *Methodist History* 28 (April 1990): 187–89.

75. Ansley, *History of the Georgia Woman's Christian Temperance Union*, 144–46.

76. Josephine Bone Floyd, "Rebecca Latimer Felton, Champion of Women's Rights," *Georgia Historical Quarterly* 30 (June 1946): 84.

77. A. Elizabeth Taylor, "The Origin of the Woman Suffrage Movement in Georgia," *Georgia Historical Quarterly* 28 (June 1944): 63.

78. Hardesty, "The Best Temperance Organization in the Land," 191–92.

79. William C. Sibley, a cotton mill owner, had also entered into third-party politics, running on the Prohibition Party ticket in 1892 with Henry Scomp.

80. Warren A. Candler, "Endangering the Church and the Temperance Cause," *Wesleyan Christian Advocate*, May 10, 1893, 2.

81. Henry A. Scomp, "A Card from Professor Scomp, He Replies to a Recent Communication from Bishop Haygood," clipping from unnamed newspaper, box 110:2, Candler Collection.

82. S. E. Sibley, "Candler Persecuted Scomp," undated *Voice* newspaper clipping, box 110:2, Candler Collection.

83. W. W. Evans to Warren A. Candler, February 15, 1894, Candler Collection.

84. J. William Jones, "Does 'Prohibition' Necessarily Mean 'Third Party'?" *Baptist and Reflector,* December 18, 1890, 3.

85. A. B. Cabaniss, "Dr. J. M. Pendleton's Prophecy," *Baptist and Reflector,* October 9, 1890, 6.

86. Quoted in L. B. Searle, "The Prohibition War," *Baptist and Reflector,* December 12, 1889, 2.

87. Marjorie Spruill Wheeler, *New Women of the New South: The Leaders of the Woman Suffrage Movement in the Southern States* (New York: Oxford University Press, 1993), 4.

88. Editorial, "Woman's Place in American Culture," *Alabama Christian Advocate,* August 23, 1888, 4.

89. Editorial, "The Discovery of Women," *Christian Index,* August 18, 1892, 4.

90. Editorial, "A Live Question," *Wesleyan Christian Advocate,* February 4, 1891, 1.

91. Quoted in John Howard Burrows, "The Great Disturber: The Social Philosophy of Alfred James Dickinson" (master's thesis, Samford University, 1970), 86.

92. G. P. Keyes, "Woman Suffrage," *Alabama Christian Advocate,* April 12, 1888, 1.

93. Editorial, "'Scourge the Preachers Back to the Pulpit,' and the Women Back to the Kitchen," *Alabama Christian Advocate,* September 15, 1887, 4.

94. Editorial, "A Live Question," 1.

95. J. W. Willis, "The New Woman," *Alabama Baptist,* August 29, 1895, 1. Willis added the warning, "Those preachers who preach against the 'new woman' had better watch out or they will get hit with a 'bloomerang,' which is a thousand times worse than a boomerang."

96. W. A. McCarty, "Woman Suffrage," *Alabama Christian Advocate,* March 22, 1888, 1.

97. Editorial, "A Live Question," 1.

98. Candler to Sibley, May 2, 1892.

99. Candler, "Endangering the Church," 2.

100. Job Harral, "Prohibition the Safety of the People," *Baptist* (Memphis), April 14, 1888, 4.

101. Lerda, "The Woman's Christian Temperance Union Reform Movement in the South," 171.

102. Keyes, "Woman Suffrage," 1.

103. McCarty, "Woman Suffrage," 1.

104. McCarty, "The Prohibition Party," 1.

105. McCarty, "Woman Suffrage," 1.

106. Candler to Sibley, May 2, 1892.

107. Editorial, "How Error Grows," *Christian Index,* July 21, 1892, 4.

108. Floyd, "Rebecca Latimer Felton," 84.

109. J. Wayne Flynt, *Alabama Baptists: Southern Baptists in the Heart of Dixie* (Tuscaloosa: University of Alabama Press, 1998), 178–79.

110. James Douglas Anderson to "The Members of the General Conference, M. E. Church, South," n.d., James Douglas Anderson Collection, Tennessee State Library and Archives, Nashville.

111. Editorial, "Woman Suffrage," *Alabama Christian Advocate*, June 21, 1888, 4.

112. Layman, "Woman's Right," *Alabama Christian Advocate*, March 24, 1910, 3.

113. E. E. Hoss to James Anderson, [May] 23, 1918, Anderson Collection.

114. Editorial, "The Woman Question in the Northern Methodist Church," *Alabama Christian Advocate*, July 5, 1888, 4.

115. For examples, see the front page of the *Alabama Baptist*, September 18, 1907, and September 8, 1909, and Bordin, *Woman and Temperance*, 80.

116. Wheeler, *New Women of the New South*, 5–8.

Conclusion

1. Ted Ownby, *Subduing Satan: Religion, Recreation, and Manhood in the Rural South, 1865–1920* (Chapel Hill: University of North Carolina Press, 1990), 210; Dewey W. Grantham, *Southern Progressivism: The Reconciliation of Progress and Tradition* (Knoxville: University of Tennessee Press, 1983).

2. See Gaines M. Foster, *Moral Reconstruction: Christian Lobbyists and the Federal Legislation of Morality, 1865–1920* (Chapel Hill: University of North Carolina Press, 2002).

3. John E. White, "Prohibition: The New Task and Opportunity of the South," *South Atlantic Quarterly* 7 (April 1908): 131.

4. John Samuel Ezell, *The South since 1865* (New York: Macmillan, 1963), 399.

5. Statewide limitations on the sale of alcohol remain as well. Today, Alabama state law still prohibits the sale of any beer with an alcohol volume greater than 6 percent or packaged in a container larger than one pint.

6. Jean Miller Schmidt, *Souls or the Social Order: The Two-Party System in American Protestantism* (Brooklyn, N.Y.: Carlson Publishing, 1991), 199.

7. Mark A. Noll, *The Old Religion in a New World: The History of North American Christianity* (Grand Rapids, Mich.: Eerdmans, 2002), 135.

8. Jeanette Keith, *Country People in the New South: Tennessee's Upper Cumberland* (Chapel Hill: University of North Carolina Press, 1995), 2.

9. George M. Marsden, *Fundamentalism and American Culture: The Shaping of Twentieth-Century Evangelicalism, 1870–1925* (New York: Oxford University Press, 1982), 185.

10. Edward Larson, *Summer for the Gods: The Scopes Trial and America's Continuing Debate over Science and Religion* (New York: Basic Books, 1997), 230, 250–53, notes that antievolution bills such as Tennessee's were almost nonexistent in the North. Despite the best efforts of fundamentalists, bills prohibiting the teaching of evolution almost invariably failed to pass in northern states. In the South, however, antievolution bills flourished both before and after Scopes. Even though conventional wisdom holds that the trial spelled the end

of such legislation, southern states and municipalities continued to restrict the teaching of evolution. Tennessee's "Monkey Law" was not repealed until 1967, and then not without considerable resistance.

11. Charles Israel's excellent study of education in Tennessee reveals how evangelical involvement in public education developed alongside the campaign for prohibition, and how the two were intertwined efforts to shape the morals and behavior of rising generations of southerners. See Charles A. Israel, *Before Scopes: Evangelicalism, Education, and Evolution in Tennessee, 1870–1925* (Athens: University of Georgia Press, 2004), 91–96.

12. John Patrick Daly, *When Slavery Was Called Freedom: Evangelicalism, Proslavery, and the Causes of the Civil War* (Lexington: University Press of Kentucky, 2002), 152–53, argues that after the Civil War, the theology of southern evangelicals turned increasingly apocalyptic and otherworldly, and the optimism and faith in moral progress that characterized antebellum evangelicalism diminished. This growing disconnect between southern religion and the natural world—a "theology of diminished expectations," Daly calls it—meant that the rise of Darwinism was much less disturbing to southern evangelicals than it was to evangelicals elsewhere.

13. Unlike the antievolution sentiment of the 1920s, the long-held prohibition attitude of southern evangelicals and their political victories on that front are not connected to the larger national conflict between fundamentalism and modernism. The kind of legislation that led to Tennessee's Scopes trial stemmed in large part from conservatives' concern over what they viewed as the growing threat of godless modernism in American schools. As Paul Keith Conkin's monograph, *When All the Gods Trembled: Darwinism, Scopes, and American Intellectuals* (Lanham, Md.: Rowman and Littlefield, 2001), 49, notes, "Only after World War I did a large body of Christians mobilize against the teaching of something called 'evolution' in the public schools."

14. Richard Hofstadter, *The Age of Reform: From Bryan to FDR* (New York: Vintage Books, 1955), 89–90. Likewise, Dewey Grantham, in *The Life and Death of the Solid South: A Political History* (Lexington: University Press of Kentucky, 1998), 79–80, attributes the rise of prohibitionism in the South to the reactionary atmosphere of the 1910s, when "fears of social change" led southerners to reconstitute the Ku Klux Klan and embrace other means of coercing racial solidarity. But in doing so, Grantham ignores the preceding three decades of prohibition activity by southerners and their long background of prohibition agitation.

15. For more on prohibitionism as a legitimate facet of progressivism, see James H. Timberlake, *Prohibition and the Progressive Movement 1900–1920* (Cambridge, Mass.: Harvard University Press, 1963).

Bibliography

Andrews, Dee E. *The Methodists and Revolutionary America, 1760–1800: The Shaping of an Evangelical Culture.* Princeton, N.J.: Princeton University Press, 2000.

Ansley, Lula Barnes. *History of the Georgia Woman's Christian Temperance Union: From Its Organization, 1883–1907.* Columbus, Ga.: Bilbert Printing, 1914.

Appleby, Joyce. "Reconciliation and the Northern Novelist, 1865–1880." *Civil War History* 10 (June 1964): 117–29.

Aptheker, Herbert. "John Brown and Heman Humphrey: An Unpublished Letter." *Journal of Negro History* 52 (July 1967): 220–27.

Arnett, Alex Mathews. *The Populist Movement in Georgia: A View of the "Agrarian Crusade" in the Light of Solid-South Politics.* New York: Longmans, Green, 1922.

Ayers, Edward L. *The Promise of the New South: Life after Reconstruction.* New York: Oxford University Press, 1992.

———. *Vengeance and Justice: Crime and Punishment in the Nineteenth-Century American South.* New York: Oxford University Press, 1984.

Bailey, Hugh C. *Liberalism in the New South: Southern Social Reformers and the Progressive Movement.* Coral Gables, Fla.: University of Miami Press, 1969.

Bailey, Kenneth K. "Southern White Protestantism at the Turn of the Century." *American Historical Review* 68 (April 1963): 618–35.

Banner, Lois W. "Religious Benevolence as Social Control: A Critique of an Interpretation." *Journal of American History* 60 (June 1973): 23–41.

Barnes, William Wright. *The Southern Baptist Convention 1845–1953.* Nashville: Broadman, 1954.

Barney, William L. *The Secessionist Impulse: Alabama and Mississippi in 1860.* Princeton, N.J.: Princeton University Press, 1974.

Bauerlein, Mark. *Negrophobia: A Race Riot in Atlanta, 1906.* San Francisco: Encounter Books, 2001.

Bauman, Mark K. "Prohibition and Politics: Warren Candler and Al

Smith's 1928 Campaign." *Mississippi Quarterly* 31 (winter 1977–1978): 109–18.

———. *Warren A. Candler: The Conservative as Idealist.* Metuchen, N.J.: Scarecrow Press, 1981.

Bederman, Gail. "'The Women Have Had Charge of the Church Work Long Enough': The Men and Religion Forward Movement of 1911–1912 and the Masculinization of Middle-Class Protestantism." *American Quarterly* 41 (September 1989): 432–65.

Berger, Peter L., Brigitte Berger, and Hansfried Kellner. *The Homeless Mind: Modernization and Consciousness.* New York: Vintage Books, 1973.

Berkley, Holly. "From Self-Made Men to Crusading Women: The Gendered Evolution of the American Temperance Movement in the Nineteenth Century." Ph.D. diss., University of Oklahoma, 2004.

Berthoff, Rowland. "Celtic Mist over the South." *Journal of Southern History* 52 (November 1986): 523–46.

———. "[Celtic Mist over the South]: A Rejoinder." *Journal of Southern History* 52 (November 1986): 548–50.

Berthoff, Rowland, Forrest McDonald, Grady McWhiney, et al. "Comparative History in Theory and Practice: A Discussion." *American Historical Review* 87 (February 1982): 131–37.

Binger, Carl A. L. *Revolutionary Doctor: Benjamin Rush, 1746–1813.* New York: Norton, 1966.

Blassingame, John W. "Sambos and Rebels: The Character of the Southern Slave." In *Historical Judgments Reconsidered: Selected Howard University Lectures in Honor of Rayford W. Logan,* ed. Genna Rae McNeil and Michael R. Winston, 57–71. Washington, D.C.: Howard University Press, 1988.

———. *The Slave Community: Plantation Life in the Antebellum South,* rev. ed. New York: Oxford University Press, 1979.

Blocker, Jack S., Jr. *American Temperance Movements: Cycles of Reform.* Boston: Twayne Publishers, 1989.

———. *Retreat from Reform: The Prohibition Movement in the United States 1890–1913.* Westport, Conn.: Greenwood Press, 1976.

Bode, Frederick A. "The Formation of Evangelical Communities in Middle Georgia: Twiggs County, 1820–1861." *Journal of Southern Religion* 60 (November 1994): 711–48.

———. *Protestantism and the New South: North Carolina Baptists and Methodists in Political Crisis, 1894–1903.* Charlottesville: University of Virginia Press, 1975.

———. "Religion and Class Hegemony: A Populist Critique in North Carolina." *Journal of Southern History* 37 (August 1971): 417–38.

Boles, John B. "Evangelical Protestantism in the Old South: From Religious Dissent to Cultural Dominance." In *Religion in the South*, ed. Charles Reagan Wilson, 13–34. Jackson: University Press of Mississippi, 1985.

———. *The Irony of Southern Religion*. New York: Peter Lang, 1994.

Bordin, Ruth. "Frances Willard and the Practice of Political Influence." *Hayes Historical Journal* 5 (1985): 18–28.

———. *Woman and Temperance: The Quest for Power and Liberty, 1873–1900*. New Brunswick, N.J.: Rutgers University Press, 1990.

Bowers, Teresa Barham. "From the Pews to the Polls: Protestants and Prohibition in Mobile, Alabama, 1880–1910." Master's thesis, University of South Alabama, 1995.

Breitenbach, William. "Sons of the Fathers: Temperance Reformers and the Legacy of the American Revolution." *Journal of the Early Republic* 3 (spring 1983): 69–82.

Bruce, Steve. *God Is Dead: Secularization in the West*. Malden, Mass.: Blackwell, 2002.

Brundage, W. Fitzhugh. Introduction to *Under Sentence of Death: Lynching in the South*, ed. W. Fitzhugh Brundage. Chapel Hill: University of North Carolina Press, 1997.

———. *Lynching in the New South: Georgia and Virginia, 1880–1930*. Urbana: University of Illinois Press, 1993.

Bryan, Ferald J. *Henry Grady or Tom Watson: The Rhetorical Struggle for the New South, 1880–1890*. Macon, Ga.: Mercer University Press, 1994.

Burns, Eric. *The Spirits of America: A Social History of Alcohol*. Philadelphia: Temple University Press, 2004.

Burrows, John Howard. "The Great Disturber: The Social Philosophy of Alfred James Dickinson." Master's thesis, Samford University, 1970.

Buss, Dietrich. "The Millennial Vision as Motive for Religious Benevolence and Reform: Timothy Dwight and the New England Evangelicals Reconsidered." *Fides et Historia* 16 (fall–winter 1983): 18–34.

Camhi, Jane. *Women against Women: American Anti-Suffragism, 1880–1920*. New York: Carlson, 1994.

Candler, Warren A. *Bishop Charles Betts Galloway: A Prince of Preachers and a Christian Statesman*. Nashville: Cokesbury Press, 1927.

Carlson, Douglas W. "'Drinks He to His Own Undoing': Temperance Ideology in the Deep South." *Journal of the Early Republic* 18 (winter 1998): 659–91.

———. "Temperance Reform in the Cotton Kingdom." Ph.D. diss., University of Illinois at Urbana-Champaign, 1982.

Cartwright, Joseph H. *The Triumph of Jim Crow: Tennessee Race Relations in the 1880s*. Knoxville: University of Tennessee Press, 1976.

Cash, Wilbur J. *The Mind of the South*. New York: Vintage Books, 1941.

Cell, John W. *The Highest Stage of White Supremacy: The Origins of Segregation in South Africa and the American South.* Cambridge: Cambridge University Press, 1982.

Chapman, James. "Alabama Baptist Biographies, 1910–1925." James Chapman Papers, Southern Baptist Historical Library and Archives, Nashville, Tenn.

Chazanof, William. *Welch's Grape Juice: From Corporation to Co-operative.* Syracuse, N.Y.: Syracuse University Press, 1977.

Clanton, Gene. *Populism: The Humane Preference in America, 1890–1900.* Boston: Twayne Publishers, 1991.

Clark, John B. *Populism in Alabama.* Auburn, Ala.: Auburn Printing, 1927.

Clark, Norman H. *Deliver Us from Evil: An Interpretation of American Prohibition.* New York: Norton, 1976.

Coker, Joe L. "The Sinnott Case of 1910: The Changing Views of Southern Presbyterians on Temperance, Prohibition, and the Spirituality of the Church." *Journal of Presbyterian History* 77 (winter 1999): 247–62.

———. "Sweet Harmony vs. Strict Separation: Recognizing the Distinctions between Isaac Backus and John Leland." *American Baptist Quarterly* 16 (September 1997): 241–50.

Colvin, David Leigh. *Prohibition in the United States: A History of the Prohibition Party, and of the Prohibition Movement.* New York: George H. Doran, 1926.

Conkin, Paul Keith. *When All the Gods Trembled: Darwinism, Scopes, and American Intellectuals.* Lanham, Md.: Rowman and Littlefield, 2001.

Cotterill, Robert S. "The Old South and the New." In *Myth and Southern History*, ed. Patrick Gerster and Nicholas Cords, 171–76. Chicago: Rand McNally, 1974.

Coulter, E. Merton. *William G. Brownlow: Fighting Parson of the Southern Highlands.* Knoxville: University of Tennessee Press, 1937.

Crider, Robert F. "The Social Philosophy of L. L. Gwaltney, 1919–1950." Master's thesis, Samford University, 1969.

Crowley, John G. *Primitive Baptists of the Wiregrass South: 1815 to the Present.* Gainesville: University Presses of Florida, 1998.

Crowther, Edward R. "Holy Honor: Sacred and Secular in the Old South." *Journal of Southern History* 58 (November 1992): 619–36.

Cummings, Diana. "Peculiar Feminism: The Georgia Woman's Temperance Union." http://www.sip.armstrong.edu/WCTU/essay.html (accessed July 18, 2007).

Curriden, Mark, and Leroy Phillips, Jr. *Contempt of Court: The Turn-of-the-Century Lynching That Launched a Hundred Years of Federalism.* New York: Faber and Faber, 1999.

Dabbs, James McBride. *Haunted by God: The Cultural and Religious Experience of the South.* Richmond, Va.: John Knox Press, 1972.

Dabney, Virginius. *Liberalism in the South.* New York: AMS Press, 1932.

Dailey, Jane. "Deference and Violence in the Postbellum Urban South: Manners and Massacres in Danville, Virginia." *Journal of Southern History* 63 (August 1997): 553–90.

Daly, John Patrick. *When Slavery Was Called Freedom: Evangelicalism, Proslavery, and the Causes of the Civil War.* Lexington: University Press of Kentucky, 2002.

Degler, Carl N. "Dawn without Noon: The Myths of Reconstruction." In *Myth and Southern History,* ed. Patrick Gerster and Nicholas Cords, 155–69. Chicago: Rand McNally, 1974.

———. *The Other South: Southern Dissenters in the Nineteenth Century.* New York: Harper and Row, 1974.

Dittmer, John. *Black Georgia in the Progressive Era, 1900–1920.* Urbana: University of Illinois Press, 1977.

Doherty, Herbert J., Jr. "Voices of Protest from the New South, 1875–1910." *Mississippi Valley Historical Review* 42 (June 1955): 45–66.

Donald, David Herbert, Jean H. Baker, and Michael F. Holt. *The Civil War and Reconstruction.* New York: Norton, 2001.

Dunlap, Leslie Kathrin. "In the Name of the Home: Temperance Women and Southern Grass-Roots Politics, 1873–1933." Ph.D. diss., Northwestern University, 2001.

Duren, William Larkin. *Charles Betts Galloway: Orator, Preacher, and "Prince of Christian Chivalry."* Atlanta: Emory University, Banner Press, 1932.

Eaton, Clement. *The Waning of the Old South Civilization, 1860–1880s.* Athens: University of Georgia Press, 1968.

Edwards, Lawrence. *The Baptists of Tennessee, with Particular Attention to the Primitive Baptists of East Tennessee.* N.p.: 1940.

Eighmy, John Lee. *Churches in Cultural Captivity: A History of the Social Attitudes of Southern Baptists,* rev. ed. Knoxville: University of Tennessee Press, 1987.

Elkins, Stanley M. *Slavery: A Problem in American Institutional and Intellectual Life,* 3rd ed. Chicago: University of Chicago Press, 1976.

Ellison, Ralph. "The World and the Jug." In *Shadow and Act,* 107–43. New York: Random House, 1964.

English, Carl Dean. "The Ethical Emphasis of the Editors of Baptist Journals Published in the Southeastern Region of the United States, 1865–1915." Th.D. thesis, Southern Baptist Theological Seminary, 1948.

Epstein, Barbara Leslie. *The Politics of Domesticity: Women, Evangelism, and Temperance in Nineteenth-Century America.* Middletown, Conn.: Wesleyan University Press, 1981.

Eskew, Glenn T. "Black Elitism and the Failure of Paternalism in Postbellum Georgia: The Case of Bishop Lucius Henry Holsey." *Journal of Southern History* 58 (November 1992): 637–66.

Eubanks, John Evans. *Ben Tillman's Baby: The Dispensary System of South Carolina 1892–1915.* N.p.: 1950.

Ezell, John Samuel. *The South since 1865.* New York: Macmillan, 1963.

Fahey, David N. *Temperance and Racism: John Bull, Johnny Reb, and the Good Templars.* Lexington: University Press of Kentucky, 1996.

Faries, Clyde J. "Carmack vs. Patterson: The Genesis of a Political Feud." *Tennessee Historical Quarterly* 38 (fall 1979): 332–47.

Farish, Hunter Dickinson. *The Circuit Rider Dismounts: A Social History of Southern Methodism 1865–1900.* Richmond, Va.: Dietz Press, 1938.

Farmer, James O. *The Metaphysical Confederacy: James Henley Thornwell and the Synthesis of Southern Values.* Macon, Ga.: Mercer University Press, 1986.

Ferrell, Henry C., Jr. "Prohibition, Reform, and Politics in Virginia, 1895–1916." *Studies in the History of the South, 1875–1922* 3 (1966): 175–242.

Fischer, David Hackett. *Albion's Seed: Four British Folkways in America.* New York: Oxford University Press, 1989.

Fitzgerald, Oscar Penn. *John B. McFerrin: Biography.* Nashville: Publishing House of the Methodist Episcopal Church, South, 1888.

Fleming, Walter L. *The Churches of Alabama during the Civil War and Reconstruction.* Montgomery, Ala.: W. M. Rogers, 1902.

———. *Civil War and Reconstruction in Alabama.* New York: Columbia University Press, 1905.

Floyd, Josephine Bone. "Rebecca Latimer Felton, Champion of Women's Rights." *Georgia Historical Quarterly* 30 (June 1946): 81–104.

Flynt, J. Wayne. "Alabama." In *Religion in the Southern States: A Historical Study,* ed. Samuel S. Hill, 5–26. Macon, Ga.: Mercer University Press, 1983.

———. *Alabama Baptists: Southern Baptists in the Heart of Dixie.* Tuscaloosa: University of Alabama Press, 1998.

———. *Alabama in the Twentieth Century.* Tuscaloosa: University of Alabama Press, 2004.

———. "Dissent in Zion: Alabama Baptists and Social Issues, 1900–1914." *Journal of Southern History* 35 (November 1969): 523–42.

———. *Introduction to the 1901 Alabama Constitution.* http://accr.constitutional reform.org/symposium/1901flint.html (accessed July 18, 2007).

Foner, Eric. *A Short History of Reconstruction, 1863–1877.* New York: Harper and Row, 1990.

Foster, Charles I. *An Errand of Mercy: The Evangelical United Front, 1790–1837.* Chapel Hill: University of North Carolina Press, 1960.

Foster, Gaines M. *Ghosts of the Confederacy: Defeat, the Lost Cause, and the Emergence of the New South, 1865–1913.* New York: Oxford University Press, 1987.

———. *Moral Reconstruction: Christian Lobbyists and the Federal Legislation of Morality, 1865–1920.* Chapel Hill: University of North Carolina Press, 2002.

Fredrickson, George M. *The Black Image in the White Mind: The Debate on Afro-American Character and Destiny, 1817–1914.* New York: Harper and Row, 1971.

Friedman, Jean. *The Enclosed Garden: Women and Community in the Evangelical South, 1830–1900.* Chapel Hill: University of North Carolina Press, 1985.

Friedman, Lawrence J. *The White Savage: Racial Fantasies in the Postbellum South.* Englewood Cliffs, N.J.: Prentice-Hall, 1970.

Frost, Dan R. *Thinking Confederates: Academia and the Idea of Progress in the New South.* Knoxville: University of Tennessee Press, 2000.

Fry, Michael. *How the Scots Made America.* New York: Thomas Dunne Books, 2005.

Fuller, Robert C. *Religion and Wine: A Cultural History of Wine Drinking in the United States.* Knoxville: University of Tennessee Press, 1996.

Gaines, Francis Pendleton. *The Southern Plantation: A Study in the Development and the Accuracy of a Tradition.* Gloucester, Mass.: Peter Smith, 1962.

Gardner, David M. "J. B. Gambrell." *Baptist Training Union Magazine* (March 1945): 5–6, 20.

Gaston, Paul M. *The New South Creed: A Study in Southern Mythmaking.* New York: Knopf, 1970.

———. "The New South Creed: A Study in Southern Mythmaking." In *Myth and Southern History: The New South,* ed. Patrick Gerster and Nicholas Cords, 49–64. Chicago: Rand McNally, 1974.

Genovese, Eugene D. *Roll, Jordan, Roll: The World the Slaves Made.* New York: Pantheon Books, 1974.

———. *The Southern Front: History and Politics in the Cultural War.* Columbia: University of Missouri Press, 1995.

George, Timothy. "Southern Baptist Ghosts." *First Things* (May 1999): 17–24.

Giele, Janet Zollinger. *Two Paths to Women's Equality: Temperance, Suffrage, and the Origins of Modern Feminism.* New York: Twayne Publishers, 1995.

Gifford, Carolyn DeSwarte. "For God and Home and Native Land: The WCTU's Image of Woman in the Late Nineteenth Century." In *Women in New Worlds: Historical Perspectives on the Wesleyan Tradition,* ed. Hilah F. Thomas and Rosemary Skinner Keller, 310–27. Nashville: Abingdon Press, 1981.

Gill, Sean. "How Muscular Was Victorian Christianity: Thomas Hughes and the Cult of Christian Manliness Reconsidered." In *Gender and Christian Religion: Papers Read at the 1996 Summer Meeting and the 1997 Winter Meeting of the Ecclesiological History Society*, ed. R. N. Swanson, 421–30. N.p.: Boydell Press, 1998.

Going, Allen Johnston. *Bourbon Democracy in Alabama, 1874–1890*. Tuscaloosa: University of Alabama Press, 1992.

Goldfield, David R. *Still Fighting the Civil War: The American South and Southern History*. Baton Rouge: Louisiana State University Press, 2002.

Goodwyn, Lawrence. *Democratic Promise: The Populist Moment in America*. New York: Oxford University Press, 1976.

Gorn, Elliott J. "'Gouge and Bite, Pull Hair and Scratch': The Social Significance of Fighting in the Southern Backcountry." *American Historical Review* 90 (February 1985): 18–43.

Grantham, Dewey W. "The Contours of Southern Progressivism." *American Historical Review* 86 (December 1981): 1035–59.

———. *Hoke Smith and the Politics of the New South*. Baton Rouge: Louisiana State University Press, 1958.

———. *The Life and Death of the Solid South: A Political History*. Lexington: University Press of Kentucky, 1998.

———. *Southern Progressivism: The Reconciliation of Progress and Tradition*. Knoxville: University of Tennessee Press, 1983.

Green, Elna. "'Ideals of Government, of Home, and of Women': The Ideology of Southern White Antisuffragism." In *Hidden Histories of Women in the New South*, ed. Virginia Bernhard, Elizabeth Fox-Genovese, et al., 96–113. Columbia: University of Missouri Press, 1994.

Greenberg, Kenneth S. *Honor and Slavery: Lies, Duels, Noses, Masks, Dressing as a Woman, Gifts, Strangers, Humanitarianism, Death, Slave Rebellions, the Proslavery Argument, Baseball, Hunting, and Gambling in the Old South*. Princeton, N.J.: Princeton University Press, 1996.

Gstohl, Mark, and Michael Homan. "Jesus the Teetotaler: How Dr. Welch Put the Lord on the Wagon." *Bible Review* 18 (April 2002): 28–29.

Gusfield, Joseph R. *Symbolic Crusade: Status Politics and the American Temperance Movement*, 2nd ed. Urbana: University of Illinois Press, 1986.

Hackney, Sheldon. *Populism to Progressivism in Alabama*. Princeton, N.J.: Princeton University Press, 1969.

Hadden, Jeffrey K. "Desacralizing the Secularization Theory." In *Secularization and Fundamentalism Reconsidered*, ed. Jeffrey K. Hadden and Anson Shupe, 3–26. New York: Paragon House, 1989.

Hahn, Steven. *The Roots of Southern Populism: Yeoman Farmers and the Transformation of the Georgia Upcountry, 1850–1890.* New York: Oxford University Press, 1983.

Hamm, Richard F. "The Killing of John R. Moffett and the Trial of J. T. Clark: Race, Prohibition, and Politics in Danville, 1887–1893." *Virginia Magazine of History and Biography* 101 (July 1993): 375–404.

———. *Murder, Honor, and Law: Four Virginia Homicides from Reconstruction to the Great Depression.* Charlottesville: University of Virginia Press, 2003.

———. *Shaping the Eighteenth Amendment: Temperance Reform, Legal Culture, and the Polity, 1880–1920.* Chapel Hill: University of North Carolina Press, 1995.

———. "Southerners and the Shaping of the Eighteenth Amendment, 1914–1917." *Georgia Journal of Southern Legal History* 1 (spring–summer 1991): 81–107.

Hardesty, Nancy A. "'The Best Temperance Organization in the Land': Southern Methodists and the WCTU in Georgia." *Methodist History* 28 (April 1990): 187–94.

Harrell, David E., Jr. "Tennessee." In *Religion in the Southern States: A Historical Study,* ed. Samuel S. Hill, 289–312. Macon, Ga.: Mercer University Press, 1983.

Harris, Carl V. *Political Power in Birmingham, 1871–1921.* Knoxville: University of Tennessee Press, 1977.

———. "Reforms in Government Control of Negroes in Birmingham, Alabama, 1890–1920." *Journal of Southern History* 38 (November 1972): 567–600.

Hart, Roger L. *Redeemers, Bourbons and Populists: Tennessee 1870–1896.* Baton Rouge: Louisiana State University Press, 1975.

Harvey, Paul. *Redeeming the South: Religious Cultures and Racial Identities among Southern Baptists, 1865–1925.* Chapel Hill: University of North Carolina Press, 1997.

Haynes, Stephen R. *Noah's Curse: The Biblical Justification of American Slavery.* New York: Oxford University Press, 2002.

Hill, Samuel S. "The South's Two Cultures." In *Religion and the Solid South,* ed. Samuel S. Hill, 24–56. Nashville: Abingdon, 1972.

———. *Southern Churches in Crisis.* New York: Holt, Rinehart and Winston, 1966.

Hilten, Robert L. *Pillar of Fire: The Drama of Holston United Methodism in a Changing World.* Johnson City, Tenn.: Commission on Archives and History, Holston Conference of the United Methodist Church, 1994.

Hofstadter, Richard. *The Age of Reform: From Bryan to FDR.* New York: Vintage Books, 1955.

Holifield, E. Brooks. *The Gentlemen Theologians: American Theology in Southern Culture 1795–1860.* Durham, N.C.: Duke University Press, 1978.

Holmes, William F. "Moonshining and Collective Violence: Georgia, 1889–1895." *American History* 67 (December 1980): 589–611.

Hyman, Michael R. *The Anti-Redeemers: Hill-Country Political Dissenters in the Lower South from Redemption to Populism.* Baton Rouge: Louisiana State University Press, 1990.

Isaac, Paul E. *Prohibition and Politics: Turbulent Decades in Tennessee 1885–1920.* Knoxville: University of Tennessee Press, 1965.

Isaac, Rhys. *The Transformation of Virginia, 1740–1790.* Chapel Hill: University of North Carolina Press, 1982.

Israel, Charles A. *Before Scopes: Evangelicalism, Education, and Evolution in Tennessee, 1870–1925.* Athens: University of Georgia Press, 2004.

Ivy, James D. *No Saloon in the Valley: The Southern Strategy of Texas Prohibitionists in the 1880s.* Waco, Tex.: Baylor University Press, 2003.

Jackson, Harvey H. "The Middle-Class Democracy Victorious: The Mitcham War of Clarke County, Alabama, 1893." *Journal of Southern History* 57 (August 1991): 453–78.

Johnson, Guion Griffis. *Ante-Bellum North Carolina: A Social History.* Chapel Hill: University of North Carolina Press, 1937.

Jones, Bartlett C. "Prohibition and Christianity, 1920–1933." *Journal of Religious Thought* 19 (1962–1963): 39–57.

Jones, Donald G. *The Sectional Crisis and Northern Methodism: A Study in Piety, Political Ethics, and Civil Religion.* Metuchen, N.J.: Scarecrow Press, 1979.

Jones, Terry Lawrence. "Attitudes of Alabama Baptists toward Negroes, 1890–1914." Master's thesis, Samford University, 1968.

Keith, Jeanette. *Country People in the New South: Tennessee's Upper Cumberland.* Chapel Hill: University of North Carolina Press, 1995.

Kerr, K. Austin. *Organized for Prohibition: A New History of the Anti-Saloon League.* New Haven, Conn.: Yale University Press, 1985.

Kiger, Joseph Charles. "Social Thought as Voiced in Rural Middle Tennessee Newspapers, 1878–1898." Ph.D. diss., Vanderbilt University, 1950.

Kirby, Jack Temple. *Darkness at the Dawning: Race and Reform in the Progressive South.* Philadelphia: Lippincott, 1972.

Kloos, John M. *A Sense of Deity: The Republican Spirituality of Dr. Benjamin Rush.* Brooklyn, N.Y.: Carlson, 1991.

Kobler, John. *Ardent Spirits: The Rise and Fall of Prohibition.* New York: G. P. Putnam's Sons, 1973.

Kousser, J. Morgan. *The Shaping of Southern Politics: Suffrage Restrictions and the Establishment of the One-Party South, 1880–1910.* New Haven, Conn.: Yale University Press, 1974.

Kuykendall, John W. *Southern Enterprize: The Work of National Evangelical Societies in the Antebellum South.* Westport, Conn.: Greenwood Press, 1982.

Lacy, Eric Russell. "Tennessee Teetotalism: Social Forces and the Politics of Progressivism." *Tennessee Historical Quarterly* 24 (fall 1965): 219–41.

Lambert, Byron Cecil. *The Rise of the Anti-Mission Baptists: Sources and Leaders, 1800–1840.* New York: Arno Press, 1980.

Lanier, Martha Louise. "Alabama Methodists and Social Issues, 1900–1914." Master's thesis, Samford University, 1969.

Larson, Edward J. *Summer for the Gods: The Scopes Trial and America's Continuing Debate over Science and Religion.* New York: Basic Books, 1997.

Lazenby, Marion Elias. *History of Methodism in Alabama and West Florida.* N.p.: 1960.

Leab, Grace. "Tennessee Temperance Activities, 1870–1899." *East Tennessee Historical Society's Publications* 21 (1949): 52–68.

Lennon, K. C. "'That Which Is Morally Wrong . . . ': A Historical Survey of the Attitudes of North Carolina Southern Baptists toward Beverage Alcohol, 1845–1988." Th.M. thesis, Southeastern Baptist Theological Seminary, 1988.

Leonard, Bill J. *Baptist Ways: A History.* Valley Forge, Pa.: Judson Press, 2003.

Lerda, Valeria Gennaro. "The Woman's Christian Temperance Union Reform Movement in the South in the Late Nineteenth Century." In *Religious and Secular Reform in America: Ideas, Beliefs, and Social Change,* ed. David K. Adams and Cornelis A. Van Minnen, 159–78. Edinburgh: Edinburgh University Press, 1999.

Lindley, Susan Hill. *"You Have Stept out of Your Place": A History of Women and Religion in America.* Louisville, Ky.: Westminster John Knox Press, 1996.

Link, Arthur S. "The Progressive Movement in the South, 1870–1914." In *Myth and Southern History: The New South,* ed. Patrick Gerster and Nicholas Cords, 65–86. Chicago: Rand McNally, 1974.

Link, William A. *The Paradox of Southern Progressivism, 1880–1930.* Chapel Hill: University of North Carolina Press, 1992.

Little, Thomas J. "The Origins of Southern Evangelicalism: Revivalism in South Carolina, 1700–1740." *Church History* 75 (December 2006): 768–808.

Litwack, Leon F. *Trouble in Mind: Black Southerners in the Age of Jim Crow.* New York: Knopf, 1998.

Logan, Rayford W. *The Negro in American Life and Thought: The Nadir, 1877–1901.* New York: Dial Press, 1954.

Loveland, Anne C. *Southern Evangelicals and the Social Order 1800–1860.* Baton Rouge: Louisiana State University Press, 1980.

Luker, Ralph E. *The Social Gospel in Black and White: American Racial Reform, 1885–1912.* Chapel Hill: University of North Carolina Press, 1991.

Lyon, Ralph M. *Julia Tutwiler.* Livingston, Ala.: Alabama-Tombigbee Rivers Regional Planning and Development Commission, 1976.

Maddex, Jack P. "From Theocracy to Spirituality: The Southern Presbyterian Reversal on Church and State." *Journal of Presbyterian History* 54 (winter 1976): 438–57.

Majors, William R. *Change and Continuity: Tennessee Politics since the Civil War.* Macon, Ga.: Mercer University Press, 1986.

———. *Editorial Wild Oats: Edward Ward Carmack and Tennessee Politics.* Macon, Ga.: Mercer University Press, 1984.

Mallary, Charles Dutton. *Memoirs of Elder Jesse Mercer.* New York: John Gray, 1844.

Mann, Harold W. *Atticus Greene Haygood: Methodist Bishop, Editor, and Educator.* Athens: University of Georgia Press, 1965.

Marsden, George M. *Fundamentalism and American Culture: The Shaping of Twentieth-Century Evangelicalism, 1870–1925.* New York: Oxford University Press, 1982.

Martin, Isaac Patton. *Methodism in Holston.* Nashville: Parthenon Press, 1945.

Mathews, Donald G. "'Christianizing the South'—Sketching a Synthesis." In *New Directions in American Religious History,* ed. Harry S. Stout and D. G. Hart, 84–115. New York: Oxford University Press, 1997.

———. "Lynching Is Part of the Religion of Our People: Faith in the Christian South." In *Religion in the American South: Protestants and Others in History and Culture,* ed. Beth Barton Schweiger and Donald G. Mathews, 153–94. Chapel Hill: University of North Carolina Press, 2004.

———. *Religion in the Old South.* Chicago: University of Chicago Press, 1977.

Mathis, James R. *The Making of the Primitive Baptists: A Cultural and Intellectual History of the Antimission Movement, 1800–1840.* New York: Routledge, 2004.

Mathisen, Robert R. "Conflicting Southern Cultures, Social Christianity, and Samuel Porter Jones." *Fides et Historia* 25 (fall 1993): 66–76.

Matthews, Terry Lee. "The Emergence of a Prophet: Andrew Sledd and the 'Sledd Affair' of 1902." Ph.D. diss., Duke University, 1989.

———. "The Voice of a Prophet: Andrew Sledd Revisited." *Journal of*

Southern Religion 6 (2003). http://jsr.as.wvu.edu/2003/Matthews.pdf (accessed July 18, 2007).

McBeth, H. Leon. *The Baptist Heritage: Four Centuries of Baptist Witness.* Nashville: Broadman Press, 1987.

McDonald, Forrest, and Grady McWhiney. "The Antebellum Southern Herdsman: A Reinterpretation." *Journal of Southern History* 41 (May 1975): 147–66.

———. "[Celtic Mist over the South]: A Response." *Journal of Southern History* 52 (November 1986): 547–48.

———. "The Celtic South." *History Today* 30 (July 1980): 11–15.

McDowell, John Patrick. *The Social Gospel in the South: The Women's Home Mission Movement in the Methodist Episcopal Church, South, 1886–1939.* Baton Rouge: Louisiana State University Press, 1982.

McLoughlin, William G. "Jones vs. Jones." *American Heritage* 12 (April 1961): 56–59.

———. *Modern Revivalism: Charles Grandison Finney to Billy Graham.* New York: Ronald Press, 1959.

McMillan, Malcolm Cook. *Constitutional Development in Alabama, 1798–1901: A Study in Politics, the Negro, and Sectionalism.* Chapel Hill: University of North Carolina Press, 1955.

McPherson, James M. *The Abolitionist Legacy: From Reconstruction to the NAACP.* Princeton, N.J.: Princeton University Press, 1975.

———. *For Cause and Comrades: Why Men Fought in the Civil War.* New York: Oxford University Press, 1997.

McWhiney, Grady. *Cracker Culture: Celtic Ways in the Old South.* University, Ala.: University of Alabama Press, 1988.

Meier, August, and Elliott Rudwick. "A Strange Chapter in the Career of Jim Crow." In *The Making of Black America: Essays in Negro Life and History*, vol. 2, ed. August Meier and Elliott Rudwick, 14–19. New York: Atheneum, 1969.

Merrill, John L. "The Bible and the American Temperance Movement: Text, Context, and Pretext." *Harvard Theological Review* 81 (April 1988): 145–70.

Minnix, Kathleen. *Laughter in the Amen Corner: The Life of Evangelist Sam Jones.* Athens: University of Georgia Press, 1993.

———. "'That Memorable Meeting': Sam Jones and the Nashville Revival of 1885." *Tennessee Historical Quarterly* 48 (fall 1989): 151–61.

Mixon, Gregory L. "The Atlanta Riot of 1906." Ph.D. diss., University of Cincinnati, 1989.

Mixon, Wayne. "Georgia." In *Religion in the Southern States: A Historical Study*, ed. Samuel S. Hill, 77–100. Macon, Ga.: Mercer University Press, 1983.

Moore, Andrew S. "To Advance the Redeemer's Kingdom: East Tennessee Southern Baptists Amid Social and Cultural Transition, 1890–1929." Master's thesis, University of Tennessee, 1994.

Moore, John Hammond. "The Negro and Prohibition in Atlanta, 1885–1887." *South Atlantic Quarterly* 69 (winter 1970): 38–57.

Moorhead, James H. *American Apocalypse: Yankee Protestants and the Civil War 1860–1869.* New Haven, Conn.: Yale University Press, 1978.

Morone, James A. *Hellfire Nation: The Politics of Sin in American History.* New Haven, Conn.: Yale University Press, 2003.

Mulder, Philip N. *A Controversial Spirit: Evangelical Awakenings in the South.* Oxford: Oxford University Press, 2002.

Murdock, Catherine Gilbert. *Domesticating Drink: Women, Men, and Alcohol in America, 1870–1940.* Baltimore: Johns Hopkins University Press, 1998.

Myrdal, Gunnar. *An American Dilemma: The Negro Problem and Modern Democracy.* New York: Harper and Brothers, 1944.

Nisbett, Richard E., and Dov Cohen. *Culture of Honor: The Psychology of Violence in the South.* Boulder, Colo.: Westview Press, 1996.

Noll, Mark A. *The Old Religion in a New World: The History of North American Christianity.* Grand Rapids, Mich.: Wm. B. Eerdmans, 2002.

Norris, Pippa, and Ronald Inglehart. *Secular and Sacred: Religion and Politics Worldwide.* Cambridge: Cambridge University Press, 2004.

Norwood, Frederick A. *The Story of American Methodism: A History of the United Methodists and Their Relations.* Nashville: Abingdon Press, 1974.

Norwood, John Nelson. *The Schism in the Methodist Episcopal Church, 1844: A Study of Slavery and Ecclesiastical Politics.* Philadelphia: Porcupine Press, 1976.

Odegard, Peter H. *Pressure Politics: The Story of the Anti-Saloon League.* New York: Columbia University Press, 1928.

Ogle, Natalie N. "Brother against Brother: Baptists and Race in the Aftermath of the Civil War." *American Baptist Quarterly* 23 (June 2004): 137–54.

O'Neill, William L. *Everyone Was Brave: The Rise and Fall of Feminism in America.* Chicago: Quadrangle Books, 1969.

Our Heritage and Our Hope: Church Street Church, 1816–1966. N.p.: n.d.

Owen, Christopher H. *The Sacred Flame of Love: Methodism and Society in Nineteenth-Century Georgia.* Athens: University of Georgia Press, 1998.

————. "Sanctity, Slavery, and Segregation: Methodists and Society in Nineteenth-Century Georgia." Ph.D. diss., Emory University, 1991.

Ownby, Ted. *Subduing Satan: Religion, Recreation, and Manhood in the Rural*

South, 1865–1920. Chapel Hill: University of North Carolina Press, 1990.

Palmer, Bruce. *"Man over Money": The Southern Populist Critique of American Capitalism.* Chapel Hill: University of North Carolina Press, 1980.

Pannell, Anne Gary. *Julia S. Tutwiler and Social Progress in Alabama.* University, Ala.: University of Alabama Press, 1961.

Parker, David B. "'Quit Your Meanness': Sam Jones's Theology for the New South." *Georgia Historical Quarterly* 77 (winter 1993): 711–27.

Parker, Harold M., Jr. *The United Synod of the South: The Southern New School Presbyterian Church.* Westport, Conn.: Greenwood Press, 1988.

Parsons, Stanley B. *The Populist Context: Rural versus Urban Power on a Great Plains Frontier.* Westport, Conn.: Greenwood Press, 1978.

Pearson, C. C., and J. Edwin Hendricks. *Liquor and Anti-Liquor in Virginia, 1619–1919.* Durham, N.C.: Duke University Press, 1967.

Peffer, William A. *Populism: Its Rise and Fall.* Lawrence: University Press of Kansas, 1992.

Pegram, Thomas R. *Battling Demon Rum: The Struggle for a Dry America, 1800–1933.* Chicago: Ivan R. Dee, 1998.

———. "Temperance Politics and Regional Political Culture: The Anti-Saloon League in Maryland and the South, 1907–1915." *Journal of Southern History* 63 (February 1997): 57–90.

Perman, Michael. *Struggle for Mastery: Disfranchisement in the South, 1888–1908.* Chapel Hill: University of North Carolina Press, 2001.

Pierce, Alfred M. *Giant against the Sky: The Life of Bishop Warren A. Candler.* New York: Abingdon-Cokesbury Press, 1948.

Posey, Roger Dale. "Anti-Alcohol City: Social, Economic, and Political Aspects of Knoxville, Tennessee, 1870–1907." Master's thesis, University of Tennessee, 1982.

Pruitt, Paul M. "Joseph C. Manning, Alabama Populist: A Rebel against the Solid South." Ph.D. diss., College of William and Mary, 1980.

Putney, Clifford. *Muscular Christianity: Manhood and Sports in Protestant America, 1880–1920.* Cambridge, Mass.: Harvard University Press, 2001.

Quist, John W. "Slaveholding Operatives of the Benevolent Empire: Bible, Tract, and Sunday School Societies in Antebellum Tuscaloosa County, Alabama." *Journal of Southern History* 62 (August 1996): 481–526.

Ragsdale, B. D. *Story of Georgia Baptists: The Convention, Its Principles and Policies, Its Allies and Agencies, Its Aims and Its Achievements,* vol. 3. Atlanta: Executive Committee of the Georgia Baptist Convention, 1938.

Reed, Avery Hamilton. *Baptists in Alabama: Their Organization and Witness.* Montgomery: Alabama Baptist State Convention, 1967.

Reed, Ralph E., Jr. "Emory College and the Sledd Affair of 1902: A Case

Study in Southern Honor and Racial Attitudes." *Georgia Historical Quarterly* 72 (fall 1988): 463–92.

Robinson, William M., Jr. "Prohibition in the Confederacy." *American Historical Journal* 37 (October 1931): 50–58.

Roblyer, Leslie F. "The Fight for Local Prohibition in Knoxville, Tennessee, 1907." *East Tennessee Historical Society's Publications* 26 (1954): 27–37.

Roche, Roberta Senechal de la. "The Sociogenesis of Lynching." In *Under Sentence of Death: Lynching in the South*, ed. W. Fitzhugh Brundage, 48–76. Chapel Hill: University of North Carolina Press, 1997.

Rogers, William Warren, Robert David Ward, et al. *Alabama: The History of a Deep South State*. Tuscaloosa: University of Alabama Press, 1994.

———. *The One-Gallused Rebellion: Agrarianism in Alabama, 1865–1896*. Baton Rouge: Louisiana State University Press, 1970.

Rohrer, James H. "The Origins of the Temperance Movement: A Reinterpretation." *Journal of American Studies* 24 (August 1990): 228–35.

Rorabaugh, W. J. *The Alcoholic Republic: An American Tradition*. New York: Oxford University Press, 1979.

———. "Estimated U.S. Alcoholic Beverage Consumption, 1790–1860." *Journal of Studies on Alcohol* 37 (March 1976): 357–64.

Rumbarger, John R. *Profits, Power, and Prohibition: Alcohol Reform and the Industrialization of America, 1800–1930*. Albany: State University of New York Press, 1989.

Sack, Daniel. *Whitebread Protestants: Food and Religion in American Culture*. New York: St. Martin's Press, 2000.

Saunders, Robert. "Southern Populists and the Negro." In *Populism: The Critical Issues*, ed. Sheldon Hackney, 51–66. Boston: Little, Brown, 1971.

Schmidt, Jean Miller. *Souls or the Social Order: The Two-Party System in American Protestantism*. Brooklyn, N.Y.: Carlson Publishing, 1991.

Scott, Anne Firor. "A Different View of Southern History." In *Unheard Voices: The First Historians of Southern Women*, ed. Anne Firor Scott, 1–71. Charlottesville: University of Virginia Press, 1993.

———. *The Southern Lady: From Pedestal to Politics, 1830–1930*. Chicago: University of Chicago Press, 1970.

Sellers, Charles. *The Market Revolution: Jacksonian America 1815–1846*. New York: Oxford University Press, 1991.

Sellers, James Benson. *The Prohibition Movement in Alabama, 1702 to 1943*. Chapel Hill: University of North Carolina Press, 1943.

Shahan, Joe Michael. "Reform and Politics in Tennessee: 1906–1914." Ph.D. diss., Vanderbilt University, 1981.

Shaw, Barton C. *The Wool-Hat Boys: Georgia's Populist Party*. Baton Rouge: Louisiana State University Press, 1984.

Sims, Anastasia. *The Power of Femininity in the New South: Women's Organizations and Politics in North Carolina, 1880–1930.* Columbia: University of South Carolina Press, 1997.

Sinclair, Andrew. *Prohibition: The Era of Excess.* Boston: Little, Brown, 1962.

Slaton, Mrs. S. T. "Fifty Years." In *The Story of the Alabama Woman's Christian Temperance Union: 1884–1959.* N.p.: 1959.

Smith, H. Shelton. *In His Image, But: Racism in Southern Religion, 1780–1910.* Durham, N.C.: Duke University Press, 1972.

Smith, John Abernathy. *Cross and Flame: Two Centuries of United Methodism in Middle Tennessee.* Nashville: Parthenon Press, 1984.

Smith, John David. *An Old Creed for the New South: Proslavery Ideology and Historiography, 1865–1918.* Westport, Conn.: Greenwood Press, 1985.

Snay, Mitchell. *Gospel of Disunion: Religion and Separatism in the Antebellum South.* Cambridge: Cambridge University Press, 1993.

Spain, Rufus B. *At Ease in Zion: Social History of Southern Baptists, 1865–1900.* Nashville: Vanderbilt University Press, 1967.

Stampp, Kenneth M. *The Peculiar Institution: Slavery in the Ante-Bellum South.* New York: Knopf, 1956.

Stark, Rodney, and William Sims Bainbridge. *The Future of Religion: Secularization, Revival, and Cult Formation.* Berkeley: University of California Press, 1985.

Stowell, Daniel W. *Rebuilding Zion: The Religious Reconstruction of the South, 1863–1877.* New York: Oxford University Press, 1998.

Strode, Hudson. *Jefferson Davis: Tragic Hero, the Last Twenty-five Years, 1864–1889.* New York: Harcourt, Brace, and World, 1964.

Summers, Martin. *Manliness and Its Discontents: The Black Middle Class and the Transformation of Masculinity, 1900–1930.* Chapel Hill: University of North Carolina Press, 2004.

Sumners, Bill. "Southern Baptists and the Liquor Question, 1910–1920." *Quarterly Review* 43 (April–June 1983): 75–85.

Szymanski, Ann-Marie E. *Pathways to Prohibition: Radicals, Moderates, and Social Movement Outcomes.* Durham, N.C.: Duke University Press, 2003.

Tankersley, Allen P. "Basil Hallam Overby: Champion of Prohibition in Ante Bellum Georgia." *Georgia Historical Quarterly* 31 (March 1947): 1–18.

Taylor, Antoinette Elizabeth. "The Last Phase of the Woman Suffrage Movement in Georgia." *Georgia Historical Quarterly* 43 (March 1959): 11–28.

———. "The Origin of the Woman Suffrage Movement in Georgia." *Georgia Historical Quarterly* 28 (June 1944): 63–79.

———. "Revival and Development of the Woman Suffrage Movement in Georgia." *Georgia Historical Quarterly* 42 (December 1958): 339–54.

———. *The Woman Suffrage Movement in Tennessee*. New York: Octagon Books, 1978.

Thompson, Ernest Trice. "Continuity and Change in the Presbyterian Church in the United States." *Austin Seminary Bulletin: Faculty Edition* 85 (April 1970): 5–86.

———. *Presbyterians in the South*, vol. 3, *1890–1972*. Richmond, Va.: John Knox Press, 1973.

———. *The Spirituality of the Church: A Distinctive Doctrine of the Presbyterian Church in the United States*. Richmond, Va.: John Knox Press, 1961.

Thompson, Harold Paul. "Race, Temperance, and Prohibition in the Postbellum South: Black Atlanta, 1865–1890." Ph.D. diss., Emory University, 2005.

Tiger, Lionel. *Men in Groups*. New York: Random House, 1969.

Timberlake, James H. *Prohibition and the Progressive Movement 1900–1920*. Cambridge, Mass.: Harvard University Press, 1963.

Tull, James E. *A History of Southern Baptist Landmarkism in the Light of Historical Baptist Ecclesiology*. New York: Arno Press, 1980.

Tyrrell, Ian R. "Drink and Temperance in the Antebellum South: An Overview and Interpretation." *Journal of Southern History* 48 (November 1982): 485–510.

———. *Sobering Up: From Temperance to Prohibition in Antebellum America, 1800–1860*. Westport, Conn.: Greenwood Press, 1979.

Vanderwood, Paul J. *Night Riders of Reelfoot Lake*. Tuscaloosa: Alabama University Press, 2003.

Velde, Lewis G. Vander. *The Presbyterian Churches and the Federal Union 1861–1869*. Cambridge, Mass.: Harvard University Press, 1932.

Ward, Margaret E. "The Early Churches and Pastors." In *Early Days of Birmingham*. Birmingham, Ala.: Birmingham Publishing, 1937.

Warnock, Henry Y. "Andrew Sledd, Southern Methodists, and the Negro: A Case History." *Journal of Southern History* 31 (August 1965): 251–71.

Webb, James. *Born Fighting: How the Scots-Irish Shaped America*. New York: Broadway Books, 2004.

Webb, Samuel L. "From Independents to Populists to Progressive Republicans: The Case of Chilton County, AL, 1880–1920." *Journal of Southern History* 59 (November 1993): 707–36.

Wedell, Marsha. *Elite Women and the Reform Impulse in Memphis, 1875–1915*. Knoxville: University of Tennessee Press, 1991.

Wells, C. A. Harwell. "The End of the Affair? Anti-Dueling Laws and Social Norms in Antebellum America." *Vanderbilt Law Review* 54 (May 2001): 1805–47.

West, Stephen A. "From Yeoman to Redneck in Upstate North Carolina, 1850–1915." Ph.D. diss., Columbia University, 1998.

Wheeler, Marjorie Spruill. *New Women of the New South: The Leaders of the Woman Suffrage Movement in the Southern States.* New York: Oxford University Press, 1993.

White, Walter. *Rope and Faggot: A Biography of Judge Lynch.* New York: Arno Press, 1969.

Wiebe, Robert H. *The Opening of American Society: From the Adoption of the Constitution to the Eve of Disunion.* New York: Knopf, 1984.

Wilke-Long, Linda. "Populists, Politics, and Prohibition." *Nebraska Lawyer* (May 1999): 12–14.

Williams, Jack K. *Dueling in the Old South: Vignettes of Social History.* College Station: Texas A&M University Press, 1980.

Williamson, Joel. *The Crucible of Race: Black-White Relations in the American South since Emancipation.* New York: Oxford University Press, 1984.

Wilson, Charles Reagan. *Baptized in Blood: The Religion of the Lost Cause 1865–1920.* Athens: University of Georgia Press, 1980.

———. "The Religion of the Lost Cause: Ritual and Organization of the Southern Civil Religion, 1865–1920." *Journal of Southern History* 46 (May 1980): 219–38.

Woodward, Comer Vann. *The Burden of Southern History,* rev. ed. New York: Mentor, 1968.

———. *Origins of the New South 1877–1913.* Vol. 10 of *A History of the South,* ed. Wendell Holmes Stephenson and E. Merton Coulter. N.p.: Louisiana State University Press, 1951.

———. *The Strange Career of Jim Crow,* 3rd ed. New York: Oxford University Press, 1974.

Wyatt-Brown, Bertram. *The Shaping of Southern Culture: Honor, Grace, and War 1760s–1880s.* Chapel Hill: University of North Carolina Press, 2001.

———. *Southern Honor: Ethics and Behavior in the Old South.* New York: Oxford University Press, 1982.

Index